Leith's

CONFIDENT COOKING

Step-by-Step Recipes and Techniques

Leith's
CONFIDENT COOKING

Step-by-Step Recipes and Techniques

Prue Leith

TED SMART

Published in Great Britain in 1993
Bloomsbury Publishing Limited, 2 Soho Square,
London W1V 5DE

This edition produced for
The Book People Ltd,
Guardian House,
Borough Road,
Godalming,
Surrey GU7 2AE.

A CIP catalogue record for this book is available from the British Library

ISBN 0 7475 1599 9

10 9 8 7 6 5 4 3 2 1

Designed by Machina

Edited by Jane Binsley

Photographed by Martin Brigdale, Clint Brown, Andy Cantouris, Nick Carman,
Chris Crofton, JJ Crofton, James Duncan, John Elliot, Paul Grater, John Heseltine,
Chris King, Dave King, Alan Marsh, Michael Michaels, Diana Miller, Paul Moon,
Hilary Moore, Vernon Morgan, Alan Newnham, Ian O'Leary, Peter Reilly,
Clive Streeter, Grant Symon, Simon Wheeler, Andrew Whittuck

Illustrated by Angela Wood, John Hutchinson, Helen Desai

Printed in Spain

DEP. LEGAL 28.299-93

CONTENTS

Foreword by Prue Leith 7

Soups & Starters **8**

Fish & Shellfish **44**

Poultry & Game Birds **66**

Meat **88**

Vegetarian **118**

Salads & Side Dishes **136**

Desserts **156**

Baking **186**

Techniques **212**

Glossary **312**

Weights & Measures **314**

Index **315**

Years of writing recipes and teaching cooking have taught me that cooks, and especially young or beginner cooks, prefer recipes with pictures. Short of tasting it, looking at a dish is the best way to decide whether it's worth the time, trouble and expense of planning, shopping and cooking. That's the joy of this book. Not only does it show you exactly how the finished dish should look, but provides the reassurance of step-by-step pictures so you can make sure you're on track every step of the way.

For the already confident cook, I hope this book will provide interesting new flavour combinations and presentation ideas and advice on professional methods and techniques. In the special techniques chapter at the back I've included all those tips and hints that the teachers at Leith's School of Food and Wine, and the professional chefs, rely on. Cooking is not a mystery art. It is a matter of being let into the secret. Once you know how, it's easy.

But the real secret of good cooking is a love of good food. A tiny touch of greed is the basic ingredient that all the best cooks have in common!

Good luck, good cooking and most of all, good eating...

SOUPS
&
STARTERS

GAZPACHO

Preparation time: 20 mins
+ chilling
Serves 6

INGREDIENTS

900 g/2 lb ripe tomatoes, peeled
1 large onion
2 red peppers
1 small cucumber
1 thick slice white bread, crusts removed
1 egg yolk
2 large cloves of garlic
6 tbls olive oil
1 tbls tarragon vinegar
450 g/1 lb tinned Italian peeled tomatoes
1 tbls tomato purée
Salt and ground black pepper
Croûtons, to serve

PRUE'S TIP

If you are using a liquidiser, blend small amounts of soup at a time to prevent the blender from clogging.

2 Put the bread, egg yolk and garlic into a blender or food processor. Turn it on and pour in the oil in a thin steady stream while the machine is running. The mixture should be the consistency of thick mayonnaise.

1 Dice a little of the fresh tomato, onion, peppers and cucumber and reserve for the garnish. Roughly chop the rest of the vegetables.

3 Pour in the vinegar. Add the tinned tomatoes, vegetables and tomato purée a little at a time blending until smooth. Add the seasoning.

4 Sieve the soup to remove the tomato seeds and adjust the seasoning if necessary. Chill covered in the fridge until required. Serve in bowls sprinkled with the diced vegetables and accompanied by a bowl of croûtons.

CREAM OF TOMATO SOUP

Preparation time: 15 mins
Cooking time: 25 mins
Serves 6

INGREDIENTS

700 g/1 lb 8 oz tomatoes
½ tbls sunflower oil
15 g/½ oz butter
1 small potato, sliced
1 onion, chopped
450 ml/¾ pt milk
450 ml/¾ pt chicken stock
2 tbls chopped fresh basil
1-2 tsp sugar
Salt and ground black pepper
150 ml/¼ pt double cream

PRUE'S TIP

Try to use ripe or over-ripe tomatoes for this recipe – firm tomatoes won't give enough colour. Even so, you won't end up with the fierce orange of tinned soup. Stir in 1 tbls tomato purée for extra colour.

1 Using a sharp knife, slice the tomatoes then chop them roughly, leaving the skins on.

2 Heat the oil and butter in a large saucepan. Add the sliced potato, chopped onion and chopped tomatoes and cook gently for 5-6 minutes or until they begin to soften.

3 Stir in the milk, chicken stock, basil, sugar, salt and pepper. Simmer, uncovered, for 15 minutes until the potatoes are cooked.

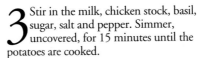

4 Allow the soup to cool then liquidise in a blender or food processor. Pour into a clean saucepan, taste and adjust seasoning if necessary. Reheat just before serving.

5 Pour the soup into individual serving bowls and add a swirl of cream to each bowl before serving.

CREAM OF SPINACH SOUP

Preparation time: 15 mins
Cooking time: 25 mins
Serves 6

INGREDIENTS

3 tbls oil
1 onion, finely chopped
1 clove of garlic, crushed
225 g/8 oz frozen spinach,
thawed and squeezed dry
3 tbls flour
600 ml/1 pt hot chicken stock
300 ml/½ pt milk, warmed
Ground black pepper
1 tsp grated nutmeg
½ a lemon

FOR THE GARNISH

6 tbls double cream
25 g/1 oz pine kernels, lightly toasted

FREEZER TIP

Freeze individual portions of soup in small plastic boxes. Defrost as needed, then reheat, garnish and serve.

1 Heat the oil, add the onion and garlic. Fry for 3-4 minutes until softened. Then add the spinach and stir well.

2 Sprinkle in the flour, stirring well for approximately 1 minute until the flour is cooked.

3 Stir the chicken stock and milk into the saucepan and bring to the boil. Simmer gently for about 20 minutes, stirring the mixture occasionally, until the soup starts to thicken in the pan. Remove from the heat and leave to cool.

4 Pour the soup into a food processor and blend until smooth. If you find the soup a little thick, add a little extra milk for a thinner consistency. Reheat and stir in the black pepper and the grated nutmeg.

5 Pour into individual soup bowls and add a squeeze of lemon juice. To garnish, swirl 1 tbls cream into each bowl and sprinkle the pine kernels on top.

CELERY & STILTON SOUP

Preparation time: 10 mins
Cooking time: 42-45 mins
Serves 6

INGREDIENTS

25 g/1 oz butter
2 heads of celery, cleaned and finely chopped
2 onions, chopped
1 small potato, diced
600 ml/1 pt milk
600 ml/1 pt chicken or vegetable stock
1 bay leaf
Salt and ground black pepper
225 g/8 oz Stilton, crumbled
½ a baguette, thinly sliced
Freshly snipped chives, to garnish

VARIATIONS

This soup can be made much richer by stirring in 2-3 tbls of cream when you add the crumbled Stilton. Follow with a light main course. Alternatively, vary the flavour by increasing the quantity of snipped chives used – stir in 1-2 tbls with the cheese.

1 Melt the butter in a large pan. Add the celery and onions. Cook for 2-3 minutes, stirring constantly. Cover the pan and cook the celery and onion for 4-5 minutes until softened.

2 Add the potato, milk, stock and bay leaf to the pan. Cover and bring to the boil. Reduce the heat and simmer for 30 minutes.

3 Remove the bay leaf. Blend or process the cooked soup until smooth, then pass through a sieve. Return to the pan and season to taste.

4 Sprinkle 100 g/4 oz Stilton onto the slices of bread and heat under a grill. Heat the soup, stirring in the remaining Stilton just before serving. Pour into individual soup bowls and top with the hot Stilton toasts. Sprinkle with chives.

MUSHROOM SOUP

INGREDIENTS
450 g/1 lb flat mushrooms, sliced
25 g/1 oz butter
600 ml/1 pt chicken stock
250 ml/8 fl oz dry white wine
250 ml/8 fl oz single cream
2 tbls cornflour
1 tsp celery salt
Ground black pepper

TO SERVE
3 tbls snipped chives
Croûtons

Preparation time: 5 mins
Cooking time: 55 mins
Serves 6

PRUE'S TIP
If you prefer a smoother texture, this soup can be cooled slightly and then liquidised before serving.

1 Put the mushrooms and butter into a large pan, cook, covered, until mushrooms are tender.

2 Add the stock and the wine, cover and simmer for 40 minutes. Stir the cream into the cornflour, then add to the pan with the celery salt and pepper. Cook, stirring, for 5 minutes.

3 Serve hot with freshly chopped chives and croûtons made from fried bread scattered over the top to add texture and colour to the soup.

CHILLI PUMPKIN SOUP

INGREDIENTS
50 g/2 oz butter
1 large onion, chopped
4 spring onions, chopped
2 tomatoes, peeled and chopped
2 cloves of garlic, crushed
2 fresh chillies, seeded and chopped
225 g/8 oz sweet potato, peeled and cubed
1.1 kg/2 lb 8 oz pumpkin, peeled, seeded and cubed
1.7 L/3 pt beef stock
1 tsp sugar
Salt and ground black pepper

TO SERVE
125 ml/4 fl oz double cream
Parmesan cheese, grated

Preparation time: 15 mins
Cooking time: 55 mins - 1 hour
Serves 8

1 Melt the butter in a large pan, add the onions and spring onions and cook for 5 minutes.

2 Stir in the tomatoes, garlic, chillies, sweet potatoes and pumpkin and cook for 5 minutes.

3 Pour over the stock and add sugar and seasoning. Bring to the boil, reduce the heat, cover and simmer for 25-30 minutes until pumpkin is soft.

4 Remove from the heat, allow to cool slightly, then liquidise. Heat for a few minutes and adjust seasoning. Swirl some cream on each serving and pass round the Parmesan separately.

LEEK & SWEET POTATO SOUP

Preparation time: 20 mins
Cooking time: 55 mins
Serves 4-6

INGREDIENTS
25 g/1 oz butter
2 tbls oil
900 g/2 lb leeks, trimmed and sliced
1 onion, finely chopped
700 g/1 lb 8 oz sweet potatoes,
peeled and chopped
1.2 L/2 pt chicken stock
Salt and ground black pepper
Finely chopped chives, to garnish

SERVING NOTE
For a thinner soup, add more stock. For a
richer version, add a swirl of cream
on top before serving.

MICROWAVE TIP
Put the butter, oil, leeks and onion in a
large microwave-proof bowl. Cover and
cook on HIGH (100%) for 2 minutes. Add
the potatoes, re-cover and cook for a
further 8 minutes. Add boiling stock and
cook for 10-15 minutes. Purée, then
reheat for 3 minutes, season and serve.

1 Melt the butter and oil in a saucepan,
add the leeks and onion and sweat for
5 minutes. Stir in the chunks of sweet
potato and cook for a further 15 minutes,
stirring frequently.

2 Add the chicken stock and plenty of
salt and pepper. Simmer for 30
minutes, or until the sweet potatoes
are very tender.

3 Leave the mixture to cool a little,
then blend to a purée in a blender or
food processor. Return the soup to
the rinsed out saucepan, adjust the
seasoning if necessary. Reheat over gentle
heat for a few minutes. Pour into bowls
and garnish with chives.

CLASSIC CONSOMME

Preparation time: 15 mins
+ soaking
Cooking time: 1½-1¾ hours
Serves 6

INGREDIENTS

2.3 L/4 pt cold brown stock (see Techniques)
225 g/8 oz lean shin of beef, minced
2 carrots, chopped
1 onion, chopped
1 bouquet garni
4 black peppercorns
2 egg whites, lightly whisked
4 tbls dry sherry
Salt and ground black pepper

"You can, of course, buy good consommé in tins. I often do. But making your own is infinitely more satisfying. It's a true chef's skill, but not as hard as they would have you believe." Prue

1 Discard any surplus fat from the cold stock. Put the minced beef in 150 ml/¼ pt water and leave to soak for 20-30 minutes.

2 Put the beef and water, carrots, onion, bouquet garni, peppercorns and egg whites into a large saucepan. Gradually add the cold stock, whisking continuously over a gentle heat.

3 Whisk thoroughly until almost boiling. Stop whisking, reduce the heat and simmer. Cover and cook for 1½ hours without stirring.

4 Meanwhile, scald a jelly bag or thick muslin cloth. Leave the consommé to stand for 15 minutes before straining through the bag. Stir the sherry into the clear amber soup and season to taste. Reheat the consommé if serving it hot.

WATCHPOINT

Do not boil the consommé quickly or it will become cloudy.

PRUE'S TIP

As a delicious variation, try Consommé Monte-Carlo, garnished with circles of thinly-sliced bread topped with butter and Parmesan cheese and toasted, or maybe Consommé à la Julienne, garnished with just-cooked neat julienne strips of carrot, turnip and celery.

FRENCH FISH SOUP

Preparation time: 20 mins
Cooking time: 25 mins
Serves 4-6

INGREDIENTS

1.1 kg/2 lb 8 oz mixed fish, including
monkfish, langoustines, red mullet and
crab, complete with shells and bones

2 tbls olive oil

2 onions, finely chopped

2 cloves of garlic, crushed

2 shallots, finely chopped

1 leek, finely sliced

1 celery stalk, sliced

1 carrot, chopped

2 tomatoes, quartered

5 cm/2 in strip of orange peel

2 sprigs of fennel

2 bay leaves

Pinch of saffron strands

Salt

Cayenne pepper

SERVING NOTE

Serve with toasted French bread covered
with rouille - a sauce made with garlic,
oil, chillies, pimientos and fresh
breadcrumbs - and then topped with
melted Gruyère cheese. For a quick and
easy rouille, combine homemade
mayonnaise with crushed garlic, pimiento
and cayenne pepper or Tabasco.

1 Chop the mixed fish into 5 cm/2 in lengths. Crack the crab shell and break into small pieces.

2 Heat the oil in a large saucepan. Add the onions, garlic, shallots, leek, celery, carrot and tomatoes and fry gently for 5 minutes until soft.

4 Using a slotted spoon, transfer all the fish (bones and all) and the crab meat and shell into a liquidiser. Grind them until they become a coarse pulp.

5 Stir the ground fish into the soup, then strain through a very fine sieve into a clean saucepan, pressing the fish with the back of a spoon to extract the liquid. Stir in the saffron and reheat gently. Season and serve.

3 Pour 1.2 L/2 pt water over the vegetables and bring to the boil. Add the fish, orange peel, fennel and bay leaves and boil for 15 minutes.

CRAB CHOWDER

Preparation time: 10 mins
Cooking time: 30 mins
Serves 6-8

INGREDIENTS

50 g/2 oz smoked streaky bacon
1 small green pepper
350 g/12 oz potatoes
25 g/1 oz butter
1 onion, finely chopped
1 tbls flour
450 ml/¾ pt fish stock
450 ml/¾ pt half cream or creamy milk
Salt and ground black pepper
Pinch of grated nutmeg
Pinch of cayenne pepper
100 g/4 oz crab meat
300 g/11 oz tinned sweetcorn, drained

SERVING NOTE

Serve the chowder with brown bread and garnish with dill. For a dinner party, substitute 150 ml/¼ pt of the fish stock with dry white wine.

1 Trim the rind from the bacon and chop the bacon finely. Remove the seeds from the green pepper and cut it into 6 mm/¼ in dice. Peel the potatoes and dice the same way.

2 Fry the bacon over a gentle heat in a large pan until the fat begins to run. Add the butter, and when melted, add the green pepper, potatoes and onion. Fry gently for 7-8 minutes until slightly softened, stirring occasionally.

3 Sprinkle the flour over the bacon and vegetables and then stir for a few minutes until the mixture becomes golden and frothy. Blend the fish stock with the cream and add to the pan with seasoning and spices. Bring to the boil, cover and simmer for 15 minutes or until the vegetables are tender.

4 Flake the crab meat and stir into the pan along with the tinned sweetcorn. Cook the soup for a few minutes so it heats through, adjust the seasoning to suit your taste and then serve.

GUACAMOLE

INGREDIENTS
2 green chillies
3 large ripe avocados
1 small onion, finely chopped
5 tbls chopped fresh coriander
Salt
1 tomato
Tortilla chips, to serve

1 Seed the chillies, then cut several thin slices and reserve for the garnish. Finely chop the rest of the chillies.

2 Peel and stone the avocados. Cut up, place in a large bowl and mash with a fork. Add the onion, chopped chillies, 4 tbls of the coriander and salt. Mash to a coarse, lumpy paste.

3 Spoon the guacamole into a large bowl. Skin, seed and finely chop the tomato. Sprinkle the tomato, reserved chilli slices and remaining coriander on top of the guacamole and serve with a bowl of tortilla chips.

Preparation time: 10 mins
Serves 6

P R U E ' S   T I P
Make the guacamole at the last possible moment before serving, as the avocado will brown on contact with air.

TARAMASALATA

INGREDIENTS
225 g/ 8 oz fresh smoked soft roe
1 slice of white bread, crusts removed
1 large clove of garlic, crushed
150 ml/¼ pt salad oil
150 ml/¼ pt olive oil
Ground black pepper
Juice of ½ a lemon
Pitta bread, to serve

1 Scrape the soft roe from the tough skin. Hold the bread slice under the tap to wet it. Squeeze dry and put it in a bowl with the soft roe and the crushed garlic. Beat well.

2 Now very slowly add the oils to the roe mixture, beating all the time. Stir in the lemon juice and season with pepper. Serve with hot pitta bread, cut into strips.

Preparation time: 15 mins
Serves 6

P R U E ' S   T I P
Adding the oil too quickly will result in an oily, curdled mixture. The more oil you add, the paler, milder and creamier the mixture becomes. Stop when you think the right balance of blandness and smoked-roe taste is achieved.

TRICOLOUR DIPS & CRUDITES

Preparation time: 35 mins
+ chilling
Serves 4

INGREDIENTS

FOR THE PRAWN AND LEMON DIP
50 g/2 oz cooked prawns, peeled
½ a lemon
150 g/5 oz mayonnaise
Ground black pepper
Whole prawns and lemon wedges, to garnish

FOR THE AVOCADO DIP
1 ripe avocado
150 g/5 oz plain yoghurt
2 tsp Dijon mustard
Pinch of cayenne pepper, to garnish

FOR THE CHINESE DIP
150 ml/¼ pt soured cream
1 tsp dark soy sauce
1 tsp dry sherry
2 spring onions, sliced
75 g/3 oz cucumber, grated

FOR THE CRUDITES
100 g/4 oz broccoli
100 g/4 oz cauliflower
3 carrots, peeled
4 sticks celery
1 green pepper
1 packet tortilla chips

1 For the prawn and lemon dip, cut the prawns into small pieces. Grate the zest of the half lemon and squeeze the juice from the same half. Mix the mayonnaise, lemon zest, lemon juice, chopped prawns and black pepper together. Cover and chill. Garnish with the whole prawn and the lemon wedges.

2 For the avocado dip, peel and halve the avocado. Remove the stone. Mash with a fork until smooth. Stir in the yoghurt and mustard. Cover and chill. Sprinkle with a pinch of cayenne pepper before serving.

3 For the Chinese dip, stir together the soured cream, soy sauce, sherry, onions and cucumber. Cover and chill. Grind black pepper over the top before serving.

4 For the crudités, break the broccoli and cauliflower into florets. Cut the carrots and celery into sticks. Halve and seed the green pepper, then cut into strips. Serve on a platter with the tortilla chips and the tricolour dips.

COARSE GARLIC PATE

INGREDIENTS
450 g/1 lb pigs' liver, trimmed
450 g/1 lb belly of pork, skinned and boned
225 g/8 oz rindless smoked streaky bacon
225 g/8 oz stewing steak
1 onion, peeled and quartered
4 tbls milk
100 g/4 oz mushrooms, chopped
3 cloves of garlic, crushed
3 tbls brandy
½ tsp grated nutmeg
Salt and ground black pepper
225 g/8 oz clarified butter

FOR THE GARNISH
Bay leaves
Pink and green peppercorns

Preparation time: 30 mins
+ chilling
Cooking time: 2 hours 5 mins
Serves 15

1 Preheat oven to 170 C/325 F/Gas 3. Process the pigs' liver, pork, bacon, steak and onion together in a food processor. Transfer to a large bowl.

2 Stir the milk, mushrooms, garlic, brandy, nutmeg and seasoning into the meat mixture. Pack into a round pâté dish and cover tightly with foil.

3 Stand the pâté dish in a roasting tin and pour in sufficient boiling water to come halfway up the sides. Bake for 2 hours.

4 Remove from the roasting tin and stand a plate and heavy weight on the pâté. Allow to cool down, then chill overnight in the fridge.

5 Melt the clarified butter in a saucepan over a gentle heat and pour over the cold pâté. Just as the butter begins to solidify slightly, garnish with the bay leaves and the peppercorns.

CHORIZO MUSHROOMS

INGREDIENTS
24 open-cup mushrooms
100 g/4 oz almonds, toasted and ground
100 g/4 oz dry white breadcrumbs
5-6 tbls olive oil
225 g/8 oz chorizo sausage, diced
Lemon wedges and juice, to serve

1 Remove the stalks from the mushrooms and put them in a blender or food processor. Reserve the mushroom cups. Add the almonds and breadcrumbs to the blender and process until evenly combined.

2 In a bowl mix together the sausage with the breadcrumb mixture. The mushroom stalks should make the mixture just moist, so that it sticks together when moulded with the fingers. If the mixture is a little dry, add a little olive oil, a tablespoonful at a time.

3 Take each mushroom and brush it lightly with oil, inside and out. Place on a baking sheet, then spoon a little stuffing into each mushroom cap using a teaspoon.

4 Preheat the grill to a medium heat and then put the mushrooms under it and cook for 3-5 minutes. The chorizo should be sizzling and the mushrooms just cooked. If you cook them for too long they will collapse. Serve piping hot garnished with lemon wedges and drizzled with lemon juice.

Preparation time: 30 mins
Cooking time: 3-5 mins
Makes 24

GARLIC MUSHROOMS

Preparation time: 20 mins
Cooking time: 6 mins
Serves 4

INGREDIENTS
25 g/1 oz flour
1 tsp dried mixed herbs
Salt and ground black pepper
275 g/10 oz button mushrooms, wiped
1 clove of garlic, crushed
1 large egg, beaten
75 g/3 oz dry white breadcrumbs
Oil, for deep frying

FOR THE DIP
75 g/3 oz Boursin cheese
with garlic and herbs
3 tbls soured cream
Freshly snipped chives, to garnish

1 Mix the flour in a large bowl with the herbs, salt and ground black pepper. Toss the mushrooms briefly in the seasoned flour mixture.

2 Beat the crushed garlic into the egg in a large bowl until well mixed. Take the mushrooms from the flour and put in with the egg mixture. Toss thoroughly until all the mushrooms are completely coated in the egg.

3 Lift out a few mushrooms with a slotted spoon and toss them in the breadcrumbs until evenly coated. To make a thicker coating, toss in egg and breadcrumbs again. Repeat with the rest of the mushrooms.

4 Heat the oil and fry half the mushrooms at a time for about 3 minutes until golden. Drain on kitchen paper and keep warm.

5 To make the dip, heat the cheese and soured cream gently until smooth and warm. Season. Pour into a serving bowl, garnish with chives and serve with the mushrooms.

MUSHROOM BOATS

Preparation time: 15 mins
+ resting
Cooking time: 15-20 mins
Makes 24-30

INGREDIENTS

40 g/1½ oz lard
90 g/3½ oz butter
75 g/3 oz mature Cheddar cheese, grated
100 g/4 oz flour
¼ tsp paprika
350 g/12 oz mixed mushrooms such as ceps, morels or field mushrooms, sliced
150 ml/¼ pt double cream
Salt and ground black pepper
2 tbls finely chopped fresh parsley

1 Preheat oven to 220 C/425 F/Gas 7. Cream together the lard and 40 g/1½ oz of the butter. Add cheese.

2 Gradually add the flour and paprika. Mix in well using a palette knife until mixture forms a ball.

3 Knead lightly for a few seconds to give a smooth dough. Cover with cling film and leave to rest for 30 minutes in the fridge.

4 Roll out the pastry thinly. Lay over a line of barquette moulds. Trim off excess pastry using a rolling-pin. Prick the pastry, line and fill with baking beans. Bake for 10-15 minutes. Remove from the moulds and keep warm.

5 Melt the remaining butter. Add the mushrooms and sauté for 2 minutes. Add the cream and boil until thickened. Remove from the heat, season and stir in the chopped parsley. Spoon into the pastry cases and serve.

MIXED MEAT ANTIPASTO

Preparation time: 10 mins
Serves 4

INGREDIENTS

1 charantais, galia or cantaloupe melon
4 fresh figs
50 g/2 oz Parma ham
50 g/2 oz salami
50 g/2 oz mortadella, cut into triangles
50 g/2 oz bresaola

PRUE'S TIP

You can vary the fruit and meats for this dish. For example, mango is quite delicious with Parma ham, as is pear or plum. Another savoury alternative is to serve the meats with a selection of pickled vegetables instead of fruit.

WINE NOTE

Serve this antipasto with an Italian wine such as Chianti or Barolo.

1 Halve the melon, remove the pips and cut the flesh into slices. Remove and discard the skin.

2 Make four deep cuts into the tops of the figs and gently open them out to make flower shapes.

3 Divide the Parma ham, salami and mortadella into four and arrange attractively on separate serving plates. Wrap a piece of bresaola around half the melon slices and arrange on the plates. Position the figs in the centres of the plates and serve.

SMOKED FISH PLATTER

Preparation time: ½ hour
Serves 10

INGREDIENTS

450 g/1 lb smoked mackerel with
peppercorns, cut into chunks
225 g/8 oz smoked salmon trout,
thinly sliced
6 tbls soured cream
225 g/8 oz taramasalata
225 g/8 oz smoked salmon pâté
Small crackers, to serve
4-6 tbls set natural yoghurt
100 g/4 oz tinned smoked oysters, drained
100 g/4 oz tinned smoked mussels, drained

FOR THE GARNISH
Tomato slices
Tiny cucumber wedges
Green peppercorns
Fresh sprigs of dill and chervil
Paprika
Shredded zest of 1 lemon

1 Arrange the smoked mackerel chunks
on large platters. Spread the smoked
salmon trout with the soured cream
and roll the slices up. Cut into 5 cm/2 in
pieces. Arrange with the mackerel.

2 Put the taramasalata and smoked
salmon pâté into small bowls to
serve with the platter.

3 Spread the crackers with the yoghurt
and top each one with an oyster or
mussel. Arrange on platter.

4 Put tomato slices on the mussel
crackers. Put cucumber wedges on
the oyster crackers. Garnish the pâté
with green peppercorns and dill. Sprinkle
paprika over the taramasalata and top with
the lemon shreds. Put tiny leaves of chervil
on top of the smoked salmon trout rolls.

SESAME TOASTS

Preparation time: 15 mins
Cooking time: 15 mins
Serves 6

INGREDIENTS

175 g/6 oz pork tenderloin, roughly chopped
175 g/6 oz frozen peeled prawns,
thawed and drained
1 tsp salt
2 tsp rice wine or dry sherry
1 spring onion, finely chopped
1 tsp fresh root ginger, finely grated
1 egg white
2 tsp cornflour
6 slices of white bread
100 g/4 oz sesame seeds
Oil, for deep frying
Unpeeled prawns, to serve

1 Mince the pork and prawn to a paste
in a blender or food processor.
Transfer to a bowl. Add the salt, wine,
spring onion, ginger, egg white and
cornflour. Mix well.

2 Remove crusts from bread and spread
the paste thickly on the six slices.
Sprinkle the sesame seeds over the
top. Set aside until ready to cook.

3 Heat oil to 180 C/350 F. Fry bread,
paste-side down for 2 minutes, or
until golden. Fry for 30 seconds on
the other side. Drain on absorbent paper.

4 When fried, cut each piece into 4
triangles. Arrange on a heated dish
and serve hot with unpeeled prawns.

RUSSIAN TARTLETS

Preparation time: 35 mins
+ chilling
Cooking time: 15-20 mins
Serves 6

INGREDIENTS

450 g/1 lb puff pastry, thawed if frozen
Beaten egg, to glaze
Bunch of fresh chervil
Zest of 1 lemon
Salt and ground white pepper
150 ml/¼ pt soured cream
3 tbls capers, drained
100 g/4 oz smoked salmon
1 tbls red lumpfish roe
1 tbls black lumpfish roe

1 Preheat oven to 200 C/400 F/Gas 6. Roll out pastry and cut into twelve 10 cm/4 in long diamonds.

2 Using a sharp knife or diamond pastry cutter, cut out the centres from 6 of the diamonds to give diamond-shaped pastry rims.

3 Brush the pastry rims with beaten egg and press, egg-side down, onto the pastry bases. Knock up the sides with a knife then arrange on a dampened baking tray with the sides touching to form a star. Chill for 30 minutes then brush the rims with beaten egg and bake for 15-20 minutes. Cool.

4 Chop the chervil, reserving some whole leaves for decoration. Mix the chopped chervil, lemon zest and seasonings with the soured cream. Arrange the pastry cases on a plate and spoon a few capers into each. Fill with the soured cream mixture. Cut the salmon into strips and lay along the centre of the filled pastry cases. Place a small spoonful of red and black lumpfish roe at the centre and outer points of the diamonds. Garnish with remaining chopped chervil.

CHICKEN GOUJONS

INGREDIENTS

700 g/1 lb 8 oz chicken breasts, skinned and boned
2 small eggs
Salt and ground black pepper
75 g/3 oz dried white breadcrumbs
Flour, for dusting
Oil, for deep frying

FOR THE DIP
6 tbls mayonnaise
4 tbls set yoghurt
1-2 cloves of garlic, crushed
Lime and parsley, to garnish

Preparation time: 30 mins
+ chilling
Cooking time: 4-6 mins
Serves 8

SERVING NOTE

As well as being a perfect party snack, chicken goujons make a delicious light lunch served with a leafy salad.

1 Cut the chicken into thin slices about 12 mm/½ in by 5 cm/2 in. Beat the eggs in a small shallow dish and season with salt and pepper. Turn the breadcrumbs out onto a large plate. Dip the chicken strips first into flour, then the eggs and finally into the breadcrumbs and set aside on a plate.

2 Heat the oil to 180 C/350 F in a deep fat fryer. Fry 6-8 strips at a time until golden. Remove with a slotted spoon and drain on absorbent paper. Check it is cooked by cutting one of the goujons in half. If it is even slightly pink fry for a little longer and increase the cooking time for the rest of the goujons.

3 When all are cooked, cool quickly, cover and keep refrigerated for no longer than 2 days.

4 Make the dip by blending together the mayonnaise and yoghurt. Stir in the garlic, cover and chill. Garnish the goujons with the lime and parsley. Serve with the dip.

CHEESE BOREK

INGREDIENTS

4 sheets of filo pastry
Salt
Ground black pepper
2 tbls freshly chopped parsley or dill, mixed with
400 g/14 oz cream cheese
Oil, for deep frying
Fresh sprig of dill, to garnish
Runny honey, for dipping

Preparation time: 20 mins
Cooking time: 10 mins
Makes 24

PRUE'S TIP

Use any kind of cream cheese for the filling provided it's not too soft. Ricotta, sieved curd or goat's cheese are best.

1 Cut doubled sheets of filo into 10 cm/4 in squares. Pipe seasoned, herby cheese onto the squares.

2 Start to roll the filo up, folding in the sides neatly as you go. Continue to roll into a thin cigarette shape. Dampen the end of the pastry with water to stick it in place.

3 Deep fry the börek in hot oil until lightly brown, tossing them in the fat to brown all over. Drain well. Garnish with dill and serve with a bowl of runny honey for dipping.

MINI SAMOSAS

Preparation time: 1 hour 15 mins
Cooking time: 35 mins
Makes About 100

INGREDIENTS

40 g/1½ oz lard
2 onions, finely chopped
900 g/2 lb lean minced beef
2-3 tsp ground coriander
3-4 tsp ground cumin
1-2 tsp cayenne pepper
1 tsp garam masala
3 carrots, grated
225 g/8 oz frozen peas
1-2 tbls chopped fresh coriander
Salt and ground black pepper
2 packets filo pastry, thawed (about 26 sheets)
100-150 g/4-5 oz butter, melted

FREEZER TIP

If cooking in advance, freeze on a plate or a baking tray and then pack into plastic bags. When ready to cook, preheat the oven to 190 C/375 F/Gas 5, place the frozen samosas on a buttered baking tray and cook for about 20 minutes or until golden.

1 Melt the lard in a large frying-pan and fry the onions for 2-3 minutes until lightly golden. Add the meat and fry, stirring occasionally, until well browned. Stir in the ground coriander, cumin, cayenne pepper and garam masala and fry over a high heat for 1 minute, then add the grated carrots, peas, fresh coriander and seasoning. Stir well, cover and cook for about 15 minutes or until the mixture has a fairly dry texture.

2 Take one sheet of filo pastry and lay on a large board. Brush with a little melted butter and lay a second sheet on top. Brush again with melted butter and then cut the rectangle widthways into 8 even strips.

3 Place a spoonful of mixture about 2.5 cm/1 in from the bottom edge and slightly to the right on each strip. Fold the bottom left hand corner over the filling to make a triangle. Fold up in neat triangles. Brush with melted butter. Continue until ingredients are finished.

4 Preheat oven to 200 C/400 F/Gas 6. Place the finished samosas on a lightly buttered baking tray and cook for about 10 minutes or until they turn a rich golden colour.

SALMON MOUSSES

INGREDIENTS
225 g/8 oz fresh salmon steak
1 bay leaf
1 strip pared lemon zest
2 eggs separated
75 ml/3 fl oz mayonnaise
2 tbls lemon juice
7 g/¼ oz powdered gelatine
1 tbls chopped fennel sprigs
Salt and ground white pepper
75 ml/3 fl oz double cream, lightly whipped
Oil, for greasing
175 g/6 oz smoked salmon slices
Lemon slices and dill sprigs, to garnish
Melba toast, to serve

Preparation time: 20 mins
+ chilling
Cooking time: 6-7 mins
Serves 4

1 Place the salmon steak, bay leaf and lemon zest in a pan and just cover with cold water. Bring to the boil slowly then cook gently for 1-2 minutes. Allow the fish to cool. Carefully remove skin and bones and mash the salmon.

2 Beat the egg yolks into the mayonnaise. Place the lemon juice in a small bowl and sprinkle over the gelatine. Dissolve the gelatine over boiling water. Cool slightly.

3 Stir the gelatine into the mayonnaise with the salmon, fennel and seasoning. Whisk the egg whites and fold into salmon mixture with the cream.

4 Oil 4 ramekin dishes and line with the smoked salmon. Spoon in the mousse and chill for 3-4 hours. Turn out. Garnish and serve with Melba toast.

PRAWN & AVOCADO BAKE

INGREDIENTS
1 small onion, finely chopped
50 g/2 oz butter
175 g/6 oz smoked back bacon, chopped, with rinds removed
450 g/1 lb cooked whole prawns or crayfish
3 large ripe avocados
2 tsp lime juice
Dash of Tabasco
Salt and ground black pepper
40 g/1½ oz fresh white breadcrumbs
2 tbls melted butter
6 lime wedges, to garnish

Preparation time: 15 mins
Cooking time: 30-35 mins
Serves 6

1 Preheat oven to 200 C/400 F/Gas 6. Sauté the onion in the butter until soft. Add the bacon and cook until all moisture has evaporated. Cool. Reserve 6 prawns or crayfish to garnish. Peel the rest.

2 Halve the avocados, remove the stones and scoop out the flesh with a spoon. Reserve shells. Dice the flesh into a bowl and add the lime juice, Tabasco, prawns or crayfish, and the onion and bacon mixture. Season and then spoon back into the avocado shells.

3 Sprinkle each filled avocado shell with a few fresh white breadcrumbs. Sit each one on a small square of foil and bring up the sides so that the avocado skin is protected. Arrange in a baking dish, dribble over the melted butter and bake for 15-20 minutes until golden.

4 Remove the foil from the baked avocados. Garnish with the reserved prawns or crayfish and lime wedges.

BAKED LANGOUSTINES

Preparation time: 10 mins
Cooking time: 5-10 mins
Serves 4

INGREDIENTS

900 g/2 lb langoustines, in the shell
Melted butter, to serve
Ground black pepper

FOR THE GARNISH
2 lemons, cut into wedges
Cucumber slices
Fresh dill sprigs

PRUE'S TIP
If live langoustines are not available, use thawed frozen crayfish tails split in half before baking. Bake in a buttered dish, cut-side down. Or use whole large raw prawn tails, and split the underside of the shell with scissors or a knife.

1 Preheat oven to 240 C/475 F/Gas 9. If you've been able to get live langoustines, put them in a frying basket and dip in a pan of boiling water for about 30 seconds. Cool them briefly under cold running water.

2 Halve the langoustines by cutting from the underside of the tail to the head with a sharp knife or a pair of kitchen scissors. Crack the claws open with nut crackers.

3 Lay the langoustines in a ovenproof dish and bake for 5-10 minutes, depending on their size. The shells will go darker pink and chalky white in patches when they are ready.

4 Serve with well-seasoned melted butter. Garnish with lemon wedges, cucumber slices and dill.

GOLDEN SQUID

Preparation time: 15 mins
Cooking time: 10 mins
Serves 4

INGREDIENTS

100 g/4 oz flour
1 egg yolk
2 egg whites
1 tbls melted butter
175 ml/6 fl oz beer
2 tbls mixed herbs, chopped
Salt and ground black pepper
Oil, for deep frying
450 g/1 lb cleaned squid, cut into thin rings
Boiled rice, to serve
Dill, to garnish

FOR THE SAUCE

6 tbls mayonnaise
2 tsp mustard powder
2 tbls Worcestershire sauce
1 onion, finely chopped
1 tsp Tabasco sauce
1 tbls dried basil
400 g/14 oz tinned tomatoes

PRUE'S TIP

Buying ready-cleaned squid tubes will save preparation time. If you can't find any, clean them yourself (see Techniques).

1 Sieve the flour into a mixing bowl making a well in the centre. Add the egg yolk, egg whites, melted butter and beer and gradually draw in the flour, using a wooden spoon. Beat well and stir in the mixed herbs and seasoning.

2 Heat oil for deep frying. Pour the batter into a large dish and add the squid rings. Coat each ring thoroughly in batter and then put a few of them at a time into a frying-basket and lower into the hot oil for 1 minute or until golden brown. As each batch is ready, drain on absorbent paper.

3 To make the sauce, combine all the ingredients in a blender, and then pass the mixture through a sieve to remove the tomato seeds. Serve the squid rings with the sauce and boiled rice. Garnish with dill.

HERBED CLAMS & PRAWNS

Preparation time: 20 mins
Cooking time: 18-19 mins
Serves 4-6

INGREDIENTS

700 g/1 lb 8 oz fresh clams
700 g/1 lb 8 oz raw unpeeled prawns
4 tbls olive oil
100 g/4 oz shallots, finely chopped
2 tbls freshly chopped mixed herbs
Pinch of paprika
1 tsp grated lemon zest
Ground black pepper
300 ml/½ pt medium or dry white wine

PRUE'S TIP

If you can't buy fresh clams use bottled ones instead (they will need only 8-10 minutes to cook), or try fresh mussels as an alternative.

1 Wash the clams thoroughly in cold running water and discard any that do not close. Chop the heads off the unpeeled prawns.

2 Heat the oil in a large pan with a tight-fitting lid and gently fry the shallots until they are just soft. Add the herbs, paprika, lemon zest and ground black pepper. Stir in the prawns and fry for 2-3 minutes.

3 Pour in the wine and bring the liquid to the boil and add the clams. Cover the pan and cook for 15 minutes, or until most of the clams have fully opened.

4 Toss the clams and prawns in the sauce. Remove any clams that have not opened and serve immediately.

MOULES MARINIERE

Preparation time: 20 mins
Cooking time: 8 mins
Serves 4

INGREDIENTS

1.8 kg/4 lb or 2.3 L/4 pt fresh mussels
2 onions, chopped
2 shallots, chopped
2 cloves of garlic, chopped
1 tbls chopped fresh parsley, plus extra to garnish
150 ml/¼ pt white wine
40 g/1½ oz butter
Salt and ground black pepper
Crusty French bread, to serve

"This is such an easy dish that it appears on every seaside bistro menu. I make it for good friends who will eat a lot of mussels and bread and little else, and who are prepared to lick their fingers." Prue

1 Clean the mussels. Throw away any that are cracked or that stay open when they are tapped.

2 Simmer the onions, shallots, garlic, parsley, wine and 150 ml/¼ pt water together for 2 minutes. Add the mussels, cover and leave to steam over a gentle heat for 5 minutes or until the shells open, shaking the pan occasionally. Drain by tipping into a colander set over a bowl.

3 Throw away any mussels that have not opened. Pour the mussel liquid from the bowl into a saucepan. Put the saucepan over a low heat, whisk in the butter and add the salt and pepper.

4 Put the mussels in a soup tureen or wide bowl. Pour the sauce over the top and sprinkle with the extra chopped parsley. Serve with the French bread to mop up the leftover sauce. Provide a large bowl for all the empty mussel shells.

PRUE'S TIP
The easiest way to get cooked mussels out of the shells is to use an empty pair of shells, which are still hinged, as pincers. Just grasp the mussel with the ends of the shells and pull.

CHINESE PANCAKE ROLLS

Preparation time: 30 mins
Cooking time: 20 mins
Serves 4

INGREDIENTS

100 g/4 oz flour	
1 tbls groundnut oil	
Pinch of salt	
Pinch of cayenne pepper	

FOR THE FILLING

2 tbls groundnut oil
100 g/4 oz minced pork
100 g/4 oz cabbage, finely sliced
50 g/2 oz leek, finely sliced
4 spring onions, sliced
50 g/2 oz bamboo shoots, cut into fine strips
50 g/2 oz mushrooms, chopped
100 g/4 oz beansprouts
100 g/4 oz frozen cooked prawns, shelled and chopped
2 tbls dark soy sauce
2 tbls dry sherry
Pinch of chilli powder
Oil, for deep frying
1 egg white, for brushing

PRUE'S TIP

To prevent the rolls from sticking, dip the frying basket in oil before frying.

1 For the pancakes, gradually beat 225 ml/8 fl oz cold water into the flour then stir in the oil, salt and cayenne pepper. Set aside for 30 minutes. Then use the batter to make 8 pancakes.

2 Meanwhile make the filling. Heat the oil in a wok or large frying-pan. Add the pork and cook for 2 minutes. Then add the cabbage, leek, spring onions and bamboo shoots and cook for 2 minutes. Add mushrooms and beansprouts and cook for 1 minute. Then add the prawns, soy sauce, sherry and chilli powder. Remove from the heat.

3 Heat the oil for deep frying to 190 C/375 F or until a small piece of bread browns in 60 seconds.

4 To assemble the pancake rolls, spoon 2 tbls filling onto each pancake. Fold over both sides and start to roll up. Brush the top flap of the pancake with a little egg white and finish rolling up.

5 Lay 4 rolls at a time in the frying basket. Fry each side for 2 minutes. Remove basket and reheat the oil. Fry for another 2 minutes on each side or until the rolls are a rich brown. Drain them on kitchen paper and serve immediately.

CRAB WONTONS

Preparation time: 30 mins
Cooking time: 15 mins
Makes 30

INGREDIENTS

175-225 g/6-8 oz white and brown
crab meat

6 spring onions, chopped

½ a red pepper, finely chopped

2.5 cm/1 in piece of root ginger, grated

15 g/½ oz butter

1 tsp chilli powder

4 tbls fresh breadcrumbs

Salt and ground black pepper

30 wonton wrappers

Oil, for deep-frying

FOR THE SAUCE

4 tbls plum sauce or jam

2 tbls tomato purée

3 tbls vinegar

1 tbls soy sauce

3 tbls brown sugar

75 ml/3 fl oz chicken stock

1 carrot, cut into strips

1 pineapple ring, cubed

PRUE'S TIP

Wonton wrappers – small squares of
fresh noodle dough – are available from
Chinese stores. Covered in cling film,
they will keep for a week in the fridge.

1 Mix white and brown crab meat
together in a bowl. Soften onions,
pepper and ginger in the butter in a
pan for 1-2 minutes. Stir in the chilli
powder and cook for ½ a minute. Cool.
Stir the vegetables into the crab meat with
the breadcrumbs and seasoning.

2 Place teaspoonfuls of the mixture on
wonton wrappers. Dampen wrappers
with water and enclose filling by
folding in half diagonally. Dampen, then
fold roughly in half again. Pinch firmly to
seal. Heat the oil and deep-fry for 1-2
minutes. Drain on absorbent paper.

3 To make the sauce, combine all the
ingredients in a pan, heat gently and
simmer for 1-2 minutes. Serve the
sauce with the wontons.

SEAFOOD BASKETS

Preparation time: 20 mins
Cooking time: 20 mins
Serves 6

INGREDIENTS

3 sheets of filo pastry

100 g/4 oz butter

1-2 tbls soy sauce

225 g/8 oz monkfish,
cut into 12 mm/½ in cubes

1 bunch spring onions, chopped

100 g/4 oz button mushrooms, sliced

12 asparagus tips, cooked

100 g/4 oz peeled prawns

12 cooked mussels

Salt and ground black pepper

PRUE'S TIP

We used jam jars to mould the filo pastry in this recipe, but if you do not have enough jam jars, heatproof mugs can be used instead.

1 Preheat oven to 200 C/400 F/Gas 6. Cut each sheet of filo pastry into six 10 cm/4 in squares. Melt the butter in a large frying-pan, remove from the heat. Brush each square with a little of the butter then place 3 squares, one on top of the other, over the base of 6 jam jars. Bake for 10 minutes. Cool slightly then remove the sheets of pastry from the base of the jars.

2 Place the pan with the remaining melted butter over the heat again and add the soy sauce and monkfish. Cook for 5 minutes, stirring constantly.

3 Add the spring onions and mushrooms and cook for a further 3 minutes. Stir in the asparagus, prawns and mussels and heat through. Season to taste with salt and pepper.

4 Spoon the filling into the baskets, transfer to warmed serving plates and serve immediately.

SALMON & TARRAGON PARCELS

Preparation time: 25 mins
Cooking time: 30 mins
Serves 4

INGREDIENTS

Four 2.5 cm/1 in thick salmon cutlets
450 g/1 lb puff pastry, thawed if frozen
1 egg, beaten

FOR THE STUFFING
225 g/8 oz cooked peeled shrimps
1 tbls fresh tarragon, finely chopped
Grated zest of 1 lemon
2 tbls double cream
1 egg yolk
2 tbls semolina
Salt and ground black pepper

WINE NOTE
A dry white wine such as a Chablis or Chardonnay would be a perfect accompanying wine.

1 Preheat oven to 200 C/400 F/Gas 6. Remove the skin and bone from each cutlet. To make the stuffing, process shrimps until finely cut up. Stir in the tarragon, lemon zest, cream, egg yolk, semolina and seasoning.

2 Roll out the pastry thinly. Cut out four 10 cm/4 in rounds and four 12.5 cm/5 in rounds. Place a salmon cutlet on each of the smaller rounds. Fill each one with a quarter of the stuffing. Dampen the pastry edges and place the larger rounds on top. Crimp the edges to seal. Cut a cross on the tops to allow the steam to escape.

3 Cut small fish shapes out of the remaining pastry and use to decorate the tops of the parcels (use beaten egg to secure them). Brush the tops with beaten egg to glaze. Place the salmon parcels on a baking sheet and bake for 25-30 minutes until golden.

SMOKED HADDOCK SOUFFLE

Preparation time: 30 mins
Cooking time: 1½ hours
Serves 4-6

INGREDIENTS

Melted butter, for greasing
2 tbls fresh white breadcrumbs
175 g/6 oz smoked haddock fillet
300 ml/½ pt milk
1 bay leaf
½ a small onion
6 peppercorns
450 g/1 lb fresh spinach
25 g/1 oz butter
25 g/1 oz flour
Salt and ground black pepper
¼ tsp mustard powder
4 large eggs, separated

1 Preheat oven to 200 C/400 F/Gas 6 and place a baking tray on the middle shelf. Brush a 1.2 L/2 pt soufflé dish with the melted butter and coat with the breadcrumbs. Lay the smoked haddock in a shallow ovenproof dish and cover with 150 ml/¼ pt of the milk. Add the bay leaf, onion and peppercorns, cover lightly with a lid or foil and bake in the oven for 30 minutes or until the fish is cooked. Strain the milk through a sieve and reserve. Mash the haddock finely with the back of a fork, then set it aside.

2 Rinse the spinach. Shake off excess water and place in a large non-aluminium pan. Set over a low heat and cook gently for 5 minutes or until soft. Drain, cool, then chop finely.

3 Melt the butter, stir in the flour and cook for 30 seconds. Take the pan from the heat and gradually add the reserved and remaining milk. Return to the heat and bring to the boil. Simmer for 1 minute, remove from the heat, season and add the mustard powder. Allow to cool slightly, then beat in the egg yolks. Stir in the mashed haddock and spinach.

4 Whisk the egg whites until they are stiff. Fold 2 large spoonfuls into the sauce to slacken it, then gently fold in the remaining egg whites. Spoon the mixture into the prepared soufflé dish, place on the heated baking tray and cook for 40-45 minutes or until well-risen and rich brown in colour. Serve immediately.

PARSLEY CHICKEN CHOUX

Preparation time: 25 mins
Cooking time: 35 mins
Serves 4

INGREDIENTS

½ quantity basic choux pastry
(see Techniques)

FOR THE FILLING

15 g/½ oz butter, plus extra for greasing
15 g/½ oz flour
150 ml/¼ pt milk
1 bay leaf
3 tbls finely chopped parsley
1 tsp chopped fresh thyme
4 tbls single cream
Salt and ground black pepper
100 g/4 oz cooked breast of chicken, diced
1 tbls melted butter
Salad leaves, to garnish

FREEZER TIP

To freeze cooked choux buns, pack in a plastic container and use within 1 month. Thaw and heat in oven to refresh the pastry before you fill it.

1 Preheat oven to 200 C/400 F/Gas 6. Grease 4 brioche moulds and divide the choux between the tins, placing a small spoonful of the dough on the top of each. Cook for 30-35 minutes until well risen and golden brown.

2 Place the butter, flour, milk and bay leaf in a pan and heat gently, whisking until the sauce thickens and boils. Remove the bay leaf.

3 Stir 2 tbls of the chopped parsley, the thyme, cream and seasoning into the sauce, then add the chicken, stir well until the chicken is coated in the sauce and heated through.

4 Remove the choux from the tins and cut off the tops. Brush the tops with melted butter and sprinkle over the remaining parsley. Spoon the filling into the choux buns and replace tops. Serve hot with a freshly arranged salad garnish.

MIXED FISH KEBABS

Preparation time: 15 mins
+ marinating
Cooking time: 6-10 mins
Serves 6

INGREDIENTS
450 g/1 lb fresh tuna, skinned
450 g/1 lb swordfish fillet, skinned
450 g/1 lb peeled raw scampi
Curly endive, to serve
Finely shredded orange zest, to garnish

FOR THE MARINADE
2 tbls olive oil
1 tbls lemon juice
½ tsp ground black pepper

FOR THE PESTO SAUCE
2 tbls chopped fresh parsley
2 tbls chopped fresh basil
1 tbls blanched almonds
2 cloves of garlic
2 tbls Pecorino cheese, grated
200 ml/7 fl oz olive oil
Salt and ground black pepper

1 Cut both fish into even chunks the same size as the scampi. Thread the fish chunks and scampi onto wooden or metal skewers.

2 Mix the marinade ingredients together. Brush over the kebabs. Marinate for 2-3 hours.

3 In a processor or blender, grind the herbs, almonds, garlic and cheese to a paste. Transfer to a bowl and blend in the oil to form a thick sauce. Season.

4 Place the kebabs under a hot grill. Cook for 3 minutes on each side, until just firm, basting with any remaining marinade liquid.

5 Serve the kebabs on a bed of curly endive with the shredded zest and a little pesto sauce spooned over.

SHISH KEBABS

Preparation time: 10 mins
+ marinating
Cooking time: 10-12 mins
Serves 6

INGREDIENTS
900 g/2 lb leg of lamb
2 cloves of garlic, crushed
Salt and ground black pepper
150 ml/¼ pt dry white wine
2 tbls olive oil
Boiled rice, to serve
Fresh bay leaves, to garnish

1 Cut the skin and fat from the meat and cut the meat into 2.5 cm/1 in cubes. Put into a bowl with the garlic, seasoning, wine and oil. Cover and leave to marinate for 6-8 hours or overnight.

2 Heat the grill. Thread the meat onto 6 skewers (allow about 6 pieces per skewer). Cook under the hot grill for 5-6 minutes on each side, or even better over a hot charcoal fire.

3 Serve the skewers of meat on a flat dish, with plain boiled rice. Garnish with bay leaves.

SWEETBREADS BONNE FEMME

Preparation time: 30 minutes
+ soaking
Cooking time: 20 mins
Serves 4

INGREDIENTS

450 g/1 lb lambs' sweetbreads
3 tbls milk
Salt and ground black pepper
6 tbls fine dry white breadcrumbs
300 ml/½ pt chicken stock
2 celery stalks, cut into fine matchsticks
1 carrot, cut into fine matchsticks
1 small swede, cut into fine matchsticks
1 leek, halved and cut into fine slices
1 tsp cornflour
6 tbls double cream
1 tbls snipped chives
50 g/2 oz butter

1 Soak the sweetbreads in cold water overnight. Plunge them into boiling water and bring back to the boil. Simmer for 1 minute, then drain and cool under running water.

2 Remove any tough membrane and fat. Season the milk with salt and pepper and dip the sweetbreads into it. Drain each one to remove excess, then coat in breadcrumbs. Set aside.

3 Bring the chicken stock to the boil. Add celery, carrot and swede. Bring back to the boil and simmer for 2 minutes. Add the leek and simmer for 30-60 seconds until the vegetables are just tender. Drain vegetables and reserve the stock. Place vegetables in a heated serving dish. Cover, set aside and keep warm.

4 Return the stock to the pan and heat until reduced to about half. Mix the cornflour with 2 tsp cold water. Add to the reduced stock with the double cream and chives. Heat the sauce gently until boiling. Season, reduce heat and simmer for 1-2 minutes.

5 Heat the butter in a large frying-pan. When it begins to bubble, add the breadcrumb-coated sweetbreads and fry for 5-6 minutes until golden. Turn them over halfway through cooking. Place some of the cooked vegetables on a hot serving plate and top with the sweetbreads. Spoon over a little of the cream and chive sauce and then serve.

FISH
&
SHELLFISH

CLAM MARINIERE

Preparation time: 10 mins
Cooking time: 20 mins
Serves 4

INGREDIENTS

900 g/2 lb fresh clams
2 tbls butter
1 large onion, finely chopped
3 cloves of garlic, crushed
1 tbls flour
300 ml/½ pt dry white wine
225 ml/8 fl oz double cream
Salt and ground black pepper
4 tbls freshly chopped parsley
Boiled spaghetti, to serve

PRUE'S TIP

Fresh clams are now widely available from fishmongers. However, if you are unable to buy them fresh, use tinned shelled clams instead. Just cook over a medium heat for 2-3 minutes or until they are heated through.

WINE NOTE

Serve with a light white wine such as Muscadet or a crisp Soave.

1 Put the clams in a large bowl and wash thoroughly in cold water, changing the water several times. Drain the clams.

2 Heat the butter in a large saucepan over a moderate heat. Add the chopped onion and crushed garlic and cook for 5 minutes or until soft and transparent. Stir in the flour using a wooden spoon and cook for 2 minutes.

3 Gradually pour in the wine, stirring constantly. Cook for 2 minutes, until smooth and slightly thickened.

4 Add the clams to the sauce, turn up the heat and shake well. Cover the saucepan with a lid. Cook, shaking the pan occasionally for 15 minutes or until all the clams have opened up.

5 Reduce the heat to low and stir in the cream. Season, sprinkle with the chopped parsley and serve on a bed of hot spaghetti.

SAFFRON MUSSELS

Preparation time: 30 mins
Cooking time: 25 mins
Serves 4

INGREDIENTS

1.8 kg/4 lb fresh mussels, in their shells
150 ml/¼ pt white wine
1 bouquet garni
350 g/12 oz pasta quills
25 g/1 oz butter
1 onion, finely chopped
50 g/2 oz button mushrooms
Pinch of cayenne pepper
Pinch of saffron strands
225 ml/8 fl oz single cream
1 egg yolk
Sprig of basil, to garnish

PRUE'S TIP

There are two golden rules to remember when cooking mussels. Discard any uncooked shells which refuse to close when you tap them, and throw away any that remain resolutely closed when cooked - this means they are bad.

WINE NOTE

A chilled Italian white wine such as Orvieto can be served with this dish.

1 Scrub and clean the mussels under cold running water. Remove the beards and discard any mussels that remain open. Place in a large pan with half the wine, 150 ml/¼ pt water and the bouquet garni.

2 Cover tightly, bring to the boil and cook for 5-7 minutes or until the mussels have opened. Remove with a slotted spoon, discarding the liquid. Cool slightly then remove the mussels from their shells. Bring a large pan of water to the boil, add the pasta, and cook for 10 minutes until just al dente.

3 In a frying-pan heat the butter then sauté the onion until softened. Slice the mushrooms, and cook for 2 minutes. Add the remaining wine, the cayenne and the saffron. Boil to reduce the wine to 50 ml/2 fl oz. Reduce the heat, then stir in the cream and mussels. Heat gently until the cream just begins to boil.

4 Remove from heat and stir in the egg yolk. Drain pasta, spoon sauce over it, garnish and serve.

SPANISH PAELLA

Preparation time: 10 mins
Cooking time: 1 hour
Serves 6

INGREDIENTS

100 g/4 oz chorizo sausage
3 tbls olive oil
6 small pieces of chicken
75 g/3 oz belly pork, diced
2 cloves of garlic, crushed
1 green pepper, halved and sliced
1 red pepper, halved and sliced
1 large Spanish onion, chopped
350 g/12 oz long grain rice
1 L/1¾ pt chicken stock
1 tsp saffron powder
¼ tsp cayenne pepper
225 g/8 oz tomatoes, skinned and quartered
Salt
100 g/4 oz unshelled prawns
225 g/8 oz mussels, cleaned
100 g/4 oz petits pois

"I love real paella, when the rice is cooked along with everything else in the classic manner. Use saffron if you can afford it. It gives an authentic Spanish flavour."
　　　　　　　　Prue

1 Heat a paella pan or frying-pan. Slice the chorizo and add to the pan. Cook for a few minutes until browned on both sides, then remove the chorizo slices from the pan with a slotted spoon. Add the oil and fry the chicken pieces and diced pork over a high heat until they are golden brown and sealed on all sides.

2 Remove the meat from the pan and keep warm. Fry the garlic, peppers and onion for 5 minutes until softened. Add the rice and stir to coat with the oil. Cook for about 2 minutes, stirring continuously.

3 Pour in the stock and stir in the saffron, cayenne and tomatoes and season with salt. Put the meat back in the pan and bring to the boil. Reduce the heat, return the chorizo and add the prawns and mussels. Carefully stir, cover loosely with foil and simmer for 30 minutes. Add the petit pois for the last 5 minutes of cooking time.

PRUE'S TIP
Saffron is very expensive to buy. A cheaper alternative is to use just a little of the Indian spice turmeric.

MONKFISH IN YOGHURT

Preparation time: 5 mins
Cooking time: 25 mins
Serves 4

INGREDIENTS

225 g/8 oz natural yoghurt
1 tbls cornflour
2 tbls milk
10 strands of saffron
1 tsp salt
1 tsp cayenne pepper
300 ml/½ pt double cream
1 large fennel, trimmed and sliced
1 large onion, sliced
700 g/1 lb 8 oz monkfish, filleted
Chopped fresh fennel leaves
Sprigs of fennel or dill, to garnish

1 Pour the yoghurt into a large heavy-based saucepan. Mix the cornflour with the milk in a cup until smooth. Mix into the yoghurt.

2 Set the pan over a medium heat and bring the yoghurt mixture to the boil. Heat for about 2 minutes, stirring continuously to prevent lumps forming. Add the saffron, salt and cayenne pepper then stir in the double cream.

3 Add the sliced fennel and onion to the pan. Bring to the boil again, cover with the lid and simmer over a low heat for 10 minutes.

4 Cut the monkfish into fairly large pieces, about 4-5 cm/1½-2 in thick. Add to the onion mixture in the saucepan and simmer for a further 10-15 minutes until the fish is cooked.

5 Finally, stir in the chopped fennel leaves. Transfer to a serving dish. Garnish with a sprig of fennel.

QUICK FISH CURRY

Preparation time: 20 mins
Cooking time: 30 mins
Serves 4

INGREDIENTS

50 g/2 oz unsweetened shredded coconut
3 tbls butter
2 onions, finely chopped
2 cloves of garlic, crushed
2.5 cm/1 in piece fresh ginger, shredded
2 tsp ground coriander
½ tsp chilli powder
½ tsp ground turmeric
1 tsp garam masala
½ tsp ground cumin
1 tbls red lentils, washed and drained
Salt and ground black pepper
50 g/2 oz creamed coconut
900 g/2 lb monkfish or cod fillets, sliced
4 tbls double cream
2 tbls chopped coriander
Boiled white rice noodles, to serve

1 Toast the shredded coconut under a medium grill for 2 minutes, until golden brown. Set aside.

2 Melt the butter in a large deep-sided frying-pan, add the finely chopped onions, garlic and ginger and fry over gentle heat for 5 minutes. Stir in the ground coriander, chilli, turmeric, garam masala, cumin and red lentils and cook for a further minute.

3 Pour over 600 ml/1 pt water and bring to the boil. Add the creamed coconut and season with salt and pepper. Lower the heat and simmer for 10 minutes until the sauce has thickened.

4 Slide in the sliced fish and cook for a further 10-15 minutes, or until the fish is cooked through. Stir in the cream and fresh coriander. Taste and adjust the seasoning.

5 Transfer the fish curry to a warmed serving platter. Garnish with the toasted coconut and serve with hot boiled white noodles.

COD IN COCONUT MILK

Preparation time: 15 mins
Cooking time: 30 mins
Serves 6

INGREDIENTS

2 tbls olive oil
1 large Spanish onion, finely sliced
4 spring onions, trimmed and chopped
2 cloves of garlic, crushed
1 green chilli, seeded and finely chopped
1 green pepper, sliced
400 g/14 oz tinned chopped tomatoes
3 tbls finely chopped fresh parsley
1 tbls finely chopped fresh coriander
Salt and ground black pepper
350 ml/12 fl oz coconut milk
700 g/1 lb 8 oz skinned cod fillets, cubed
Boiled rice, to serve

PRUE'S TIP
Make coconut milk by melting blocks of creamed coconut in boiling water. Use three-quarters of a block for 600 ml/1 pt water.

1 Heat the oil in a large flame-proof casserole. Gently fry the sliced Spanish onion. Add the spring onions, garlic cloves, chilli and green pepper. Cook for 2 minutes.

2 Add the tomatoes and cook for 5 minutes. Stir in the parsley and coriander. Season to taste with salt and ground black pepper.

3 Pour over enough of the coconut milk to make a thick sauce. Stir. Gently bring to the boil, then reduce the heat and stir again.

4 Add the fish fillets and simmer for 15 minutes. Season to taste. Serve immediately with rice.

ITALIAN FISH STEW

Preparation time: 10 mins
Cooking time: 35-40 mins
Serves 6

INGREDIENTS

2 tbls olive oil
2 onions, thinly sliced
2 cloves of garlic, thinly sliced
175 g/6 oz bacon, diced
1 red pepper, seeded and thinly sliced
1 yellow pepper, seeded and thinly sliced
125 ml/4 fl oz red wine
450 g/1 lb tinned tomatoes
450 g/1 lb new potatoes, scrubbed and halved
1 tsp thyme
2 bay leaves
Salt and ground black pepper
450 g/1 lb fillet of firm fleshed white fish
225 g/8 oz squid, cut into 12 mm/½ in rings
3 tbls fresh parsley, finely chopped

1 Heat the oil in a large flameproof casserole. Add the onions and garlic and fry over a low heat for 5 minutes. Stir in the bacon and peppers and cook for 5 more minutes.

2 Add the wine, tomatoes, potatoes, thyme and bay leaves and season with salt and pepper. Bring to the boil, then simmer for 15 minutes.

3 Stir in the fish and squid and simmer for 10-15 minutes or until the fish is cooked. Just before serving, taste and adjust the seasoning if necessary. Sprinkle the fresh parsley over the top of the stew.

FAMILY FISHCAKE

Preparation time: 20 mins
+ chilling
Cooking time: 45 mins
Serves 4-6

INGREDIENTS

350 g/12 oz smoked haddock
300 ml/½ pt milk
350 g/12 oz potatoes, peeled
Salt and ground black pepper
65 g/2½ oz butter
1 egg, beaten
1 tbls chopped parsley, plus extra to garnish
1 tbls chopped chives
1½ tbls oil
Green salad, to serve

1 Put the smoked haddock into a frying-pan, cover with the milk and cook gently over a low heat for 10-15 minutes or until the fish is firm, and cooked through. Remove the fish from the milk, cool and then remove any skin and bones and flake the flesh.

2 Cut up the potatoes roughly and boil in salted water until soft. Drain and mash with 25 g/1 oz of the butter until smooth. Season with salt and pepper, stir in the flaked fish and add a little egg. The mixture should be soft but not too sloppy. Stir in the chopped parsley and chives. Chill. When firm, heat the remaining butter and the oil in a non-stick frying-pan. Add the mixture and press it down with the back of a fork.

3 Fry over a moderate heat for about 10 minutes or until golden brown. To turn it over, place a large plate over the pan and, holding it down with the palm of your hand, flip the fishcake onto the plate. Slide it back into the pan and cook the other side for 10 minutes. Slide it onto a serving dish, garnish with parsley and cut into wedges. Serve with a salad of oakleaf lettuce and endive.

SOLE WITH LEMON SAUCE

Preparation time: 20 mins
Cooking time: 35-45 mins
Serves 4

INGREDIENTS

900 g/2 lb fresh lemon sole fillets
Juice of 1 lemon
Salt and ground white pepper
225 g/8 oz fresh asparagus,
cut into 5 cm/2 in lengths
25 g/1 oz butter

FOR THE SAUCE

300 ml/½ pt chicken stock
Grated zest of ½ a lemon
1 tbls cornflour
Juice of 1½ lemons
2 egg yolks, lightly beaten
2 tsp sugar
1 tbls finely chopped fresh tarragon
Pinch of ground ginger

FOR THE GARNISH

Lemon slices
Fresh tarragon sprigs

MICROWAVE TIP

Arrange the rolled fish fillets in a shallow microwave-proof dish. Cover and cook on HIGH (100%) for 10-15 minutes, rearranging 3 times, or until fish flakes. Stand for 2 minutes and then serve.

1 Wash the fish fillets and pat dry with absorbent paper. Pour over the lemon juice and season with salt and pepper.

2 Boil the asparagus for 5 minutes. Drain then rinse under cold water. Dry on absorbent paper. Put 2 asparagus pieces onto each fillet and roll up. Grease a large plate with butter then place the fish on the plate. Dot with the remaining butter. Cover with foil and place over a saucepan half-filled with boiling water. Steam for 15-20 minutes.

3 Meanwhile make the sauce. Put the chicken stock and lemon zest into a saucepan. Bring to the boil. Lower the heat and simmer for 5 minutes. Mix the cornflour with the lemon juice and add to the stock. Cook over a low heat for 5 minutes, stirring constantly.

4 Put the egg yolks and sugar into a heatproof bowl or the top of a double boiler. Gradually pour in the stock mixture, beating with a wooden spoon as you pour. Heat over a pan of boiling water and cook for 5-10 minutes, until the sauce thickens, stirring frequently. Add the tarragon and ginger. Adjust the seasoning.

5 Transfer to a warmed serving platter, pour over the sauce and garnish with lemon slices and fresh tarragon sprigs.

GRILLED FISH STEAKS

Preparation time: 10 mins
+ marinating
Cooking time: 8 mins
Serves 4

INGREDIENTS

2 tbls fresh mixed Mediterranean herbs, including thyme, basil, marjoram and rosemary, chopped
3 tbls extra virgin olive oil
1 tbls black peppercorns
Juice of 1 lemon
2 leaves of fennel, sliced
Four 350 g/12 oz halibut steaks
Sea salt
Fresh herbs, to garnish

PRUE'S TIP
You can use dried mixed or Provençal mixed herbs in place of fresh herbs, but do not add as much as dried herbs have a more concentrated flavour than fresh.

1 To make the marinade, mix together the herbs, oil, fennel, peppercorns and lemon juice. Turn the steaks in the marinade and chill for 8 hours.

2 Preheat the grill until really hot. Lift the fish steaks from the marinade and grill for about 2 minutes each side.

3 Spoon over the rest of the marinade, including the fennel slices and grill the fish again until the fennel strips are just beginning to blacken at the edges.

4 Sprinkle the fish with sea salt and any pan juices. Garnish with fresh herbs and serve immediately.

PROVENCAL PLATTER

Preparation time: 45 mins
Cooking time: 25 mins
Serves 8

INGREDIENTS

8 fresh tuna steaks

Extra virgin olive oil,
for shallow frying and dressing

20 fresh rosemary leaves, chopped

1 head of fennel

2 small courgettes, sliced

16 small tomatoes

16 tiny new potatoes, scrubbed and halved

1 clove of garlic, crushed

Sea salt

2 large yellow peppers

Juice of ½ a lemon

12 coriander seeds, finely crushed

225 g/8 oz small French beans,
cooked until tender

16 quails' eggs, hard-boiled and peeled

50 g/2 oz black olives

Ground black pepper

1 Brush the tuna steaks with the olive oil and scatter with the fresh rosemary. Heat the grill to maximum and grill the steaks for 2 minutes on each side. Brown the outside while leaving the middle of the fish moist.

2 Slice the fennel into very fine strips and put in a bowl of icy water. This will make it go crisp.

3 Fry the courgette slices very fast in olive oil to slightly singe them. Cool. Make deep parallel cuts in the tomatoes without cutting right through and insert the courgette slices.

4 Boil the potatoes for 15 minutes. Drain them and toss in a little olive oil, garlic and sea salt while hot.

5 Grill the peppers until black. Cool in a polythene bag, then rub the skins off under cold water. Slice. Toss in 1 tbls oil, 1 tsp lemon juice and the crushed coriander seeds.

6 Drain and dry the fennel and dress it lightly with oil and 1 tsp lemon juice. On a large platter, arrange all the ingredients in neat clumps or rows. Add olives and sprinkle over the remaining lemon juice. Season with pepper.

SOLE FLORENTINE

Preparation time: 15 mins
Cooking time: 12-17 mins
Serves 4

INGREDIENTS

4 whole Dover sole,
with black skin removed (see Techniques)

1 tbls vegetable oil

1 small onion, finely chopped

2 cloves of garlic, crushed

8 button mushrooms, chopped

50 g/2 oz pine kernels, plus extra to garnish

450 g/1 lb spinach,
cooked, drained and chopped

50 g/2 oz grated Parmesan cheese

Salt and ground black pepper

25 g/1 oz butter, melted

6 tbls fine breadcrumbs

Sprigs of mint, to garnish

1 Trim off any fins and untidy edges from the sole using a pair of scissors. Heat the oil in a frying-pan. Fry the onion and garlic until soft. Add the mushrooms and pine kernels and cook for a further 3 minutes, then remove the pan from the heat.

2 Add the chopped spinach to the mushroom mixture and heat thoroughly. Stir in the Parmesan and season to taste. Remove from the heat and leave to cool.

3 Take a sharp pointed kitchen knife and use it to make a cut down the central line of the fish where the fillets meet, making sure that you cut right through to the backbone of the fish.

4 Use the knife to scrape the fillets from the bone to form two pockets. Roll back the fillets. Snip the backbone with scissors in three places so you can free it and remove the pieces (see Techniques).

5 Season inside the fish cavities. Divide the cooled stuffing among the sole. Brush the fish with melted butter. Scatter the breadcrumbs over the fish and press down.

6 Grill the sole for 5-10 minutes or until it is firm and just cooked. Sprinkle the pine kernels over the spinach and garnish with sprigs of mint before serving.

SPINACH-STUFFED TROUT

Preparation time: 20 mins
+ chilling
Cooking time: 45-55 mins
Serves 4

INGREDIENTS

175 g/6 oz fillet whiting
300 ml/½ pt milk
Salt and ground black pepper
100 g/4 oz frozen spinach,
thawed and squeezed dry
75 ml/3 fl oz double cream
2 tbls lemon juice
4 tbls fresh white breadcrumbs
1 egg white, whipped
Four 200 g/7 oz rainbow trout,
cleaned and gutted (see Techniques),
with tails and heads left on
75 g/3 oz butter
6 tbls chopped fresh watercress

FOR THE GARNISH
Sprigs of watercress
Lemon slices

1 Preheat oven to 180 C/350 F/Gas 4. Arrange whiting in a frying-pan and pour over the milk. Season. Gently poach for 5-10 minutes.

2 Drain, skin, bone and flake the whiting. Put in a food processor with the spinach, cream, 1 tbls lemon juice, breadcrumbs and seasoning.

3 Process the mixture in short bursts until smooth, then pour into a clean bowl. Allow the mixture to cool, then gently fold in the whipped egg white until it is thoroughly combined. Cover and chill for 1 hour.

4 Make sure the trout is dry, then stuff with the spinach mousse, using a spoon. Do not overfill. Lay the fish in an ovenproof dish. Melt the butter in a saucepan. Stir in the rest of the lemon juice with the chopped watercress. Season.

5 Pour the sauce over the fish, cover the dish with foil and bake in the oven for about 40 minutes. Remove the foil and transfer the fish to the serving plates. Reshape if necessary. Garnish with watercress and lemon and serve.

RED MULLET IN ORANGE

Preparation time: 10 mins
Cooking time: 15 mins
Serves 4

INGREDIENTS

Four 225 g/8 oz red mullet
Salt and ground black pepper
Juice of 2 oranges
1 tbls olive oil
50 g/2 oz butter
1 tsp sugar
1 tbls chopped fresh coriander
FOR THE GARNISH
Sprigs of fresh coriander
Orange slices

1 Clean the mullet leaving the head and tail on. Season with salt and black pepper and sprinkle with a little of the orange juice.

2 Heat the oil in a frying-pan and add the butter. When the butter has melted, brown the fish on each side, reduce the heat and cook for about 5 minutes on each side.

3 When the fish are cooked, transfer to a heated serving dish and keep warm. Pour the remaining orange juice into the sizzling pan, bring to the boil and reduce until syrupy.

4 Add the sugar and check the seasoning. Stir in the chopped coriander. Pour the sauce over the fish, garnish with the coriander and orange slices and serve immediately.

PRUE'S TIP
If you don't have a frying-pan large enough to hold all the fish, brown them one at a time, transfer to a baking dish and bake in the oven for 10 minutes at 190 C/375 F/Gas 5.

SERVING NOTE
Sauté potatoes or new potatoes oozing in butter, and some lightly-cooked green beans will go well with the red mullet.

WINE NOTE
Try serving a well-chilled bottle of Vinho Verde with this tasty dish.

THAI-BAKED FISH

Preparation time: 5 mins
+ marinating
Cooking time: 40 mins
Serves 4

INGREDIENTS

1.1 kg/2 lb 8 oz sea bass

FOR THE MARINADE

1 tsp sugar
1 tsp salt
1 tbls groundnut oil
2.5 cm/1 in fresh root ginger, shredded
2 cloves of garlic, crushed
1 red chilli, sliced
Squeeze of lemon
4 spring onions, chopped

FOR THE SAUCE

4 tbls dry white Vermouth
2 tbls sunflower oil
4 tbls groundnut oil
2 tbls dark soy sauce
Fresh coriander leaves
2 spring onions, chopped
50 g/2 oz peanuts, toasted

1 Make the marinade by mixing the sugar, salt, groundnut oil, shredded ginger, garlic, chilli, lemon juice and chopped spring onions. Pour this over the fish. Cover with foil and refrigerate for approximately 4 hours.

2 Preheat oven to 180 C/350 F/Gas 4. Bake the fish in the oven for 35 minutes or until a skewer will slide easily into the flesh.

3 Just before serving, put the Vermouth, sunflower oil, groundnut oil and soy sauce into a pan, boil briefly and pour over the fish. Sprinkle the coriander leaves, spring onions and peanuts over the top.

SALMON CHAUDFROID

Preparation time: 40 mins
+ setting
Cooking time: 28 mins
Serves 25

INGREDIENTS

3.2 kg/7 lb salmon

6 batches court bouillon (see Techniques)
3 batches chaudfroid sauce (see Techniques)
900 ml/1½ pt prepared aspic, using 40 g/1½ oz aspic jelly powder

FOR THE GARNISH

3 carrots, sliced lengthways
½ a cucumber, sliced lengthways
1 tsp green peppercorns
Flat-leaved parsley
Fresh coriander sprigs
Fresh dill springs
100 g/4 oz peeled and unpeeled prawns
1 lemon, sliced

"I like to do this dish when I'm really showing off because it looks so very professional. It takes some time and patience, but really isn't very difficult" Prue

1 Rinse and wipe the cavity of the salmon clean. Place in a large fish kettle and pour in the cooled court bouillon. Cover, bring to the boil, then turn down the heat so the liquid is agitating a little, but not bubbling. Poach gently for 4 minutes per 450 g/1 lb. The fish is cooked when the dorsal fin comes away easily. Cool for at least 3 hours in the liquid, and then leave to chill overnight.

2 Carefully remove the fins and peel off the skin with a palette knife, leaving the head and tail intact. Put the fish on a wire rack set over a baking tray. Pour the chaudfroid sauce evenly over the salmon, leaving the head and tail clear. Chill until set.

3 Put the salmon on a large oval platter. Cut heart shapes out of the carrot and cucumber with aspic cutters. Dip in aspic before putting on the salmon and on the platter. Garnish with peppercorns and tiny sprigs of parsley. Chill until decorations are firmly set.

4 Chill the remaining prepared aspic jelly until it is on the point of setting and then spoon it all over the salmon and the platter to make a thin coating. Chill, then decorate the platter with herbs, prawns and lemon and serve.

SALMON EN CROUTE

Preparation time: 1 hour
+ chilling
Cooking time: 1 hour
Serves 6

INGREDIENTS

450 g/1 lb puff pastry, thawed if frozen
1 egg, beaten, for glazing
3 tbls semolina
1.8 kg/4 lb salmon, skinned and filleted
Zest of ½ a lemon
Juice of ½ a lemon
Few sprigs of fresh tarragon
Salt and ground black pepper
75 g/3 oz butter

FOR THE GARNISH

Watercress sprigs
Lemon slices

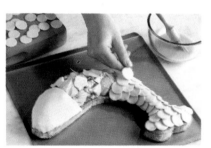

1 Preheat oven to 200 C/400 F/Gas 6. Roll out two-thirds of the pastry into a large oval, approximately 35.5 cm/14 in length. Cut out a curved fish shape with a sharp knife and lift onto a baking tray. Cut narrow strips from the trimmings. Brush with beaten egg and position around the edge of the pastry fish, egg side down. Prick the base with a fork and chill in the fridge for 10 minutes.

2 Bake the pastry fish for 12 minutes or until the sides are well risen and golden brown. Leave to cool, then sprinkle the base with semolina.

3 Cut the salmon into large chunks and mix with the lemon zest, lemon juice and tarragon leaves and season with salt and plenty of ground black pepper. Pack into the pastry case, heaping the filling up along the centre. Cut the butter into pieces and press into the salmon.

4 Roll out the rest of the pastry thinly. Brush the top with egg. Cut out pastry to cover the fish head and press firmly onto the sides of the pastry case, egg side down. Stamp the rest of the pastry into small circles.

5 Starting at the tail end, arrange the circles like scales, overlapping them and pressing them egg side down to stick them to the pastry case. Position one circle for an eye then chill for 15 minutes.

6 Brush all over with beaten egg and bake for 15 minutes. Lower the oven temperature to 150 C/275 F/Gas 1 for a further 30 minutes. If the pastry browns too quickly cover loosely with foil. Slide onto a serving plate and garnish with watercress and lemon slices.

MIXED FISH PIE

Preparation time: 25 mins
Cooking time: 35 mins
Serves 6

INGREDIENTS

50 g/2 oz butter
8 queen scallops
225 g/8 oz monkfish, cut in 2.5cm/1 in chunks
225 g/8 oz cod fillet, cut in 2.5 cm/1 in chunks
225 g/8 oz fresh salmon fillet, cut in 2.5 cm/1 in chunks
300 ml/½ pt Müller-Thurgau white wine
225 g/8 oz peeled prawns
3 tbls flour
150 ml/¼ pt milk
1 tbls whisky
2 tbls chopped parsley
Salt and ground black pepper
450 g/1 lb puff pastry (see Techniques)
1 egg, beaten, to glaze

1 Melt the butter in a frying-pan. Add the scallops and monkfish, toss in the butter for 2-3 minutes to cook slightly. Remove from the pan using a slotted spoon and put into a 1.2 L/2 pt oval pie dish. Reserve the remaining butter in the frying-pan.

2 Place the cod and salmon in a saucepan and pour over the wine. Bring slowly to the boil. Turn off the heat and leave the fish in the wine for 5 minutes. Remove the fish from the pan with a slotted spoon and place in the pie dish. Add prawns.

3 Sprinkle the flour over the butter left in the frying pan and cook for 2 minutes. Pour over the wine that the fish was cooked in, stirring all the time, then stir in the milk. Bring to the boil stirring until thickened, simmer for 2 minutes then stir in the whisky, parsley and seasoning. Allow to cool slightly then pour over the fish and set aside.

4 Preheat oven to 200 C/400 F/ Gas 6. Roll out the pastry to 6 mm/¼ in thick, cut 12 mm/½ in strips from around the pastry and lay around dampened edges of the dish. Wet the pastry edge and lay remaining rolled pastry on top. Trim off the excess pastry, knock up and crimp the edges.

5 Cut a hole in the top of the pastry and decorate with any trimmings. Brush top with beaten egg and bake in the oven for 25 minutes or until the pastry is risen and golden brown.

POULTRY
&
GAME BIRDS

STUFFED DRUMSTICKS

INGREDIENTS
16 chicken drumsticks
Sunflower oil, for brushing
Salt and ground black pepper
Lime wedges, to garnish
Coriander sprigs, to garnish

FOR THE STUFFING
4 limes
100 g/4 oz fresh breadcrumbs
8 tbls chopped fresh coriander
1 tsp cayenne pepper

Preparation time: 35 mins
Cooking time: 15-20 mins
Serves 8

1 Grate the zest from the limes. Cut limes in half and squeeze the juice into a bowl. Add the zest and other stuffing ingredients. Mix all the stuffing ingredients well to combine.

2 Insert the blade of a knife, or just a finger, carefully under the chicken skin on the fattest part of each drumstick. Loosen the skin from the flesh, making sure that you don't pierce the skin. This allows space for stuffing.

3 Divide the stuffing mixture evenly among the drumsticks. Hold back the skin and spoon the stuffing under it. Fold the skin back and carefully rub the drumsticks to spread the stuffing evenly under the skin.

4 Before cooking on the barbecue, brush the drumsticks with oil and season well. Cook for 15-20 minutes, or until the juices run clear when pierced in the thickest part with a sharp skewer. Garnish with lime wedges and sprigs of coriander and serve.

CHICKEN PANCAKE ROLLS

INGREDIENTS
8 pancakes (see Techniques)

FOR THE FILLING
3 skinless chicken breasts, cubed
3 tbls sunflower oil
1 leek, sliced
3 sticks celery, sliced
25 g/1 oz flour
150 ml/¼ pt chicken stock
300 ml/½ pt milk
Ground black pepper
75 g/3 oz Gruyère cheese, grated
Chopped parsley, to garnish
Celery leaves, to garnish

Preparation time: 20 mins
Cooking time: 50 mins
Serves 4

1 Preheat oven to 220 C/425 F/Gas 7. Fry the chicken in hot oil for 5 minutes. Drain and put aside. Then fry the leek and celery for 3 minutes until tender, not browned.

2 Add the flour, stock and milk. Bring to the boil, stirring continuously until thickened. Add the chicken and simmer, covered, for 20 minutes, or until the chicken is cooked and tender. Season with black pepper.

3 Divide the chicken filling evenly among 8 pancakes. Spread it along the centre of each one and roll up. Put the pancakes side by side in an ovenproof dish. Sprinkle over the grated Gruyère cheese and reheat in the oven for 20 minutes, or until golden brown. Sprinkle the chopped parsley over the top and garnish with celery leaves.

CORONATION CHICKEN

Preparation time: 20 mins
Serves 4-6

INGREDIENTS

1 large firm ripe mango
50 g/2 oz sultanas
1 kg/2 lb 4 oz chicken breast, cooked, skinned and cut into 12 mm/½ in strips
150 ml/¼ pt mayonnaise
1-1½ tsp mild curry powder
1 tbls mango chutney
1 tsp lemon juice
Salt and ground black pepper
100 g/4 oz cashew nuts, toasted

PRUE'S TIP

If you chop the mango and the chicken into smaller pieces this makes a delicious, moist sandwich filling for a packed lunch.

SERVING NOTE

Serve with a rice salad or arranged on a bed of crispy green salad.

1 Remove the skin from the mango. Chop the flesh off either side of the stone, and slice into strips.

2 Put the sultanas, the chicken and half the mango strips together in a large bowl.

3 Mix the mayonnaise with the curry powder, chutney and lemon juice. Season. Pour over the chicken mixture and toss gently. Add half the nuts and mix in well.

4 Transfer to a serving dish and garnish with the remaining mango strips and cashew nuts.

YOGHURT-BAKED CHICKEN

INGREDIENTS
450 g/1 lb Greek strained yoghurt
½ an onion, roughly chopped
Juice of ½ a lemon
2.5 cm/1 in piece fresh root ginger, peeled and chopped
½ fresh green chilli, seeded
1 tsp ground turmeric
2 tsp ground cumin
¼ tsp cayenne pepper
½ tsp ground cardamom
1 tsp salt
1.1 kg/2 lb 8 oz chicken pieces

Preparation time: 5 mins
+ marinating
Cooking time: 20-25 mins
Serves 6

1 Put all the ingredients except for the chicken into a food processor or liquidiser and process until smooth.

2 Skin the chicken pieces and make a couple of diagonal slashes across each piece with a sharp knife. Lay the pieces in a large, shallow dish. Then pour over the marinade, turn the pieces once, cover and leave for up to 8 hours or in the fridge overnight.

3 Preheat oven to 220 C/425 F/Gas 7. Line a large shallow oven tray with plenty of foil and set a rack over it. Remove the chicken from the marinade and shake off the excess mixture. Lay the chicken on the rack meatiest side uppermost and bake, turning once, for 20-25 minutes or until the juices run clear when the meat is pierced.

THAI BARBECUE CHICKEN

INGREDIENTS
10 boned chicken breasts

FOR THE MARINADE
1 large onion, quartered
2 cloves of garlic, halved
75 ml/3 fl oz olive oil
150 ml/¼ pt white wine
3 tbls soy sauce

FOR THE PEANUT SAUCE
225 g/8 oz creamed coconut
600 ml/1 pt boiling water
350 g/12 oz peanut butter
1 large onion, grated
4 cloves of garlic, crushed
2 tsp chilli powder
1 tsp brown sugar
2 tbls oil
2 tbls lemon juice
Salt

Preparation time: 20 mins
+ marinating
Cooking time: 20 mins
Serves 10

1 Make two or three slashes over both sides of each chicken breast, and put them in a bowl.

2 To make the marinade, blend the onion, garlic and olive oil in a blender or food processor. Add the wine and soy sauce then coat the chicken breasts. Cover and chill for 6 hours.

3 For the peanut sauce, dissolve the coconut in the boiling water. Add the peanut butter, onion, garlic, chilli powder, sugar, oil, lemon juice and salt. Slowly bring to the boil. Simmer until the sauce is a thick pouring consistency.

4 Lift the chicken out of the marinade. Cook about 10 cm/4 in above the hot coals for 6-8 minutes on each side or until the meat is cooked through. Baste with marinade while cooking.

CHICKEN KORMA

Preparation time: 20 mins
Cooking time: 45 mins
Serves 4-6

INGREDIENTS

700 g/1½ lb chicken breasts
100 g/4 oz ground almonds
4 cm/1½ in piece of fresh ginger, peeled and roughly sliced
1 large clove of garlic, peeled
2 fresh green chillies, seeded
2 tbls ghee or vegetable oil
1 onion, chopped
½ tsp ground turmeric
4 green cardamom pods
4 cloves
2.5 cm/1 in piece of cinnamon stick
1 tsp coriander seeds
1 tsp cumin seeds
1 tsp cornflour
225 g/8 oz Greek strained yoghurt
Juice of ½ a lemon
2 tbls coriander, chopped
25 g/1 oz creamed coconut
Salt

PRUE'S TIP

Ghee is a kind of clarified butter used in Indian cooking. If you don't have any, use vegetable oil instead.

1 Skin the chicken and cut into 2.5 cm/1 in cubes. Put the almonds, ginger, garlic and chillies in a blender with 150 ml/¼ pt cold water and blend to make a paste.

2 Heat the ghee or vegetable oil in a large frying-pan and fry the onion over a moderate heat until lightly coloured. Add the turmeric, cardamom, cloves, cinnamon, coriander and cumin seeds. Fry for 1 minute.

3 Mix the cornflour with the yoghurt. Return the frying-pan to the heat and gradually add the yoghurt mixture, stirring well.

4 Add the nut paste, 50 ml/2 fl oz water and the chicken and bring to simmering point. Simmer for 30 minutes or until the chicken pieces are cooked through.

5 Add the lemon juice, chopped coriander, creamed coconut and salt to taste. Heat for 1 minute to dissolve the coconut, then serve.

CANTON LEMON CHICKEN

Preparation time: 20 mins
Cooking time: 10-15 mins
Serves 6

INGREDIENTS
700 g/1 lb 8 oz chicken breast fillets, skinned
1 large egg white
2 tsp cornflour
Groundnut oil, for deep frying

FOR THE SAUCE
125 ml/4 fl oz chicken stock
3 tbls lemon juice
2 tsp sugar
2 tsp light soy sauce
1-2 tbls dry sherry
1 clove of garlic, crushed
1 red chilli, seeded and chopped
1 tsp cornflour

1 Cut the chicken into 2.5 cm/1 in cubes and place in a bowl. Lightly beat the egg white with the cornflour to slacken slightly. Pour over the chicken. Cover and refrigerate for 30 minutes.

2 Heat the oil in a wok or deep frying-pan. Cook the chicken pieces in two batches for 3-4 minutes each. Drain the first on absorbent paper while cooking the second. Keep the cooked chicken hot.

3 To make the sauce, place the stock, lemon juice, sugar, soy sauce, sherry, garlic and finely chopped chilli in a medium saucepan. Bring to the boil, stirring continuously.

4 Mix the cornflour with 1-2 tsp of water then stir this paste into the boiling sauce. Continue to cook for 2-3 minutes stirring until thickened then add the chicken and stir to coat. Cook for a further minute then turn onto a warmed serving dish and serve.

CHICKEN WITH PRAWNS

Preparation time: 15 mins
Cooking time: 25 mins
Serves 4

INGREDIENTS
4 boned chicken breasts
1 tbls freshly chopped parsley
1 tbls freshly chopped coriander
225 g/8 oz frozen prawns,
thawed and drained
Juice of 1 lemon
Butter, for greasing
3 tbls fresh white breadcrumbs
Salt and ground black pepper
25 g/1 oz butter, melted

1 Preheat oven to 190 C/375 F/Gas 5. Using a sharp knife, make a slit in the side of each chicken breast. Mix together half the parsley and coriander, half the prawns and half the lemon juice in a small bowl.

2 Open the slits up carefully and push as much of the prawn mixture as possible inside.

3 Scatter the rest of the prawns in a small buttered baking dish. Lay the chicken fillets on top. Sprinkle with rest of the lemon juice, coriander, breadcrumbs, seasoning and butter.

4 Bake for 25 minutes or until firm and golden. Sprinkle the rest of the parsley on top and garnish with prawns, lemon and coriander.

DUCK IN BITTER ORANGE

Preparation time: 10 mins
Cooking time: 50 mins
Serves 4

INGREDIENTS

1 tbls vegetable oil
25 g/1 oz butter
4 duck breasts, skinned
4 shallots, finely chopped
2 large oranges
60 ml/2½ fl oz red wine
Juice of ½ a lemon
5 tbls bitter orange marmalade
50 g/2 oz blanched almonds
1 tbls arrowroot
Salt and ground black pepper
Thyme sprigs, to garnish

PRUE'S TIP

Before cutting the almonds into slivers, soak them for 2 minutes in a little hot water to prevent them splintering and breaking when sliced. Shake the tray occasionally while toasting to make sure they all brown evenly.

1 Preheat oven to 180 C/350 F/Gas 4. Heat the oil and butter in a large frying-pan and fry the duck breasts on both sides until brown. Transfer to a casserole dish. Fry the chopped shallots in the fat until tinged with brown. Remove the pan from the heat.

2 Using a potato peeler, pare the zest from 1 of the oranges and add to the casserole. Squeeze the juice from the orange and add to the shallots in the frying-pan along with the red wine, lemon juice and marmalade. Bring to the boil, then pour over the duck breasts. Cover and cook in the oven for 1½ hours.

3 Meanwhile chop the almonds into slivers, sprinkle on a baking tray and toast in the oven for 5 minutes or until brown. Cut the second orange into slices, then halve the slices.

4 When the duck is tender, drain all liquid into a small saucepan and remove and discard the zest. Keep the duck warm. Bring the cooking liquid to the boil. Blend the arrowroot with 1 tbls water to make a paste and stir into the sauce. Boil hard until syrupy then season with salt and pepper. Pour over the duck and garnish with almonds, orange slices and thyme sprigs.

ITALIAN-STYLE CHICKEN

Preparation time: 5 mins
Cooking time: 1 hour
Serve 4

INGREDIENTS

4 large chicken breasts, skinned
2 cloves of garlic, crushed
2 tsp chopped tarragon
Salt and ground black pepper
15 g/½ oz butter
3 tbls oil
1 onion, finely chopped
2 shallots, finely chopped
400 g/14 oz tinned tomatoes, chopped
2 tbls tomato purée
2 tsp sugar
1 tsp oregano
150 ml/¼ pt chicken stock
150 g/5 oz mozzarella cheese, sliced
Black olives and mint leaves, to garnish

"This is one of my all-time favourite family meals – so fragrant and well-flavoured that everyone loves it, and so easy you can prepare it in no time."　　Prue

1 Season the chicken breasts with the garlic, tarragon, salt and pepper. Melt the butter and 1 tbls oil in a frying-pan and gently fry the chicken for 3 minutes on each side. Transfer to a flameproof dish.

2 Heat the remaining oil in a saucepan, add the onion and shallots and fry for 5 minutes. Add the tomatoes, tomato purée, sugar, oregano and chicken stock. Season to taste with salt and pepper and cook for 15 minutes over low heat.

3 Preheat oven to 180 C/350 F/Gas 4. Spoon the tomato sauce over the chicken breasts, cover with foil and cook in the oven for 25 minutes.

4 Set the grill to high. Remove the chicken from the oven and cover with the sliced mozzarella cheese. Place under the grill for 3-5 minutes, or until the cheese has melted. Garnish with olives and mint leaves and serve.

PRUE'S TIP
If you can't buy mozzarella try using Gouda or Gruyère instead.

CHICKEN & ONION QUICHE

Preparation time: 20 mins
Cooking time: 40 mins
Serves 8

INGREDIENTS

Butter, for greasing
350 g/12 oz shortcrust pastry
(see Techniques)
225 g/8 oz cooked chicken breast,
roughly chopped
100 g/4 oz ham, diced
8 spring onions, cut into 4 cm/1½ in slices
100 g/4 oz sage Derby cheese, grated
300 ml/½ pt milk
3 eggs, beaten
Salt and ground black pepper

1 Preheat oven to 200 C/400 F/Gas 6. Grease a 23 cm/9 in loose-bottomed flan tin. Roll out the pastry and use it to line the tin. Cover the base of the pastry with the chicken, ham, onions and cheese.

2 Beat together the milk, eggs and seasoning. Pour the mixture over the filling and bake for 40 minutes until golden and firm.

PRUE'S TIP
Try these alternative fillings: pineapple, gammon and pine kernels, or calabrese and cheese.

SERVING NOTE
Serve this Chicken & Onion Quiche hot or cold, with potatoes and a fresh salad. Make the salad with lettuce, cucumber, spring onions, celery and green pepper, and toss in a vinaigrette dressing.

WINE NOTE
White wine is usually drunk with chicken, so try a dry white wine such as a Sauvignon or Alsace. If you prefer red wine, choose a young one such as Beaujolais-villages.

TURKEY & CRANBERRY PIE

Preparation time: 40 mins
+ chilling
Cooking time: 35 mins
Serves 6-8

INGREDIENTS

275 g/10 oz flour, plus extra for dusting
½ tsp salt
175 g/6 oz butter
1 egg
1 egg yolk

FOR THE FILLING

3 tbls fresh chopped parsley
700 g/1 lb 8 oz cooked turkey meat, chopped
½ quantity béchamel sauce (see Techniques)

FOR THE TOPPING

175 g/6 oz cranberries, thawed if frozen
4 tbls cranberry jelly
1 tbls orange juice
Zest of 1 orange

1 To make the pastry, sieve the flour and salt into a bowl. Rub in the butter, stir in the egg and yolk to form a soft dough. Wrap and chill in the fridge. Stir the parsley and turkey into the béchamel sauce. Roll out two-thirds of the pastry on a floured surface and use this to line an 18 cm/7 in spring-form tin. Spoon the filling into the tin, pressing down with the back of a spoon.

2 Roll out the remaining pastry and cut into 6 mm/¼ in strips. Brush the underside of the strips with water, then lay them over the turkey filling. Press onto the pastry edge, then press on another layer of pastry strips to form a lattice pattern. Trim away any excess pastry from around the edges.

3 Place on a baking tray and bake for 35 minutes in an oven preheated to 200 C/400 F/Gas 6. Cool.

4 Place the cranberries and 4 tbls water in a pan, cover and bring to the boil. Simmer gently for 2-5 minutes then drain well. Place the cranberry jelly, orange juice and zest in a small pan and heat slowly, stirring, until the jelly has dissolved. Allow to cool. Spoon a few berries into the space between each lattice. Spoon the cooled cranberry jelly over the top, garnish and chill until required.

CHICKEN & LEEK GALANTINE

Preparation time: 25 mins
+ chilling
Cooking time: 1¼ hours
Serves 6-8

INGREDIENTS

1.6 kg/3 lb 8 oz chicken, boned (see Techniques)
Salt and ground black pepper
1 tbls chopped fresh thyme
7 small whole leeks, cooked
Juice of 1 lemon
2 courgettes
4 sticks of celery
6 juniper berries
Dill sprigs, to garnish
Quartered lemon slices, to garnish

PRUE'S TIP

If you want a short cut to this dish your butcher will usually bone the chicken when asked in advance. Ask him not to trim the bird, so it will cover the leeks when folded.

1 Lay out the boned chicken, skin-side down on a board and season with salt, pepper and thyme. Lay 6 of the leeks lengthways down the middle of the chicken, three one way and three the other, so that both ends have alternate green and white parts of the leek. Sprinkle with salt, pepper and thyme, and add lemon juice.

2 Fold the sides of the chicken over the leeks to make a neat parcel and then wrap it tightly in a double piece of muslin, tying the ends of the muslin together. Secure with string.

3 Coarsely chop the remaining leek, courgettes and celery and put them in a flameproof casserole with the juniper berries. Season. Just cover the vegetables with water and then rest the chicken on top, cover tightly and gently simmer for 1¼ hours.

4 Remove the chicken from the casserole, tighten the muslin and leave to cool. Refrigerate for at least 6 hours to firm up. Remove muslin, slice and arrange on a platter. Garnish with dill and lemon to serve.

COUNTRY STUFFED CHICKEN

Preparation time: 30 mins
+ resting
Cooking time: 1 hour 35 mins-
2 hours 5 mins
Serves 6

INGREDIENTS

1.6 kg/3 lb 8 oz chicken
100 g/4 oz pork sausage meat
Salt and ground black pepper
50 g/2 oz butter

FOR THE MINT AND ROSEMARY STUFFING

25 g/1 oz butter
1 onion, finely chopped
1 stick of celery, finely chopped
100g/4 oz fresh white breadcrumbs
1 tbls fresh chopped rosemary
1 tbls mint sauce
Grated zest of 1 orange
1 egg yolk

FOR THE CHESTNUT STUFFING

100 g/4 oz tinned, cooked chestnuts, drained
100 g/4 oz no-soak dried apricots
25 g/1 oz butter
1 onion, finely chopped
100 g/4 oz fresh white breadcrumbs
1 egg white, lightly beaten

1 Open bone the chicken (see Techniques) keeping the wing and leg bones still attached, but removing the rest of the carcass.

2 Make mint and rosemary stuffing. Melt the butter in a pan and fry onions and celery for 3-4 minutes. Stir in rest of stuffing ingredients. Cool.

3 Make the chestnut stuffing. Coarsely chop the chestnuts and apricots and place in a bowl. Melt the butter in another pan and add the onion. Stir until softened. Add the breadcrumbs to the chestnuts with the onion. Stir in egg white and season with salt and pepper.

4 Lay out the chicken skin-side down. Spread the herb stuffing over the flesh. Top with a layer of chestnut stuffing. Roll the sausage meat out to a sausage to fit along the bird.

5 Preheat oven to 180 C/350 F/Gas 4. Bring sides up over the sausage meat and sew together. Truss the legs and wings (see Techniques). Place the bird breast-side up in a roasting tin, spread the butter over the top.

6 Cook at 180 C/350 F/Gas 4 for 1½-2 hours or until the juices run clear when the flesh is pierced with a knife. Rest for 5 minutes before carving.

FRENCH ROAST CHICKEN

Preparation time: 15 minutes
Cooking time: 1¼ hours
Serves 4-6

INGREDIENTS

15 g/½ oz butter
1 tbls vegetable oil
1.6 kg/3 lb 8 oz whole chicken
Celery salt
Ground black pepper
2 cloves of garlic, peeled
12 rosemary sprigs
12 thyme sprigs
150 ml/¼ pt chicken stock
3 tbls double cream

"This was one of the first dishes I learnt to cook, and I've been doing it regularly ever since. It's very simple to do and results in some of the juiciest and most delicious roast chicken I've ever tasted." Prue

1 Preheat oven to 200 C/400 F/Gas 6. Melt the butter with the oil in a large frying-pan, add the chicken and cook, turning constantly, for 5 minutes or until golden brown. Transfer to a medium-sized casserole dish. Reserve the cooking juices in the frying-pan.

2 Season the chicken with the celery salt and pepper. Tuck the cloves of garlic and about 4 sprigs of both rosemary and thyme under the legs. Pour 50 ml/2 fl oz of the chicken stock over the chicken, cover and cook for 45 minutes. Uncover and continue to cook for a further 15 minutes.

3 Remove from the oven, transfer the chicken to a warmed serving dish and keep warm in a low oven while you prepare the sauce.

4 Strain the juices from the casserole into the frying-pan. Pour in the reserved stock and bring to the boil, stirring constantly. Continue boiling until it is reduced by half then allow it to cool slightly before stirring in the cream. Serve the chicken surrounded by the remaining thyme and rosemary sprigs with the sauce served separately in a small sauce boat.

PRUE'S TIP
When you pour in the cold stock add 2 tbls white wine or brandy at the same time for a richer flavour.

CHICKEN WITH OLIVES

INGREDIENTS
1.4 kg/3 lb oven-ready chicken

Sea salt

6 tbls groundnut oil

6 tbls butter, melted

2 large onions, finely chopped

2 cloves of garlic, crushed

Pinch of saffron strands

1 tsp ground ginger

1 tsp hot pepper sauce

Peel of 1 preserved lemon, rinsed and cut into strips

225 g/8 oz green olives

1-2 tbls lemon juice

2 tbls finely chopped flat-leaved parsley

Preparation time: 10 mins + resting
Cooking time: 1½-2 hours
Serves 4

1 Wash the chicken inside and out, pat dry and rub the outside with salt. Leave for an hour.

2 In a large flameproof casserole dish, heat the oil and butter until sizzling. Add the chicken and brown lightly.

3 Add the onions, garlic, spices and 250 ml/8 fl oz water and stir. Cover the casserole dish and cook over a low heat, stirring occasionally for 1½-2 hours, adding more water during cooking if necessary. Fifteen minutes before the end of cooking, stir in the preserved lemon peel and the olives.

4 Before carving the chicken, adjust the seasoning of the sauce to taste and stir in the lemon juice and the chopped parsley.

TURKEY WITH PECANS

INGREDIENTS
4 kg/8 lb 8 oz oven-ready turkey

100 g/4 oz butter

Ground black pepper

FOR THE STUFFING

50 g/2 oz butter

2 onions, chopped

6 spring onions, trimmed and chopped

225 g/8 oz fresh white breadcrumbs

150 g/5 oz pecan nuts, chopped

225 g/8 oz cranberry sauce

2 tbls finely chopped fresh thyme

Grated zest and juice of 1 orange

Salt and ground black pepper

Preparation time: 20 mins
Cooking time: 3-3½ hours
Serves 8

PRUE'S TIP
If using fresh cranberries for the stuffing, simmer 225 g/8 oz with 1 tbls orange juice and 50 g/2 oz sugar in a saucepan for 10 minutes.

1 Preheat oven to 190 C/375 F/Gas 5. Wash and dry the cavity of the turkey with absorbent paper. To make the stuffing, melt the butter in a pan, add the onions and fry for 5 minutes.

2 Stir in the spring onions and cook for a further 3 minutes. Add the breadcrumbs, pecan nuts, cranberry sauce, thyme, orange zest and juice and salt and pepper. Mix together well.

3 Allow to cool, then stuff the turkey. Place in a large roasting tin and dot the top of the bird with the butter. Season with pepper.

4 Cover with foil and place in the oven. Cook for 2½-3 hours, basting frequently. Remove the foil for the last 30 minutes. Lower the heat if necessary. Serve garnished with orange slices and pecan nuts.

ROAST GOOSE WITH SAGE

Preparation time: 45 mins
Cooking time: 3¼-3½ hours
Serves 6

INGREDIENTS
4.7-5.5 kg/11-13 lb oven-ready goose
Salt, for sprinkling

FOR THE STUFFING
15 g/½ oz butter
1 onion, finely chopped
4 rashers rindless bacon, finely diced
1 medium cooking apple, peeled, cored and diced
175 g/6 oz no-soak prunes, pitted and chopped
100 g/4 oz fresh wholemeal breadcrumbs
2 tbls freshly chopped sage
2 tbls port
1 egg
Ground black pepper

FOR THE GARNISH
1 red apple, cut into small wedges
Fresh watercress

1 Preheat oven to 200 C/400 F/Gas 6. Prick the goose skin all over with a fork. Remove any excess fat from inside the bird's cavity and rub the salt thoroughly all over.

2 For the stuffing, melt the butter in a frying-pan. Add the onion and bacon. Cook for a further 2-3 minutes until the onion has softened. Add the apple and prunes and stir until the apple has softened slightly. Remove from the heat and stir in the breadcrumbs, sage, port, egg and black pepper.

3 Stuff and truss the goose. Weigh it to calculate the cooking time – allow 15 minutes per 450 g/1 lb plus 15 minutes extra.

4 Put the goose on a wire rack set in a roasting tin. Cover with foil and cook in the oven according to weight. Uncover for the last 30 minutes. Put the goose on a serving dish. Garnish with apple and watercress.

PEKING DUCK

Preparation time: 1 hour
+ drying
Cooking time: 1½ hours
Serves 4

INGREDIENTS

2.3 kg/5 lb oven-ready duck, fresh or frozen
3 tbls brandy
5 tbls clear honey
3 tbls soy sauce
1 bunch of spring onions
10 cm/4 in piece cucumber

FOR THE CHINESE PANCAKES

250 g/9 oz flour, plus extra for dusting
200 ml/7 fl oz boiling water
3 tbls sesame oil

FOR THE SAUCE

1 tbls sesame oil
2.5 cm/1 in piece ginger, peeled and sliced
2 tbls soya paste
200 g/7 oz plum jam
1 tsp chilli powder
25 g/1 oz caster sugar

WATCHPOINT
Don't attempt this dish on a hot day as
you must hang the duck up. The air
circulating around it will dry the skin
making it more crisp when it is cooked.
A cool, breezy day is ideal.

1 Place the duck in a colander in a pan.
Pour over a kettle full of boiling
water. This helps to loosen the skin.
Leave for 5 minutes then pat dry, inside
and out, with absorbent paper.

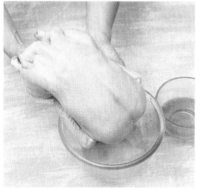

2 Brush the brandy over the duck – the
alcohol has a drying effect on the skin
and will help to make it really crispy.
Tie a piece of string around the wings and
hang the duck up in a cool airy place. Put
a tray underneath to catch any drips.

3 Leave the duck for 4 hours until the
skin is very dry. Mix together the
honey and soy sauce and brush over
the duck. Leave to dry for 1 hour then
brush over again and leave to dry for a
further 3 hours.

4 Meanwhile make the pancakes: sift the flour into a mixing bowl, gradually add the water to make a soft dough. Place on a lightly floured surface and knead well until smooth. Place in a bowl, cover with a clean damp tea-towel and leave to rest for 30 minutes.

5 Knead the dough again for 5 minutes, dust with a little flour if it is sticky. Roll out to a roll about 40 cm/16 in long and about 2.5 cm/1 in in diameter. Mark the roll of dough into sixteen 2.5 cm/1 in segments with the blade of a knife. Cut the dough into segments and then roll each of the segments into a smooth round ball.

6 Work with 2 dough balls at a time. Dip one side of one ball in sesame oil. Place the oiled side on top of the other ball, then flatten the balls together slightly with the palm of your hand. Lightly flour your work surface then roll the dough out to a circle about 15 cm/6 in in diameter. Repeat with remaining balls.

7 Heat a heavy based frying-pan over a low flame. Place a double pancake in the pan and cook for about 1 minute, or until dry on one side. Turn over and cook for 1 minute on the other side. Pull pancakes apart and stack on a plate. Cooking the pancakes together will keep them moist making them easier to roll around the filling.

8 To make the sauce, heat the oil in a small pan, fry the ginger for 2 minutes to flavour the oil lightly. Remove the ginger with a slotted spoon. Add the soya paste, plum jam, chilli powder and caster sugar and heat gently until smooth. Pour into serving bowl and then set aside.

9 Preheat oven to190 C/375 F/Gas 5. Place the duck on a rack in a roasting tin and roast for 1½ hours. It is essential that the duck is placed on a rack otherwise the fat in the pan will stop the skin browning underneath. Do not open the door during the cooking time.

10 Meanwhile, cut the spring onions into 5 cm/2 in pieces and shred lengthwise into thin strips. Cut the cucumber into two 5 cm/2 in pieces then remove the skin or leave it on as you wish. Cut into single or double strips and arrange on a serving dish. Garnish the dish with tomato roses and mint leaves.

11 Transfer the duck to a board. Carve the meat into slices and place on a serving dish. To serve, dip a little meat in the plum sauce and brush over a pancake. Then put the meat, and a little spring onion and cucumber in the middle of the pancake and roll up.

POUSSINS WITH GRAPES

Preparation time: 20 mins
Cooking time: 1 hour 10 mins-
1 hour 25 mins
Serves 4

INGREDIENTS

50 g/2 oz butter
4 small poussins
4 tbls Cointreau
Fresh sprig of thyme
4 rashers of rindless bacon, diced
2 cloves of garlic, crushed
2 tsp cornflour
225 ml/8 fl oz white wine
100 g/4 oz red seedless grapes
Salt and ground black pepper
Fresh thyme, to garnish
Green salad, to serve

P R U E ' S   T I P

If the poussins seem too large, cook two, then cut in half down the breast and backbone. Serve half a poussin each.

1 Preheat oven to 200 C/400 F/Gas 6. Heat the butter in a large frying-pan. Add the poussins and cook over a high heat until golden.

2 Pour the Cointreau over the poussins in the pan. Ignite and heat until flames die down.

3 Put the poussins into a roasting tin with any juices from the frying-pan and the fresh thyme. Cover and cook for 45 minutes-1 hour until poussins are tender. Set aside and keep warm.

4 Drain any cooking juices in the roasting tin into a saucepan. Heat until the juices have reduced and only the fat remains. Add the bacon and cook until just brown. Add the garlic and fry briefly. Blend the cornflour with a little wine, then pour into the pan with rest of the wine. Halve the grapes and add to sauce with seasoning.

5 Bring the sauce to the boil, stirring. Simmer for 5 minutes then spoon over the poussins. Garnish with thyme and serve with green salad.

ROAST PHEASANT

Preparation time: 10 mins
Cooking time: 1 hour 5 mins
Serves 4

INGREDIENTS

2 young pheasants
Salt and ground black pepper
50 g/2 oz butter
6 rashers streaky bacon, rind removed
2 pomegranates
50 ml/2 fl oz dry sherry
225 ml/8 fl oz chicken stock
2 tsp cornflour
½ tsp red wine vinegar

PRUE'S TIP
Pheasants are traditionally served with a stuffing made by cooking the livers in butter, sprinkling with Cognac and mashing with a handful of fresh breadcrumbs.

WATCHPOINT
Take care when carving the pheasants to remove any stray gun shot that is still in the birds.

SERVING NOTE
Serve with roast potatoes, courgettes and green beans. Garnish with watercress.

1 Preheat oven to 220 C/425 F/Gas 7. Season pheasants well with salt and pepper. Heat the butter in a roasting tin in the oven, then turn the birds in the melted butter, lay 3 bacon rashers over each bird and roast for 15 minutes. Reduce the oven temperature to 180 C/350 F/Gas 4 and roast for a further 40 minutes. Transfer the birds to a plate. Cover and keep warm.

2 Remove the juice from one of the pomegranates using a lemon squeezer, or scoop the flesh into a sieve set over a bowl and press out the juice, using a wooden spoon.

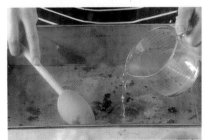

3 To make the sauce, spoon off any excess fat from the cooking juices in the roasting tin and place over direct heat for a few minutes. When sizzling, stir in the sherry, chicken stock and pomegranate juice. Mix the cornflour with a little water and stir into the pan. Add the vinegar and season to taste.

4 Stir half the seeds of the remaining pomegranate into the sauce. Serve the pheasants sprinkled with the rest of the seeds.

MEAT

SIZZLING BARBECUE RIBS

Preparation time: 10 mins
+ marinating
Cooking time: 45 mins - 1 hour
Serves 4

INGREDIENTS

1 kg/2 lb 4 oz pork spare ribs
4 tbls vegetable oil
2 tbls light soy sauce
2 tbls clear honey
1 tsp Dijon mustard
1 tbls tomato purée
1 tbls orange marmalade
1 clove of garlic, crushed
Salt and ground black pepper

1 Place the pork ribs in a shallow dish. Mix the oil, soy sauce, honey, mustard, tomato purée, orange marmalade, garlic, salt and pepper together in a bowl. Pour over the ribs and turn them to coat. Cover and chill for 6 hours or overnight.

2 To oven-cook, preheat oven to 200 C/400 F/Gas 6. Remove the ribs from the marinade and cook for 45 minutes-1 hour or until tender, brushing regularly with the marinade.

3 Alternatively, prepare the barbecue, heating the coals for about 30 minutes until a grey, ashy colour. Oil the grill and place the ribs on it. Cook for 30-35 minutes, turning occasionally and brushing with the marinade until crisp and tender.

PRUE'S TIP
If Chinese spare ribs (as they are often called) are not available, use spare rib pork chops instead. These are more meaty with a small central bone.

WATCHPOINT
Keep an eye on the spare ribs towards the end of the cooking time. The honey and particularly the sugar of the marmalade in the marinade could start to burn if the ribs are cooked for too long.

WINE NOTE
Summertime food requires summertime wine. Try a really icy cold white Rioja with the ribs.

MIDDLE EASTERN KEBABS

Preparation time: 30 mins
+ soaking
Cooking time: 25 mins
Serves 4

INGREDIENTS

50 g/2 oz basmati rice
450 g/1 lb minced lamb
1 large onion, grated
1 tbls chopped dill
1 tbls chopped coriander
1 tbls chopped chives
1 tbls chopped parsley
½ tsp ground fenugreek
1 tsp ground turmeric
Salt and ground black pepper
2 tbls raisins
1 small egg, beaten
100g/4 oz Feta cheese, diced

FOR THE TZATZIKI

½ a medium-sized cucumber, diced
142 g/5 oz firm set natural yoghurt
2 tsp olive oil
1 tbsp chopped fresh mint
1 garlic clove, skinned and crushed
Salt and ground black pepper

FOR THE GARNISH

Spring onions, sliced
Fresh coriander

1 Rinse the rice under cold running water, then soak in hot water for 30 minutes. Drain. Cover with cold water and bring to the boil. Cover the pan and simmer for 10-12 minutes.

2 Drain the rice well and put in a bowl with the minced lamb. Add the onion, herbs, spices, seasoning, raisins and egg. Mix together well, then knead so it forms a ball.

3 Divide the mince mixture into 16 equal-sized pieces. Push a cube of Feta cheese into the centre of each piece. Enclose the cheese in the meat and roll into smooth oval shapes between the palms of your hands.

4 Thread 4 balls of meat onto each skewer. Cook under the grill for 5 minutes. Turn over and cook for a further 5 minutes or until golden brown.

5 To make the tzatziki, place all the ingredients together in a serving bowl. Mix well, then cover and chill before serving with the kebabs. Garnish with sliced spring onions and sprigs of fresh coriander.

BEEF CANNELLONI

Preparation time: 40 mins
Cooking time: 1 hour 15 mins
Serves 3

INGREDIENTS

1 tbls oil
25 g/1 oz butter, plus extra for greasing
1 onion, chopped
1 clove of garlic, crushed
250 g/1 lb lean minced beef
200 g/7 oz tinned chopped tomatoes
225 g/8 oz frozen spinach
1 tsp dried basil
Salt and ground black pepper
6 cannelloni tubes
Basil sprigs, to garnish

FOR THE SAUCE

25 g/1 oz butter
25 g/1 oz flour
450 ml/¾ pt milk
75 g/3 oz Cheddar cheese, grated

1 Preheat oven to 180 C/350 F/Gas 4. Heat the oil and butter in a large frying-pan and fry the onion and garlic for 3-4 minutes.

2 Add the mince and brown evenly, then add the tomatoes, spinach, basil and seasoning. Cover with a lid and simmer for 15 minutes, stirring occasionally. Remove the lid and cook for 5 minutes to thicken the liquid. Cool.

3 Meanwhile bring a pan of salted water to the boil and cook the cannelloni for 8-10 minutes until tender. Drain and rinse each tube, inside and out, under cold running water. Place in a single layer on a dampened tea-towel.

4 Lightly grease a shallow ovenproof dish with butter. Spoon teaspoonfuls of the meat and spinach mixture into the cannelloni tubes and place them, side-by-side, in the ovenproof dish.

5 To make the sauce, melt the butter in a saucepan, stir in the flour and cook over a low heat for 1 minute. Gradually add the milk, stirring continuously until thickened and smooth. Take off the heat and add 50 g/2 oz of the cheese and season with salt and pepper. Stir until well blended.

6 Pour the sauce over the cannelloni and sprinkle with the remaining 25 g/1 oz cheese. Bake in the oven for 30-35 minutes. Garnish with basil.

MUSTARD BEEF ROLLS

Preparation time: 15 mins
Cooking time: 1 hour 15 mins
Serves 3-4

INGREDIENTS

700 g/1 lb 8 oz topside, cut into 6-8 thin slices
6-8 tsp wholegrain mustard
50 g/2 oz mushrooms, finely chopped
25 g/1 oz butter
1 small onion, chopped
2 rindless bacon rashers, chopped
2 tbls flour
800 g/1 lb 12 oz tinned tomatoes, chopped
2 tbls fresh chopped parsley
Pinch of sugar
Salt and ground black pepper

WINE NOTE

A robust red wine, such as a Cabernet Sauvignon, will complement the full flavour of these appetising meat rolls.

1 Preheat oven to 180 C/350 F/Gas 4. Spread each topside slice with 1 tsp of the mustard, and then sprinkle with the chopped mushrooms. Roll up the slices very carefully, securing the joins with cocktail sticks. Place the rolls in an ovenproof dish.

2 Meanwhile melt the butter in a saucepan, add the onion and bacon and fry for 2-3 minutes or until the onion has softened. Add the flour and cook for a further minute. Gradually stir in the tomatoes. Simmer until the sauce has thickened slightly.

3 Remove from the heat and sieve the sauce. Return the sauce to the pan, add the parsley, sugar and seasoning. Pour over the beef rolls in the ovenproof dish and cover with foil. Cook in the oven for 1 hour, turning the beef rolls occasionally. Remove the cocktail sticks before serving.

LAMB NOISETTES

Preparation time: 25 mins
Cooking time: 35 mins
Serves 6

INGREDIENTS

2 medium aubergines
450 g/1 lb tomatoes
300 ml/½ pt stock
225 g/8 oz onions, sliced
175 g/6 oz mushrooms, sliced
4 tbls oil
1 clove of garlic, crushed
4 sprigs of fresh mint
Salt and ground black pepper
1 tbls tomato purée
18 lamb noisettes
Mint leaves, to garnish

1 Preheat oven to 200 C/400 F/Gas 6. Bake the aubergines until soft (approximately 15-20 minutes). Scoop out and mash the flesh.

2 Skin and seed the tomatoes, then chop them roughly. Reserve half of them and put the rest with the aubergine flesh in a saucepan. Add the stock and boil until thickened.

3 Fry the onions and mushrooms one after the other in half the oil. Then add the garlic and fry for a further minute. Add to the aubergine and tomato sauce. Chop the fresh mint and add with the seasoning and tomato purée.

4 Pour the remaining oil into a large frying-pan and fry noisettes until brown. Transfer to a flameproof dish and pour over sauce.

5 Cover the dish and simmer the lamb in the sauce for 5 minutes. Transfer to a serving dish, garnish with the reserved chopped tomato and sprinkle with mint leaves.

NECTARINE PORK CHOPS

Preparation time: 30 mins
Cooking time: 1 hour
Serves 4

INGREDIENTS

4 pork loin chops, 2 cm/¾ in thick
2 rindless smoked back bacon rashers, diced
15 g/½ oz pine kernels
50 g/2 oz long grain rice, rinsed
Pinch of ground turmeric
2 tsp chopped fresh parsley
1 tsp chopped fresh sage
Pinch of cinnamon
Salt and ground black pepper
2 nectarines
2 tbls beaten egg
50 g/2 oz butter
50 ml/2 fl oz pineapple juice
50 g/2 oz brown sugar
1 tsp wine vinegar
Fresh coriander, to garnish

PRUE'S TIP

Pine kernels are available from most supermarkets and health-food shops.

1 Preheat oven to 190 C/375 F/Gas 5. Using a small sharp knife, cut a pocket into the fat side of the chops, then set them aside. Place the bacon and pine kernels in a frying-pan and dry fry until golden and crisp.

2 Cover the rice and turmeric in 2.5 cm/1 in water. Cook for 10 minutes, drain and mix with the bacon, pine kernels, parsley, sage, cinnamon and seasoning. Finely chop half of 1 nectarine and add to the rice mixture with the beaten egg. Stir well. Slice the remaining fruit, set aside.

3 Spoon the stuffing into the pockets of the chops. Heat 25 g/1 oz of the butter in a frying-pan, add the chops and brown on both sides. Place in a baking dish. Pour all but 2 tbls of the pineapple juice over the chops. Cover with foil and bake for about 40 minutes.

4 Add the remaining butter to the frying-pan with the brown sugar and reserved pineapple juice. Heat gently until the sugar has dissolved. Add the sliced nectarines and cook gently until the fruit has softened slightly and the sauce has thickened and become a glaze. Add a little of the chop cooking liquid, and the vinegar, stir to make a sauce. Garnish the chops with coriander.

TARRAGON LAMB CHOPS

Preparation time: 10 mins
Cooking time: 30 mins
Serves 4

INGREDIENTS

4 butterfly lamb chops
Salt and ground black pepper
1 tbls oil
2 tbls rowan jelly
1 clove of garlic, crushed
1 tbls flour
150 ml/¼ pt soured cream
2 tbls finely chopped tarragon
50 g/2 oz chopped spinach, thawed if frozen
150 ml/¼ pt vegetable stock
Pinch of nutmeg

1 Preheat oven to 190 C/375 F/Gas 5. Season the chops with the salt and pepper. Heat the oil in a frying-pan, then quickly fry the chops on both sides to seal in the juices.

2 Melt the jelly in a pan, add the garlic and paint over the chops. Put the chops in a roasting tin and cook in the oven for 10-15 minutes.

3 Transfer to a hot serving dish and keep warm. Add flour to the meat juices and stir over a low heat. Add the soured cream, tarragon, spinach, stock and nutmeg and bring to the boil, stirring continuously. Blend the sauce until smooth. Pour over the chops and serve.

PRUE'S TIP
Chopped spinach can be bought in packets of individual portions. Use these, rather than the large blocks, so that there is no waste.

SERVING NOTE
Serve with buttered new potatoes, carrots and sliced courgettes. Garnish with fresh tarragon.

WINE NOTE
This lamb dish goes delightfully with a bottle of Beaujolais.

SIRLOIN IN WHISKY SAUCE

Preparation time: 5 mins
Cooking time: 20 mins
Serves 4

INGREDIENTS
4 sirloin steaks
Sunflower oil, for frying
4-6 tbls whisky
150 ml/¼ pt homemade beef stock or water
2 tsp green peppercorns
150 ml/¼ pt double cream
Salt and ground black pepper

1 Trim the steak of fat if desired and cut into 4 pieces. Brush a frying-pan with oil and place over high heat. When the oil starts to smoke, put the steaks in the pan. Fry for 3 minutes each side, lifting them now and again to stop them from sticking.

2 Spoon the whisky over the steaks and cook for a few minutes. Take the steaks out of the pan, put them on a plate and keep warm.

3 Add the stock or water to the pan, then add the peppercorns and cream. Season and simmer for a few minutes, stirring continuously.

4 Stir the juices that have oozed from the steaks into the sauce. Serve poured over the steaks.

SWEET & SOUR PORK

Preparation time: 25 mins
+ marinating
Cooking time: 15 mins
Serves 4

INGREDIENTS

350 g/12 oz lean pork
1 tbls dry sherry
1 tbls light soy sauce
Pinch of salt
50 g/2 oz green pepper
50 g/2 oz red pepper
50 g/2 small carrots, peeled
4 spring onions
75 g/3 oz water chestnuts
Rice, to serve

FOR THE SAUCE

150 ml/¼ pt chicken stock
1 tbls light soy sauce
Pinch of salt
1½ tbls white wine vinegar
2 tbls soft brown sugar
1 tbls tomato purée
1 tsp cornflour
½ tbls oil

FOR THE BATTER

100 g/4 oz flour
Pinch of salt
2 tsp vegetable oil, plus extra for deep-frying
2 eggs, separated

1 Cut the pork into 2.5 cm/1 in cubes. Put them in a small bowl with the sherry, soy sauce and salt. Stir so the pork is completely coated. Leave to marinate for 20 minutes.

2 Cut the green and red peppers and carrots into thin slices. Boil them for 2 minutes, drain and refresh in cold water. Slice the spring onions across on a slant into 2.5 cm/1 in long pieces. Slice the water chestnuts.

3 For the sauce, mix everything but the oil in a jug. Heat the oil in a wok and stir-fry the peppers for 1 minute. Add the rest of the vegetables and stir-fry for 1 minute. Pour in the sauce and stir until it boils and thickens.

4 For the batter, sift the flour and salt into a bowl and make a well. Pour in the oil and yolks and mix them together. Gradually stir in 175 ml/6 fl oz water, beating to a smooth batter. Whisk the egg whites until stiff and gently fold into the mixture.

5 Heat the oil in a wok to 190 C/375 F or until a cube of stale bread browns in 50 seconds. Using a slotted spoon, lift the pork cubes out of the marinade and drop them one by one into the batter and the oil. Fry for 2 minutes then drain on absorbent paper. Mix with the sauce and vegetables and serve.

BEEF CURRY

Preparation time: 25 mins
Cooking time: 1 hour 45 mins -
2 hours 15 mins
Serves 4-6

INGREDIENTS
900 g/2 lb lean braising steak,
cut into 2.5 cm/1 in cubes

| 3 tbls seasoned flour |
| 5 tbls sunflower oil |
| 1 tsp ground cumin |
| 1 tsp ground coriander |
| ½ tsp ground ginger |
| 1 tsp ground turmeric |
| ¼ tsp ground mace |
| 1-2 fresh chillies, seeded and finely chopped |
| 2 onions, chopped |
| 3 cloves of garlic, crushed |
| 150 ml/¼ pt rich beef stock |
| 400 g/14 oz tinned tomatoes |
| Salt and ground black pepper |
| 25 g/1 oz butter |
| 50 g/2 oz flaked almonds |
| 225-350 g/8-12 oz basmati rice, to serve |
| Fresh coriander, to garnish |

1 Coat the cubed braising steak in the seasoned flour. Heat the oil in a large frying-pan. Sear the meat in batches, using a slotted spoon or spatula to transfer the browned meat to a plate.

2 Add the spices to the pan and stir over a moderate heat. Cook for 1 minute, then add the chillies, onions and garlic. Stir in the meat and the stock, then the tinned tomatoes and seasoning to taste. Bring to the boil, then reduce to a simmer, cover and cook for 1½-2 hours, stirring occasionally, until the meat is tender. Remove the lid for the final 30 minutes of the cooking time to allow the sauce to reduce.

3 Just before serving, melt the butter in a frying-pan and sauté the almonds until golden. Serve the curry on a bed of basmati rice and sprinkle the almonds over the top. Garnish with fresh coriander.

BEEF IN GUINNESS

Preparation time: 10 mins
Cooking time: 1¾-2¼ hours
Serves 4

INGREDIENTS

50 g/2 oz flour
1 tsp salt
Ground black pepper
½ a tsp grated nutmeg
900 g/2 lb chuck steak, cut into 2.5 cm/1 in cubes
3 tbls oil
25 g/1 oz butter
2 large onions, finely sliced
2 cloves of garlic, crushed
1 tsp brown sugar
600 ml/1 pt Guinness
Juice and zest of 1 orange
3 bay leaves

"I don't like obviously boozy stews, but the Guinness in this one gives richness to the sauce without being overpowering. The dish reheats brilliantly too" Prue

1 Preheat oven to 180 G/350 F/Gas 4. Sift the flour into a shallow dish and stir in the salt, pepper and nutmeg. Coat the meat in the flour.

2 Heat half the oil and half the butter in a flameproof casserole. Add half the meat and fry for 2-3 minutes until evenly browned. Transfer to a plate, add the remaining oil and butter to the casserole and brown the remaining meat. Transfer to the plate.

3 Put the onions and garlic in the casserole and fry gently for 5 minutes, stirring constantly. Then add the sugar and cook over a moderate heat for a further minute, stirring constantly, until the sugar caramelises.

4 Return the beef to the casserole and pour the Guinness over the top. Add the orange juice and half the zest together with 1 bay leaf and bring to the boil. Cover and cook for 1½-2 hours, stirring occasionally and adding a little extra water to the casserole if the liquid becomes too thick.

5 When the meat is tender, discard the bay leaf and adjust the seasoning, adding a little more nutmeg if necessary. Sprinkle the remaining orange zest over the meat, garnish with the remaining bay leaves and serve.

PRUE'S TIP
Stout can be used instead of Guinness. Because it has a sweeter flavour you may wish to omit the sugar.

HAM & CHEESE GOUGERE

Preparation time: 20 mins
Cooking time: 1 hour
Serves 6

INGREDIENTS

40 g/1½ oz butter, plus extra for greasing
40 g/1½ oz flour
300 ml/½ pt milk
175 g/6 oz mature Cheddar cheese, grated
400 g/14 oz tinned pineapple chunks, drained
2 tbls finely chopped fresh parsley
Salt and ground black pepper
225 g/8 oz cooked ham, unsliced

FOR THE CHOUX PASTRY
75 g/3 oz butter
95 g/3¾ oz flour, sifted
Pinch of salt
3 large eggs, beaten
50 g/2 oz mature Cheddar cheese, grated

1 For the filling, melt the butter in a medium-sized pan and then stir in the flour and cook for 30 seconds. Take the pan off the heat and gradually add the milk, beating well after each addition until thoroughly mixed.

2 Return the pan to the heat and slowly bring to the boil stirring continuously until it becomes thick and smooth. Remove from the heat. Add the cheese, pineapple chunks and parsley. Season to taste with salt and ground black pepper. Cut the ham into cubes the same size as the pineapple chunks and stir into the cheese mixture.

3 For the pastry, preheat the oven to 200 C/400 F/Gas 6. Put the butter and 215 ml/7½ fl oz water in a heavy-based pan. Heat gently to melt the butter then bring to a rolling boil. Stir in the flour and salt, remove the pan from the heat and beat vigorously until the paste leaves the sides of the pan. Cool slightly, then gradually add the beaten eggs, mixing well between each addition. You may not need to add all the eggs, just enough to make a smooth glossy paste that drops reluctantly from the spoon. Beat in the grated cheese.

4 Grease a 28 cm/11 in oval oven-proof dish and place spoonfuls of the choux paste around the edge of the dish. Spoon the filling into the middle of the dish and bake in the centre of the oven for 45 minutes or until the pastry has puffed up and turned a rich golden colour. Serve immediately.

STEAK & KIDNEY MINI PIES

Preparation time: 1½ hours
Cooking time: 2¾ hours
Serves 8

INGREDIENTS

700 g/1 lb 8 oz chuck steak, trimmed and cut into chunks
225 g/8 oz ox kidney, finely sliced with sinew removed
Oil or dripping, for frying
1 onion, chopped
100 g/4 oz mushrooms, sliced
25 g/1 oz flour, plus extra for dusting
300 ml/½ pt beef stock
1 tsp tomato purée
Salt and ground black pepper
450 g/1 lb puff pastry (see Techniques)
1 egg, beaten
25 g/1 oz butter
1 tbls chopped parsley
Watercress, to garnish

1 In a large saucepan brown first the chuck steak, then the kidney in the oil or dripping. Fry fast to brown meat all over, lifting out as done.

2 Brown the onion in the pan, add the mushrooms and fry for 3-4 minutes. Mix in the flour and add the stock and tomato purée. Bring to the boil, stirring continuously.

3 Put the steak and kidney and any juices back into the pan, season with salt and pepper, then cover. Simmer gently for 2 hours or until tender.

4 Take off the heat and leave until tepid, then strain the gravy into a separate small saucepan. Cover the meat loosely until stone cold. Chill.

5 Preheat oven to 200 C/400 F/Gas 6. Roll the pastry out thinly and cut into 8 ovals, about 13.5 cm/5½ in long and 9 cm/3½ wide. Cut another 8 ovals 12 mm/½ in larger all round. Put the smaller ovals onto a floured baking tray. Moisten meat with a little cold gravy and divide among 8 smaller ovals. Brush edges with egg and lay the larger pieces on top. Seal the edges and decorate with the back of a knife.

6 Cut 3 slashes in each pie. Decorate with plaited pastry trimmings. Brush with egg and bake for 30 minutes. Bring the extra gravy to the boil and add the butter and parsley. Garnish the pies with watercress.

HOT GAME PIE

Preparation time: 20 mins
+ chilling
Cooking time: 2 hours 30 mins -
3 hours 5 mins
Serves 6

INGREDIENTS

1 large carrot, chopped
1 onion, chopped
1 stick of celery, chopped
2 cloves of garlic, crushed
2 flat mushrooms, chopped
2 tbls oil
75 ml/3 fl oz port
450 g/1 lb venison, off the bone
450 g/1 lb pheasant, off the bone
225 g/8 oz hare, off the bone
25 g/1 oz butter
15 g/½ oz flour
450 ml/¾ pt stock
1 tsp redcurrant jelly
Pinch of thyme
Salt and ground black pepper
350 g/12 oz shortcrust pastry
(see Techniques)
Beaten egg, to glaze

1 Cook the carrot, onion, celery, garlic and mushrooms in oil. Add the port and allow to cool.

2 Cut all the meats into pieces and mix well with the vegetables and port. Chill overnight.

3 Next day, remove the meat from the vegetables and pat dry on kitchen paper. Fry the meat in the butter in a deep flameproof casserole. Fry a few pieces at a time, browning them on all sides.

4 When the meat is browned return it all to the pan and sprinkle the flour over the top. Mix thoroughly, then add the vegetables, stock, jelly, thyme and plenty of salt and ground black pepper. Cover and cook very gently for 2-2½ hours or until it is tender.

5 With a slotted spoon, lift out the meat. Boil the liquid down fast, until syrupy. Pour over the meat, and allow the meat and gravy to cool before refrigerating. Put the meat and gravy into the pie dish.

6 Preheat oven to 200 C/400 F/Gas 6. Cover the pie with the pastry and use any trimmings to decorate. Brush well with egg. Bake the pie in the oven for 25-30 minutes.

PORK & PEAR PIE

Preparation time: 20 mins
Cooking time: 1 hour 15 mins
Serves 4

INGREDIENTS

700 g/1 lb 8 oz pork, cubed
1 large onion, sliced
1 bay leaf
1 clove of garlic, crushed
1 tbls tomato purée
1 tbls freshly chopped sage
Salt and ground black pepper
300 ml/½ pt chicken stock
450 g/1 lb pears, peeled, cored and thickly sliced

FOR THE TOPPING

450 g/1 lb flaky pastry, thawed if frozen
1 egg, for glazing

1 Preheat oven to 180 C/350 F/Gas 4. Put the cubed pork into a large casserole. Add the onion, bay leaf, garlic, tomato purée, sage, stock and salt and ground black pepper.

2 Cook in the oven for 45 minutes. Put the pork into a 1.2 L/2 pt pie dish and insert a pie funnel in the centre of the dish. Arrange the pear slices on top of the pork.

3 Increase the oven heat to 200 C/400 F/Gas 6. Roll out the pastry. Lay a thin strip around the edge of the dish, dampen with water and lay the remaining pastry on top. Trim off any excess and reserve for decoration.

4 Knock up the edges (see Techniques). Flute the edges and cut out 4 pear shapes from the leftover pastry. To decorate, dampen the pie top with a little water and stick the pastry pears on top. Glaze the pastry with beaten egg. Bake for 25-30 minutes or until the pastry is light golden in colour.

VEAL, CHESTNUT & APRICOT PIE

Preparation time: 30 mins
Cooking time: 2 hours
Serves 6-8

INGREDIENTS

2 tbls sunflower oil
900 g/2 lb pie veal, cubed
450 ml/¾ pt brown stock (see Techniques)
300 ml/½ pt fresh orange juice
225 g/8 oz tinned chestnuts
225 g/8 oz no-soak, dried apricots
1 tsp chopped fresh tarragon
2 tbls cornflour
Butter, for greasing
1½ quantities rich shortcrust pastry (see Techniques)
Milk, for glazing

"I think this recipe personifies English cooking at its best – a heady combination of juicy filling, crumbly pastry and the pleasant tang of fruit." Prue

1 Heat the oil in a large saucepan, add the pie veal and fry for 5 minutes until brown. Pour in the stock and orange juice. Add the tinned chestnuts, apricots and chopped tarragon. Bring to the boil, cover the saucepan and simmer for 30 minutes.

2 Lift the cooked veal, chestnuts and apricots into a bowl with a slotted spoon, and set aside to cool. Blend the cornflour with a little cold water until smooth and pour into the pan with the stock and orange juice. Bring to the boil, stirring constantly until thickened. Reserve 150 ml/¼ pt sauce. Leave the remaining sauce covered in a bowl until it is needed.

3 Preheat oven to 200 C/400 F/Gas 6. Roll out two-thirds of the pastry and line a greased 20 cm/8 in round spring-form tin. Trim away the excess pastry. Spoon in the cooled veal filling and add the reserved 150 ml/¼ pt sauce. Roll out the remaining pastry to form a lid for the pie. Moisten the edges with water and set the lid on the pie. Trim and pinch the edges together to seal well. Make a hole in the centre to allow steam to escape from the pie. Use pastry trimmings to decorate. Glaze with milk.

4 Bake in the oven for 30 minutes, then reduce the temperature to 180 C/350 F/Gas 4 for an hour longer. Leave to cool. Remove the pie carefully from the tin and set on a warmed serving plate. Reheat the remaining liquid and serve with the pie.

PRUE'S TIP

If the pie sides aren't brown but the top is, return to the tin, cover with foil and bake for a further 10-15 minutes.

LAMB IN A JACKET

Preparation time: 1 hour
+ chilling
Cooking time: 1 hour 15 mins
Serves 4

INGREDIENTS

650 g/1 lb oz best end of neck lamb joint,
chined

1 onion, unpeeled and roughly chopped

2 tbls oil

400 g/14 oz puff pastry, thawed if frozen

1 egg, beaten

Salt and ground black pepper

50 g/2 oz cold butter, diced

Marjoram, flat-leaved parsley
and mint sprigs, to garnish

FOR THE STUFFING

40 g/1½ oz fresh breadcrumbs

25 g/1 oz mixed parsley, thyme
and rosemary, finely chopped

1 small egg, beaten

Grated zest of ½ a lemon

SERVING NOTE

Carve the lamb through the bone into
cutlets, and serve with seasonal
fresh vegetables.

1 Preheat oven to 230 C/450 F/Gas 8. Trim the excess fat from the lamb and scrape the flesh from the top of the bones (see Techniques). Save the trimmings for making the gravy. Roast for 10 minutes then cut off the chine bone and leave the rack until cold.

2 To make the gravy, fry the chine bone, trimmings and onion in the oil until browned. Add 1.2 L/2 pt cold water, bring to the boil, then simmer for 30 minutes. Strain the gravy into a clean saucepan and leave to cool. Discard the bone, trimmings and onion.

3 To make the stuffing, mix together the herbs, breadcrumbs, egg and lemon zest. Spoon onto the scooped side of the meat.

4 Roll the pastry out to an oblong large enough to cover the lamb. Save trimmings for pastry leaves. Wrap the lamb, piercing the pastry with the bones and sealing the joins under the base of the rack with some of the beaten egg. Place on a baking tray, seams down. Decorate and chill.

5 Preheat oven to 220 C/425 F/Gas 7. Brush the pastry with more of the beaten egg. Cook for 15-20 minutes. Reduce the heat to 190 C/375 F/Gas 5 and cook for a further 15 minutes. Meanwhile, remove the layer of fat from the gravy then reduce by half over a high heat. Season, then whisk in the cold butter. Garnish the lamb with the herb sprigs and serve with the gravy.

WALNUT-STUFFED LAMB

Preparation time: 40 mins
Cooking time: 1 hour 30 mins
+ standing
Serves 6-8

INGREDIENTS

1.8 kg/4 lb shoulder of lamb, boned
Salt and ground black pepper
Oil, for brushing

FOR THE STUFFING

15 g/½ oz butter
1 small onion, chopped
50 g/2 oz fresh white breadcrumbs
1 tsp freshly chopped thyme
1 tbls freshly chopped parsley
2 small apples, peeled, cored and chopped
225 g/8 oz walnuts, chopped
Salt and ground black pepper
2-3 tbls lemon juice

FOR THE GRAVY

1 tbls flour
450 ml/¾ pt lamb stock

VARIATION

Equally delicious is rosemary and peach stuffing. Take 50 g/2 oz breadcrumbs, 1 tsp chopped rosemary, 2 chopped tinned or fresh peaches, a pinch of salt and bind with half an egg.

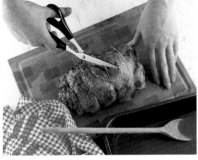

1 Preheat oven to 190 C/375 F/Gas 5. To make the stuffing, melt the butter in a small frying-pan and fry the onion for a few minutes until slightly softened. Place in a bowl with the breadcrumbs, thyme, parsley, apples and walnuts. Season and then stir in enough lemon juice to bind.

2 Spread out the lamb and remove excess fat. Season with salt and pepper. Spread the stuffing evenly over the meat. Roll up the joint and tie securely with string. Weigh the joint and then place in a roasting tin. Brush with oil then cook in the oven for 20 minutes per 450 g/1 lb, plus 15 minutes.

3 When the joint is cooked, remove the string, transfer to a serving plate and allow to stand in a warm place for 10-15 minutes. Meanwhile make the gravy: spoon off the excess fat from the meat juices in the roasting tin, add the flour and stir over the heat until smooth. Add stock, stirring until boiling. Season. Use less stock for thicker gravy.

FRENCH ROAST LAMB

Preparation time: 30 mins
+ soaking
Cooking time: 3 hour 15 mins
Serves 6

INGREDIENTS

450 g/1 lb dried haricot beans
Salt
25 g/1 oz butter
1 large onion, sliced
1 tbls tomato purée
2.3 kg/5 lb leg of lamb
20 small rosemary sprigs
3 cloves of garlic, peeled and finely sliced
1 glass of sweet red wine
450 g/1 lb French beans, topped and tailed

"This combination of haricot beans and lamb is a marriage made in heaven, and the addition of garlic and rosemary makes it irresistible. I like the lamb cold too, and leftover juices and beans can be liquidised for a very good soup" Prue

1 Soak the haricot beans for 12-24 hours. Put the soaked beans into a heavy-based saucepan and cover with water. Add a pinch of salt, cover and simmer gently until tender – about 1½ hours. Discard any remaining liquid.

2 Preheat oven to 190 C/375 F/Gas 5. Melt the butter and gently sauté the onion, stirring until soft and very pale brown. Stir in the tomato purée then mix with the cooked haricot beans, taking care not to break them up.

3 Cut and pull the skin from the leg of lamb and cut away any excess fat, leaving only a thin layer over the meat. With the tip of a knife, make small holes in the lamb at 2.5 cm/1 in intervals, and push a tiny sprig of rosemary and a sliver of garlic into each hole. Put the leg in a roasting tin and pour over the wine. Roast for about 1½ hours.

4 Lift the meat onto a platter and keep warm. Meanwhile, bring a large pan of water to the boil, add salt and simmer the French beans for about 6 minutes. Then drain.

5 Pour off and discard most of the surplus fat from the juices in the roasting tin. Add the haricot and French beans and shake the tin over a high heat to mix and heat. Tip beans and juices into a serving dish. Push the beans to the edge and place the leg of lamb in the middle, then carve and serve.

PRUE'S TIP
To find out if the meat is cooked, prick it deeply and look at the juice as it runs off: red is too rare, pale pink is medium-rare and clear means the meat is well-done.

SERVING NOTE
Serve French Roast Lamb with roast potatoes, or with the more unusual accompaniment of French bread and green salad.

WINE NOTE
Bordeaux wine complements this delicious meat dish perfectly.

FILO PORK & APRICOTS

Preparation time: 1 hour
Cooking time: 40 mins
Serves 4

INGREDIENTS
450 g/1 lb pork fillet
1 tbls oil
15 g/½ oz butter
6 sheets filo pastry, thawed
Melted butter, for brushing

FOR THE STUFFING
15 g/½ oz butter
2 rashers rindless smoked streaky bacon, chopped
½ small onion, finely chopped
40 g/1½ oz fresh wholemeal breadcrumbs
50 g/2 oz dried apricots, soaked overnight and chopped
15 g/½ oz pine kernels
1 tbls chopped fresh parsley
Salt and ground black pepper
1 egg yolk

1 Preheat oven to 200 C/400 F/Gas 6. Make the stuffing: melt the butter and fry the bacon gently until the fat begins to run. Add the onion and fry until softened. Mix together the breadcrumbs, apricots, pine kernels, parsley, seasoning and egg yolk in a bowl.

2 Trim the pork of any membrane and make a deep slit along the length but without cutting right through. Open the meat out, place between two sheets of cling film and beat out gently with a rolling-pin.

3 Make a sausage of the stuffing and place it in the centre of the pork. Bring the sides together, tuck in the ends like an envelope and secure with wooden cocktail sticks or fine string.

4 Heat the oil and butter in a large frying-pan and brown the pork evenly on all sides. Allow to cool then remove the cocktail sticks or string.

5 Lay the sheets of filo pastry one on top of the other, brushing each layer with melted butter. Cut four or five 2 cm/¾ in strips from one of the shorter sides and reserve for garnish.

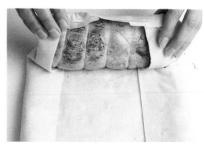

6 Place the pork at one end of the filo pastry and roll up, tucking in the sides as you go. Dampen one side of each filo strip and wrap around the roll. Brush with melted butter and then bake in the oven for 15 minutes. Reduce the oven temperature to 180 C/350 F/Gas 4 and cook the pork for a further 15 minutes.

MILK ROASTED PORK

Preparation time: 5 mins
+ marinating
Cooking time: 1 hour 40 mins
Serves 6

INGREDIENTS

1.2 kg/2 lb 12 oz boned, skinned and rolled
loin of pork

1.2 L/2 pt milk

1 sprig of flat-leaved parsley, to garnish

FOR THE MARINADE

150 ml/¼ pt olive oil

1 tbls white wine vinegar

2 cloves of garlic, crushed

2 sprigs of rosemary

1 tbls juniper berries

Salt and ground black pepper

WATCHPOINT

Make sure you have removed the rind
from the loin before cooking. Left on, it
will go unpleasantly soft and flaccid.

SERVING NOTE

Serve with crispy roast potatoes and
Romanesco cauliflower – a variety which
looks as if it has been dyed green badly!
Glazed carrots and a sprig of flat-leaved
parsley complete the dish.

1 Put the pork into a deep, close fitting casserole. Mix the marinade ingredients together and pour over the pork. Cover and leave the pork in the fridge to marinate for 24 hours, turning it every now and then.

2 The next day, preheat the oven to 180 C/350 F/Gas 4. Pour the milk into the casserole and roast the pork, uncovered, for 1 hour. Then increase the oven temperature to 200 C/400 F/Gas 6 and cook for another 30 minutes or until the juices run clear (not pink) when the meat is pierced with a skewer.

3 Transfer the joint to a plate, cover with foil and keep hot while making the sauce. Skim off the oil from the surface of the liquid left in the casserole. Strain the remaining liquid into a saucepan and boil rapidly until it is reduced to a thick and syrupy sauce. Carve the pork into thickish slices and serve with the sauce. Garnish with parsley.

PORK WITH APPLE CUPS

Preparation time: 20 mins
Cooking time: 2-2¼ hours
Serves 6-8

INGREDIENTS

1.6-1.8 kg/3 lb 8 oz-4 lb leg of pork
2 tbls clear honey
Salt
6 green or red apples

FOR THE STUFFING

60 g/2½ oz butter
1 small onion, finely chopped
2 tsp dried sage
100 g/4 oz fresh white breadcrumbs
2 tbls raisins

FOR THE GRAVY

1 tbls cornflour
300 ml/½ pt cider
1 tbls honey

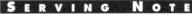

SERVING NOTE

Garnish the roast pork with watercress and serve with carrots and boiled new potatoes in parsley butter.

1 Preheat oven to 220 C/425 F/Gas 7. Run a knife under the pork fat to separate it from the flesh. Carefully spread the honey under the fat. Sprinkle the top of the pork fat with salt. Put the pork in a roasting tin, cover with foil and cook for 30 minutes, then reduce the heat to 200 C/400 F/Gas 6. Continue to cook for a further 1½ hours.

2 To make the stuffing, melt 50 g/2 oz of the butter in a pan, add the onion and fry for 5 minutes. Stir in the sage, breadcrumbs and raisins and cook for 30 seconds. Remove from the heat. Core the apples, making large cavities. Make zig-zag cuts around the top of each apple.

3 Chop the apple tops and add to the stuffing. Divide the stuffing among the apples. Dot with remaining 15 g/½ oz butter.

4 Forty minutes before the meat is cooked, remove the foil to crisp the crackling. Add the apples to the roasting tin.

5 Transfer the pork to a warmed serving dish and surround it with the apples. Keep warm while you make the gravy. Pour out most of the fat from the roasting tin. Mix the cornflour with 4 tbls of the cider. Pour the remaining cider into the tin. Add the honey and bring to the boil, stirring constantly. Add the cornflour mixture and cook for a few more minutes, until the sauce is smooth and thick. Pour into a sauce boat and serve with the meat and the apples.

GLAZED GAMMON

Preparation time: 25 mins
+ soaking and cooling
Cooking time: 2 hours 15 mins
Serves 8-10

INGREDIENTS

1.8 kg/4 lb gammon joint
3-6 bay leaves
1 tsp peppercorns
225 g/8 oz cranberries
100 g/4 oz sugar
50 ml/2 fl oz port
1-2 tbls whole cloves
400 g/14 oz tinned apricots
Watercress, to garnish

V A R I A T I O N

As an alternative to cranberry glaze, try this honey and ginger glaze. Blend 3 tbls of clear honey with 2 tbls demerara sugar, ½ tsp Dijon mustard and ½ tsp ginger powder. Brush the syrup over the joint before baking and baste regularly.

W I N E   N O T E

Chianti, a fruity red wine, is the perfect complement to this dish.

1 Soak the gammon joint in cold water overnight then put the joint in a large pan and cover with fresh cold water. Bring to the boil, drain, cover with cold water again and add the bay leaves and peppercorns. Bring to the boil, cover and simmer for 30 minutes.

2 Cook cranberries and sugar in 150 ml/¼ pt water for 5 minutes. Drain. Reserve fruit. Boil juice for a minute until syrupy, add port.

3 Preheat oven to 200 C/400 F/Gas 6. Remove the joint from the pan, cut off the rind. Score the fat into diamonds. Insert a clove into the points of each diamond. Brush the syrup over the top and bake in the oven for 1¾ hours, basting regularly with the syrup. Serve the reserved cranberries and apricot halves with the joint. Garnish with watercress.

MIGNON FILLETS & SAUCES

Preparation time: 15 mins
Cooking time: 25 mins
Serves 4

INGREDIENTS

Four 150 g/5 oz mignon fillets

Salt and ground black pepper

Tarragon and chervil sprigs, to garnish

FOR THE RED PEPPER SAUCE

25 g/1 oz butter

1 onion, diced

1 clove of garlic, crushed

¼ tsp celery seeds

1 large red pepper, deseeded and sliced

1 bouquet garni

150 ml/¼ pt vegetable stock

Salt and ground black pepper

FOR THE BEARNAISE SAUCE

1 shallot, finely diced

1 bay leaf

1 sprig of tarragon

1 sprig of chervil

3 tbls white wine vinegar

6 peppercorns

2 egg yolks

100 g/4 oz butter, melted

4 tsp tarragon, chopped

4 tsp chervil, chopped

1 To make the red pepper sauce, melt the butter in a saucepan and soften the onions and garlic. Add the celery seeds, red pepper, bouquet garni and stock. Cover and simmer for 10-15 minutes until tender. Remove and discard bouquet garni. Liquidise sauce until smooth. Season and keep warm.

2 To make the Béarnaise sauce, put the shallot, bay leaf, tarragon and chervil in the pan with the vinegar and peppercorns. Boil until reduced to 1 tbls. Strain and discard the shallots, the herbs and the peppercorns.

3 Blend the egg yolks and reduced vinegar mixture for 30 seconds. While blending, pour in the melted butter in a thin stream.

4 Add the chopped tarragon and chervil to the sauce and keep warm in a bain-marie. Slightly flatten the mignons. Season and grill them quickly according to taste.

5 Swirl equal quantities of the red pepper sauce and Béarnaise sauce on opposite sides of each plate so that they meet in the middle. Lift the steaks onto the plates and serve garnished with the sprigs of tarragon and chervil.

PEPPERED SIRLOIN STEAK

Preparation time: 5 mins
Cooking time: 40-50 mins
Serves 4

INGREDIENTS

900 g/2 lb piece of sirloin steak
1 tbls crushed, mixed black, green
and pink peppercorns
1 tbls clarified butter (see Techniques)

FOR THE SAUCE
1 tbls brandy
50 ml/2 fl oz beef stock
150 ml/¼ pt cream
1 tsp ready-made English mustard
Pinch of salt
Watercress leaves, to garnish

1 Trim all but a thin layer of fat from the meat and then press the peppercorns over the meat.

2 Heat the butter in a heavy-based frying-pan and quickly fry the steak on all sides. It should be well-browned but not cooked in the middle. Allow to cool and then refrigerate.

3 To make the sauce, pour off all but 1 tsp fat from the pan, but leave any sediment and peppercorns in it. Add the brandy and cook rapidly until the liquid is reduced to 1 tbls. Add the stock or water and swirl about, scraping the pan with a wooden spatula to incorporate any sediment from the bottom. Add the cream and mustard, and stir until thick and bubbling. Season with salt, then set aside.

4 Thirty minutes before serving, transfer the steak to an oven preheated to 220 C/425 F/Gas 7. This will give you rare steak. Allow 35 minutes for medium steak and 45 minutes for well done.

5 Carve the steak just before serving (or at the table) in thin diagonal slices. Pour over the hot sauce, and garnish with the watercress.

VEGETARIAN

VEGETABLE CHOW MEIN

Preparation time: 10 mins
+ soaking
Cooking time: 7 mins
Serves 4

INGREDIENTS

900 ml/1½ pt vegetable stock
75 g/3 oz or 2 sheets Chinese egg noodles
4 tbls sesame oil
1 large onion, sliced
2 cloves of garlic, crushed
5 cm/2 in cube fresh ginger, shredded
2 carrots, sliced diagonally
175 g/6 oz baby sweetcorn
1 red pepper, sliced
1 green pepper, sliced
6 spring onions, sliced
225 g/8 oz tinned water chestnuts, sliced
175 g/6 oz beansprouts
2 tsp cornflour
3 tbls dark soy sauce
3 tbls dry sherry
1 tsp clear honey
½ tsp five spice powder
Spring onion, to garnish
1 tomato, to garnish

PRUE'S TIP

Make the tomato rose by peeling
a firm tomato, using a small sharp
knife, in one strip. Carefully roll up the
strip to form a rose.

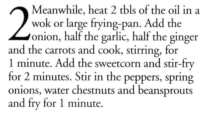

1 Bring the stock to the boil. Add the
noodles, remove from the heat and
allow to soak for 5 minutes.

2 Meanwhile, heat 2 tbls of the oil in a
wok or large frying-pan. Add the
onion, half the garlic, half the ginger
and the carrots and cook, stirring, for
1 minute. Add the sweetcorn and stir-fry
for 2 minutes. Stir in the peppers, spring
onions, water chestnuts and beansprouts
and fry for 1 minute.

3 Mix the cornflour with the soy sauce
and sherry and stir in the honey.
Pour onto the vegetables and stir
until thickened. Drain the noodles. Heat
the remaining oil in another pan with the
rest of the garlic and ginger and the five-
spice powder. Toss with the noodles to
coat. Transfer to a serving platter and top
with the vegetables. Garnish with a spring
onion tassel and tomato rose and serve.

PLANTAINS & AUBERGINES

Preparation time: 20 mins
Cooking time: 15-20 mins
Serves 6

INGREDIENTS

1 aubergine
Salt
225 g/8 oz pumpkin
1 plantain
1 red pepper
1 beefsteak tomato
3 tbls groundnut oil
1 onion, chopped
1 green chilli, seeded and finely sliced
2 cloves of garlic, crushed
100 ml/3½ fl oz vegetable stock
Salt and ground black pepper
½ tsp ground cumin
½ tsp ground coriander
Rice, to serve

FOR THE GARNISH

Coriander leaves
Spring onion

1 Trim the ends from the aubergine, slice and cube, then sprinkle with salt and set aside. Similarly peel and cut the pumpkin into same-sized cubes. Peel and slice the plantain. Deseed and cut the red pepper into dice. Skin the tomato and cut into chunks.

2 Heat the oil in a heavy-based frying-pan, add the onion, chilli and garlic and fry till soft and transparent. Rinse the aubergine and dry well on absorbent paper then add to the pan and cook for 2 minutes, stirring all the time, then add the pumpkin and plantain. Reduce the heat and cook gently for 2-3 minutes then add the pepper and tomato, stock, seasoning and spices.

3 Cover and cook gently for about 10-12 minutes until the vegetables are just tender. Do not overcook. Taste for seasoning and serve on a bed of rice, garnished with fresh coriander leaves and shredded spring onion.

CHICKPEAS IN COCONUT

INGREDIENTS
50 g/2 oz coarsely shredded coconut
1 onion, chopped
50 g/2 oz butter
2 cloves of garlic, crushed
1 tbls ground coriander
400 g/14 oz tinned chickpeas, drained
1 tsp finely chopped dried red chillies
Juice of 1 lemon or 2 limes
Salt
1 tsp garam masala

Preparation time: 5 mins
Cooking time: 20 mins
Serves 4

1 Toast the coarsely shredded coconut under the grill until the strands are golden. Be careful to watch it carefully and stir it regularly as it burns easily. Leave to cool.

2 Cook the onion in the butter until softened. Add the garlic, the ground coriander, the chickpeas, the chillies and the lemon juice. Season, cover and cook gently for 10 minutes.

3 Add the garam masala and half the coconut. Cook uncovered until the liquid evaporates.

4 Transfer to a shallow serving dish, sprinkle with the remaining toasted coconut and serve.

LEMON & MINT DHAL

INGREDIENTS
2 medium onions
4 tbls oil
5 cm/2 in cinnamon stick
2.5 cm/1 in fresh root ginger
450 g/1 lb split red lentils
600 ml/1 pt vegetable stock
600 ml/1 pt boiling water
½ tsp cayenne pepper
Salt
Juice and finely grated zest of 1 lemon
2 bay leaves
1 clove of garlic, crushed
3 tbls chopped fresh mint
Mint sprig, to garnish

Preparation time: 5 mins
Cooking time: 40-50 mins
Serves 4

PRUE'S TIP
Wash the lentils thoroughly and remove any grit or small stones before cooking.

1 Chop one onion and cook in 2 tbls of the oil until tender. Stir in the cinnamon, peeled and grated ginger and lentils. Cook for 2 minutes.

2 Add the stock and boiling water, season with the cayenne pepper and salt. Bring to the boil, stirring.

3 Add the lemon juice, zest, bay leaves and garlic, cover and simmer for 30-40 minutes. Stir often to prevent the dhal from sticking.

4 Slice the remaining onion and cook in the 2 tbls oil until lightly browned all over.

5 Stir 2 tbls of chopped mint and the browned onions into the dhal. Transfer to a serving dish and sprinkle with the rest of the chopped mint. Garnish and serve.

SPICY MIXED VEGETABLES

Preparation time: 20 mins
Cooking time: 32-40 mins
Serves 4

INGREDIENTS

50 g/2 oz ghee or clarified butter
2 cloves of garlic, crushed
8 spring onions, chopped
3 tbls ground coriander
1 tbls ground cumin
2 tsp ground turmeric
Pinch of chilli powder
5 cm/2 in piece fresh root ginger, peeled and chopped
450 g/1 lb potatoes, peeled and chopped into 2.5 cm/1 in cubes
1 large aubergine cut into 2.5 cm/1 in cubes, blanched and drained
225 g/8 oz courgettes, sliced
100 g/4 oz green beans, trimmed and cut into 2.5 cm/1 in lengths
450 g/1 lb tomatoes, skinned, seeded and sliced
400 ml/14 fl oz coconut milk
150 ml/¼ pt vegetable stock
Flat-leaved parsley, to garnish

1 Melt the ghee or butter in a large saucepan. Add the garlic, spring onions, spices and ginger. Cook, stirring frequently, for about 5 minutes. Add the potatoes and aubergine and cook for 2-3 minutes. Stir in the courgettes and beans. Cook for 3-5 minutes, then add the sliced tomato.

2 Add the coconut milk and stock. Stir well, then cover and cook for 20-30 minutes over a medium heat until the vegetables are tender.

3 Remove the lid and continue to cook for 5-10 minutes, to thicken the sauce. Serve garnished with flat-leaved parsley.

VEGETABLE & CASHEW CURRY

Preparation time: 30 mins
Cooking time: 35-45 mins
Serves 4-6

INGREDIENTS

2 tbls peanut oil

2 cloves of garlic, crushed

¼ tsp ground coriander

2 tsp ground cumin

1 tsp ground turmeric

2 cm/¾ in fresh root ginger, finely chopped

2 potatoes

2 aubergines, cut into 12 mm/½ in cubes

1 small cauliflower,
trimmed and divided into florets

100 g/4 oz green beans,
cut into 2.5 cm/1 in lengths

1 green chilli, very finely chopped

175 ml/6 fl oz coconut milk

450 g/1 lb tomatoes,
seeded, skinned and chopped

Salt and ground black pepper

100 g/4 oz cashew nuts, toasted

Rice, to serve

Coriander sprig, to garnish

Natural yoghurt, to serve

"This is easily my favourite vegetarian supper – so mild that children will eat it, but spicy and interesting enough to please grown-up palates too." Prue

1 Heat the oil in a heavy-based pan. Fry the crushed garlic, spices and chopped ginger for 3-4 minutes until soft but not brown.

2 Cook the potatoes for 5 minutes, drain and cut into cubes. Add to the spices along with the remaining vegetables and chilli. Fry for 7-10 minutes, stirring occasionally.

3 Stir in the coconut milk and the tomatoes. Season, then simmer for 15-20 minutes.

4 Stir the cashews into the curry and then arrange on a bed of rice. Garnish with a coriander sprig and serve with a bowl of natural yoghurt.

PRUE'S TIP

This vegetable curry can be made up to 2 days in advance and kept covered in the fridge. Add the cashew nuts once the curry is reheated and just before serving.

STUFFED VINE LEAVES

INGREDIENTS
225 g/8 oz vine leaves in brine,
or 16 fresh blanched leaves

FOR THE STUFFING
100 g/4 oz easy-cook rice
50 g/2 oz pine kernels, toasted
1 onion, finely chopped
1 tbls fresh chopped dill
1 tbls finely chopped fresh mint
Freshly ground black pepper
50 ml/2 fl oz olive oil
1 tbls lemon juice

FOR THE COOKING LIQUID
50 ml/2 fl oz olive oil
1 tbls lemon juice

FOR THE GARNISH
Mint sprig
Dill sprig

Preparation time: 30 mins
Cooking time: 55 mins
Serves 4

1 Drain the vine leaves and if brined rinse well to remove excess salt. Separate the leaves carefully.

2 Put the rice into a dish, add boiling water to cover and leave 5 minutes. Drain. Place in a bowl with the pine kernels and stuffing ingredients. Mix well.

3 Spread out a vine leaf, rib side up. Place 2 tbls of stuffing near its stalk. Fold the bottom in, then the sides, and roll to form a parcel, keeping the ends underneath. Repeat with the other leaves.

4 Arrange in a layer in a pan, add 150 ml/5 fl oz hot water, oil and lemon juice. Cover and simmer for 50 minutes. Drain and garnish.

STUFFED TOMATOES

INGREDIENTS
Six 225 g/8 oz beefsteak tomatoes
Salt and ground black pepper
1 tsp caster sugar
1 large onion, finely chopped
6 tbls olive oil
175 g/6 oz long-grain rice
2 tbls chopped fresh mint
2 tbls chopped fresh parsley
25 g/1 oz currants
25 g/1 oz pine kernels or almonds
Sprigs of flat-leaved parsley, to garnish

Preparation time: 30 mins
Cooking time: 30 mins
Serves 6

1 Slice the tops off the tomatoes and scoop out the cores and seeds. Save this pulp for the filling and sauce. Season the inside of the tomatoes, sprinkle with the sugar and leave to stand while preparing the filling.

2 Cook the onion in 4 tbls of the olive oil until tender and golden. Add the rice and cover with boiling water. Cook for 10-12 minutes until tender.

3 Add the herbs, seasoning, currants, pine kernels or almonds. Strain the tomato pulp. Reserve 150 ml/¼ pt and chop the fleshy pieces discarding any seeds. Add the chopped pulp to the rice and season to taste.

4 Fill the tomatoes and cover with their lids. Arrange in a shallow ovenproof dish, brush with remaining oil and pour over reserved tomato juice. Bake at 180 C/350 F/Gas 4 for half an hour. Garnish with parsley.

CURRIED PUMPKIN

Preparation time: 20 mins
Cooking time: 25 mins
Serves 6

INGREDIENTS

2 tbls oil
1 onion, sliced into rings
1 clove of garlic, crushed
1 tsp ground cumin
1 tsp mild curry powder, or to taste
½ a red chilli, seeded and chopped
Pinch of ground cloves
Juice of ½ a lime
Salt
450 g/1 lb pumpkin, peeled, seeded and cut into 2.5 cm/1 in cubes
4 tomatoes, skinned, seeded and sliced
Fresh herbs, to garnish

PRUE'S TIP

Try hollowing out a second pumpkin to act as a novel container in which to serve the curry. Make sure you don't pierce the skin of the pumpkin, or the juices from the curry will escape.

VARIATION

Sprinkle chopped fresh coriander over the curry before it is served. This will add an unusual piquant flavour to the pumpkin dish.

1 Heat the oil in a large frying-pan and sauté the onion and garlic until soft and lightly browned. Stir in the cumin, curry powder, chilli, ground cloves, lime juice and salt to taste. Cook for 1 minute.

2 Add the cubes of pumpkin flesh to the mixture and cook for about 15 minutes or until the pumpkin is just tender.

3 Add the tomatoes, stir and cook for another 3-4 minutes. Transfer the curry to a serving dish and garnish with fresh herbs.

AUBERGINES IN OLIVE OIL

Preparation time: 25 mins
+ standing
Cooking time: 1 hour 5 mins
Serves 8

INGREDIENTS
8 aubergines
Salt and ground black pepper
450 g/1 lb onions, sliced
200 ml/7 fl oz olive oil
4 cloves of garlic, crushed
4 tbls finely chopped fresh parsley
450 g/1 lb ripe tomatoes
1½ tsp sugar
Juice of 1 large lemon

FOR THE GARNISH
Sprigs of parsley
Tomato slices

1 Pull the leaves from the stalk end of the aubergines, but leave 12 mm/½ in of the stalk attached.

2 Peel strips of skin lengthways down the aubergines with a potato peeler, leaving narrow, alternate stripes of peeled and unpeeled flesh. Make a lengthways slit right down each aubergine. Sprinkle the inside and out heavily with salt and leave to stand for 1 hour to extract some of the juices.

3 Preheat oven to 190 C/375 F/Gas 5. Rinse the aubergines, dry and scoop out the flesh. Keep the shell intact. Chop the flesh.

4 Gently fry the onions in 3 tbls of the oil until soft. Add the aubergine flesh. Stir for 30 seconds, then add the garlic and chopped parsley. Skin, seed and chop the tomatoes and add to the pan. Season. Mix, then spoon into the aubergines.

5 Pack the aubergines, split-side up, in a roasting tin and cover with the remaining olive oil. Sprinkle with the sugar and pepper to taste. Add 150 ml/¼ pt water. Sprinkle with the lemon juice. Cover and cook in the oven for 1 hour or until very soft. Leave the stuffed aubergines to cool until they are lukewarm, then carefully transfer onto a serving dish. Garnish with sprigs of fresh parsley and sliced tomato.

STUFFED MARROW

Preparation time: 40 mins
+ soaking
Cooking time: 40 mins
Serves 4-6

INGREDIENTS

15 g/½ oz couscous
25 g/1 oz butter, plus extra for greasing
2 cloves of garlic, crushed
1 leek, thinly sliced
50 g/2 oz mushrooms, sliced
50 g/2 oz adzuki beans, soaked overnight and cooked
2 tsp chopped parsley
1 tbls chopped thyme
1 large marrow
Flat-leaved parsley, to garnish

FOR THE SAUCE
25 g/1 oz butter
4 spring onions, sliced
25 g/1 oz flour
300 ml/½ pt milk
50 g/2 oz red Leicester cheese
1 spring onion, chopped

PRUE'S TIP

Look for a ripe marrow – this should be firm and feel heavy. Store in a cool dry place for up to 3 days.

1 Soak the couscous for 30 minutes then drain. Preheat the oven to 190 C/375 F/Gas 5. Melt the butter in a pan and sauté the garlic and leek for 1 minute. Add the mushrooms and sauté for a further minute. Stir in the beans, herbs and couscous. Set aside.

2 Grease a roasting tin. Slice the marrow and remove and discard the centres. Fill with stuffing, place in the tin and add 125 ml/4 fl oz water. Cover the tin and bake the marrow in the oven for 30 minutes.

3 To make the sauce, melt the butter and sauté the onions for 2 minutes. Stir in the flour and gradually stir in the milk, off the heat. Return the pan to the heat and cook, stirring, until the sauce thickens. Grate cheese, stir in and heat gently to melt.

4 Spoon the sauce over the bases of serving plates. Drain the marrow well. Put a slice of marrow onto each plate, sprinkle onion around the outside and garnish with parsley.

TACOS WITH SAUCES

Preparation time: 20 mins
Cooking time: 1 hour 30 mins
Serves 6

INGREDIENTS

2 large potatoes
40 g/1½ oz butter
Salt and ground black pepper
Twelve 15 cm/6 in tortillas
Oil, for shallow frying
450 g/1 lb Mozzarella cheese,
grated coarsely
150 ml/¼ pt soured cream
150 ml/¼ pt fromage frais
100 g/4 oz Feta cheese, crumbled

FOR THE GREEN SAUCE

1 onion, chopped
2 cloves of garlic, crushed
2 green chillies, seeded and chopped
2 tbls oil
450 g/1 lb green tomatoes,
seeded and chopped
4 tbls vegetable stock
1 small ripe avocado
2 tbls chopped fresh coriander
Cayenne pepper

FOR THE RED SAUCE

1 onion, chopped
2 cloves of garlic, crushed
2 red chillies, seeded and chopped
2 tbls oil
450 g/1 lb ripe tomatoes,
skinned, seeded and chopped
1 large red pepper, seeded and chopped
4 tbls vegetable stock

1 To prepare the tacos, peel the potatoes and boil for 20 minutes. Drain and mash with the butter, salt and pepper. Soften the tortillas by frying for a few seconds in shallow oil. Drain and then place 1 tbls of mashed potato and a few strips of Mozzarella in the centre of each one. Roll up and secure with a cocktail stick. Chill.

2 For the green sauce, fry the onion, garlic and chillies in the oil until soft. Add the tomatoes and stock. Cover and cook for 30 minutes. Cool. Liquidise with the avocado and coriander. Season with cayenne pepper.

3 For the red sauce, fry the onion, garlic and chillies in the oil until soft. Add the remaining ingredients, cover and cook for 30 minutes. Cool, then liquidise until smooth.

4 To cook the tacos, shallow fry until crisp and golden. Drain on absorbent paper. To serve, remove the cocktail sticks from the tacos and put 2 in the centre of each plate. Spoon green sauce onto one side of the plate and red sauce onto the other. Mix the soured cream and fromage frais together and spoon a little over each taco. Sprinkle Feta cheese over the top and serve immediately.

SPINACH & SORREL RAVIOLI

Preparation time: 25 mins
Cooking time: 2-5 mins
Serves 4

INGREDIENTS
100 g/4 oz cooked fresh spinach, chopped
100 g/4 oz cooked fresh sorrel, chopped
50 g/2 oz Parmesan, grated
25 g/1 oz pine kernels
Salt and ground black pepper
450 g/1 lb basic pasta dough
(see Techniques)
Melted butter, for greasing

TO SERVE
25 g/1 oz melted butter
1 tbls chopped fresh parsley
25 g/1 oz Parmesan cheese, grated
Parsley sprigs, to garnish

P R U E ' S   T I P
Sorrel can be difficult to find but by increasing the amount of spinach to 225 g/8 oz and adding the zest of 1 lemon you can approximate its tangy lemon flavour.

1 In a large bowl mix together the chopped fresh spinach and the sorrel with the grated Parmesan cheese and pine kernels. Season to taste by adding plenty of salt and ground black pepper.

2 Roll out half the pasta dough until about 4 mm/⅙ in thick. Using the rolling-pin to help, lay the dough carefully over the top of a well-greased indented ravioli tin.

3 Spoon the spinach mixture into each pasta indent. Roll out the rest of the pasta dough and lay it on top. Roll a rolling-pin across the top and cut the ravioli into squares.

4 Bring a large saucepan of water to the boil and add the spinach and sorrel ravioli. Simmer the ravioli for 2-5 minutes or until it is cooked but still firm to the bite.

5 Drain the cooked ravioli thoroughly and toss in the melted butter, parsley and Parmesan cheese. Garnish with parsley and serve.

SAVOURY EASTER PIE

Preparation time: 50 mins
Cooking time: 1 hour
Serves 6

INGREDIENTS

450 g/1 lb flour
½ tsp salt
3 tbls olive oil, plus extra for layering

FOR THE FILLING

350 g/12 oz chopped frozen spinach, thawed
350 g/12 oz ricotta cheese
1 tbls grated Parmesan cheese
2 tbls olive oil
7 eggs
1 tbls fresh marjoram
Salt and ground black pepper
Pinch of nutmeg
400 g/14 oz tinned artichoke hearts, drained
Flat-leaved parsley, to garnish

"This very pretty pie is surprisingly simple to make. I make it for my foodie friends. Full of fashionable ingredients, it looks a treat and they won't have had it before." Prue

1 To prepare the pastry, sieve the flour and salt into a bowl. Add 3 tbls of olive oil and 150 ml/¼ pt water and stir until it forms a soft dough. Cover and chill.

2 Squeeze out as much liquid as possible from the thawed spinach. Place in a mixing bowl with the ricotta and Parmesan cheeses and olive oil. Beat in two of the eggs with the marjoram. Season with salt, pepper and nutmeg and beat together until combined. Quarter the artichoke hearts and fold in.

3 Preheat oven to 190 C/375 F/Gas 5. Lightly grease a 20 cm/8 in loose-bottomed cake tin with olive oil. Divide the pastry in half and roll out one half large enough to line the tin, but do not trim the pastry edges. Divide remaining pastry in four and roll each into a 20 cm/8 in circle. Brush each layer with oil and sandwich one on top of the other.

4 To assemble the pie, spoon the filling into the pastry-lined tin and make four indentations. Break one egg into each recess. Cover with the layered pastry circle and trim off excess pastry with a knife. Decorate the top with attractive pastry shapes made from the trimmings. Beat the remaining egg and glaze the pie. Bake in the centre of the oven for 1 hour. Allow to cool before turning out and garnishing.

SPINACH & CHEESE PASTIES

INGREDIENTS

350 g/12 oz new potatoes
Salt
Ground black pepper
1 tbls oil
25 g/1 oz butter, plus extra for greasing
1 large onion, chopped
350 g/12 oz frozen spinach, thawed and drained well
175 g/6 oz ricotta cheese
50 g/2 oz Parmesan cheese, grated
2 quantities of rich shortcrust pastry (see Techniques)
Milk, for brushing

Preparation time: 45 mins
Cooking time: 55-60 mins
Serves 8

1 Preheat oven to 190 C/375 F/Gas 5. Scrub the potatoes and cut into 6 mm/¼ in cubes. Cook in salted boiling water for about 10 minutes or until tender. Drain. Heat the oil and butter and fry the onion until soft, then set aside. Add the spinach to the onions. Stir in cheeses, seasoning and potatoes.

2 Divide the pastry into 16 small balls. Roll out each ball into a 10 cm/4 in round and place 1 heaped tbls of filling in the centre of each.

3 Bring the edges together like a Cornish pasty and seal with a little milk. Flute the edges with a knife and place on a greased baking tray. Brush with a little more milk and cook in the oven for 35-45 minutes until pale golden. Cool on a rack and chill until required.

ONION & CARAWAY FLAN

INGREDIENTS

60 g/2½ oz margarine
150 g/5 oz flour, plus extra for dusting
50 g/2 oz mature Cheddar, grated
100 g/4 oz small onions, sliced into thin rings
2 eggs
150 ml/¼ pt single cream
150 ml/¼ pt milk
Salt and ground black pepper
1 tsp caraway seeds

Preparation time: 20 mins
Cooking time: 30 mins
Serves 4

1 Preheat oven to 200 C/400 F/Gas 6. Rub margarine into flour and stir in Cheddar. Add sufficient water to form a dough. Roll out on a floured surface, then line a 20 cm/8 in fluted flan tin.

2 Separate the onion rings and arrange evenly over the pastry base. Stir in the cream, milk, salt and ground black pepper. Pour over the onion rings and sprinkle the top evenly with the caraway seeds. Bake in the preheated oven for 30 minutes or until firm to the touch and golden.

VEGETARIAN KOULIBIACA

Preparation time: 50 mins
Cooking time: 1 hour 45 mins
Serves 8

INGREDIENTS

1 quantity of brioche dough (see Techniques).
1 tbls milk

FOR THE TOMATO LAYER
175 g/6 oz onions, peeled
3 cloves of garlic, crushed
1 tbls oil
400 g/14 oz tinned tomatoes
Salt and ground black pepper
1 tbls chopped marjoram

FOR THE SPINACH RICOTTA LAYER
450 g/1 lb fresh spinach,
cooked and finely chopped
175 g/6 oz ricotta cheese
Freshly grated nutmeg

FOR THE MUSHROOM LAYER
1 large onion, finely chopped
2 tbls oil
350 g/12 oz aubergine, diced
100 g/4 oz button mushrooms

FOR THE RICE LAYER
50 g/2 oz butter
225 g/8 oz long-grain rice

1 First make the fillings. For the tomato layer, fry the onions and garlic in the oil. Add tomatoes and simmer to reduce liquid. Season and stir in marjoram. Cool. Then for the spinach layer, mix spinach with ricotta cheese. Add nutmeg and season. Set aside.

2 For the mushroom layer, sauté the onion in the oil until soft. Add the aubergine and cook gently until pulpy. Transfer to a food processor and process until smooth. Season, return to the pan and add mushrooms. Cook until tender.

3 For the rice layer, melt butter, stir in the rice, and 475 ml/16 fl oz salted boiling water. Cook for 15 minutes, until the water is absorbed. Cool.

4 Preheat oven to 200 C/400 C/Gas 6. To assemble the koulibiaca turn out the brioche dough and knead for 2 minutes. Roll out a large rectangle and use to line a well-oiled 30 cm/12 in by 11.5 cm/4½ in clip-sided loaf tin, leaving some dough overhanging.

5 Spoon half the rice into the base of the tin and press down. Layer over the tomato, spinach and mushroom fillings, and finish with the rest of the rice. Fold over the overhanging dough neatly and seal the joins of the dough with milk. Leave to rest for 20 minutes.

6 Bake for 1-1¼ hours, covering the top of the dough with a piece of foil after 30 minutes to prevent it browning any further. Serve in slices, either hot or cold.

SALADS
&
SIDE DISHES

CARROT & AVOCADO SALAD

INGREDIENTS
450 g/1 lb carrots
100 g/4 oz pine kernels
4 ripe avocados
Juice of 1 orange
Grated zest of 1 orange
Classic vinaigrette dressing (see Techniques)

Preparation time: 30 mins
Cooking time: 2 mins
Serves 6-8

PRUE'S TIP

Ripe avocados bruise very easily and turn an unattractive brown, so when you add them to the salad, mix lightly and as little as possible.

1 Grate the carrots. Dry fry the pine kernels in a frying-pan until golden brown and set aside.

2 Slice the avocados in half and remove the stone. Slice in half again. Remove the peel and cut the flesh into even-sized pieces. Put the avocados in a bowl with the orange juice.

3 Just before serving add the pine kernels to the carrots, reserving a few to garnish. Mix well. Stir the orange zest into the vinaigrette. Pour the vinaigrette over the carrots and pine kernels and toss thoroughly. Drain the orange juice from the avocados and discard. Put the avocados in a serving bowl with the carrot mixture. Stir very gently. Garnish with remaining pine kernels.

ORIENTAL SALAD

INGREDIENTS
1 cucumber
1 red pepper
1 green pepper
1 bunch of spring onions
350 g/12 oz beansprouts
4 tbls sesame seeds, toasted

FOR THE DRESSING
6 tbls oil
3 tbls white wine vinegar
3 tbls soy sauce
2 cloves of garlic, crushed

Preparation time: 15 mins
+ chilling
Serves 6-8

1 To make the dressing, put the oil, vinegar, soy sauce and garlic into a jam jar. Shake vigorously to blend, then set aside.

2 Cut the cucumber in half lengthways and scoop out the seeds. Then cut into 1 cm/⅓ in pieces and put into salad bowls.

3 Remove the seeds and cores from the red and green peppers. Cut the peppers into 1 cm/⅓ in by 5 cm/2 in pieces. Add to the salad bowls. Thinly slice the spring onions and add to the salad along with the beansprouts.

4 Pour the dressing over the top and toss the salad gently. Chill for at least 1 hour or for up to 6 hours. Add the toasted sesame seeds just before serving, and toss again.

LAMB'S LETTUCE SALAD

INGREDIENTS

| 1 onion |
| 50 g/2 oz watercress |
| 3 tbls salad oil |
| 1 tbls olive oil |
| ½ tsp English mustard |
| Pinch of sugar |
| 1 tbls wine vinegar |
| Salt and ground black pepper |
| 350 g/12 oz lamb's lettuce |

Preparation time: 15 mins
Serves 6-8

V A R I A T I O N

For a slightly different salad, add a Zesty Lime Dressing (see Techniques) instead of the vinaigrette described here, or try adding other green leaves such as curly endive or chicory.

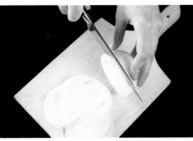

1 Slice the onion into paper-thin rings using a sharp kitchen knife. Rinse and then set aside.

2 To make the dressing, combine the salad and olive oil, mustard, sugar, vinegar and seasoning.

3 Wash lettuce, removing roots. Toss together the lettuce, watercress and onion. Dress and serve.

LETTUCE & CHIVE SALAD

INGREDIENTS

| 1 butterhead or round lettuce |
| 1 bunch of chives |
| 1 yellow or orange pepper |
| 125 ml/4 fl oz olive oil |

Preparation time: 20 mins
+ marinating
Cooking time: 5 mins
Serves 4

1 To make the dressing, cut the pepper into quarters, deseed it and grill the pieces, skin-side up, until wrinkled and blistered. Peel off the outer skin, and cut the pepper into strips or dice. Leave to soak for as long as possible, covered in the olive oil in the fridge. After a day the oil will be mildly flavoured, after a week the flavour will be wonderfully powerful.

2 Tear the lettuce leaves into small pieces. Put into a salad bowl. Cut the chives into 12 mm/½ in lengths and sprinkle over the lettuce.

3 Spoon the oil, including a few pieces of the sliced pepper over the salad leaves. Toss and serve.

TABOULI

INGREDIENTS
100 g/4 oz bulgar wheat
50 g/2 oz fresh parsley
4 spring onions, thinly sliced
2 tbls chopped fresh mint
2 large beefsteak tomatoes, finely diced
Salt and ground black pepper
2 tbls lemon juice
2 tbls olive oil
Lettuce, to serve

Preparation time: 15 mins
+ soaking
Serves 4

2 Mix the parsley and wheat together in a bowl. Add the onions, mint and diced tomatoes. Season well with salt and pepper. Stir in the lemon juice and oil. Serve with lettuce leaves torn into bite-sized pieces.

1 Soak the bulgar wheat in 600 ml/1 pt warm water for 20 minutes until it is soft. Drain well. Finely chop parsley.

FETA & TOMATO SALAD

INGREDIENTS
½ a cucumber
1 green pepper
225 g/8 oz tomatoes
1 small onion
2 tbls olive oil
Salt and ground black pepper
1 tbls chopped fresh oregano
100 g/4 oz Feta cheese
25 g/1 oz black olives

Preparation time: 10 mins
+ chilling
Serves 4

1 Thinly slice the cucumber and arrange around the edge of the serving dish. Deseed the pepper and slice thinly, cutting the rings in half. Cut each tomato into 6-8 wedges.

2 Peel and slice the onion into thin rings. Combine the sliced pepper, tomato wedges and onion. Mix well and spoon into the centre of the cucumber slices. Pour over the olive oil, season to taste. Sprinkle the oregano on top.

3 Cut the Feta cheese into 1 cm/⅓ in cubes and add to the top of the salad, along with the black olives. Chill well before serving.

AVOCADO & GRAPE SALAD

Preparation time: 10 mins
+ chilling
Serves 6

INGREDIENTS

1 curly endive (frisée lettuce)
1 bunch of watercress
100 g/4 oz seedless white grapes
Juice of 1 lemon
4 firm, ripe avocados
1½ tbls finely chopped mint
50 ml/2 fl oz classic vinaigrette
(see Techniques)
6 sprigs of mint, to garnish
Wholemeal bread, to serve

VARIATION

You can make this salad more substantial for a main course by adding chopped cooked chicken. Dress with mayonnaise instead of vinaigrette.

1 Pick off only the crisp leaves of the curly endive and tear into small pieces. Wash and dry thoroughly. Remove stalks from the watercress and toss leaves with the curly endive. Chill.

2 Halve the grapes and toss in the lemon juice. Cover and chill in the fridge until required.

3 Half an hour before serving, cut the avocados in half. Remove the stones and cut each half in two. Peel away the skin. Cut the flesh of the avocados into chunks and toss with the grapes and lemon juice.

4 To serve, drain the grapes and avocados. Mix the chopped mint with the vinaigrette. Toss the rest of the mint with the salad leaves. Put the salad leaves to one side of a small plate and spoon a little avocado and grape mixture beside it. Garnish each plate with a sprig of mint and serve immediately with fresh wholemeal bread.

SALMON & VEGETABLE SALAD

INGREDIENTS
450 g/1 lb fresh salmon fillets, skinned
3 tbls fresh lemon juice
150 ml/¼ pt dry white wine
Salt and ground black pepper
Sprigs of fresh tarragon
225 g/8 oz courgettes, trimmed
225 g/8 oz carrots
1 large turnip

FOR THE DRESSING
6 tbls extra virgin olive oil
4 tbls tarragon wine vinegar
Salt and ground black pepper
2 tbls snipped fresh chives

Preparation time: 15 mins
Cooking time: 5-6 mins
Serves 4-6

1 Place the salmon fillets in a poaching pan or roasting tin. Pour the lemon juice and wine over top. Season with salt and pepper and the tarragon sprigs. Place over a medium heat, bring to a gentle simmer and cook for 4-5 minutes, until they are firm to the touch. Lift out of the poaching liquid and then set aside to cool. Discard the liquid.

2 Cut the courgettes, carrots and turnip into very fine long julienne strips. Blanch for 1 minute in boiling water then drain and rinse under cold running water to cool.

3 Turn the vegetables on to a serving platter. Flake the cooled fish into large chunks and scatter it over the top of the vegetables.

4 Put the dressing ingredients in a screw-top jar and shake to combine. Pour over the salad and serve.

HALLOUMI & TOMATO SALAD

INGREDIENTS
2 large beefsteak tomatoes
2 tbls chopped fresh mint
8 tbls olive oil
Salt and ground black pepper
100 g/4 oz Halloumi cheese
Flour, for dusting
Mint sprigs, to garnish

Preparation time: 10 mins
Cooking time: 5 mins
Serves 4

PRUE'S TIP
If possible use extra virgin olive oil for this dish to give the very best flavour.

1 Slice the tomatoes and arrange them on plates. Sprinkle with 1 tbls of the oil, mint, salt and pepper.

2 Slice the Halloumi cheese thickly and flour lightly. Heat the remaining olive oil. Fry cheese on both sides until golden. Drain on absorbent paper.

3 Arrange the cheese decoratively on the tomatoes. Garnish with mint sprigs and serve while still hot.

HOT SICILIAN BEAN SALAD

INGREDIENTS
450 g/1 lb fresh green beans
4 tomatoes
3 tbls extra virgin olive oil
1 onion, sliced
1 clove of garlic, crushed
1 yellow pepper, seeded and sliced
Salt and ground black pepper
1 tbls chopped fresh oregano, to garnish

1 Trim the beans and cook in boiling water for 10 minutes. Meanwhile, place the tomatoes in hot water for a few seconds, then cool under cold water and peel off the skins. Halve, remove the seeds and then slice.

2 Drain beans. Heat the oil in a large frying-pan. Add the onion, garlic and yellow pepper slices and fry gently for 5 minutes until tender but not beginning to brown.

3 Add the tomato slices and beans to the onion and pepper mix. Stir together, cover and cook gently for 10 minutes. Transfer to a warm dish, season with salt and black pepper. Sprinkle with oregano and serve.

Preparation time: 10 mins
Cooking time: 25 mins
Serves 4

PRUE'S TIP
This dish is also tasty chilled and served cold with savoury dishes.

PROVENCAL PEPPER SALAD

INGREDIENTS
3 tbls extra virgin oil
12 black peppercorns, crushed
12 coriander seeds, crushed
1 sprig of rosemary, bruised
1 red and 1 green chilli, slightly bruised
2 large red peppers
2 large yellow peppers
2 large green peppers
Crusty Italian bread, to serve

1 Gently heat 2 tbls of the oil in a pan with the rosemary, coriander seeds, peppercorns, and chillies. Warm, but do not fry, for 10 minutes. Cool.

2 Cut the peppers into large pieces and discard the seeds. Grill, skin-side up to brown and blister the skin. Cool.

3 Peel the peppers, then layer in a dish with the flavoured oil spooned between the layers. Spoon the remaining olive oil over the top. Marinate for at least 24 hours at room temperature.

4 Garnish with the chillies from the oil. Serve the pepper salad with crusty fresh Italian bread.

Preparation time: 10 mins
+ marinating
Cooking time: 20 mins
Serves 6

PRUE'S TIP
Store the peppers covered with olive oil in a jar in the fridge.

FRENCH PETITS POIS

INGREDIENTS
25 g/1 oz butter

2 bunches of spring onions

1 clove of garlic, crushed

450 g/1 lb frozen petits pois

100 g/4 oz smoked lean bacon, cubed

2 sprigs of mint

Salt and ground black pepper

Preparation time: 5 mins
Cooking time: 20 mins
Serves 8

1 Melt the butter in a saucepan. Roughly chop the spring onions, reserving the green tops. Add the chopped onions to the butter and cook gently until semi-soft. Add the garlic to the pan and cook for 30 seconds.

2 Tip in the petits pois, cubed smoked bacon and the sprigs of mint. Season with a little salt and plenty of ground black pepper. Cover the saucepan with a lid and simmer very gently for 10-15 minutes or until the liquid has almost evaporated and the peas are very soft.

3 Meanwhile, chop the green spring onion tops finely. Just before serving, remove and discard the mint and mix the onion tops with the peas.

CABBAGE IN MUSTARD SEEDS

INGREDIENTS
700 g/1 lb 8 oz cabbage

50 g/2 oz butter

1 tbls white mustard seeds

1 tbls black mustard seeds

Salt

Ground black pepper

Preparation time: 5 mins
Cooking time: 11 mins
Serves 6

PRUE'S TIP
You can shred the cabbage up to 24 hours in advance and keep it in a polythene bag in the fridge.

1 Remove any damaged outer leaves, then cut the cabbage into quarters. Cut out the hard inner core and discard. Slice the cabbage very finely.

2 Heat the butter in a large saucepan. When it begins to foam, add the mustard seeds. As soon as they begin to pop, stir in the cabbage and seasoning. Add 2 tbls water. Cover and cook gently until the cabbage is just softened.

STIR-FRIED VEGETABLES

Preparation time: 20 mins
Cooking time: 10 mins
Serves 4

INGREDIENTS

100 g/4 oz broccoli florets
100 g/4 oz mangetout
100 g/4 oz asparagus spears
2 leeks
2 courgettes
1 green chilli
1 tbls cornflour
300 ml/½ pt vegetable stock
1 tbls hoisin sauce
Pepper strips, to garnish

VARIATIONS

You can flavour the vegetables with other sauces such as yellow bean sauce or chilli sauce or the ever-popular oyster sauce instead of hoisin sauce.

MICROWAVE TIP

Mix the cornflour with 2 tbls stock. Put the remaining stock in a microwave-proof bowl and cook on HIGH (100%) for 2 minutes. Add the vegetables, cover and cook for 2 minutes. Stir in the cornflour and hoisin sauce. Cook for 1 minute then serve.

1 Cut the vegetables diagonally into 7.5 cm/3 in lengths. Deseed the chilli and cut into thin slices.

2 Mix the cornflour with 2 tbls of the stock. Pour the remaining stock into a wok and boil. Add the vegetables and cook, stirring constantly for 5 minutes. Using a slotted spoon, remove vegetables and keep warm.

3 Add the cornflour and hoisin sauce to the stock and continue to boil for 1 minute or until the sauce thickens. Return the vegetables to the wok and cook for a further 2 minutes or until heated through but still crisp. Transfer to a heated serving dish, garnish and serve immediately.

SPINACH WITH NUTMEG

INGREDIENTS
900 g/2 lb spinach
50 ml/2 fl oz fromage frais
Freshly grated nutmeg
Salt and ground black pepper

Preparation time: 10 mins
Cooking time: 10 mins
Serves 6

MICROWAVE TIP
Place washed spinach in a large microwave-proof bowl. Cover and cook on HIGH (100%) for 4-5 minutes. Proceed from step 2.

1 Strip any tough stalks from the spinach leaves and discard. Rinse the leaves well and, while still wet, put in a large saucepan and shake. Turn over a medium heat until the spinach has wilted and collapsed.

2 Tip the spinach leaves out into a colander set over a dish and press with the back of a ladle to force out most of the moisture.

3 Add the fromage frais to the leaves, toss briefly, and serve with a grating of nutmeg and a good sprinkling of salt and pepper.

AUBERGINES WITH OLIVES

INGREDIENTS
450 g/1 lb aubergines
Salt
6 tbls olive oil
1 large onion, chopped
1 small head of fennel, chopped
1 clove of garlic, crushed
400 g/14 oz chopped tinned tomatoes
2 tbls tomato purée
1 bay leaf
1 tsp sugar
Pinch of allspice
Salt and ground black pepper
100 g/4 oz black olives
100 g/4 oz green olives

FOR THE GARNISH
Chopped fresh basil
Sprig of fresh basil

Preparation time: 30 mins
+ salting
Cooking time: 1 hour
Serves 6-8

1 Trim the tops from the aubergines and cut them into 12 mm/½ in slices. Put the slices in a colander. Cover with a sprinkling of salt and leave for about 1 hour.

2 Wash and dry the aubergines thoroughly and cut the slices into quarters. Heat the oil in a pan and fry the onion, fennel, garlic and aubergine until just softened.

3 Add the tomatoes, tomato purée, bay leaf, sugar and allspice and season well. Stir until well mixed, cover and simmer gently for 30 minutes. Add the olives and simmer for a further 10 minutes. Turn out into a serving bowl. Sprinkle with chopped basil and top with the sprig of basil.

CELERY HEARTS & BACON

Preparation time: 5 mins
Cooking time: 15 mins
Serves 4

INGREDIENTS

2 celery hearts
3 tbls oil
2 slices rindless bacon, diced
1 potato, diced and blanched
Pinch of salt
1 lemon
150 ml/¼ pt single cream
1½ tbls Dijon mustard
½ tsp ground ginger

PRUE'S TIP

If you can't find pre-packaged celery hearts, buy whole celery from the greengrocer. Wash it well and peel until you get to the heart.

WATCHPOINT

Make sure you rinse the potato well after blanching to remove the starch, otherwise it will stick to the pan and washing-up will be even more of a chore!

SERVING NOTE

Succulent slices of ham are the perfect complement to this dish.

1 Trim the celery hearts to even lengths and cut in half lengthways. Nick off some top leaves and reserve. Do not trim the bases.

2 Heat the oil in a frying-pan and fry the bacon until crisp. Remove from the pan and fry the potato for 5-7 minutes until crisp and golden. Drain both on absorbent paper.

3 Bring a large pan of salted water to the boil. Halve the lemon. Squeeze the juice into the water and drop the lemon halves in. Add the celery and cook for about 3 minutes. Drain, trim off ends and keep the celery warm.

4 Pour the cream into a small pan and stir in the mustard and ginger. Heat gently until hot.

5 Pour the sauce over the celery and sprinkle the bacon and potato pieces over the top. Garnish with the reserved celery leaves and serve.

BUTTERY VEGETABLE LAYERS

INGREDIENTS

2 heads broccoli

1 small cauliflower

25 g/1 oz melted butter, to coat,
plus extra for greasing

Salt and ground black pepper

Preparation time: 10 mins
Cooking time: 8 mins
Serves 6

PRUE'S TIP

Fill the centre of the moulds with the less
perfect-looking florets.

1 Using a sharp knife, carefully cut the
broccoli and cauliflower into small
even-sized florets.

2 Cook the two vegetables in separate
pans of salted water until just tender,
but still bright. Drain, rinse under
cold water and drain well. Turn in melted
butter and season with salt and pepper.

3 Butter individual cups or individual
pudding moulds and arrange the
florets, rounded sides out, inside the
moulds. Make sure you keep the coloured
layers of vegetables separate, layering from
the bottom upwards. Press down firmly
as you go. Cover the tops of the vegetables
with buttered foil.

4 Reheat the dishes in a steamer. Turn
out carefully onto a large serving
plate. Arrange the buttery vegetable
layers in a neat circle on the plate.

VEGETABLE DOLMAS

INGREDIENTS

575 g/1 lb 4 oz lean minced lamb or beef

1 large onion, finely chopped

75 g/3 oz long-grain rice, cooked

1 tbls chopped fresh mint

1 tbls chopped fresh coriander

Salt and ground black pepper

1 tbls tomato purée

7 even-sized small red peppers
or round courgettes

2 tbls olive oil

Fresh mint sprigs, to garnish

Preparation time: 25 mins
Cooking time: 30 mins-1 hour
Serves 6

1 Preheat oven to 180 C/350 F/Gas 4.
Dry fry the meat over a high heat
until the moisture has evaporated. In
a bowl, combine the meat, onion, herbs,
cooked rice, seasoning and tomato purée.

2 Using a sharp knife, carefully slice the
stalk end from the peppers and
remove the seeds. Reserve the tops
for lids. Cut the stalk ends off the round
courgettes. Hollow out carefully, leaving
the skin and a 6 mm/¼ in wall of flesh
intact. Discard the hollowed-out flesh.

3 Fill the hollow vegetables with meat
mixture and cover with their lids.
Arrange in a shallow ovenproof
dish, brush with oil and pour about
250 ml/8 fl oz water into the dish. Cover
with foil and bake for ½-1 hour or until
tender. Leave to cool. Serve cold,
garnished with fresh mint sprigs.

COURGETTES ITALIENNE

Preparation time: 10 mins
Cooking time: 20 mins
Serves 4-6

INGREDIENTS

450 g/1 lb tomatoes
4 tbls olive oil
2 small onions, thinly sliced
2 cloves of garlic, crushed
450 g/1 lb courgettes, sliced
125 ml/4 fl oz chicken stock
1 tsp chopped fresh marjoram
or ½ tsp chopped fresh oregano
Salt and ground black pepper
75 g/3 oz roast almonds

PRUE'S TIP

Tinned chopped tomatoes can be used instead of fresh tomatoes when time is short. If the flavour of the tinned tomatoes is a little too overpowering, add a pinch more marjoram or oregano.

1 Blanch the tomatoes for about 10-12 seconds then peel off the skin. Cut the tomatoes into quarters. Remove and discard the seeds.

2 Heat the olive oil in a large frying-pan and gently fry the sliced onions and crushed garlic until slightly softened.

3 Add courgettes and fry gently for 6-7 minutes until lightly browned, stirring all the time.

4 Add the prepared tomatoes and chicken stock. Stir in marjoram or oregano and seasoning. Cover with foil and simmer gently for 4 minutes or until the courgettes are tender.

5 Quickly stir the almonds into the tomato mixture and turn into a warmed serving dish. Serve at once.

PARSNIP CHIPS

INGREDIENTS
450 g/1 lb parsnips
Oil, for deep frying
Pinch of salt

Preparation time: 15 mins
Cooking time: 15 mins
Serves 6

1 First peel the parsnips with a potato peeler, then slice them into thin wide ribbons, using the peeler. It is best to keep the strips as thin as possible, but make sure they remain a reasonable length. If they are too short the effect won't be so good.

2 Half fill a deep pan with the oil and heat enough for a crumb to sizzle in it, then spoon in the parsnip ribbons a few at a time.

3 Fish them out and drain on kitchen paper as soon as they are brown and crisp. Repeat with remaining strips. Pile them into a serving dish. Add salt.

POTATO & CARROT BAKE

INGREDIENTS
225 g/8 oz onions
225 g/8 oz carrots
225 g/8 oz potatoes
40 g/1½ oz butter, plus extra for greasing
1 clove of garlic, crushed
Salt and ground black pepper

Preparation time: 10 mins
Cooking time: 1½ hours
Serves 6

1 Preheat oven to 170 C/325 F/Gas 3. Cut vegetables into thin matchsticks. Mix together.

2 Melt the butter in a large saucepan and cook the garlic for 30 seconds. Add the vegetables, season and mix well. Remove the vegetables from the heat.

3 Put into an 18 cm/7 in greased cake tin, pressing down well to flatten into a round cake. Bake for 1¼ hours or until the vegetables are crisp at edges and tender in the middle.

ORANGE-GLAZED POTATOES

INGREDIENTS
450 g/1 lb new potatoes
25 g/1 oz butter
½ tsp sugar
1 small orange
1 tbls chopped fresh mint

Preparation time: 15 mins
Cooking time: 35 mins
Serves 4

P R U E ' S   T I P

Pare the zest from the orange before you squeeze out the juice. Cut into fine strips and sprinkle over the potatoes to garnish. Top with an extra sprig of mint

1 Scrub the potatoes thoroughly to remove most of the skins. Place them in a saucepan of cold water, bring to the boil and cook for 15-20 minutes until they are cooked but still firm.

2 Melt the butter in a pan with the sugar and juice of the orange. Drain the potatoes well and add them to the butter mixture. Toss them over a high heat until lightly browned.

3 Add the mint to the potatoes. Tip into a serving dish and serve immediately.

LEMONY POTATOES

INGREDIENTS
450 g/1 lb small, scrubbed new potatoes
15 g/½ oz butter
1 tbls flour
150 ml/¼ pt hot vegetable stock
1 egg
Juice of 1 small lemon

Preparation time: 10 mins
Cooking time: 30 mins
Serves 4

1 Cook the potatoes, drain and keep warm. Melt the butter in a pan, stir in the flour, add the stock, stir until boiling and thickened.

2 Break the egg into a bowl and beat thoroughly. Whisk the lemon juice and 1 tbls cold water into it.

3 Pour the hot sauce onto the egg mixture in the bowl. Mix well and return to the pan. Stir the sauce continuously as it heats through, and do not allow to boil or it will curdle.

4 Pour the hot sauce over the potatoes and mix gently to cover them evenly. Serve either hot or cold.

GLAZED VEGETABLES

Preparation time: 20 mins
Cooking time: 15-20 mins
Serves 4

INGREDIENTS

450 g/1 lb uncooked beetroot

450 g/1 lb turnips

450 g/1 lb carrots

40 g/1½ oz butter

4½ tbls sugar

Salt

2.5 cm/1 in piece fresh root ginger,
peeled and finely grated

PRUE'S TIP

The turnip and carrot can be cooked in the same pan if you are short of saucepans, but keep the beetroot separate or the colour will bleed into the other vegetables.

WATCHPOINT

Test the vegetables are tender with a sharp knife. If they are still hard, add some more hot water and boil down again to obtain the glaze.

1 Cut the vegetables into 5 cm/2 in long pieces and square off sides to give a rectangular block.

2 Using a small sharp knife shave off the corner lengthways, to give barrel shapes. Place the different vegetables in separate bowls of cold water until required.

3 Place the vegetables in separate saucepans to prevent the colours and flavours mingling. Add water to just cover the vegetables. Add 15 g/½ oz butter, 1½ tbls sugar, salt and a third of the ginger to each pan.

4 Bring the pans to the boil, swirling the liquid around. Leave the pans uncovered and boil vigorously for 15-20 minutes until all the liquid has evaporated, a glaze has formed over the vegetables and they are tender.

5 To serve, arrange the vegetables in three separate layered rows on a hot serving plate.

POTATO GRATIN

Preparation time: 30 mins
Cooking time: 1-1½ hours
Serves 4-6

INGREDIENTS
40 g/1½ oz butter
900 g/2 lb potatoes, peeled and thinly sliced
2 large onions, thinly sliced
175 g/6 oz Gruyère cheese, grated
Salt and ground black pepper
Freshly grated nutmeg
225 ml/8 fl oz milk
225 ml/8 fl oz double cream

PRUE'S TIP
Use a food processor with a slicing blade, or a mandolin, to slice the potatoes really thinly.

MICROWAVE TIP
Layer the ingredients in a microwave-proof dish. Cover and place on an upturned plate. Cook on MEDIUM (50%) for 40-45 minutes, turning the dish 4 times during cooking. Place under a pre-heated grill until golden.

1 Preheat oven to 180 C/350 F/Gas 4. Grease a large, shallow ovenproof dish with the butter. Layer the potatoes in the dish with the onions and 100 g/4 oz of the cheese. Sprinkle each layer with a little salt, pepper and nutmeg, and finish with a layer of overlapping potato slices.

2 Mix the milk with the cream and pour over the potatoes and then sprinkle the top with the remaining grated cheese.

3 Place the dish on a baking tray and bake, uncovered, for 1-1¼ hours or until the potatoes are tender when pierced with a skewer. Increase the temperature of the oven to 200 C/400 F/Gas 6 for the last 10-15 minutes to brown the cheese.

YELLOW RICE

INGREDIENTS
700 g/1 lb 8 oz long-grain rice

300 ml/½ pt coconut milk

1 tsp ground turmeric

1 tbls chopped fresh coriander,
plus extra to garnish

Salt

1 Wash the rice several times in cold water, then drain well. Place in a large saucepan.

2 Add the coconut milk, turmeric and 600 ml/1 pt of water. Cover and bring to the boil. Remove the lid and simmer for 15-20 minutes.

3 When the rice is cooked and all the liquid is absorbed, stir in the chopped coriander and season with salt. Transfer to a serving dish and sprinkle extra chopped coriander over the top to garnish before serving.

Preparation time: 5 mins
Cooking time: 15-20 mins
Serves 8

V A R I A T I O N
For a slightly different flavour, fry a large, thinly sliced onion in 1 tbls of oil until crisp then stir into the cooked rice instead of the chopped coriander.

CARAWAY-SPIKED WILD RICE

INGREDIENTS
900 ml/1½ pt chicken stock

225 g/8 oz wild rice

½ tsp salt

25 g/1 oz butter, softened

1 tsp caraway seeds

Flat-leaved parsley, to garnish

1 Bring the chicken stock to the boil and pour in the wild rice then sprinkle with salt.

2 Bring back to the boil, stirring, then cover and simmer for 35 minutes. The rice is done when the dark outer skins of the grains start to burst open, and the rice is tender but not mushy. Taste, and if not done, give the rice another 5-10 minutes.

3 Drain well, then gently fork in the butter and the caraway seeds. Garnish with flat-leaved parsley.

Preparation time: 10 mins
Cooking time: 40-45 mins
Serves 4

P R U E ' S   T I P
If you don't have the time to make the chicken stock from bones, a bouillon cube will do just as well.

NASI GORENG

Preparation time: 15 mins
Cooking time: 15-10 mins
Serves 6

INGREDIENTS

1 tbls oil
3 tbls melted butter
3 shallots or 1 medium onion, finely chopped
2 cloves of garlic, crushed
225 g/8 oz chicken breast fillets, skinned and cut into 2.5 cm/1 in cubes
3 carrots, peeled and diced
100 g/4 oz mushrooms, sliced
1 tsp paprika
½ tsp chilli powder
2 tsp tomato purée
2 tbls soy sauce
350 g/12 oz long-grain rice, cooked
1 tbls chopped fresh coriander
Salt and ground black pepper

FOR THE GARNISH

1 tbls oil
1 tbls milk
1 egg, beaten
Sprigs of fresh herbs

1 Heat the oil and butter in a large frying-pan. Add the shallots and the garlic. Cook for 2-3 minutes, until softened, then stir in the chicken and carrots. Cook for a further 3-4 minutes, stirring to prevent sticking.

2 Add the mushrooms and cook for a further 2 minutes. Stir in the paprika, chilli powder, soy sauce and tomato purée.

3 Preheat oven to 110 C/225 F/Gas ¼. Add the rice to the pan and cook for 5 minutes to heat through. Stir in coriander and season. Spoon mixture onto an ovenproof platter and using the back of a spoon, pat into a mound. Cover with foil and place in the oven to keep warm.

4 To make the garnish, heat the oil in a small frying-pan. Mix the milk with the beaten egg and pour into the pan. Cook on one side until golden, then turn over and cook the other side.

5 Tip the omelette onto a board and slice into 12 mm/½ in strips. Lay omelette strips over the warm rice. Garnish with herbs.

DESSERTS

PEACHES IN CARAMEL

Preparation time: 5 mins
Cooking time: 20 mins
Serves 6

INGREDIENTS
6 large firm ripe peaches
90 g/3½ oz caster sugar
3 tbls Armagnac
6 large ripe figs
½ tsp rose water

TO DECORATE
50 g/2 oz unsalted pistachio nuts, shelled
Fresh mint leaves

1 Place the fresh peaches in a large mixing bowl and pour in boiling water. Leave for a few minutes, then drain and rinse under cold water. Using a sharp knife, carefully peel away the skin.

2 Pour 450 ml/¾ pt of water into a pan, add 3 tbls of the sugar and the Armagnac. Bring to the boil, add the peaches and simmer for 5 minutes, turning gently. Using a slotted spoon, transfer them to a plate.

3 Add the figs to the cooking liquid and poach them for 5 minutes. Transfer them to a sieve set over a bowl. Reserve the liquid. Press the figs through the sieve into the bowl, using the back of a spoon. Stir in the rose water.

4 Spoon the fig coulis onto 6 individual plates and carefully place a peach in the centre of each plate.

5 Add the remaining sugar to the fruit cooking liquid and bring to the boil. Boil vigorously for 5 minutes, or until the mixture has reduced by half and is starting to caramelise. Do not let it burn.

6 Spoon the caramel over the peaches, decorate with the pistachio nuts and mint leaves before serving.

FIG & APRICOT NECTAR

Preparation time: 10 mins
Cooking time: 20 mins
Serves 8

INGREDIENTS

Butter, for greasing
900 g/2 lb fresh apricots
700 g/1 lb 8 oz fresh ripe figs
Juice of 1 lemon
4 tbls runny honey
300 g/11 oz honeycomb honey
450 g/1 lb strained Greek yoghurt

V A R I A T I O N

You can cook any fruit that bakes well using this method. Try with pears and peaches or nectarines and apples. Avoid soft fruits, though – they will go too mushy.

1 Preheat oven to 220 C/425 F/Gas 7. Grease an ovenproof dish with the butter. Wash figs and drain. Peel the apricots. Prick the figs with a fork so their juice will mix with the honey during baking. Slice figs in half.

2 Arrange the figs and apricots in the dish. Sprinkle with lemon juice and spoon the runny honey over the fruit.

3 Bake for 20 minutes or until the honey is bubbling. Test that the fruit is tender using a skewer.

4 Serve the fruit hot with the yoghurt and the honeycomb honey. Pour a little of the honey sauce around the sides of the plates.

SAUTERNES PEARS

Preparation time: 40 mins
+ cooling
Cooking time: 35 mins
Serves 6

INGREDIENTS
6 even-sized ripe pears
2 tbls lemon juice
Zest of 2 oranges, cut into fine julienne strips
600 ml/1 pt Sauternes
600 ml/1 pt fresh orange juice
50 g/2 oz caster sugar

FOR THE SAUCE
6 egg yolks
50 g/2 oz caster sugar
4 tbls Grand Marnier
25 g/1 oz unsalted butter, softened

1 Peel the pears, leaving the stalks intact and trimming the bases so they stand upright. Sprinkle with lemon juice. Put the orange zest, Sauternes and orange juice into a pan. Slowly bring to the boil.

2 Reduce the liquid to a simmer and lower the pears carefully into the pan. Cover and poach until just soft – about 20 minutes. Remove them with a slotted spoon, stand them upright in a serving dish, cool and chill.

3 Strain the cooking liquid into a jug. Reserve 300 ml/½ pt for the sauce. Return the rest to a pan with the julienne strips and sugar. Boil until syrupy. Pour over the pears and return to fridge.

4 To make the sauce, whisk the yolks and sugar together until pale and thick. Slowly whisk in reserved cooking liquid. Set the bowl over a pan of simmering water and whisk until the mixture thickens. Remove bowl from heat, whisk in the Grand Marnier and then set over cold water. Gradually whisk in small pieces of the softened butter. Cool and chill until needed. Whisk again before serving with the pears.

PASSIONFRUIT HEARTS

Preparation time: 25 mins
+ setting
Cooking time: 2 mins
Serves 6

INGREDIENTS
4 passionfruit
3 tsp gelatine
225 g/8 oz fromage frais
150 ml/¼ pt double cream
75 g/3 oz icing sugar
2 egg whites
Double cream, to decorate

FOR THE STRAWBERRY COULIS
225 g/8 oz strawberries
1-2 tbls icing sugar, to taste

1 Halve the passionfruit and scoop out the fruit. Place in a sieve and press out all the juice into a bowl. Sprinkle on the gelatine and dissolve over a pan of simmering water.

2 Put fromage frais and double cream in a bowl and beat until very smooth. Stir in the passionfruit juice and gelatine mixture with the sugar. Whisk the egg whites until stiff and then fold into the cheese and passionfruit mixture.

3 Line the base of 6 heart-shaped moulds with muslin. Spoon the mixture into the moulds. Refrigerate for at least 2 hours or up to 24 hours.

4 Make the strawberry coulis by blending the strawberries and pressing them through a fine sieve. Sweeten to taste with icing sugar. Spoon over 6 serving plates, then unmould the hearts onto the centre of the plates. Pipe small blobs of cream in the strawberry coulis and then draw a cocktail stick through the cream to make tiny heart shapes. Decorate with strawberry slices.

ZABAGLIONE

Preparation time: 20 mins
+ cooling
Cooking time: 15 mins
Serves 4

INGREDIENTS

4 egg yolks
50 g/2 oz caster sugar
8 tbls Marsala dessert wine
Grated chocolate, to decorate
Orange zest, to decorate

FOR THE LANGUES DE CHAT

50 g/2 oz butter, plus extra for greasing
50 g/2 oz caster sugar
1 egg
Finely grated zest of 1 orange
50 g/2 oz self-raising flour
50 g/2 oz chocolate, melted

1 Preheat oven to 220 C/425 F/Gas 7. Grease and line 2 baking trays. To make the langues de chat, cream together the butter and sugar until pale and fluffy. Beat in the egg and orange zest and add the flour until the mixture has a thick, piping consistency.

2 Snip about 1 cm/⅓ in off the end of a paper piping bag and spoon the mixture into the bag. Pipe the fingers onto the baking trays. Each should measure 7.5 cm/3 in and be spaced about 5 cm/2 in apart. Bake in the oven for 5 minutes or until pale golden in colour. Transfer the biscuits onto a cooling rack.

3 Dip one end of each langues de chat into the melted chocolate and leave to set on baking parchment.

4 To make the zabaglione, put egg yolks, sugar and Marsala into a large bowl. Set over a pan of simmering water and beat for 8-10 minutes, until thick and fluffy.

5 Pour the warm mixture into 4 wine glasses. Top with grated chocolate and orange zest and serve with the langues de chat.

BRANDYSNAP BASKETS

Preparation time: 1 hour
+ freezing
Cooking time: 25-30 mins
Serves 4

INGREDIENTS

100 g/4 oz fresh brown breadcrumbs
50 g/2 oz soft brown sugar
300 ml/½ pt double cream
150 ml/¼ pt single cream
1 tbls rum
25 g/1 oz icing sugar

FOR THE BASKETS

25 g/1 oz butter
25 g/1 oz caster sugar
1 tbls golden syrup
25 g/1 oz flour
¼ tsp ground ginger

FOR THE DECORATION

2-3 pieces of stem ginger, cut into shreds
Mint leaves

"I've been making brandysnaps all my cooking life, and this recipe produces by far the crispest, lightest and thinnest of any I've tried." Prue

1 Make the ice cream the day before it is needed. Preheat the oven to 200 C/400 F/Gas 6. Mix together the breadcrumbs and soft brown sugar and spread over a baking tray. Bake in the oven for about 10 minutes. Cool, then crumble between your fingers.

2 Whisk together the double and single cream until just stiff. Fold in the rum and icing sugar, spoon into a container. Freeze for 2 hours.

3 Place the cream mixture in a mixing bowl and beat well until smooth. Stir in the breadcrumbs, return to container. Freeze until firm.

4 Preheat oven to 180 C/350 F/Gas 4. Line a baking tray with baking parchment. Melt butter, sugar and syrup over low heat. Beat in flour and ginger, leave to cool.

5 Divide the mixture into 4, roll into balls and place on a baking tray about 10 cm/4 in apart. Flatten each ball into 10 cm/4 in rounds and bake for 7-10 minutes or until golden and bubbly. Set out 4 teacups upside down.

6 Allow the biscuits to cool slightly. Then, quickly and carefully, remove each one with a palette knife and lay it over an upturned teacup. Mould the biscuits into basket shapes and then leave them to cool and harden. To serve, scoop 2-3 balls of ice cream into each basket and decorate with the stem ginger and mint leaves.

P R U E ' S   T I P
If your brandysnaps harden before you have time to mould them, pop the tray back in the oven for 1 minute and try again.

RHUBARB ICE CREAM

Preparation time: 20 mins
+ freezing
Cooking time: 35 mins
Serves 6

INGREDIENTS

450 g/1 lb fresh rhubarb, cut into chunks
60 g/2½ oz caster sugar
¼ tsp ground allspice
3 tbls stem ginger syrup
4 tbls brandy
25 g/1 oz stem ginger, chopped
600 ml/1 pt double cream

FOR THE CIGARETTES RUSSES
2 egg whites
100 g/4 oz caster sugar
50 g/2 oz flour
50 g/2 oz butter, melted
2-3 drops vanilla essence

PRUE'S TIP

Bake one biscuit first to try the mixture.
If it is too runny add a little more flour.
If it is too crisp add more melted butter.

1 Put the rhubarb in a pan with the sugar, allspice and syrup. Cover and stew gently until the rhubarb is soft and pulpy. Leave to cool.

2 Stir the brandy and ginger into the cooled rhubarb. Whisk the cream until peaks form. Stir the rhubarb mixture into the cream, pour into an airtight container and freeze.

3 Meanwhile make the Cigarettes Russes. Preheat the oven to 190 C/375 F/Gas 5. Mix the egg whites and caster sugar together. Stir in the flour, melted butter and vanilla essence. Spread six 10 cm/4 in by 4 cm/1½ in oblongs of the mixture onto a baking tray lined with baking parchment.

4 Put the tray on the top shelf of the oven and bake for 5-6 minutes until the biscuits turn golden in the centre and brown around the edges.

5 Let the biscuits cool for a few seconds, then carefully peel away from the baking parchment and curl around pencils. Leave to cool completely on a wire rack.

6 Stand the ice cream in the fridge to soften for 30 minutes before serving with the Cigarettes Russes.

PORT JELLIES

Preparation time: 40 mins
+ setting
Cooking time: 15 mins
Serves 6

INGREDIENTS

350 g/12 oz sugar
700 g/1 lb 8 oz blackcurrants
300 ml/½ pt ruby port
25 g/1 oz gelatine
150 ml/¼ pt single cream

PRUE'S TIP

If the serving plates are wetted before unmoulding the jellies, it is easier to shift the jellies to the middle of the plate should they end up slightly off centre.

SERVING NOTE

Decorate the tops of the jellies with 50 g/2 oz whole blackcurrants, and some pretty-coloured leaves.

1 Gently heat the sugar and blackcurrants in a saucepan until the fruit collapses. Push the mixture through a sieve. Add the port and enough water to bring the liquid up to 1.65 ml/2¾ pt.

2 Put 9 tbls water in a small saucepan and sprinkle the gelatine over it. Soak for 5 minutes. Heat gently until clear, but do not boil. Pour into the fruit liquid and stir well.

3 Wet six 300 ml/½ pt jelly moulds. Reserve 6 tbls of the jelly mixture and pour the remainder into the moulds. Chill in the fridge for 6 hours or until set.

4 To turn out, briefly dip the moulds into hot water then invert onto 6 dessert plates.

5 Melt the reserved jelly mixture then allow it to cool. Surround the jellies with the cream. When the reserved jelly mixture is cool but not set, pipe small blobs around the jellies onto the cream. Drag a cocktail stick through the blobs in a wavy line to produce a feathered effect.

FRUITY MERINGUE RINGS

Preparation time: 30 mins
Cooking time: 2¼-3¼ hours
Makes 15

INGREDIENTS

6 egg whites
300 g/11 oz caster sugar
1½ tbls vanilla essence

FOR THE FILLING

175 g/6 oz strawberries, hulled
175 g/6 oz redcurrants, topped and tailed
175 g/6 oz sweet cherries, stoned
175 g/6 oz raspberries
175 g/6 oz blackcurrants or blueberries
2 kiwi fruit, peeled and sliced
Fruit leaves, to decorate
Whipped cream, to serve

P R U E ' S T I P

Meringue rings look very impressive and are perfect for summertime parties.

W A T C H P O I N T

If the meringues are colouring too much when cooking, open the oven door to allow it to cool down a little, then close it again.

1 Preheat oven to 160 C/300 F/Gas 2. Cover several baking trays with baking parchment. Whisk the egg whites in a large bowl until very stiff. Still whisking, gradually add all the sugar and the vanilla essence until the meringue has become glossy and thick.

2 Spoon two-thirds of the mixture into a piping bag fitted with a star nozzle. Spoon a teaspoonful of the remaining mixture on the tray and spread out in a circle about 7.5 cm/3 in across. Repeat, leaving about 10 cm/4 in between each, until you have 15 meringue bases.

3 Using the mixture in the piping bag, pipe rosettes around each circle of meringue to form little nests. Bake for 15 minutes, then reduce the oven temperature to 100 C/200 F/Gas ¼ and leave for 2-3 hours, until they have dried out completely. Allow the nests to cool for a few minutes before peeling them off the baking parchment. At this stage the nests can either be stored in air-tight containers for 3-4 days or packed in rigid containers and frozen for up to 3 months.

4 To serve, place a selection of fruit, in the nests. Decorate with the fruit leaves. The nests can sit like this for several hours. Serve the nests with a large bowl of whipped cream.

BERRYFRUIT BASKETS

Preparation time: 35 mins
Cooking time: 30-35 mins
Makes 12-14

INGREDIENTS

50 g/2 oz butter, plus extra for greasing
60 g/2½ oz caster sugar
2 egg whites
50 g/2 oz flour
Grated zest of 1 orange
25 g/1 oz flaked almonds
300 ml/½ pt double cream
225 g/8 oz mixed fruits including blackcurrants, redcurrants and loganberries
Icing sugar, to dust

1 Preheat oven to 190 C/375 F/Gas 5. Grease a baking tray and set aside 2 ramekin dishes or, alternatively, 2 wide-mouthed teacups.

2 Cream together the butter and sugar. In a separate bowl break up the egg whites with a fork. Add the egg and flour to the butter and sugar, a little at a time, mixing well until they are both incorporated. Stir in the grated orange zest and the almonds.

3 Place 2 tsp of the mixture well apart on the baking tray. Using the back of a teaspoon spread them out to form 2 circles, 10 cm/4 in across.

4 Bake for about 5 minutes until golden at the edges. Then working quickly loosen the biscuits with a palette knife and ease each one into a ramekin or wide-mouthed teacup, fluting the edges as you do so. Remove when cool and crisp, ready for the next ones. Continue in the same way with the remaining mixture.

5 Just before serving, whip the double cream until stiff and pipe a generous swirl into each tuile cup. Top with a selection of the fresh fruit. Dust the fruit and the tuiles with icing sugar and serve immediately.

STRAWBERRY GRATIN

Preparation time: 10 mins
Cooking time: 15-20 mins
Serves 6

INGREDIENTS

900 g/2 lb strawberries, hulled

3-4 tbls vodka

FOR THE SABAYON SAUCE

2 large eggs

2 egg yolks

75 g/3 oz caster sugar

V A R I A T I O N

Any soft fruit could be used as an alternative if strawberries aren't available. Raspberries or cherries, for example, would work well.

1 Check the strawberries and discard any which are damaged. Cut them in half, or into quarters if they seem particularly large, and divide among six 11.5 cm/4½ in round shallow gratin dishes. Sprinkle with the vodka. Set aside.

2 Set the grill to high and then proceed with the sabayon sauce. Put the eggs, yolks and sugar into a large bowl. Set over a pan of simmering water and whisk vigorously for 10-15 minutes until the mixture is very thick and creamy. If you prefer, use an electric whisk to make it easier.

3 As soon as the sauce has thickened, spoon it over the fruit and place under the grill until evenly browned. Watch closely as it will burn easily. Serve immediately while still hot.

APRICOT TARTES TATIN

Preparation time: 30 mins
Cooking time: 25-30 mins
Serves 6

INGREDIENTS

60 g/2½ oz butter

50 g/2 oz soft light brown sugar

9-10 small ripe apricots

FOR THE VANILLA CREAM SAUCE

½ a large vanilla pod,
split in half lengthways

250 ml/9 fl oz double cream

3 egg yolks

3 tbls caster sugar

FOR THE PASTRY

75 g/3 oz butter, softened

50 g/2 oz caster sugar

115 g/4½ oz flour

75 g/3 oz skinned hazelnuts,
toasted and finely chopped

5 tbls apricot jam,
warmed and sieved, to decorate

1 To make the vanilla sauce, put the vanilla pod and cream in a small pan and bring to just below boiling point. Whisk the yolks and sugar until frothy. Remove the vanilla pod, and gradually add cream to the egg mixture, beating all the time.

2 Return the mixture to the pan and heat gently, stirring all the time until thickened. Strain into a bowl, cover the surface and chill.

3 Preheat oven to 200 C/400 F/Gas 6. Cream the butter and soft light brown sugar and spread over the bottom of 6 large ramekins. Cut the apricots in half and remove the stones. Cut the fruit into thick wedges and arrange them over the butter and sugar in the ramekin dishes.

4 For the pastry, cream the butter and sugar together with a wooden spoon. Work in the flour and the hazelnuts until the mixture forms a soft dough. Press into a ball and divide into 6. Shape into small rounds and flatten slightly. Arrange on top of the fruit in the ramekins and press down firmly. Bake on a baking tray for 20-25 minutes until golden. Remove from the oven.

5 Pour the sauce over the serving plates. Spoon the warm apricot glaze into a piping bag and pipe a circle of glaze around each plate. Feather it using the tip of a cocktail stick or fine skewer. Run a knife around the edge of each of the pastries and turn out of the ramekin dishes and onto the pools of vanilla cream sauce. Serve immediately.

APPLE CREME BRULEE

Preparation time: 15 mins
+ chilling
Cooking time: 35-40 mins
Serves 6

INGREDIENTS

450 g/1 lb dessert apples, peeled and chopped
2 tbls lemon juice
25 g/1 oz sultanas
600 ml/1 pt double cream
1 cinnamon stick
3 egg yolks
50 g/2 oz caster sugar
4 tbls demerara sugar

VARIATION

To make a classic Crème Brûlée, all you have to do is omit the apple and sultana mixture from this recipe.

WATCHPOINT

It is important that the grill is really hot. If not, the cream mixture will begin to melt before the sugar does.

2 Bring 450 ml/¾ pt of the cream to the boil with the cinnamon stick. Cover and set aside for 10 minutes then remove the cinnamon.

3 Whisk together the egg yolks and caster sugar until pale, then whisk in the remaining 150 ml/¼ pt cream. Stir this into the heated cream and cook, stirring, over moderate heat for 15 minutes until the mixture has thickened in the pan.

1 Put the apples, lemon juice and 4 tbls water in a pan. Cover and simmer over a gentle heat, stirring, for 15-20 minutes, until the apples have pulped. Stir in the sultanas and set aside.

4 Divide the apple and sultana mixture equally among 6 ramekin dishes, then pour the cream mixture on top to fill each dish. Chill well.

5 Top each ramekin with demerara sugar. Place under a fierce grill for 2-3 minutes, or until the sugar has melted and is bubbling on the top. Leave to cool, then chill for 1 hour before serving.

CHOCOLATE MOUSSE

Preparation time: 10 mins
+ chilling
Cooking time: 3-5 mins
Serves 6-8

INGREDIENTS

6 eggs
100 g/4 oz sugar
300 ml/½ pt double cream
225 g/8 oz plain chocolate
1 tbls Cointreau
Grated zest of 1 orange

FOR THE DECORATION
Grated orange zest
Chocolate leaves (see Techniques)

MICROWAVE TIP

Place broken chocolate in a small microwave-proof bowl and cook on **MEDIUM HIGH (75%)** for 3 minutes, stirring often. This will melt the chocolate ready for use.

WINE NOTE

For a special dinner party, serve a bottle of Marsala dessert wine as an accompaniment to the chocolate mousse.

1 Separate the eggs and whisk the yolks with the sugar until pale and creamy. Beat the cream until slightly thickened then stir in the yolks and sugar. Melt the chocolate in a bowl over a pan of warm water. Cool slightly then stir into the cream mixture.

2 Whisk the egg whites until stiff. Stir a little into the chocolate mixture then fold in the rest. Add the Cointreau and orange zest.

3 Spoon into individual dishes and chill for about 4 hours or until set. Decorate with orange zest and chocolate leaves.

CHOCOLATE SOUFFLES

Preparation time: 15 mins
Cooking time: 40 mins
Serves 4

INGREDIENTS
50 g/2 oz plain chocolate
100 ml/3½ fl oz milk
25 g/1 oz caster sugar
2 tbls flour
2 egg yolks
2 egg whites
Sieved icing sugar, for dusting

FOR THE SAUCE
75 ml/3 fl oz evaporated milk
25 g/1 oz plain chocolate
25 g/1 oz soft brown sugar

1 Preheat oven to 200 C/400 F/Gas 6. To make the sauce, put the sauce ingredients into a saucepan and heat gently, stirring until the sugar has dissolved. Bring to the boil and simmer until thick.

2 Spoon 1 tbls of the sauce into the base of four individual soufflé dishes. Make sure you coat the dishes evenly.

3 Put the chocolate into a small bowl and melt over a saucepan of hot water. Reserve 2 tbls of milk and put the rest into another saucepan, together with the caster sugar. Slowly bring to the boil, stirring steadily to make sure the sugar is melted. Stir the chocolate into the milk mixture.

4 Mix the flour with the 2 tbls milk and add to the chocolate mixture in the pan.

5 Bring the chocolate mixture to the boil, stirring constantly. Cook until the mixture has thickened. Remove from heat, cool slightly and add the egg yolks individually.

6 Whisk the egg whites until stiff and carefully fold into the chocolate mixture. Spoon into the dishes and cook in the oven for 30 minutes or until the soufflés are well risen and set. Remove from the oven, lightly dust with icing sugar and serve immediately.

HOT TOFFEE SOUFFLES

Preparation time: 20 mins
+ cooling
Cooking time: 25 mins
Serves 6

INGREDIENTS

FOR THE PRALINE
Oil, for greasing

25 g/1 oz blanched, peeled almonds

25 g/1 oz caster sugar, plus extra for dusting

Butter, for greasing

FOR THE TOFFEE SAUCE
15 g/½ oz butter

20 g/¾ oz soft brown sugar

2 tbls golden syrup

FOR THE SOUFFLE BASE
300 ml/½ pt milk

3 large eggs, separated

50 g/2 oz caster sugar

25 g/1 oz flour

1 Oil a baking tray. Make the praline by putting the almonds and caster sugar into a small heavy-based pan and placing over a low heat. Leave until the sugar has melted and turned golden brown, then pour onto the baking tray. Allow to harden then grind coarsely in a food processor.

2 Preheat oven to 220 C/425 F/Gas 7. Position a baking tray on the centre shelf. Brush six 9 cm/3 ½ in ramekins with butter and then dust the inside of each one with caster sugar.

3 To make the toffee sauce, put the butter, soft brown sugar and golden syrup in a small saucepan and set over a low heat until melted. Boil for 2 minutes, then cool slightly.

4 Meanwhile quickly bring the milk to the boil and set aside. Beat the egg yolks and half the caster sugar until pale. Beat in the flour and then the hot milk. Pour the mixture back into the saucepan and simmer for 2 minutes, stirring constantly. Remove from heat to cool slightly. Then mix in the toffee sauce.

5 Whisk the egg whites until stiff and then whisk in the remaining caster sugar. Fold a large spoonful of the egg white mixture into the toffee mixture, then lightly fold in the remainder.

6 Spoon the mixture into the prepared ramekins and sprinkle the top of each with 1 tsp of the praline. Place on the pre-heated baking tray and bake for 10-12 minutes.

GINGER PUDDINGS

Preparation time: 45 mins
Cooking time: 1-1½ hours
Serves 6

INGREDIENTS
FOR THE SPONGE

100 g/4 oz butter, plus extra for greasing
100 g/4 oz caster sugar
2 eggs
100 g/4 oz self-raising flour
50 g/2 oz stem ginger, drained and chopped
6 tbls maple syrup

FOR THE SAUCE

1 tbls freshly peeled, grated ginger
300 ml/½ pt milk
25 g/1 oz butter
25 g/1 oz flour
50 g/2 oz caster sugar

1 Grease and base line 6 dariole moulds. Cream the butter and sugar together until light and fluffy. Beat in the eggs one at a time, adding a little of the flour with each egg.

3 Steam the puddings for 1-1½ hours. To make the sauce, add the ginger to the milk in a pan and bring to scalding point. Leave to infuse for 30 minutes then strain. Melt the butter, add the flour and cook for 1 minute, add the milk and cook, stirring, until thickened. Stir in the sugar.

4 When the sauce is ready, turn the puddings out onto serving plates. Spoon over the ginger sauce just before serving.

2 Fold the remaining flour into the mixture. Add the chopped stem ginger. Spoon 1 tbls maple syrup into the bottom of each mould, then spoon the sponge mixture on top. Cover each mould with buttered foil.

PECAN-STUFFED CREPES

Preparation time: 25 mins
+ standing
Cooking time: 25 mins
Makes 8

INGREDIENTS

FOR THE CREPES

1 tbls vanilla essence
2 eggs, beaten
1 egg yolk
300 ml/½ pt milk
2 tbls Cognac
25 g/1 oz butter, melted
175 g/6 oz flour
Butter, for frying

FOR THE FILLING

300 ml/½ pt double cream
4 tbls maple syrup
100 g/4 oz pecan nuts, chopped
Maple syrup, to serve
Pecan nuts, to decorate

1 First make the crêpes. Mix the vanilla essence, eggs, egg yolk, milk, Cognac and melted butter together. Sift the flour into a bowl.

2 Make a well in the flour and pour in the milk and butter mixture, whisking until smooth. Stand, covered, for half an hour.

3 Melt a little butter in a small crêpe pan and pour in enough batter to just cover the base of the pan. Cook for a few minutes until the underside is golden, then flip over. Transfer to a plate while you make the remaining crêpes. Place absorbent paper between crêpes. Cool.

4 Make the filling. Whisk the double cream until stiff. Fold in the maple syrup and pecan nuts.

5 Divide the filling evenly among the crêpes and fold into quarters. Pour over extra maple syrup and decorate with pecan nuts. Chill in the fridge until required.

HAZELNUT PROFITEROLES

Preparation time: 40 mins
+ cooling
Cooking time: 35-40 mins
Makes 40

INGREDIENTS
Oil, for greasing
75 g/3 oz butter
95 g/3¾ oz flour, sifted
Pinch of salt
3 eggs, beaten
75 g/3 oz hazelnuts,
toasted, skinned and coarsely chopped

FOR THE CREAM FILLING
300 ml/½ pt double cream
1 tbls icing sugar, sifted
75 g/4 oz hazelnuts,
toasted, skinned and coarsely chopped

FOR THE CHOCOLATE SAUCE
175 g/6 oz plain chocolate,
broken into pieces
4 tbls golden syrup
25 g/1 oz butter

V A R I A T I O N

For a hint of extravagance, beat 1-2 tbls brandy into the chocolate sauce when removed from the heat.

1 To make the choux pastry, line 2 baking trays with greaseproof paper and brush with oil. Melt the butter in 215 ml/7½ fl oz water then bring to the boil. Quickly tip the flour in and take the pan off the heat. Beat hard until the mixture forms a soft ball. Cool for 5 minutes, then beat the eggs into the choux mixture, a little at a time, until it is a dropping consistency. Stir in the chopped hazelnuts.

2 Form rounded shapes between 2 teaspoons and put well apart on the baking trays. Bake for 20-25 minutes or until evenly browned and crisp. Make a small hole in each one to release the steam, then return to the oven for 5 minutes. Allow to cool.

3 For the filling, whip the cream until it stands in peaks. Fold in the icing sugar and nuts. Pipe into profiteroles.

4 For the chocolate sauce, melt the chocolate, syrup and butter in a pan. Off the heat beat until smooth. Cool, then serve.

AMARETTO CHOUX

Preparation time: 30 mins
+ cooling
Cooking time: 35-40 mins
Serves 6

INGREDIENTS

Oil, for greasing

1 quantity choux pastry (see Techniques)
50 g/2 oz caster sugar
50 g/2 oz almonds, peeled
300 ml/½ pt double cream
2 tbls amaretto liqueur

FOR THE TOPPING
100 g/4 oz caster sugar

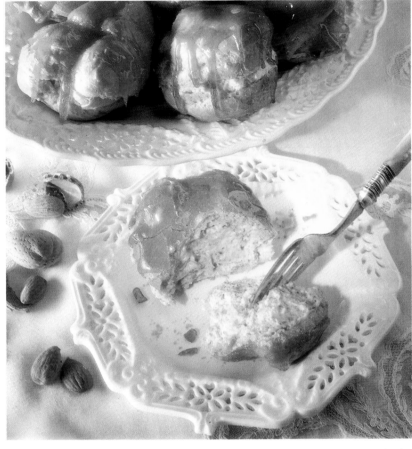

1 Preheat oven to 200 C/400 F/Gas 6. Grease a baking sheet and then place six egg-sized spoonfuls of choux pastry onto it. Bake in the oven for 25-30 minutes until the pastry is well risen and golden-brown in colour. Pierce each choux ball, then return to the oven for 5 minutes. Cool on a wire rack.

2 Oil a baking sheet. Place the sugar in a heavy-based pan and heat very gently until it has caramelised. Add the almonds. Cook until the almonds begin to crack and the caramel is a rich golden colour. Pour onto the baking sheet and leave until cold and hard. Remove from the baking sheet and process until broken up into pieces but not too fine.

3 Whip the cream and amaretto together until peaks form. Fold in the praline. Cut the choux balls in half and fill with cream mixture.

4 To make the topping, heat the sugar and 4 tbls water together over a low heat until the sugar is dissolved. Increase the heat and cook for 5 minutes or until golden brown. Spoon the topping over each choux bun and leave to set.

CHOCOLATE & NUT LOAF

Preparation time: 20 mins
+ chilling
Cooking time: 5 mins
Serves 6-8

INGREDIENTS

225 g/8 oz plain chocolate
150 ml/¼ pt double cream
6 digestive biscuits, roughly crushed
Oil, for greasing
50 g/2 oz Brazil nuts, sliced
50 g/2 oz glacé cherries, halved
50 g/2 oz angelica, diced
50 g/2 oz glacé pineapple, diced

1 Melt the chocolate over a pan of simmering water. Remove from heat and pour into a mixing bowl. Add the cream and crushed digestive biscuits.

2 Oil a 450 g/1 lb loaf tin and line with greaseproof paper or foil. Spoon a third of the mixture into the tin and smooth it down with a spoon. Cover with half the sliced Brazil nuts, glacé cherries, diced angelica and diced glacé pineapple.

3 Spoon on another layer of the chocolate mixture, smooth down and cover with the remaining nuts and fruit. Spread over the last of the mixture and smooth down using a knife.

4 Cover the loaf tin with cling film. Chill in the fridge for at least 2 hours, then turn the cake out onto a rectangular serving plate. Slice thinly and serve.

VARIATION
For a richer loaf add 2-3 tbls brandy or rum to the chocolate mixture before spooning it into the loaf tin.

SERVING NOTE
Decorate with rows of piped cream alternated with glacé cherries and Brazil nuts. Sprinkle with angelica.

RICH CHOCOLATE TORTE

Preparation time: 45 mins
+ cooling
Cooking times: 25-30 mins
Serves 6

INGREDIENTS

FOR THE MACAROON BASE

100 g/4 oz ground almonds
175 g/4 oz caster sugar
1 tsp flour
2 egg whites
2 drops of vanilla essence
Rice paper

FOR THE TOPPING

350 g/12 oz plain chocolate
50 g/2 oz hazelnuts
50 g/2 oz blanched almonds
75 g/3 oz unsalted butter
2 tbls brandy or rum
50 g/2 oz walnut pieces
50 g/2 oz double cream

FOR THE GLAZE

100 g/4 oz plain chocolate
25 g/1 oz unsalted butter
2 tbls milk

1 Preheat oven to 180 C/350 F/Gas 4. To make the base, mix together the almonds, sugar, flour, egg whites and vanilla essence.

2 Line the base of a 23 cm/9 in spring-form tin with rice paper. Spoon in the mixture and spread to cover the base. Bake for 20-25 minutes until it is a rich golden colour. Leave until completely cool.

3 To make the topping, melt the chocolate with 125 ml/4 fl oz of water. Leave to cool.

4 Toast the hazelnuts and almonds. Cool. Chop roughly. Cream the butter. Then beat in the melted chocolate, brandy or rum and all the nuts.

5 Whip 215 ml/7½ fl oz of the cream until it begins to thicken. Fold into the chocolate mixture and pour onto the base. Smooth, cover and chill in the fridge until firm.

6 To make the glaze, melt together chocolate, butter and milk. Cool. Pour over torte in tin.

7 Spoon little blobs of cream at regular intervals around the edge and then, using the tip of a fine skewer, swirl in the cream. Chill to allow glaze to set. Then run a knife around the tin, unmould and serve.

CHOCOLATE PUDDING

Preparation time: 15 mins
Cooking time 2¼-2½ hours
Serves 6

INGREDIENTS
FOR THE TOPPING

50 g/2 oz plain chocolate
2 tbls double cream
Butter, for greasing

FOR THE SPONGE

175 g/6 oz butter
175 g/6 oz caster sugar
3 large eggs, beaten
175 g/6 oz self-raising flour
100 g/4 oz plain chocolate
2 tbls milk

FOR THE BRANDY SAUCE

2 tbls soft brown sugar
2 tbls caster sugar
1 tbls cornflour
150 ml/¼ pt milk
15 g/½ oz butter
4 tbls brandy
Grated zest of 1 orange

MICROWAVE TIP
Use a 1.7 L/3 pt microwave-proof bowl, cover with cling film and cook on **MEDIUM HIGH (75%) for 8-10 minutes** until risen and spongy.

1 For the topping, melt the chocolate in a bowl set over hot water. Stir in the cream. Grease a 1.1 L/2 pt pudding basin with butter and spoon in the chocolate mixture.

2 For the sponge, beat the butter and sugar together until light and fluffy. Add the eggs, one at a time, beating well between each addition. Fold in the flour. Melt the chocolate in a bowl over a pan of hot water, beat in the milk, then fold into the sponge mixture.

3 Spoon the mixture into the pudding basin over the chocolate mixture. Cover with greaseproof paper and then foil and secure with string. Place in a steamer over a pan of boiling water, cover and cook for 2-2¼ hours, topping up the water as required.

4 For the sauce, place the sugar and cornflour in a saucepan. Gradually whisk in the milk over a low heat, then stir until the mixture comes to the boil. Beat in the butter gradually, then stir in the brandy and orange zest. Turn the pudding out onto a plate and serve with the sauce.

CHOCOLATE CHEESECAKE

Preparation time: 25-30 mins
+ chilling
Cooking time: 5 mins
Serves 10-12

INGREDIENTS

FOR THE BASE

225 g/8 oz digestive biscuits
100 g/4 oz butter, melted

FOR THE FILLING

225 g/8 oz cream cheese
150 ml/¼ pt thick set natural yoghurt
26 g/1 oz caster sugar
Finely grated zest and juice of 1 orange
1 egg white
275 g/10 oz white chocolate

FOR THE TOPPING

75 g/3 oz chocolate caraque (see Techniques)
Icing sugar, to sprinkle

PRUE'S TIP

White chocolate melts much more easily if grated rather than just broken up. The best way to guarantee success is to use white cooking chocolate. For extra creaminess, spread 150 ml/¼ pt whipped cream over the cheesecake before adding the chocolate caraque.

1 Crush the biscuits and stir in the melted butter. Mix until smooth and transfer to the base of a 23 cm/9 in spring-form tin. Use the back of a spoon to press the biscuits firmly into place. Chill in the fridge for 30 minutes.

2 To make the filling, beat the cream cheese, yoghurt, caster sugar, orange zest and 2 tbls juice until smooth.

3 Grate the white chocolate and melt over a bowl of simmering water. Add to the cream cheese mixture and stir in thoroughly.

4 Whisk the egg white until stiff and fold into the mixture until fully blended. Pour into the prepared tin and chill overnight.

5 When the cheesecake is firm, remove it from the tin. Arrange the chocolate caraque on top of the cake and sprinkle with a dusting of icing sugar. Chill until ready to serve.

CHEESECAKE WITH STRAWBERRIES

Preparation time: 40 mins
+ chilling
Cooking time: 20 mins
Serves 6

INGREDIENTS

FOR THE SPONGE

Butter, for greasing
3 eggs
100 g/4 oz caster sugar
100 g/4 oz flour
Grated zest of 1 lemon

FOR THE FILLING

200 g/7 oz low-fat cream cheese
150 ml/¼ pt soured cream
300 ml/½ pt double cream
225 g/8 oz tinned pineapple pieces, in natural juice
4 tbls kirsch
225 g/8 oz Alpine strawberries
Strawberry leaves, to decorate

FOR THE SAUCE

225 g/8 oz fresh raspberries
Icing sugar, to taste

"There's no doubt that cheesecake is not at all good for the waistline, so I try not to make it too often. But whenever I do, it never lasts very long." Prue

1 Preheat oven to 180 C/350 F/Gas 4. Grease and line a deep 20 cm/8 in round cake tin. Whisk the eggs with an electric mixer until pale, then add the sugar and whisk until the mixture will hold the trail of the whisks.

2 Sift the flour several times, then lightly fold into the egg mixture with the lemon zest. Pour into the prepared tin and bake in the oven for about 20 minutes until golden and springy to the touch. Turn out and cool on a wire rack, then split horizontally.

3 Meanwhile, mix together the cream cheese and soured cream. Whip half the double cream and fold into the cheese mixture. Drain the pineapple, reserving the juice. Stir the kirsch into the juice and sprinkle over the sponge halves.

4 Spread one-third of the cheese mixture over the bottom sponge, scatter half the strawberries and the pineapple over the top. Cover with half the remaining cheese mixture. Add the top layer of sponge and then the remaining cheese mixture. Chill in the fridge for about 1 hour until firm.

5 Whip the remaining double cream until it holds soft peaks and spread over the top of the cake. Decorate with remaining strawberries and strawberry leaves. Push the raspberries through a nylon sieve into a bowl, then stir in icing sugar to taste. Serve sauce with the chilled cheesecake.

HEDGEROW CRUMBLE

INGREDIENTS
900 g/2 lb mixed prepared hedgerow fruits,
including blackberries, cooking plums,
apples, blueberries and Alpine strawberries

Grated zest of 1 orange

Juice of ½ an orange

50 g/2 oz sugar

FOR THE CRUMBLE TOPPING
175 g/6 oz flour

75 g/3 oz butter

75 g/3 oz sugar

25 g/1 oz rolled oats

Preparation time: 15 mins
Cooking time: 40-50 mins
Serves 6

1 Place all the prepared fruit in a pan with the orange zest and juice. Cover the pan and simmer. Cook for 5-10 minutes or until the apples and the firmer fruits are tender. Stir in the sugar to taste. Remove the lid and cook for a further 5 minutes.

2 Preheat oven to 200 C/400 F/Gas 6. To make the crumble topping, sift the flour into a bowl and rub in the butter until it resembles coarse crumbs. Stir in the sugar and oats.

3 Spoon the fruit into the base of a pudding dish and top with the crumble mixture, pushing down the crumble around the sides. Bake in the oven for 25-30 minutes until golden.

CARAMELISED RICE PUDDING

INGREDIENTS
175 g/6 oz pudding rice

1 L/1¾ pt milk

1 vanilla pod, cut in half lengthways

150 g/5 oz caster sugar

5 egg yolks

Pinch of ground cinnamon

Pared zest of 1 lemon

225 ml/8 fl oz double cream

FOR THE CARAMEL
4 tbls soft brown sugar

Preparation time: 20 mins
+ chilling
Cooking time: 1 hour
Serves 6

VARIATION
If the topping is too sweet for your taste, sprinkle rice with a little ground cinnamon before serving.

1 Wash the rice and boil in a saucepan of water for 5 minutes. Drain and rinse again. Then gently heat 500 ml/17 fl oz milk and add the rice, 50 g/2 oz of the sugar and one half of the vanilla pod. Simmer for about 15 minutes until the rice is tender. Remove the half vanilla pod and set the rice aside to cool.

2 In a large bowl, cream the egg yolks with 75 g/3 oz sugar. Heat the remaining milk with the remaining half of vanilla pod in a separate pan until warm. Pour the milk into the egg mixture, remove the vanilla pod and blend well. Return to a heavy-based saucepan. Heat gently, stirring until the custard thickens and coats the back of a wooden spoon.

3 Stir the cooked rice into the custard, add the cinnamon and set aside. Blanch the lemon zest for 1 minute in boiling water. Rinse under cold water, dry with absorbent paper and stir into the rice. Chill rice in fridge until cold.

4 Whisk the cream until stiff and fold it into the rice. Turn the grill to maximum. Spoon the rice into a flameproof serving dish and sprinkle the sugar evenly over the top. Put it under the hot grill, watching it carefully, until the sugar caramelises. Do not allow the sugar to burn. Serve immediately.

BREAD & BUTTER PUDDING

Preparation time: 20 mins
+ soaking
Cooking time: 1¼ hours
Serves 6

INGREDIENTS

150 g/5 oz dried apricots
50 g/2 oz sultanas
25 g/1 oz butter
450 g/1 lb white loaf, sliced
Oil, for greasing
225 ml/8 fl oz milk
225 ml/8 fl oz single cream
1 vanilla pod
175 g/6 oz caster sugar
3 eggs, beaten
1-2 tsp lemon juice

V A R I A T I O N

Sprinkle each layer of bread generously with grated nutmeg or cinnamon to add a spicy flavour.

1 Soak the apricots overnight in 600 ml/1 pt water. Preheat oven to 180 C/350 F/Gas 4. Soak the sultanas in hot water for 10 minutes, drain and mix with 50 g/2 oz apricots. Butter the bread slices, remove crusts and cut into triangles. Arrange in a 1.3 L/2¼ pt greased soufflé dish, buttered side up. Sprinkle sultanas and apricots between the layers.

2 Put the milk, cream, vanilla pod and 100 g/4 oz of the sugar in a saucepan and bring to just below boiling point. Remove the vanilla pod and add the eggs.

3 Pour the custard through a sieve onto the bread. Leave to soak in. Lightly oil a piece of foil and cover the dish.

4 Sit the dish in a small roasting tin and pour in hot water to come half-way up the sides. Bake in the centre of the oven for 50 minutes or until set firm.

5 To make the apricot sauce, place the remaining apricots and the soaking liquid in a pan, cover and simmer for 15 minutes. Add the remaining 50 g/2 oz sugar and the lemon juice and stir until the sugar dissolves. Blend in a liquidiser until smooth. Pour into a jug. Keep warm.

6 When the pudding is cooked remove from the tin and leave to cool for 10 minutes. Turn out. Serve the sauce separately.

BAKING

VIENNESE BISCUITS

INGREDIENTS
Oil, for greasing
75 g/3 oz butter, softened
25 g/1 oz icing sugar
75 g/3 oz flour, sieved
¼ tsp baking powder
225 g/8 oz plain chocolate,
broken into pieces

Preparation time: 20 mins
Cooking time: 20 mins
Makes 8

FREEZER TIP

These can be made in advance and frozen for 1 month, without the chocolate coating.

1 Preheat oven to 190 C/375 F/Gas 5. Lightly grease a baking tray with oil. Put the butter and sugar in a large bowl and cream until pale and fluffy. Beat in the flour and baking powder until the mixture is completely smooth and thoroughly combined.

2 Using a piping bag fitted with a star-shaped nozzle, pipe eight S-shaped biscuits on the baking tray. Bake in the centre of the oven for 15-20 minutes until crisp and golden. Remove the biscuits from the heat and allow to cool on a wire rack.

3 Melt the chocolate in a bowl set over a pan of simmering water. Remove the pan from the heat. Taking one biscuit at a time, dip both ends into the melted chocolate. Allow the biscuits to cool on a plate.

PALMIERS

INGREDIENTS
375 g/13 oz puff pastry (see Techniques)
Flour, for dusting
100 g/4 oz caster sugar
Butter, for greasing
150 ml/¼ pt double cream, whipped

Preparation time: 10 mins
+ cooling
Cooking time: 13-15 mins
Makes 12

FREEZER TIP

These will freeze for up to 2 months either cooked or uncooked. Defrost then bake.

1 Preheat oven to 220 C/425 F/Gas 7. Roll out the pastry on a lightly floured surface to a 30 cm/12 in by 25 cm/10 in rectangle, 6 mm/¼ in thick. Dredge with 25 g/1 oz sugar. Fold both long sides halfway towards the centre.

2 Dredge with another 25 g/1 oz sugar and fold again lengthways, taking the sides right to the centre.

3 Dredge with the remaining sugar and fold in half to make one long strip. Press lightly. Cut the strip into 24 slices. Arrange on a greased baking tray, flattening the biscuits slightly. Bake for 8-10 minutes until golden. Remove from the oven, turn the pastry over and cook for a further 5 minutes. Transfer to a wire rack and allow to cool.

4 Fill a piping bag with cream and pipe over half the palmiers. Sandwich the palmiers together and dredge with extra sugar if liked.

FLORENTINES

Preparation time: 20 mins
Cooking time: 20 mins
Makes 15

INGREDIENTS

50 g/2 oz butter, plus extra for greasing
50 g/2 oz flour, plus extra for dusting
50 g/2 oz sugar
1 tbls clear honey
50 g/2 oz glacé cherries, chopped
25 g/1 oz mixed candied peel
25 g/1 oz almonds, chopped
100 g/4 oz plain chocolate

1 Preheat oven to 180 C/350 F/Gas 4. Grease two baking sheets, sprinkle with flour then shake off any excess.

2 Put the butter, sugar and honey in a pan and melt slowly. Remove from the heat and stir in the flour, cherries, candied peel and almonds.

3 Drop spoonfuls of the mixture onto the baking sheets, leaving enough space for them to spread while cooking. Smooth over slightly.

4 Bake for about 10 minutes or until browned and crisp. Cool on a wire rack. Melt the chocolate in a small bowl over simmering water and spread over the underside of the florentines. When nearly set, mark wavy lines with a fork. Leave until set.

ECCLES CAKES

INGREDIENTS

225 g/8 oz puff pastry, thawed if frozen
Flour, for dusting
15 g/½ oz butter, plus extra for greasing
75 g/3 oz currants
25 g/1 oz demerara sugar,
plus extra for topping
½ tsp ground nutmeg
Milk, to glaze

Preparation time: 20 mins
Cooking time: 20 mins
Makes 12

PRUE'S TIP

Once cut, the pastry rounds may shrink a little, so roll to the original size again before filling. This will make them much easier to fill.

1 Roll out the puff pastry on a lightly floured surface until it is 3 mm/⅛ in thick. Cut out nine 7.5 cm/3 in rounds with a plain cutter and set aside. Stack pastry trimmings on top of one another and roll out once more. Stamp out another 3 rounds with the cutter.

2 Preheat oven to 220 C/425 F/Gas 7. Gently melt the butter in a saucepan, then stir in the currants, sugar and nutmeg. Mix well. Divide the mixture among the pasty rounds. Dampen pastry edges with milk and draw up to enclose the filling, pinching the edges together. Turn the pastries over and roll back into 7.5 cm/3 in rounds.

3 Arrange the rounds on greased baking trays. Make 3 small cuts in the top of each and then brush with milk. Sprinkle with a little sugar and bake at the top of the oven for 15 minutes. Cool on a wire rack.

MINT BROWNIES

INGREDIENTS

100 g/4 oz butter
175 g/6 oz sugar
225 g/8 oz flour
100 g/4 oz cocoa powder
3 tbls golden syrup
½ tsp baking powder
Pinch of salt
2 eggs
225 g/8 oz semi-sweet chocolate, chopped
225 g/4 oz pecan nuts, chopped
16 square chocolate-covered,
soft-centred mints

Preparation time: 15 mins
Cooking time: 30-35 mins
Makes 16

1 Preheat oven to 180 C/350 F/Gas 4. Line a 23 cm/9 in square baking tin with baking parchment.

2 Beat the butter and sugar until light and fluffy. Add the flour, cocoa powder, golden syrup, baking powder, salt, and eggs. Beat until mixed.

3 Stir in the chopped chocolate pieces and nuts. Spoon the mixture into the prepared tin and bake for 25-30 minutes.

4 Remove the tin from the oven and cover the top of the brownies with the squares of chocolate-covered soft-centred mints.

5 Return the tin to the oven and bake for a further 5 minutes. Remove from the oven and place brownies onto a wire rack. When cool, cut into 16 squares.

CHELSEA BUNS

Preparation time: 30 mins
+ rising
Cooking time: 25 mins
Makes 9-12

INGREDIENTS

10 g/⅓ oz dried yeast
75 g/3 oz caster sugar
1 egg, beaten
215 ml/7½ fl oz warm milk
75 g/3 oz butter, plus extra for greasing
450 g/1 lb flour, sifted
½ tsp salt, sifted
1 tsp mixed spice, sifted
50 g/2 oz no-soak dried apricots, chopped
15 g/½ oz glacé cherries, chopped
25 g/1 oz sultanas
1 tsp demerara sugar

FREEZER TIP

When cold, open freeze on a baking sheet. Wrap when frozen and then keep for up to 3 months.

1 Preheat oven to 200 C/400 F/Gas 6. Mix the yeast with 1 tsp of the sugar. Add the egg and milk and put in a warm place until frothy. Rub half the butter into the flour, salt and spice in a bowl, then stir in half of the remaining caster sugar.

2 Make a well in the centre of the flour, pour in the yeast mixture and mix to make a soft dough.

3 Knead until smooth on a floured surface, then put in a large bowl, cover and leave in a warm place for approximately 1 hour or until the dough has doubled in bulk.

4 Knead the dough again until elastic, then roll out into a 23 cm/9 in square. Spread the rest of the butter over the surface and sprinkle with the remaining sugar. Scatter the dried fruit over the surface and roll up into a sausage.

5 Cut into 2.5-5 cm/1-2 in slices and arrange in rows .5 cm/¼ in apart in a greased baking tin. Sprinkle with the demerara sugar. Leave to prove for 15 minutes then bake for 20-25 minutes. Cool on a wire rack before separating.

STREUSEL TRAY BAKE

Preparation time: 15 mins
Cooking time: 55 mins-1 hour
Makes 14

INGREDIENTS

Oil, for greasing
100 g/4 oz butter
50 g/2 oz caster sugar
100 g/4 oz flour, sifted
6 tbls seedless raspberry jam

FOR THE TOPPING
150 g/5 oz flour
½ tsp baking powder
100 g/4 oz butter
75 g/3 oz brown sugar
40 g/1½ oz blanched almonds, chopped
Grated zest of ½ a lemon

SERVING NOTE
Reheat these biscuits and serve with whipped cream as a dessert.

FREEZER TIP
These can be made in advance and frozen for up to 6 months.

1 Preheat oven to 180 C/350 F/Gas 4. Lightly oil a 19.5 cm/7½ in square baking tin.

2 To make the base, beat the butter and caster sugar together until pale. Then slowly stir in the flour to form a soft dough. Press the mixture down into the prepared tin with a spoon. Bake for 15 minutes. Remove from the oven. Spread the jam over the top.

3 To make the topping, place the flour in a mixing bowl and stir in the baking powder. Rub in the butter thoroughly until the mixture resembles large, even-sized breadcrumbs. Stir in the brown sugar, the blanched almonds and the lemon zest.

4 Sprinkle the topping over the jam. Bake for 40-45 minutes until golden. Allow to cool before cutting into 14 even-sized fingers.

PEACH & APPLE TRAY BAKE

Preparation time: 25 mins
+ chilling
Cooking time: 45 mins
Serves 8

INGREDIENTS

100 g/4 oz butter, plus extra for greasing
225 g/8 oz flour, plus extra for dusting
50 g/2 oz caster sugar
2 egg yolks
400 g/14 oz tinned peach halves, drained and sliced
2 red-skinned apples, cored and sliced
4 tbls strawberry jam, melted and sieved
2 tsp demerara sugar
25 g/1 oz blanched almonds, split

1 Preheat oven to 180 C/350 G/Gas 4. Grease a baking tray. Rub the butter into the flour until it resembles fine breadcrumbs. Stir in the sugar and add the egg yolks with 2 tbls water. Bring the mixture together with the finger tips to form a soft dough, wrap and chill.

2 Roll out the pastry on a floured surface to 6 mm/¼ in thick. Use to line a 23 cm/9 in by 33 cm/13 in Swiss roll tin. Trim edges and prick all over with a fork. Bake blind (see Techniques) for 20 minutes. Remove from the oven and allow to cool.

3 Arrange the peach and apple slices in rows on top. Blend together the jam and 1 tbls water and brush over the fruit. Sprinkle with demerara sugar and almonds. Bake for a further 25 minutes until golden.

4 Remove from the oven and cut into bars while still warm. Serve either hot or cold.

APRICOT BAKLAVA

Preparation time: 40 mins
Cooking time: 40-45 mins
Serves 6

INGREDIENTS

175 g/6 oz unsalted butter, melted
450 g/1 lb filo pastry
225 g/8 oz chopped almonds
225 g/8 oz dried apricots, minced
700 g/1 lb 8 oz sugar
2 tbls lemon juice
Strained Greek yoghurt, to serve

PRUE'S TIP

The oils in the lemon help prevent the almond and apricot mixture from sticking to the filo pastry. If you don't have one to hand, use a spoon instead.

1 Preheat oven to 180 C/350 F/Gas 4. Brush a Swiss roll tin measuring 41.5 cm/15½ in by 25 cm/10 in with a little of the melted butter. Place one sheet of filo pastry on the base of the tin, brush with more butter and layer up three more sheets of pastry in this way.

2 Mix the chopped almonds and apricots together and place an even layer over the pastry. Use a lemon to roll the filling over the pastry.

3 Cover with a sheet of pastry and layer up with melted butter and three more sheets of pastry as before, finishing with butter. (Keep the pastry covered at all times as it will dry out quickly.) Freeze any remaining pastry.

4 Cut right through the pastry into diamond shapes. Bake in the oven for 40-45 minutes, until the pastry has turned golden brown.

5 Put the sugar, lemon juice and 250 ml/8 fl oz water into a pan. Dissolve over a gentle heat, then simmer for 15 minutes. Pour the liquid over the baklava while it is still hot. Leave to cool before serving the baklava accompanied by yoghurt.

CURD TARTLETS

Preparation time: 30 mins
Cooking time: 25-30 mins
Serves 8

INGREDIENTS

1 quantity rich shortcrust pastry
(see Techniques)

Flour, for dusting

FOR THE FILLING

2 nectarines

50 g/2 oz butter

50 g/2 oz caster sugar

2 egg yolks, lightly beaten

225 g/8 oz curd cheese, sieved

PRUE'S TIP

Take some peeled slices of nectarines brushed with lemon juice, and reserve in a sealed container. These can be fanned out to garnish the tartlets.

1 Roll out the shortcrust pastry thinly on a floured surface and use to line eight 10 cm/4 in fluted tartlet tins.

2 Peel and stone the nectarines. Purée them in a food processor. Pour into a dish and set aside. Beat together the butter and sugar, add egg yolks and cheese. Beat well.

3 Spoon a little of the puréed nectarines into each of the pastry cases. Top with the cheese mixture and bake in the oven for 25-30 minutes until the filling is set. Allow to cool in the oven first, then store in a cool place.

BAKED LEMON & LIME PIE

Preparation time: 30 mins
+ macerating
Cooking time: 30-40 mins
Serves 6

INGREDIENTS

2 thin-skinned lemons, sliced
2 limes, thinly sliced
200 g/7 oz caster sugar
250 g/9 oz flour
½ tsp salt
175 g/6 oz butter
5-6 tbls cold milk
2 tsp arrowroot
3 eggs, beaten, plus 1 extra for glazing

FOR THE DECORATION

1 lime
1 lemon
2 tbls caster sugar

1 Combine the sliced lemons and limes with the caster sugar and leave overnight or until the sugar has completely dissolved.

2 Preheat oven to 230 C/450 F/Gas 8. Sieve the flour and salt into a bowl. Rub in the butter. Add milk to bind the mixture well. Knead the dough briefly.

3 Using just over half the pastry, roll out and line a 23 cm/9 in pie plate. Roll the remaining pastry into a circle to cover the top. Save trimmings which will be used later to decorate the pie.

4 Stir a little fruit juice into the arrowroot. Add to the fruit with the beaten egg. Pour into the pastry shell. Brush the edge with egg and lay the round of pastry on top. Press the edges together.

5 Cut around the edge of the pie at 2.5 cm/1 in intervals. Shape the trimmings into balls. Lay one in the bottom right-hand corner of each section. Fold the top left-hand corner over the pastry ball and press down. Brush with beaten egg and bake for 10 minutes. Reduce heat to 180 C/350 F/Gas 4 and bake for 20 minutes until pale golden.

6 Pare the peel and pith from lime and lemon, then segment them both. Arrange the fruit on top of the pie, put the finely chopped zest in the middle and sprinkle with caster sugar.

HONEYED PEAR PIE

Preparation time: 30 mins
+ chilling
Cooking time: 1 hour
Serves 4

INGREDIENTS
700 g/1 lb 8 oz small ripe pears
3 tbls honey
Juice of ½ a lemon
225 g/8 oz flour, plus extra for dusting
50 g/2 oz walnuts, finely chopped
Finely grated zest of ½ an orange
75 g/3 oz caster sugar, plus extra for dusting
100 g/4 oz firm butter
1 egg, beaten
Thick yoghurt or cream, to serve

1 Peel the pears from top to bottom, halve and remove their cores. Place the pears in a saucepan, cover with cold water and add the honey and lemon juice. Cover and simmer for 20 minutes. Allow to cool in the syrup.

2 To prepare the pastry, sieve the flour into a mixing bowl, add the walnuts, orange zest, sugar and butter and rub together or use a food processor until the mixture resembles large breadcrumbs. Add the egg and combine into a soft dough. Cover and leave to chill for 20 mins.

3 Roll out two thirds of the chilled pastry on a lightly floured surface and then use to line a 23 cm/9 in pie dish. Trim the edges of the pastry using a knife. Reserve the trimmings and set aside. Remove the pears from the honey syrup and arrange the halves in the bottom of the pastry-lined dish.

4 Preheat oven to 200 C/400 G/Gas 6. Roll out the remainder of the pastry to the size of the pie dish and cut a slit in the centre. Moisten the edges of the lined dish with water and cover with the pastry top. Crimp the pastry edges. Decorate with leftover scraps of pastry. Brush the pastry top with egg and sprinkle with caster sugar.

5 Bake the pie for 35-40 minutes until golden. Serve with yoghurt or whipped cream.

PEACH & ALMOND TART

Preparation time: 20 mins
Cooking time: 1 hour
Serves 6

INGREDIENTS
1 quantity almond pastry (see Techniques)
Flaked almonds, to decorate

FOR THE FILLING
4 ripe peaches
40 g/1½ oz flaked almonds
½ tsp ground cinnamon

FOR THE CUSTARD
3 eggs
50 g/2 oz sugar
2 drops vanilla essence
1 tsp cornflour
300 ml/½ pt milk

1 Preheat oven to 180 C/350 G/Gas 4. Line a 23 cm/9 in flan tin with pastry and bake blind (see Techniques) for about 15 minutes. Remove paper and beans and cook for 5 minutes.

2 Meanwhile make the filling. Put the peaches in a bowl, pour boiling water over the top and leave to stand for 1 minute. Remove the peaches carefully with a fork and peel off the skins. Cut the peaches in half, remove the stones and place the peaches in the pastry case. Sprinkle over the almonds and cinnamon.

3 To make the custard, beat the eggs, sugar and vanilla essence together in a heatproof bowl until thick. Mix the cornflour with a little cold water and add it to the eggs. Heat the milk until warm, then stir it into the egg mixture. Put the bowl containing the egg mixture over a pan of boiling water and stir until it has thickened. Allow to cool.

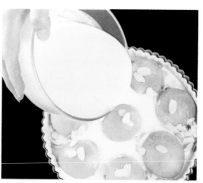

4 Pour the custard over the peaches and return the tart to the oven for 30 minutes. Decorate with more flaked almonds. Serve hot or cold.

CHERRY CLAFOUTIS

Preparation time: 15 mins
+ macerating
Cooking time: 45 mins
Serves 6

INGREDIENTS

450 g/1 lb bottled black cherries,
stoned and drained

4 tbls kirsch or cherry brandy

25 g/1 oz butter, melted,
plus extra for greasing

75 g/3 oz flour

25 g/1 oz cocoa powder

50 g/2 oz caster sugar,
plus extra for dredging

3 eggs

150 ml/¼ pt milk

150 ml/¼ pt single cream

1 Macerate the black cherries in the kirsch or cherry brandy for at least an hour, preferably longer.

2 Preheat oven to 190 C/375 F/Gas 5. Generously butter a shallow 23 cm/9 in ovenproof dish. Spread the cherries evenly over the bottom, reserving any accumulated juices, which can be used later.

3 Sieve the flour and cocoa powder into a bowl. Stir in the caster sugar. Make a well in the centre and break in the eggs. Beat the eggs, incorporating the flour mixture until you have a smooth batter. Beat in the milk, the cream, the melted butter and any remaining cherry and alcohol juices.

4 Pour the batter over the cherries. Bake in the centre of the oven (so that the batter cooks evenly) for 45 minutes until puffed up and golden.

5 Remove from the oven and leave to cool a little. Dredge with sugar. Serve while warm.

FRENCH APPLE TART

Preparation time: 40 mins
Cooking time: 55 mins
Serves 8

INGREDIENTS

350 g/12 oz rich shortcrust pastry, made with wholemeal flour (see Techniques)
5 apples
25 g/1 oz caster sugar
50 g/2 oz butter, melted
3 tbls smooth apricot jam
1 tbls kirsch

"I find this version of the classic French flan easier to do than the usual Tarte Maison. You don't need to use a flan ring, and laying the apples in this way takes less time and skill than laying them in rows."   Prue

1 Preheat oven to 200 C/400 G/Gas 6. Roll the pastry out very thinly into a large round about 30 cm/12 in in diameter. Place the round on an upturned baking tray and trim the edges using a small sharp knife to make a neat circle.

2 Peel the apples, remove the cores, and halve them lengthways. Place the apple halves, cut side down, on a board and slice them thinly.

3 Roughly chop any small and broken pieces of apple and pile them up in the centre of the pastry. Then arrange the sliced apple in circles over the pastry, starting 2.5 cm/1 in from the outside and working towards the centre, overlapping the slices as you go.

4 Fold the pastry edge over to make a rim around the apples. Sprinkle with sugar and drizzle over the melted butter. Cook for 45 minutes or until the top is golden. Then melt the jam with the kirsch and paint the apples. Cook for another 5-10 minutes until slightly caramelised. While still slightly warm, slide the tart onto a large plate and serve.

VARIATION
You can use plain flour or half plain and half wholemeal flour for the base instead of all wholemeal.

WATCHPOINT
Take care when transferring the tart to a plate. Use a metal spatula and an extra pair of hands.

SERIOUS CHEESECAKE

Preparation time: 20 mins
+ cooling
Cooking time: 1 hour 45 mins
Serves 10

INGREDIENTS

175 g/6 oz shortcrust pastry, thawed if frozen
100 g/4 oz butter, softened
150 g/5 oz caster sugar
25 g/1 oz flour
3 eggs, beaten
400 g/14 oz cream cheese
Grated zest and juice of 2 lemons
1 tsp vanilla essence
100 g/4 oz pecan nuts

PRUE'S TIP
Pecan nuts are now available in supermarkets and health-food shops. They look similar to walnuts but are softer to the bite.

1 Preheat oven to 200 C/400 F/Gas 6. Roll out the pastry into a 23 cm/9 in circle and use to line the base of a 20 cm/8 in spring-form tin. It will come half-way up the tin. Prick the pastry and bake blind (see Techniques) for 12-15 minutes. Allow to cool. Lower the oven temperature to 150 C/275 F/Gas 1.

2 Cream the butter and sugar together until light and stir or whisk in the flour with a little egg.

3 Beat the cheese until soft, then add to the butter mixture. Gradually add the rest of the egg, the lemon zest and juice and the vanilla essence and pour into the pastry base.

4 Arrange the pecan nuts in two circles on top of the filling and bake in the oven for 1¼-1½ hours until firm.

5 Turn off the oven and leave the door ajar. Let the cheesecake cool slowly in the oven for 30 minutes, then take out of the oven and leave until cold. Remove from the tin and serve.

WALNUT & ORANGE TART

Preparation time: 20 mins
+ chilling
Cooking time: 45-50 mins
Serves 6-8

INGREDIENTS

250 g/9 oz flour, plus extra for dusting
1 egg yolk
175 g/6 oz butter, diced
150 g/5 oz brown sugar
150 g/5 oz maple syrup
3 eggs, beaten
25 g/1 oz butter, melted
100 g/4 oz walnut halves
1 orange

1 Sift the flour into a bowl. Mix the egg yolk with 1 tbls water. Make a well in the centre of the flour and add the egg mixture. Add the butter. Knead together until it is a soft pliable dough. Transfer to a floured surface and knead again. Cover and chill.

2 Preheat oven to 200 C/400 F/Gas 6. Roll out the pastry to line a 20 cm/8 in round, loose-based flan tin and trim off edges.

3 Heat the sugar and syrup slowly until sugar is dissolved. Leave to cool. Beat in eggs and melted butter. Chop half the walnuts and add to the mixture. Pour into the flan dish and bake for 10 minutes. Remove from the oven and reduce the heat to 180 C/350 F/Gas 4.

4 Put one slice of orange in the centre of the tart and cut another into small triangles. Zest the remaining fruit. Decorate the top of the tart with walnut halves and orange pieces and bake for 30-35 minutes or until just set. Sprinkle zest over the top and serve.

DUNDEE CAKE

Preparation time: 25 mins
Cooking time: 2-2½ hours
Serves 9

INGREDIENTS

150 g/5 oz softened butter, plus extra for greasing
150 g/5 oz soft brown sugar
3 large eggs, lightly beaten
225 g/8 oz flour
1 tsp baking powder
100 g/4 oz currants
100 g/4 oz raisins
100 g/4 oz sultanas
50 g/2 oz mixed peel
50 g/2 oz glacé cherries, quartered
50 g/2 oz ground almonds
Grated zest of 1 lemon
Grated zest of 1 orange
50 g/2 oz whole blanched almonds

1 Preheat oven to 170 C/325 F/Gas 3. Grease a 20 cm/8 in round cake tin and line with greaseproof paper.

2 Cream the butter and sugar until fluffy, then gradually beat in the eggs. Sift the flour and baking powder and fold into the egg mixture.

3 Gently fold the currants, raisins, sultanas, glacé cherries, mixed peel, ground almonds and lemon and orange zests into the flour mixture using a metal spoon.

4 Spoon the mixture into the greased and lined cake tin. Smooth the top of the cake with a palette knife or the back of a spoon.

5 Arrange the whole almonds in circles over the top of the cake, lightly pressing them into the mixture. Bake the cake in the centre of the oven for 2-2½ hours, covering it with greaseproof paper if it begins to get too dark. Cool in the tin before removing.

CARROT & WALNUT CAKE

Preparation time: 30 mins
Cooking time: 2-2½ hours
Serves 9

INGREDIENTS

225 g/8 oz flour
2 tsp bicarbonate of soda
1 tsp cinnamon
Pinch of grated nutmeg
½ tsp salt
400 g/14 oz soft brown sugar
350 ml/12 fl oz vegetable oil
4 eggs, beaten
400 g/14 oz grated carrots
275 g/10 oz chopped walnuts
Butter, for greasing

FOR THE FROSTING

100 g/4 oz cream cheese
40 g/1½ oz butter, softened
100 g/4 oz caster sugar
3 drops of vanilla essence
1 tinned pineapple ring, drained and chopped

1 Preheat oven to 180 C/350 F/Gas 4. Sift the flour, bicarbonate of soda, cinnamon, nutmeg and salt together in a large bowl.

2 Mix the sugar and oil together in another bowl, then add the eggs. Make a well in the flour, stir in the liquid, then the carrots and walnuts.

3 Grease and base line an 18 cm/7 in square cake tin. Spoon in the cake mixture and bake for 2-2½ hours or until a skewer inserted into the cake comes out clean.

4 Leave the cake to cool in the tin, then turn out onto a wire rack. When cold, wrap in foil and leave for a day.

5 To make the frosting, mash the cheese, butter, sugar and vanilla essence together. Stir in the pineapple, making sure it is drained thoroughly or the frosting may curdle. Spread over the top of the cake and serve cut into squares.

COFFEE GATEAU

Preparation time: 50 mins
Cooking time: 40 mins
Serves 8-12

INGREDIENTS

1 quantity genoese sponge mixture
(see Techniques) flavoured with
1 tbls instant coffee granules
and chicory essence

4 tbls coffee liqueur

50 g/2 oz flaked almonds, toasted

FOR THE CREME AU BEURRE

4 egg yolks

100 g/4 oz sugar

275 g/10 oz butter, softened

2 tsp instant coffee granules

PRUE'S TIP
Add the dissolved coffee to the sponge
mixture before adding the flour so it
blends in well.

1 Preheat oven to 190 C/375 F/Gas 5.
Using a 20 cm/8 in round tin, bake
the sponge for 30-35 minutes. Cut
the cake in half horizontally and sprinkle
the centre with coffee liqueur.

2 To make the crème au beurre, whisk
the yolks in a bowl. Dissolve the
sugar in 125 ml/4 fl oz water in a
pan. Boil until the syrup forms a short
thread between your index finger and
thumb. Whisk the syrup into the yolks
until the mixture turns pale and fluffy.

3 Whisk softened butter into the egg
mixture. Dissolve the coffee granules
in 2 tsp water and whisk into the
crème au beurre. Sandwich the cake with
one quarter of the crème. Reserve one
quarter for piping and spread the rest
over the top and sides.

4 Press the almonds onto the sides of
the cake. Fill a piping bag fitted with
a large star nozzle with the remaining
crème au beurre and use to pipe spirals
around the top edge and in the centre of
the cake. Leave to cool for at least
30 minutes before serving.

CHOCOLATE PIZZA

Preparation time: 25 mins
+ cooling
Cooking time: 20 mins
Serves 10-12

INGREDIENTS

100 g/4 oz butter, plus extra for greasing
100 g/4 oz flour, plus extra for dusting
225 g/8 oz golden syrup
225 ml/8 fl oz double cream
225 g/8 oz chocolate
100 g/4 oz sugar
½ tsp vanilla essence
2 eggs, beaten
Pinch of salt
50 g/2 oz walnuts
75 g/3 oz strawberries
75 g/3 oz kiwi fruit
75 g/3 oz raspberries
75 g/3 oz banana, sliced

1 Preheat oven to 180 C/350 F/Gas 4. Grease two 25 cm/10 in diameter pizza tins and dust with flour.

2 Bring 50 ml/2 fl oz of the cream and the golden syrup to the boil. Lower the heat, add the chocolate and stir until melted.

3 Remove 150 ml/¼ pt of the sauce and set it aside. Add the butter and sugar to the chocolate mixture in the pan. Stir until melted. Take the pan off the heat. With a whisk, beat in the vanilla essence and the eggs, then gradually add the flour, salt and walnuts.

4 Pour the mixture into the prepared tins and bake for 20 minutes. Cool for 5 minutes and then turn out onto two wire racks.

5 Whip the remaining cream and spread it over the surface of the pizza. Leave a 2.5cm/1 in border. Slice the strawberries, kiwi fruit, raspberries and banana and decorate. Warm the reserved sauce and drizzle it over the top. Serve cut into wedges.

RICH CHOCOLATE CAKE

Preparation time: 20 mins
Cooking time: 1 hour
Serves 6-8

INGREDIENTS

Butter, for greasing
3 tbls cocoa powder
3 tbls warm water
225 g/8 oz soft margarine
225 g/8 oz caster sugar
4 eggs
1 tsp vanilla essence
225 g/8 oz self-raising flour, sifted
Chocolate leaves, to decorate

FOR THE ICING
175 g/6 oz butter
225 g/8 oz caster sugar
350 g/12 oz icing sugar, sifted
100 g/4 oz drinking chocolate

"This cake comes into what I call the Death by Chocolate category. I don't recommend you bake it every day of the week, but for high days and holidays, who can resist?"　Prue

1 Preheat oven to 180 C/350 F/Gas 4. Grease and line a 20 cm/8 in spring-form tin with greaseproof paper. Blend the cocoa with the water. In a separate bowl, cream together the margarine and sugar until light and fluffy. Beat in the cocoa mixture, eggs and vanilla essence. Fold in the flour.

2 Spoon the mixture into the tin. Bake for 50-60 minutes or until cooked. Allow to stand for 5 minutes then turn out and cool on a wire rack.

3 For the icing, gently heat the butter, 6 tbls water and the caster sugar until the sugar has dissolved. Bring to the boil then pour over the icing sugar and drinking chocolate. Beat well until smooth. Cool for 15 minutes.

4 Cut the cake into 3 layers then sandwich together with some of the icing. Reserve 2 tbls of icing, smooth rest over the cake. Decorate with the reserved icing and chocolate leaves.

PRUE'S TIP
To make chocolate leaves, brush washed, non-toxic leaves with melted chocolate. Allow to dry, then peel away the leaf.

MICROWAVE TIP
Line a deep 20 cm/8 in microwave-proof cake dish with baking parchment. Spoon in the mixture, smooth the top and cook on MEDIUM HIGH (75%) for 11 minutes. Stand for 10 minutes before turning out.

CHOCOLATE ROULADE

Preparation time: 25 mins
Cooking time: 15 mins
Serves 4-6

INGREDIENTS

Oil, for greasing
Flour, for dusting
5 eggs, separated
175 g/6 oz caster sugar
175 g/6 oz dark, sweetened chocolate
1 tsp instant coffee granules
3 tbls boiling water
Icing sugar, for dredging
300 ml/½ pt double cream, whipped

FOR THE DECORATION

150 ml/¼ pt double cream, whipped
Chocolate caraque (see Techniques)

1 Line a 33 cm/13 in by 23 cm/9 in Swiss roll tin with oiled and floured greaseproof paper, sticking well up round the sides.

2 Whisk yolks and sugar together until they leave a thin ribbon trail from the whisk.

3 Melt the chocolate and coffee in the water in a bowl over a pan of simmering water. Fold the chocolate mixture into the whisked yolks.

4 Whisk whites and fold in. Spread the mixture evenly in the tin. Bake for 12-15 minutes until the top is dry to the touch and an inserted skewer comes out clean.

5 Dredge a sheet of greaseproof paper with icing sugar. Place the roulade in the tin on a wire rack and cover with a just-damp tea-towel to cool. Flip the cake onto the greaseproof paper. Trim the edges. Peel away the lining paper. Slide the paper and cake onto the wire rack.

6 Spread with cream, leaving a 4 cm/1½ in border along one short edge. Roll up, removing paper as you go. Pipe the whipped double cream along the length of the roulade, then top with caraque and serve.

BLACK FOREST GATEAU

Preparation time: 20 mins
+ cooling
Cooking time: 40-50 mins
Serves 8

INGREDIENTS

Butter, for greasing
100 g/4 oz caster sugar,
plus extra for dusting
4 eggs
75 g/3 oz flour
25 g/1 oz cocoa powder
Pinch of salt

FOR THE FILLING

425 g/15 oz tinned, stoned black cherries
3 tbls kirsch
450 ml/¾ pt double cream, whipped
50 g/2 oz plain chocolate, grated

1 Preheat oven to 180 C/350 F/Gas 4. Grease a 20 cm/8 in round cake tin, line the base with greased greaseproof paper and dust with caster sugar.

2 To make the sponge, beat the eggs and sugar together over a pan of simmering water until thick and mousse-like. Sift the flour with the cocoa and salt onto the egg and sugar mixture. Carefully fold in. Pour into the prepared tin. Bake in the oven for 40-50 minutes. Turn onto a wire rack and leave until completely cool.

3 Slice the sponge into three and put the bottom layer onto a circle of card. Drain the black cherries, reserving 8 cherries for the decoration. Roughly chop the remainder.

4 Sprinkle the kirsch and 2 tbls of cherry juice over the bottom two layers. Sandwich the gateau together with one-third of the whipped cream and the chopped black cherries.

5 Put 2 tbls of the remaining cream into a piping bag fitted with a fluted nozzle. Use the rest to coat the top and sides of the gateau. With a palette knife press most of the grated chocolate onto the side of the gateau. Transfer to a serving dish.

6 Pipe rosettes of cream on top of the gateau. Sprinkle each one with a little of the remaining grated chocolate and top with a black cherry.

TECHNIQUES

HERBS

The importance of herbs in cooking can't be stressed strongly enough. By adding their own special flavour, they subtly give a dish its essential character, and they are often as important as the main ingredient.

Types of Herb

1 Coriander This has a particularly fragrant smell and superb flavour. Stir into meat or chicken curries or sprinkle over lamb kebabs.

2 Bay Essential for stock and court bouillon, bay has a musty-sweet smell and adds a distinct resinous flavour. Use also in casseroles, sauces and soups.

3 Thyme With its warm, earthy flavour, thyme is excellent in casseroles, stuffings, pâtés and with Mediterranean vegetables.

4 Mint Perfect with boiled new potatoes, or in many sweet dishes and fruit drinks.

5 Parsley This has a mild flavour and can be used as a garnish or added to soups, fish dishes and sauces.

6 Flat-leaved parsley Ideal for decoration.

7 Chives With their delicate onion flavour, these are excellent snipped into omelettes or onto baked potatoes and used as a garnish.

8 Basil This has a delightfully sweet smell

and flavour and is particularly suited to tomato-based dishes.

9 Rosemary This is slightly sweet and goes well with lamb, veal, pork and rabbit.

10 Marjoram Sweet and fragrant, the fresh leaves of this herb are good sprinkled into salads or onto lamb kebabs.

11 Oregano This heady-scented herb adds that distinct Italian flavour to a variety of pizza and pasta dishes.

12 Tarragon Tasting faintly of aniseed and vanilla, tarragon is excellent with chicken, ham, fish and in egg or cream dishes.

13 Dill This tastes faintly of aniseed and has an affinity with fish. It is also often used in pickling.

14 Sage Harsh, dry but fragrant, this is used for stuffings for roast pork and goose and in making sausages and pork pies.

Using Herbs

Freezing

Parsley, thyme, tarragon, marjoram, chives, dill, coriander and mint all freeze well. Don't bother to freeze rosemary, sage or bay, they are better simply dried.

Freeze single or mixed chopped herbs in ice cube trays. Half fill the trays with herbs, top up with water and freeze. Then simply stir into soups and casseroles.

Drying

Marjoram, thyme, rosemary, sage, bay and mint dry well. Tarragon, chives, dill and coriander don't. If you can rely on the weather, herbs can be dried out of doors. However, the more usual method is to dry them indoors. Choose a spell of fine

weather and pick before the sun is too strong. It is best to dry most herbs on their stalks to prevent bruising and for easy handling. Tie them into small bunches and hang in a warm, shady, airy place for at least a week.

To dry herbs in an oven, arrange on cooling racks. Don't allow the oven temperature to exceed 30 C/90 F and keep the door ajar. Once the herbs are dried, strip off the leaves and store them in labelled darkened glass or earthenware jars.

Any soft-leaved herb can be dried in the microwave. Before drying, remove stalks or break into small sprigs. Line a shallow dish with absorbent paper and stand a cup of cold water in the centre.

Place about 25 g/1 oz of any herb around the edge of the dish and microwave on HIGH (100 %) for 6 minutes until the herbs are just dry, moving them a little every minute. Leave on absorbent paper until cool, then crumble and store in airtight jars in a cool, dry dark place. Use within 3-6 months.

Drying concentrates flavour so use only half the amount you would for fresh herbs.

Making a Bouquet Garni

To make a bouquet garni take a bay leaf, a sprig each of parsley and tarragon or thyme and some peppercorns and tie them inside a little muslin parcel. Alternatively, tie between two sticks of celery.

SPICES

Like herbs, spices can add far more to the flavour of a dish than the small quantities used would suggest.

Types of Spices

Allspice This is used in baking, pickling and savoury dishes. It tastes like cloves, cinnamon and nutmeg mixed together.

Caraway seeds These have a strong flavour and are used in savoury dishes and cheeses.

Cardamom This comes in either small green pods which contain tiny dark seeds and have a lemony flavour, or larger brown pods with a stronger less tangy taste.

Cayenne pepper Made from ground red chilli peppers and should be used sparingly in curries, soups and stews.

Chillies Fresh green and red chillies should be sliced before cooking. They add a fierce spiciness to food – for a milder flavour, discard the seeds before use. Whole dried chillies are hotter still. Ground chilli powder is a bright orange-red if fresh, and similar in flavour to cayenne pepper.

Chinese five spice powder This tastes something like licorice but is used by the Chinese in savoury dishes. To make your own, mix ground star anise, anise pepper, cassia, cloves and fennel seeds.

Cinnamon This is available ground or in sticks which are dried quills of bark from the cinnamon tree. It is used to flavour meat and rice dishes, cakes and desserts.

Cloves The dried buds of the clove tree can be used whole or in powder form to flavour baking, pickles and hot drinks.

Coriander The beige-coloured seeds of the coriander plant are an important ingredient in curries, whole or ground.

Cumin seeds These can be used whole or ground in curries and pickles. Can be beige-brown or smaller dark brown seeds.

Fenugreek seeds Often used in Indian cooking. The leaves can also be used.

Ginger This zesty, fragrant spice is available as a root, ground into a powder or pickled. It is used as a root to flavour oriental dishes, as a powder in baking and pickles and in pickled form for desserts.

Juniper berries Traditionally used as a flavouring for pork and game dishes.

Mustard seeds Both yellow and reddish-brown varieties are available – and add a pleasant spiciness to dishes.

Nutmeg and mace These sister-spices come from the same plant. Nutmeg is the nut, mace the lacy husk which grows around it. They taste very similar, but ground nutmeg is traditionally used for sweet dishes and ground mace for savoury.

Paprika Related to chilli and cayenne, but without the heat. Used to add a subtle flavour and a red colour to savoury dishes.

Pepper Black pepper is most common, but the milder white is used in white sauces. Pink and green are also available.

Saffron strands The dried stigmas of a variety of crocus. They are very expensive but a little goes a long way to colour and flavour. Also available in powder form.

Star anise These distinctive star-shaped seeds are used in Chinese cooking.

Turmeric A bright yellow powder. It adds colour to vegetable, rice and chicken dishes.

Using Spices

Commercial curry powders sold in tins are convenient and easy to use, but by mixing your own blends you can create the exquisite flavourings used in authentic Indian and Asian cooking. Make up a batch, store in airtight jars and use instead of commercial brands. Garam masala is a mix of ground spices which have strong but not necessarily hot flavours such as cinnamon, cloves and peppercorns. It is used in many meat and vegetable dishes.

Dry Roasting

Seeds should be dry roasted before grinding to strengthen their flavour and make them easier to grind. Heat a heavy-based pan over a low heat, then add the seeds, cover with a lid and shake over the heat for 1-2 minutes. Take care not to let the seeds burn in the pan and let them cool before grinding.

WATCHPOINT

If grinding spices in a coffee grinder, be sure to clean it thoroughly after use or your coffee will taste very exotic!

GARAM MASALA

Preparation time: 5 mins + grinding

INGREDIENTS

1 small stick of cinnamon
1 tsp black peppercorns
6 whole cloves
½ tsp grated nutmeg
1 tbls cardamom seeds, dry roasted
2 tsp cumin seeds, dry roasted
1 small dried bay leaf
¼ tsp mace
2 tsp coriander seeds, dry roasted

1 Mix all the ingredients and grind to a fine powder using a coffee grinder, food processor or pestle and mortar.

CURRY POWDER

Preparation time: 5 mins + grinding

INGREDIENTS

4 tbls coriander seeds, dry roasted
2 tbls cumin seeds, dry roasted
1 tsp cardamom seeds, dry roasted
2 tsp ground turmeric
2 dried red chillies, chopped
½ tsp salt

1 Mix all the ingredients and grind using a coffee grinder, food processor or pestle and mortar.

ONIONS & GARLIC

Of all the vegetables used in cooking, onions and garlic are so central to most cuisines they deserve a special mention. Although both have their share of bad press, most people who hate onions and garlic are not cooks. Cooks would be hard-pressed to manage without them. Indeed, many an onion-hater doesn't realise that their favourite sauce or stew, mince or pickle depends heavily on the addition of these piquant ingredients.

Know your onions

For centuries onions have been highly regarded for their culinary and medicinal properties – ancient Egyptians even used them as offerings to the gods. Nowadays we have more humble uses for them!

There a several different types of onion. Spanish onions are large, juicy, mild, all-purpose onions. Egyptian onions are medium-sized, strong flavoured, and excellent for cooking. If you want a small, dry and mild type of onion use shallots. They are excellent raw and in sauces. Even smaller are button onions or pickling onions. They are good whole in cooking, or can be pickled raw. Spring onions are perfect for salads, while red onions make a colourful garnish for many dishes.

Garlic goodness

Garlic is known to have antibiotic and antiseptic properties, and it's widely believed to prevent blood clots, but you must eat it raw to gain medicinal benefits. The ancient Greeks fed it to their athletes, while in Britain people carried garlic to ward off evil spirits and even the plague.

The most important thing about garlic is that it should be fresh, and preferably not sprouting. The perfect garlic head is very firm and quite difficult to break apart. The cloves are firm and bright white inside – not fibrous, grey or soft. When fresh like this, garlic has a clean pleasant smell, with no ammonia overtones.

Don't buy strings of garlic – buy little and often for freshness. And don't keep it in a stoppered container or polythene bag. Keep it in a cool airy place.

Other onions

Chives and leeks are also members of the onion family. Only the leaves of chives are eaten. They are good for decoration and flavour. Leeks are wonderful cooked in soups and quiches and on their own.

PRUE'S TIP
Do onions make you cry? Try peeling them under a running tap to reduce the vapour in the air, or dip them in cold water as you slice. Alternatively, try sucking a sweet – it's hard to salivate and cry at the same time!

Using Onions & Garlic

Preparing Garlic

1 To break open a head of garlic, put it on a board and whack it with a heavy object.

2 To get the skin off a clove without getting garlic in your fingernails, put the garlic on cling film on a board. Lay a large knife blade over it flat and crack down with your fist. Then peel.

3 Put the garlic on a bit of paper or foil to chop it, or add a little salt and crush with a knife.

Roasting Garlic

Whole cloves of garlic roasted in their skins have a mild, nutty flavour and are delicious. Place them around a joint of meat halfway through the cooking time. Baste with the meat juices.

PRUE'S TIP
Raw parsley combats garlic breath. But the real trick is to give everyone garlic, then they won't be able to smell it on you!

Dicing Onions

1 Slice the unpeeled onion lengthways through the core. Peel back the skin and remove, leaving the root on to hold the layers together. Put each piece flat on the board and make parallel cuts from near the root end to the stalk end.

2 Cut into the parallel cuts to make fine dice. Finish close to the root. For onion slices make only the crosswise cuts.

OILS & VINEGARS

Of the many styles of cooking to be found worldwide, there are few, if any, that do not depend on a variety of oils and vinegars flavoured with indigenous herbs and spices. With a basic knowledge of which flavours combine most effectively with certain oils and vinegars, we can create for ourselves the very essence of international cuisine. Flavoured oils and vinegars are easy to make at home.

Strike oil

Cooking oils are made from a variety of seeds, kernels and nuts which are pressed to release their natural oils. The oils that are produced invariably taste of their original fruit, so care should be taken to use the appropriate oil for each purpose.

Olive oil has a fruity, often nutty, olive taste. Depending on your budget, it can be used for shallow frying to impart a delicate scent of fresh olives. Blended with less pungent oils such as groundnut, grapeseed and sunflower oils, olive oil is ideal for use in salad dressings.

Walnut oil is rich, with a strong nutty flavour, and best when used in special salad dressings. Groundnut oil has a light neutral taste. It is suitable for shallow and deep frying and for making mayonnaise. Safflower oil has a delicate taste with a light texture.

Vinegar varieties

There are many different varieties of vinegar readily available, including red wine, white wine, cider, malt and tarragon vinegars. So-called malt vinegars are widely used for preserving and pickling. Wine, sherry and cider vinegars are less acid and are best suited to use in salad dressings.

Flavouring Oils & Vinegars

Keep a selection of flavoured oils and vinegars on hand. Wait at least 2 weeks before use to let the flavour infuse fully.

Hot Chilli Oil

Put five chillies in a bottle or jar, cover with 250 ml/9 fl oz of olive or groundnut oil and leave to stand for 2-3 weeks. Use sparingly to pep up spicy dishes.

Peppercorn Oil

Heat 3 tbls groundnut or safflower oil in a small frying-pan, add 1 tbls of black peppercorns and sizzle lightly for about 4 minutes to release their flavour. Transfer to a bottle or jar, add 1 pricked clove of garlic, top up with 175 ml/6 fl oz oil and leave for 2-3 weeks. Try a mixture of black, green and pink peppercorns for a colourful alternative. This oil will impart a wonderful flavour to roasts and marinades.

Herbal Oils

To make herbal oils, place your chosen herbs in a bottle or jar, top up with oil and leave to infuse for 3-4 weeks. Try olive oil with garlic, rosemary and bay for use in Mediterranean and barbecue cooking. For use with grilled white meats, combine groundnut oil or sunflower oil with sage, thyme and winter savoury. For cooking fish and shellfish try safflower oil with fennel stem, dill, garlic and thyme.

Herb Vinegars

Capture the sweet aroma of fresh herbs by preserving their flavour in vinegar. Herb vinegars are perfect for giving salads an extra lift in the winter, and if made in a attractive bottles make excellent home-grown gifts.

Vinegars that blend well with herbs and flavourings are red wine, white wine, cider, and malt vinegars. Flavour them with a variety of home-grown herbs. Try using tarragon, thyme, rosemary, oregano, basil, mint, bay leaves or dill. If you don't have a herb garden, many supermarkets now have a wide selection of fresh herbs to choose from. Place the herb sprigs in a bottle or jar, add a good quality wine or cider vinegar, seal and leave to infuse for 3-4 weeks. Use in dressings, mayonnaise and marinades.

RASPBERRY VINEGAR

Preparation time: 5 mins
+ marinating
Makes 750 ml/1¼ pt vinegar

INGREDIENTS
450 g/1 lb fresh raspberries
600 ml/1 pt white wine vinegar

1 Reserve 6 raspberries and put the rest in a bowl. Bruise them lightly to release their juices. Pour the vinegar over the berries, cover with a clean tea-towel and leave at room temperature for 24 hours. Strain the vinegar.

2 Put the 6 reserved raspberries into the bottom of a 750 ml/1¼ pt bottle and cover with the strained vinegar. Seal the bottle and allow to stand for 2-3 days before using.

SALADS & DRESSINGS

The most important rule to remember when making a salad is not to overdo it. Many a salad has been ruined by the addition of ingredients that are weird and less-than-wonderful. Stick to simple combinations like chicken and tarragon, celery and cheese, potato and onion, or tomato and garlic and you can't go wrong.

Clean green

The wonderful array of interesting salad leaves now available has given that old favourite 'the green salad' a huge fillip. You can use them in just about any combination you fancy. Almost any leaf, from crisp Chinese leaves to tender lamb's lettuce will do excellently. But just any old dressing certainly won't.

Get the dressing right

Vinaigrettes (or French dressings) don't have to be rigidly classical. I use a tasteless vegetable oil like peanut oil or corn oil for most salads, but vary the flavourings to suit the salad ingredients and my mood. I like to add mustard to the dressing for potatoes, chopped fresh coriander for fish, garlic and mint for beans, and so on.

Crisp & dry

Remember not to use too much dressing. Use enough to coat each leaf, but not enough to collect in the bottom of the salad bowl. Which brings me to the commonest problem with salads – soggy leaves. If every leaf is not thoroughly dried after washing, the dressing will become watery and insipid, and the leaves will go glassy and limp at the bottom of the bowl.

Types of Salad Leaves

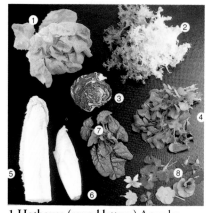

1 Iceberg lettuce A crisp lettuce that keeps well, with a high proportion of tender, pale inner leaves. Not much taste but an excellent texture.
2 Rocket Dark, pretty leaf with a strong peppery taste. Excellent when used to spike bland salads.
3 Oak-leaf A tender, expensive variety which doesn't keep long, but is delicious and very pretty.
4 Cos Sweet and crisp, with long large leaves. Keeps excellently. The inner leaves have the best flavour.
5 Lamb's lettuce (corn salad) Tender mini-plants with a mild flavour. Wash carefully, keeping the leaves attached to each other to preserve their pretty shape.
6 Lollo rosso Similar to oak-leaf but frillier and less tender. Wash gently and spin in a salad spinner.
7 Little gem Related to cos but much smaller. All the leaves are crisp and delicious. Split in half, then separate.

1 Hothouse (round lettuce) A tender lettuce and even the darkest leaves are edible. Wash and dry as for oak-leaf.
2 Curly endive (Frisée lettuce) Use the pale leaves. Discard the dark bitter ones.
3 Radicchio Pretty, round-headed chicory. Keeps well. Slightly bitter.
4 Watercress Store upside down (leaves submerged) in cold water in the fridge. Rinse under water while still in the bunch, but untied. Use only the the leafy ends.
5 Chinese leaves Insipid tasting, but has wonderfully crisp, firm heads. Keeps well.
6 Chicory (Belgian endive) Split lengthways with a knife and peel off the leaves. Very slightly but pleasantly bitter.
7 Spinach Young spinach leaves are excellent raw, but the old leaves are too tough. Detach the stalk by folding the leaf along the rib, tearing away the stalk.
8 Edible flowers Young leaves of edible flowers like nasturtium, polyanthus and pansies add a peppery flavour to salads.

Preparing Salad Leaves

1 To wash tender leaves such as oak-leaf or soft hothouse lettuce, hold by the stalk and submerge in a bowl or sink of cold water. Plunge gently up and down. Wipe chicory heads with a damp cloth, but don't bother to wash every leaf.

2 Iceberg, radicchio and any cabbage-like crisp lettuce can simply be pulled apart. Don't ever cut lettuce or wring it to break up the leaves, as both methods result in bruising. Gently tear the leaves to bits with your fingers, then wash them and dry them thoroughly.

3 Prepare a dressing of your choice. Not more than half an hour before serving, give the dressing a shake and pour over the salad. Toss the salad in the dressing using your hands – salad servers bruise tender leaves. Transfer to a bowl, leaving behind any excess dressing.

PRUE'S TIP
Use a salad spinner to get your delicate salad leaves really dry without any danger of bruising them.

Vinaigrette Dressings

Add different flavourings, such as mustard, garlic and ginger, to this basic oil and vinegar dressing (called a vinaigrette), and then use it to enhance many dishes.

CLASSIC VINAIGRETTE

INGREDIENTS
4 tbls oil

1 tbls white wine vinegar

½ tsp salt

Freshly ground black pepper

1 Put the oil, the vinegar, the salt and plenty of pepper in a screw-top jar and shake vigorously.

YOGHURT DRESSING

This dressing goes well with warm cooked vegetable or fish salads.

INGREDIENTS
4 tbls salad oil

2 tbls Greek yoghurt

1 tbls chopped chives, parsley, tarragon, mint or chervil, or a combination of any or all

A good pinch of rock salt or sea salt

10 twists of a black peppermill

1 Whisk the oil into the yoghurt drop by drop to produce a semi-emulsion. Add the chopped herbs and the seasonings and stir together well.

ZESTY LIME DRESSING

Serve Zesty Lime Dressing with a crunchy combination of cabbage, celery and apples or with Asian-influenced salads.

INGREDIENTS
1 fresh lime

2 tbls salad oil

1 tbls walnut oil

A good pinch of rock salt or sea salt

10 twists of a black peppermill

1 Grate only the green part of the lime skin (not the white pith) extremely finely. Squeeze out the lime juice.

2 Combine the grated zest, juice, two oils and the seasonings in a screw-top jar and shake well.

VARIATIONS
Use flavoured vinegars to pep up salad dressings. Try red wine vinegar with added rosemary for Italian-influenced salads or white wine vinegar with tarragon for light, summery salads.

Mayonnaise Dressings

Mayonnaise, a delicate mixture of egg yolks and oil, has many simple variations and can be used to transform a wide range of meat, fish and salad dishes. For a Mediterranean-style dressing, use pure olive oil and add plenty of garlic. For a richer flavoured mayonnaise, substitute half the quantity of salad oil with walnut or hazelnut oil and add chopped fresh herbs such as tarragon, thyme and chives.

WATCHPOINT
Raw eggs have been found to contain the salmonella food-poisoning organism. To reduce the risk, keep the mayonnaise cool at all times. It also helps to make sure it has a good dash of lemon juice or vinegar in it.

PRUE'S TIP
To make mayonnaise in a blender or food processor, use the same ingredients as for Classic Mayonnaise. Whizz the yolks, seasoning, vinegar or lemon juice together, then gradually pour in the oil in a thin, steady stream.

CLASSIC MAYONNAISE

INGREDIENTS
2 egg yolks

1 tsp Dijon mustard

175 ml/6 fl oz salad oil

1½ tbls vinegar or lemon juice

Salt

Ground white pepper

1 Place the egg yolks in a bowl (warm over hot water if they are straight from the fridge). Beat with a teaspoon of Dijon mustard.

2 Gradually add the salad oil, drip by drip, beating all the time. The mixture will gradually thicken as the oil is added. If it starts to curdle, beat in 1-2 tsp of boiling water before adding any more oil.

3 Add the vinegar or lemon juice, then salt and pepper to taste. If the mayonnaise is too thin, add more oil, beating well between each addition. If it is too thick, add 1 tbls of water just before serving and stir well.

GRAINS & RICE

Rice and cereals have made a fashionable comeback. Once people shunned them because they were thought to be fattening and stodgy, but now we are told they are good for us. And indeed they are, providing varying amounts of E and B vitamins, iron, protein, phosphorus and of course carbohydrate, plus (especially if the bran is not removed) fibre. But my main affection for rice and cereals is less concerned with health than it is with the wealth of interesting and varied flavours they offer.

Grains galore

A visit to a good wholefood shop can have me unwisely staggering home laden like a pack-camel with bulgar wheat and kasha, millet, buckwheat and groats, couscous and maybe even the fine cornmeal masa harina for tortillas. This is not a practice I recommend. It is far better not to buy too much at once. Surprisingly, flours and grains go stale in a warm storecupboard, and their flavour is much better if they are cooked and eaten while they are fresh.

Rice ratios

Versatile and handy as rice is, it's often difficult to gauge how much of it you need to allow for your guests. For savoury rice, served as a vegetable, allow 2 tbls per person; to go with curry, 4 tbls per person; for risotto and plain rice, 5 tbls per person. If you are serving pudding rice, 5 tbls to 600 ml/1 pt milk will serve 4-5 people.

And don't forget that rice (uncooked of course) is traditionally thrown at newly-weds. In this case you can use as much as you like!

Types of Rice

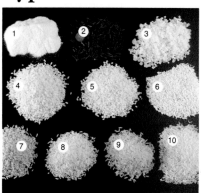

1 **Rice flour** This is used in catering as a thickening agent.
2 **Wild rice** This is not really rice at all, but a grain formed by a grass. It needs to be cooked for at least 30 minutes.
3 **Rice flakes** You use these in the same way as pudding rice.
4 **Italian risotto rice** This is generally a medium-grained rice and perfect for use in making risotto.
5 **Pudding rice** A round-grained starchy rice that will stick together easily.
6 **Glutinous rice** Japanese sticky rice used for making sushi.

7 **Brown rice** This has the husks removed but is otherwise untreated. It takes longer to cook than white rice does, but is better for you.
8 **White (polished) rice** This has been treated to remove all the outer skin, and with it the thiamine (Vitamin B1) and some protein and oil. It cooks quickly.
9 **Easy-cook rice** This is polished, pre-steamed and convenient. The grains remain beautifully separate when cooked.
10 **Basmati rice** This Indian rice needs a good washing and soaking for at least 20 minutes before rinsing and cooking.

Cooking Rice

Absorption Method

This is the most nutritious method of cooking long-grain rice. First rinse the rice, then put it into a heavy-based pan and shake level. Pour in water to twice the depth of the rice (3 times the depth for brown rice). Add salt. Cover and simmer until the water is absorbed.

Microwave Method

Put the rice and twice its volume of liquid in a bowl and microwave on HIGH (100%) for 10-20 minutes, stirring occasionally until the liquid is completely absorbed.

Fried Rice

Fry the dry grains in a little oil, shaking and stirring until brown. Then add the liquid and continue as for the absorption or excess water methods.

Excess Water Method

Ideal for poor quality long-grain varieties. First wash the rice. Bring a large pan of salted water to the boil. Tip in the rice. Stir. Cook 10 minutes. Taste. If still chewy boil 2 more minutes. (Brown rice will take 35-40 minutes to cook and should be a little chewy.) Drain and rinse. Spread out on a shallow tin to dry in an oven preheated to 90 C/190 F/Gas 1 for 10 minutes. Fluff up with a fork.

RICE PUDDING

INGREDIENTS

600 ml/1 pt milk
3 tbls double cream
75 g/3 oz pudding rice
25 g/1 oz vanilla sugar
Grated nutmeg
15 g/½ oz butter

1 Preheat oven to 160 C/300 F/Gas 2. In a saucepan heat the milk and the double cream to just below boiling point. Take off the heat and stir in the pudding rice and vanilla sugar and leave to stand for 15 minutes.

2 Pour into a well buttered 1.2 L/2 pt baking dish, sprinkle the top with grated nutmeg and dot with the butter. Bake for about 2 hours, stirring every 30 minutes for the first hour.

Types of Grain

Corn

Farmers refer to grain crops (be it barley, wheat, oats or whatever) as corn, whereas to cooks, corn means maize.

1 Popcorn As it is heated the starchy inside swells and bursts its skin.
2 Cornflour Purified starch extracted from the corn and used for thickening.
3 Corn on the cob Eat boiled, with butter.
4 Polenta This is similar to cornmeal, but finer. Goes well with stews.
5 Cornmeal This can be fine or coarse and is simply milled maize.
6 Maize meal (flour) This is popular in America for making porridge, puddings and bread.

Rye

This is the deep-flavoured greyish grain used in rye bread and pumpernickel.

Barley

1 Pearl barley This has the bran removed, and is used for thickening soups or stews.
2 Barley water
3 Barley flour Ideal for simple griddle cakes, but not for bread.
4 Barley flakes Perfect for biscuits and muesli-type cereals.
5 Pot barley Use as for pearl barley.

Oats

1 Oat groats (grains) These are gluten-free and are milled fine, medium or coarse.
2 Jumbo oats These are best for biscuits and muesli-type cereals.
3 Fine oatmeal Use in porridge or oatcakes.
4 Coarse oatmeal Perfect for coating herrings or fried trout.
5 Quick porridge oats As its name suggests, this is good for a quick breakfast.

Wheat

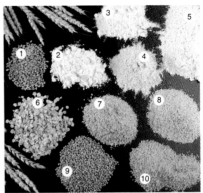

1 Wholewheat grains Excellent for adding to casseroles, or for using in rice salads.
2 Strong plain flour Its high gluten content makes dough elastic so it rises well.
3 Self-raising flour This has baking powder added. Use for non-yeast bread and cakes.
4 Wholemeal flour This includes the nutritious wheatgerm and the bran.
5 Plain flour This is better for pastries, cakes and non-yeasted items.
6 Wheat flakes Fine flakes of wheat.
7 Bran The outer layer of wheatgrain.
8 Wheatgerm This is the ground kernel of the wheat and is highly nutritious.
9 Buckwheat This is not wheat, but the seed of a plant related to rhubarb.
10 Bulgar Wheat or cracked wheat grains.

Cooking with Grains

CHOC-CHIP OATIES

Preparation time: 15 mins
Cooking time: 10-12 mins
Makes 20-24 biscuits

INGREDIENTS

100 g/4 oz butter, plus extra for greasing
100 g/4 oz soft brown sugar
75 g/3 oz self-raising wholemeal flour, sifted
100 g/4 oz rolled oats
50 g/2 oz dark chocolate chips

1 Preheat oven to 180 C/350 F/Gas 4. Cream butter and sugar until light and fluffy. Beat in the flour, and then stir in the oats, followed by the chocolate chips.

2 Take heaped teaspoons of the mixture and roll into balls between the palms of your hands. Place the oat balls well apart on a greased baking tray and flatten down with the back of a fork.

3 Bake for 10-12 minutes. Remove from the oven and allow the biscuits to cool slightly before placing on a wire rack to finish cooling.

PULSES

Full of goodness and easy to store, pulses are probably the world's first convenience food. Yet, like rice and cereals, they have tended to go in and out of fashion, perhaps because, the more elegant tables of Europe considered pulses rather common – an opinion aided by the way pulses have often been over-cooked to an unappetising sludge. But, when cooked well, they are not only a good source of protein, carbohydrate and fibre, but full of flavour and texture too.

Little & often

Contrary to popular belief, pulses will not keep on the shelf forever. They should not be stored for longer than 6-9 months since they harden and shrivel with age and become difficult to cook. So it's not worth bulk-buying beans or lentils unless you plan to eat lots of them very regularly.

Types of Bean

1 Butter beans These are also known as Lima beans and have a distinctive mealy texture and taste.
2 Mung beans Can be bought whole, split and skinned. They can be either cooked or sprouted.
3 Black-eyed beans Small and cream in colour with a black splodge in the centre. A favourite in many American recipes.

4 Adzuki beans Known as the 'king of beans' in Japan, these are the most expensive type.
5 Haricot beans These are used for tinned baked beans and are very high in fibre.
6 Pinto beans This mottled, pink bean is used in many Mexican stews and casseroles.
7 Red kidney beans Essential in chilli con carne, these beans have a rich floury taste.

8 Cannellini beans The Italian haricot bean. These keep their firm texture even after cooking.
9 Soya beans The most nutritious of all beans, these are very high in protein. They can be cooked or used for sprouting.
10 Flageolet beans These have a fine delicate flavour which is superb in salads.
11 Broad beans When dried, these are used in Middle Eastern dishes like falafel.

Other Pulses

Lentils

Whether spilt or whole, lentils are just as nutritious as beans but they do not need to be soaked in water before cooking. They also cook faster than dried beans.

1 Green lentils Sometimes called continental lentils, these taste slightly less earthy than the brown variety, but still have a nutty texture. In France, they are eaten with garlic and lemon and served with salt pork.
2 Split red lentils These are probably the most familiar of all the lentils and are

commonly available. Green, yellow and brown split lentils are less easy to find, although they can usually be bought from Asian foodstores. None require soaking and they cook fairly quickly. Since they tend to break up during cooking, they are best combined with other ingredients for pâtés and vegetable purées.
3 Brown lentils These are red lentils with the outer skin attached. They have a nutty flavour and a good texture, provided they are not overcooked. They go well in casseroles or can be served as a side dish.

Chick Peas

The pea that is really a bean. With their distinctive crunchy texture and nutty flavour, chick peas are eaten and enjoyed around the world. They are served sprinkled with salt (Greece) or fiery spices (India) or dressed with oil and garlic (Italy) to make a heady starter. In the Middle East they are combined with tahini, lemon juice and garlic to make hummus.

Peas

Dried peas can be added to casseroles or stews, puréed to make soups or pâtés or even milled into a flour for thickening.

1 & 2 Split peas Green and yellow split peas have a pleasant sweet flavour. They do not require soaking and cook relatively quickly. Split peas tend to turn into a purée when cooked and are best in soups and pâtés.
3 Whole peas These can be cooked and served as a vegetable, made into pea and ham soup or added to stews and casseroles.

Cooking Pulses

It is a good idea to pick over pulses before soaking or cooking to remove any broken pieces, husks or small stones that may occasionally creep into the packets. Then rinse thoroughly in cold water.

Soaking

Apart from lentils and split peas, all dried beans and peas should be soaked before cooking. (Lentils and split peas may be soaked for 10 minutes to speed up cooking time.) There are two methods for soaking pulses. If you have plenty of time, cover the rinsed beans with cold water, allowing room for them to swell, and leave to soak overnight. Flageolets are the exception – soak 1 hour only. If time is short, however, place the peas or beans in a pan of unsalted water, bring to the boil and simmer for 5 minutes. Leave for 1 hour and then drain and rinse. Soya beans and chick peas will need to stand for 2 hours before being drained. Flageolets and lentils should be soaked in cold water.

Timing

The time pulses take to cook depends on type, age and quality. The fresher the beans, the less time they will take. If after the given time, the pulse is sill hard in the centre, continue cooking until it is soft and quite tender.

Cooking

It is best not to add salt to beans until the end of the cooking time. If they are salted at the beginning, the skins will split open and the insides will harden. Skim off any

TIMINGS FOR COOKING PULSES

	QUICK SOAK	BOILING	PRESSURE COOKING
Adzuki beans	1 hour	30-45 mins	10 mins
Black beans	1 hour	1-1¼ hours	15 mins
Black-eyed beans	1 hour	¾-1 hour	15 mins
Broad beans	1 hour	1-1½ hours	15 mins
Butter (Lima)	1 hour	1-1½ hours	15 mins
Cannellini	1 hour	1-1½ hours	15 mins
Chick peas	2 hours	1-1½ hours	20 mins
Dried peas	1 hour	45 mins	10 mins
Flageolets	–	¾-1 hour	10 mins
Ful medames	1 hour	1¼-1½ hours	20 mins
Haricot beans	1 hour	1 hour	15 mins
Lentils	–	30 mins	8 mins
Pinto beans	1 hour	1¼ hours	15 mins
Red kidney beans	1 hour	1¼-1½ hours	15 mins
Soya beans	2 hours	2-4 hours	1 hour
Split lentils	–	20 mins	5 mins
Split peas	–	30 mins	8 mins

surface scum from lentils, peas and beans when they come to the boil. Pulses are best when cooked (and soaked) in soft water. If your tap water is hard, you should be able to soften it by adding a good pinch of bicarbonate of soda.

Pressure cooking cuts cooking times by at least a half. If in doubt, it is better to undercook pulses rather than overcook them to a mush. And remember to watch out for froth which can clog the valve.

If there's no fat in the recipe, add 2 tbls oil to the liquid. Remember too, that all pulses swell during cooking, so don't reduce liquid as you would when pressure cooking vegetables.

PRUE'S TIP
However it may euphemistically be said, the plain truth is that pulses cause wind. This is because they contain hard-to-digest sugars which may react violently when they reach the lower intestine. You can reduce the effects by adding a pinch of anise, fennel or caraway seeds to the recipe or by drinking an infusion of any of these seeds.

WATCHPOINT
Red kidney and black beans <u>must</u> be boiled for 10-15 minutes before eating to kill any toxins. Never casserole them slowly unless they have been boiled first.

Pulse Recipes

Chick peas can be used to make falafel – a kind of vegetarian meatball – or a delicious dip called hummus.

FALAFEL

INGREDIENTS
225 g/8 oz tinned chick peas
1 large onion, chopped
2 cloves of garlic, crushed
5 tbls fresh white breadcrumbs
1 egg, beaten
1 tbls chopped fresh coriander
1 tbls chopped fresh parsley
Large pinch of ground cumin
½ tsp baking powder
Salt and ground black pepper
Vegetable oil, for frying
Pitta bread and mixed salad, to serve

1 Blend together the chick peas, onion, garlic, breadcrumbs, egg, coriander, parsley, cumin, baking powder and salt and pepper in a food processor and form into small balls or patties with wetted hands.

2 Heat the oil and deep fry the balls or patties for 3 minutes. Alternatively, fry in shallow oil for 5 minutes, turning constantly to brown all over. Drain. To serve, stuff into pitta bread with mixed chopped salad and hummus.

HUMMUS

INGREDIENTS
400 g/14 oz tinned chick peas, drained
3 cloves of garlic, chopped
Juice of 2 lemons
175 g/6 oz tahini paste
Salt and ground black pepper
2 tbls olive oil
2 tbls finely-chopped fresh parsley

1 Purée the chick peas, garlic, lemon juice and tahini paste together in a food processor or blender until they form a smooth purée. Season to taste with salt and pepper. Serve covered with a thin coating of olive oil and sprinkled with parsley. Use as a sauce or a dip.

SHELLFISH

1 Brown shrimps 2 Whelks 3 Scallops 4 Lobster 5 Crayfish 6 Prawns 7 Mussels
8 Oysters 9 Crab 10 Clams 11 Winkles

Shellfish, almost any kind of shellfish, gives any meal or snack an instant lift. A few scallops fried with a little garlic and tipped hot onto a salad is the sort of starter for which restaurants charge the earth, and a prawn sandwich is more than a cut above a sardine one.

Fresh is best

With shellfish, freshness is all. The delicate but distinctive flavours of crab, scallop, mussel or prawn vanish if the shellfish is not totally fresh. Besides which, seafood poisoning is very unpleasant, so steer clear of anything with even the faintest whiff of ammonia. All shellfish should smell clean, pleasant, and of the sea.

Treat with a light touch. Too much cooking will produce tough, rubbery flesh or too much flavouring, such as a strong curry sauce, will overpower the flavour.

Always buy shellfish from a fishmonger with a good, quick turnover, or from a busy supermarket. Do not store for long and cook and eat as soon as possible.

WATCHPOINT
Avoid any shellfish that smells suspect. Don't buy it or eat it. Life's too short for food poisoning.

Lobster

Lobster is the undisputed king of shellfish. Magnificent to look at, wonderful to eat and, believe it or not, simple to cook.

Lobsters are generally sold cooked in their shells, so you still have the job of cutting and cleaning them at home. Sometimes you can buy them split and cleaned, either fresh or frozen. Personally, I like to order mine freshly cooked from the fishmonger. I reckon if you are going to the expense of serving lobster then it's worth making the effort to get the freshest one possible.

Some fishmongers keep live lobsters but if you buy one you are then faced with the macabre task of killing and cooking it yourself. Never buy a dead uncooked lobster, because the intestinal contents can go bad very quickly once the creature is dead. The best weight of lobster to buy is between 450-900 g/1-2 lb.

Preparing Cooked Lobster

Once cooked, lobsters still have to be split and cleaned. The flesh has to be removed from the body and claws in preparation for use in your recipe.

1 Split the lobster in half and extract the glassy-looking stomach sac near the head. Pull away and discard the thread-like intestine running from head to toe. Remove the pink roe and use for a sauce or to make lobster butter. Leave the soft greenish tomalley (liver) in place near the head or spoon out and use for sauce.

2 Crack the claws and legs with a lobster cracker, or by tapping with a hammer through a sheet of polythene or a cloth to stop bits of shell flying. Use a lobster pick or skewer to extract the flesh from the legs.

3 Using a large dessertspoon, extract the flesh from the tail in one piece, and cut into slices.

Molluscs

Shellfish, unless they are frozen or precooked, must be alive when you buy or cook them. The fishmonger will open scallops or oysters for you, but mussels, cockles, and clams are usually cooked in the shell. Whelks and winkles are only available ready-cooked.

Double-sided shellfish – mussels, cockles and clams – should shut tightly when tapped. Throw away any that stay open. An hour under cold water before cooking helps to 'purge' them of grit.

Preparing & Cooking

To prepare mussels, clams or cockles, scrub the shells thoroughly and remove any 'beards' from mussels. Discard any shellfish which remain open. Steam or simmer gently in plenty of water in a closed pan. Once the shells open, the shellfish is cooked. Discard any which refuse to open.

To open scallops, slide a sharp knife between the shells and cut through the hinge. Remove any black matter and trim off the fibrous muscle opposite the roe. Fry briefly in garlic butter (15 seconds a side for small ones, 30 seconds for large).

To open oysters, wedge a strong blade between the shells at the hinge end and lever open. Serve raw on the deeper half of the shell on a bed of salt or ice.

The Shrimp Family

In Britain, only the tiniest of all prawns are known as shrimps. The prawns that you are most likely to find at the fishmonger's will be cooked and frozen, peeled or unpeeled and will be a pink colour. If they are to be cooked, fresh or live prawns will give the best results.

1 Dublin Bay prawn, scampi, langoustine or saltwater crayfish
2 Jumbo or king prawn
3 Tiger prawn
4 Freshwater crayfish or écrevisse
5 Shrimp (brown and pink)

Freezing

Prawns keep well in the freezer and freeze well in cooked mixtures and sauces. But don't re-freeze them, as freezing does not destroy micro-organisms. Besides, prawns lose moisture every time they thaw, and end up becoming tough.

Thawing

Frozen shellfish should be thawed slowly. For minimum water loss and best flavour and texture, thaw overnight in the fridge. Cooked, frozen prawns should be spread out on absorbent paper in the fridge (covered with more paper). They will be well drained but still juicy. Remember that once thawed, prawns weigh quite a bit less. A 450 g/1 lb pack will thaw and drain to 400 g/14 oz. Once thawed, keep in the fridge and eat within 24 hours.

Cooking

All seafood cooks quickly, but be especially careful when using ready-cooked prawns as overcooking makes them tough and dry. Always add them last. If the prawns and shrimps are to be eaten by themselves, then they are best fried and served with their buttery pan juices. Or serve with a thick sauce for dipping, such as garlic mayonnaise. Grilled prawns can be flavoured with butter, chilli, pepper, garlic, ginger and herbs while cooking. Both prawns and shrimps make wonderful soup and you can use the shells to flavour the liquid. Chefs often pound seafood shells to provide extra flavour for soups and sauces.

Preparing

1 Pinch off the legs and head. Remove and keep the eggs to add to a sauce or soup. Open up the shell from underneath and peel it off.

2 To remove the unsightly intestinal tract from large prawns, slit the back open. Pull out the tract carefully. Ignore it on any small prawns.

3 To butterfly prawns, pinch off the heads and legs but leave the shells on. Split through the length of the prawn, leaving the tail intact.

Crabs

Crabs are absolutely delicious, but a bit intimidating to cook and shell for the first time. Your fishmonger may sell them boiled, in which case you must extract the flesh, or live, requiring both boiling and preparing.

When buying crabs, a weight of approximately 700-900 g/1 lb 8 oz-2 lb is ideal, giving the maximum proportion of flesh to shell. It will yield 225-350 g/8-12 oz flesh, some of it soft creamy-brown meat, the rest firm, white meat. Both are delicious, but the white meat, which is less strongly flavoured, is considered superior. Allow about 50 g/2 oz of flesh per person.

Crab is good hot in soups and crab-cakes, or cold, dressed or with mayonnaise.

Cooking

To cook live crabs, bring a large, deep saucepan of well-salted water to the boil. When it is boiling briskly, drop in the crabs. They will die within seconds and the shells will turn orangey-red. Once this has happened, turn the heat down and simmer for 8 minutes for every 450 g/1 lb of weight. Lift the crabs out of the water and allow to cool for at least 2 hours before continuing with your recipe.

Preparing Crabs

Crabs can be bought from the fishmonger ready 'dressed' but it's easier than it looks to do it yourself and well worth the effort. To remove cooked crab meat from the shell for use in other recipes, follow these same steps but omit step 8.

DRESSED CRAB

Preparation time: 45 mins
Serves 2

INGREDIENTS

1 large crab
2 tbls mayonnaise
1 tbls lemon juice
2 tbls chopped fresh parsley
1 large hard-boiled egg

1 If using live crab, cook in boiling, salted water. Drain and leave to cool. Then lay the crab on its back and twist off the legs and claws.

2 Crack the legs and claws by tapping with a hammer or rolling pin. (Cover with polythene or cloth to prevent shell flying.) Pick out the crab flesh using a pick or skewer and place in a bowl. Discard the membrane and cartilage.

3 With the crab on its back, push with thumbs to force up 'apron' and separate it from the shell.

4 Pull the body away with the 'apron'. Remove and discard the spongy gills, or dead man's fingers as the crab's lungs are sometimes called.

5 Using a skewer, begin the somewhat laborious job of picking out the white meat. Place in bowl.

6 Press down on the mouth part of the large shell. It will crack off, bringing with it the stomach sac, which you discard. Also discard the cartilaginous membrane which is found in the shell.

7 Remove the soft brown meat from the shell. Crack the inner edge of the shell which will break along the fine visible line running round near the edge. Wash out the shell.

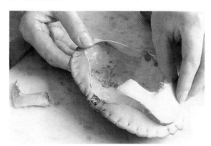

8 Mix the dark meat with the mayonnaise and sprinkle the white meat with lemon juice. Fill the middle of the shell with dark meat, and the two ends with white. Separate the egg white from the yolk, finely chop the white and push the yolk through a sieve. Cover the dark meat with lines of chopped parsley, egg white and egg yolk.

FISH

In today's world full of health-conscious people, fish is climbing high in the gastronomic popularity poll. It's low in fat and high in protein, quick and easy to cook and brilliant in the microwave.

Many exotic fish from all parts of the world are now readily available. Round fish cover many different varieties including herring, sea bass and mullet. The traditional British favourites salmon and trout still shine out and are delicious baked, poached, sautéed and grilled.

From a cooking point of view, the essential difference between round and flat fish is that flat fish yield four fillets, and round fish only two. The fillets of small flat fish, like sole, plaice and John Dory, can be rolled and stuffed. They are also delicious fried or grilled in breadcrumbs.

Something fishy

Whatever sort of fish you choose, freshness is vital. To tell if fish is fresh, look at the gills – ideally, they should be shiny and protruding, not dull and sunken. The belly should feel firm rather than flabby. The skin and scales should be bright and shiny. There should be no fishy smell, only a pleasant tang of the sea. Of course if you are buying pre-packed fish, in the CAP (controlled atmospheric pack) see-through boxes in a supermarket, you will have to trust the date-stamp.

Safe storing

Ideally, fish should be eaten on the day it is bought. If you have to buy fish for Sunday on, say, Friday, then I would recommend buying it from a supermarket

in a CAP box. If you intend keeping fresh fish more than 2 days at home, freeze it and then thaw it. To keep fish overnight, put it in the coldest part of the fridge wrapped in a damp J-cloth or covered loosely in cling film. Or prepare the fillets, then dip them in oil, or brush them all over with melted, but cooled butter. This will keep out the air and keep the fish fresh.

Freezing fish

Fish should be frozen when absolutely fresh. Firmer-textured fish freeze best. Freeze fillets or small fish wrapped separately so that they do not stick together in the freezer. To thaw, put the whole pack in an airtight polythene bag and dunk in cold water. If thawing in the microwave take care not to overcook.

Types of Flat Fish

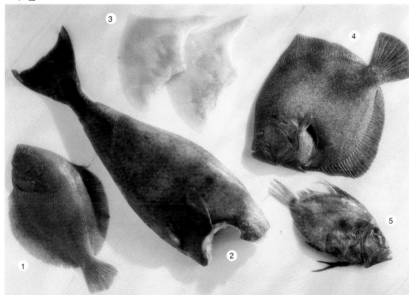

Small Flat Fish

1 Brill The flesh is softer and more inclined to break up than that of turbot and halibut, but has an excellent flavour. Take care not to overcook it.
2 Halibut A huge fish, generally sold in steaks cut through the backbone, and then, if large, halved. Halibut has an excellent firm texture and wonderful flavour.
3 Skate This is not strictly a flat fish, its body being small and round, but its huge fins (or wings) both top and bottom give it a flat appearance. Only

the wings are eaten. The fishmonger will remove the skin from the wings and cut them into more manageable portions.
4 Turbot This is the professional chef's favourite for its firm flesh and delicious flavour. Excellent served with a sauce or plainly steamed or grilled.
5 John Dory Called St Peter's fish because the round mark on its side is said to be St Peter's thumb-print. Its firm flesh has a nutty flavour and is quite delicious simply fried or grilled and eaten either hot, or cold with mayonnaise.

1 Plaice A tender-fleshed fish with a delicate flavour. Best eaten really fresh, and lightly cooked.
2 Dover Sole This has a wonderful flavour and firm texture. The king of the small flat fish and one of the few fish to survive being frozen or refrigerated for a few days. Excellent plainly cooked or served with French sauces.
3 Lemon Sole Cheaper than Dover sole, with less flavour and a softer texture. Cook this fish as simply as possible to preserve its gentle flavour.
4 Small John Dory Cook and serve as for large John Dory (see left).
5 Pomfret Full flavoured and best cooked very simply by poaching or grilling.
6 Flounder Best when freshly caught as it becomes tasteless when it has been frozen or refrigerated. Good firm flesh.

Large Round Fish

1 Sea trout Looks like a thinner version of salmon. Its delicate pink flesh combines the best of both salmon and trout.

2 Freshwater trout Now available all year round all around the world. It has a delicate, slightly earthy taste. There are many varieties to choose from, but the most commonly available is the ordinary rainbow trout.

3 Salmon Has a dense pink flesh with a unique flavour. A single fish can weigh up to 13.5 kg/30 lb but the best fish weigh about 3.6 kg/8 lb and are available whole, or as steaks or tailpieces. Scottish salmon is considered the finest quality although Canadian, Norwegian and Greenland salmon are also good buys. Salmon is delicious, but expensive, smoked. When buying smoked salmon, remember it should never be dry, hard or salty. Very dark red salmon is likely to be over-cured or dyed.

Small Round Fish

1 Mackerel These have steely blue and black tiger markings. Available all year round, they are inexpensive and have a rich nutritious flesh with a strong flavour. Fresh mackerel are best just plainly grilled or set off with a sharp-flavoured sauce. Smoked mackerel are delicious peppered and lightly grilled.

2 Grey mullet This is a silvery grey fish with a grey scaly back and a pale almost white belly. It varies in size from medium to quite large, and has soft white flesh. Best cooked whole, either grilled, pan fried or stuffed and baked. The cured roe is used for making taramasalata.

3 Red mullet No relation to grey mullet, red mullet is thought to be a far superior fish. It has a pretty red colouring and an excellent flavoured, firm flesh. It is an ideal fish for barbecuing or grilling and is at its best during the summer.

1 Whiting This has a pale grey or olive green back with a silvery underbelly. The flesh is sweet and crumbly and tends to be rather bony. It can be poached and baked whole, or filleted, coated and fried. Perfect for use in fish cakes, quenelles and terrines.

2 Whitebait These are young herrings. They freeze well and are usually bought frozen. Whitebait are generally coated in seasoned flour and deep-fried until crisp.

3 Sardines These are small silvery fish with copper-coloured heads. They have a delicate flesh and a strong flavour. Best when absolutely fresh. Cook whole or gutted and split, under the grill or on the barbecue and serve with a squeeze of lemon juice.

4 Herring Silvery fish with lots of fine bones and a delicately flavoured flesh. They can be plainly grilled or coated in oats and fried in butter. They are also often filleted and soused. Make sure you buy herrings that are firm and shiny.

Other Popular Round fish

Sea bass These have firm, delicately-flavoured milky-white flesh. Available whole, or in steaks or fillets, all year round but check with the fishmonger – you may need to order it and it can sometimes cost more to buy than salmon.

Smelt These belong to the salmon family and spawn in fresh water. They have a faint smell of cucumber when fresh, a delicate flesh and require careful handling. Served whole, lightly dipped in flour and fried, they are a special treat. They are best in winter and spring.

Sprats These are small fish similar to the herring. They are plentiful and therefore very cheap. You will find them in the shops during the winter and they can be cooked in the same way as herring.

The Great Fish

The large ocean fish almost all come from the warmer waters of the world. Their flesh is firm and meaty and inclined to be dry, so in general they can all be improved by marinating.

If you are going to grill or bake great fish, ask the fishmonger to cut it into 4 cm/1½ in steaks. A moderately large steak will weigh about 900 g/2 lb and will serve 4 people. Marinate in oil and lemon juice for at least an hour before cooking.

To grill, sprinkle the fish with herbs and cook 8-10 minutes on each side. To bake, cover with vegetables and place in a moderate oven for an hour. To barbecue,

cook in one piece or thread chunks onto skewers. Grill over charcoal for 10 minutes.

Types of Great Fish
1 Tuna Tuna can grow to an enormous size and are consequently always sold as steaks. The more common blue-fin variety has a dark-reddish flesh and a close-grained texture.

2 Swordfish The meaty flesh of swordfish has a slightly aromatic flavour and, like tuna, is close-grained and best marinated or cooked with oil or a sauce.

3 Shark Porbeagle shark has the best flavour and is good for grilling or braising. Fresh shark has a slight ammonia smell, but this is nothing to worry about – it will disappear during cooking.

Squid & Octopus

These strange creatures, which are known collectively as cephalopods, have been popular in the cuisines of Mediterranean countries for centuries. They are also used in Oriental cooking.

Their most distinctive feature is their texture. Though admittedly unusual, it should never be unpleasantly chewy. Properly cooked, a young specimen should be tender with just a little 'bite' to it. Badly cooked, however, the flesh will be as tough as the proverbial rubber band.

PRUE'S TIP

All cephalopods contain ink sacs, which lie behind the head in squid and octopus and inside the body of cuttlefish. The ink is used in many Mediterranean recipes.

Types of Cephalopods
1 Squid These are at their most tender and sweet when small, and they are ideal for simply boiling and using in a seafood salad. Marinate large squid in lemon juice or wine vinegar, onion and seasoning for several hours. The tentacles are the most delicate part of the squid; on young squid these can be dipped in butter and fried. Slice the pocket into rings and deep fry, or stuff and bake. The main rule to remember, however, is that the cooking time should be either very brief or very long or the squid will be very tough.

2 Octopus Large specimens are best stuffed and then stewed for several hours. If very small, they can be grilled or sautéed whole.

Cuttlefish (not pictured) The largest, but most tender, of the cephalopods. Prepare as for squid, except that it is simplest to open the body pouch with a knife in order to remove the cuttle-bone and viscera. Cook as for squid and octopus. Tiny specimens can be deep fried.

Preparing Octopus
To prepare an octopus, cut away the tentacles and cut off the suckers. Invert the body sac to remove the viscera (entrails). Parboil to remove mottled skin. If the octopus is large it may be tough, so beat with a mallet until soft.

Preparing Squid

1 Hold the body in one hand and the head, just below the eyes, in the other and pull apart gently.

2 Carefully pull away the mottled skin and discard it along with the head and the viscera. Feel inside the body for the cartilage or 'quill'. Pull firmly, but gently, and remove.

3 Wash the body thoroughly inside and out and then separate the two 'fins' from the body.

4 Cut the tentacles from the head and chop. Use the body for stuffing or cut into rings. Slice the fins.

Preparing Flat Fish Whole

Scaling

Most small flat fish do not require scaling because they are normally eaten skinned. To scale larger fish, hold under water in the sink and scrape with a large knife blade from tail to head.

Gutting

Make an incision just behind the head and scrape out the innards with a small sharp kitchen knife.

Skinning

1 With the fish still whole, cut a slit at the tail end. Dip your thumbs in salt and ease them under the skin to separate it from the flesh.

2 Turn the fish over and repeat the skinning process described above on the other side.

Boning

1 Cut through the flesh along the backbone and ease part of the fillets away from the bone. Roll back both fillets to expose the backbone.

2 Cut through the backbone at the head and tail and lift out. Trim round the fish to cut off the fringe-like fins.

Preparing Flat Fish in Fillets

Filleting

1 Lay the fish on a board, tail towards you. Cut along the backbone down the length of the fish.

2 With a sharp flexible knife cut one fillet away from the bone, keeping the blade almost flat against the bones of the fish.

3 Turn the fish so the head is towards you and repeat the above steps for the second fillet. Turn the fish over and repeat for the other side.

Double Filleting

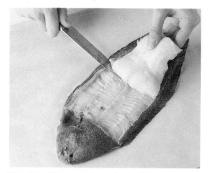

Flat fish fillets can be left whole. Working from the head, lift the double fillet with one hand as you ease the flesh off the bone with a small filleting knife.

PRUE'S TIP

Filleting knives have thin flexible blades which make it easy to ease the flesh away from the bones. When skinning fish, keeping the knife almost upright reduces the danger of cutting the skin, but with practice you will be able to flatten the knife and slide it forward to remove the fillet, without the sawing motion.

Skinning a Fillet

Dip your fingers in salt to get a firm grip on the tail end. With the skin side down and tail towards you, cut through the flesh close to the tip, taking care not to cut through the skin. Work the flesh from the skin with a gentle sawing motion (pushing rather than cutting). It's easiest if you use a large, heavy knife rather than a thin filleting knife. Hold the knife at right angles to the fillet with the blade's point tilting slightly downwards.

Cleaning & Gutting Round Fish

Use a sharp flexible knife or a pair of kitchen scissors for preparing round fish. Fresh fish are slippery and slimy; a cloth, a little salt and frequent washing will help you keep a good firm hold.

PRUE'S TIP
If the fish eyes worry you, remove before or after cooking – it is easier after – and replace with a caper or a tiny sprig of parsley before serving. Alternatively, cover them with a quartered lemon slice or another garnish.

Cleaning

Hold the fish firmly by the tail and scrape it, using a shell or the back of a knife, from tail to head to remove the excess scales. Trim the fins with scissors and cut the tail into a neat 'V'.

Gutting

Lay the fish on greaseproof paper. With a sharp knife slit the belly and scrape the gut onto the paper and discard. (Save the roe to souse or serve on toast.) Rinse the fish in salty water, rubbing with a little extra salt to remove any clots of blood.

Boning & Stuffing Round Fish

Boning Through the Belly

1 With a sharp knife, slit the belly and remove the gut. Lay the fish open on a board, skin side up. Sprinkle the tail with salt and hold firmly with one hand. Press firmly with the thumb all the way along the backbone to flatten the fish.

2 Turn the fish over skin side down on the work surface. Snip the tail end of the backbone using a pair of scissors. Free the backbone with the point of a knife and snip at the head end to release it.

Boning Through the Back

1 To stuff the fish through the back, cut down the back, from head to tail, right through to the bone. Slide the knife down either side of the backbone keeping the blade very close to the bone.

2 Open the fish out and then carefully prise out the backbone and gut. Snip the backbone off at the head and tail with scissors. Remove any remaining small bones that you can still see in the fish using a pair of tweezers.

Stuffing the Back

Spoon the stuffing in through the opening you have made in the back. With the belly intact the fish will keep a perfect shape.

Stuffing the Belly

Fill the belly with stuffing – not too much as it will swell during cooking. Gently press the fish into a neat shape; the stuffing will hold it together so sewing is not necessary.

Poaching & Steaming Flat Fish

Poaching and steaming are two of the quickest and healthiest methods of cooking flat fish. Any small flat fish fillets can be cooked using these methods.

Steaming

Plain steamed fish is easy to digest, being free of fats and sauces. It is also highly nutritious as the fish cooks quickly in its own juices. But there are pitfalls. Unadorned steamed fish, which depends entirely on itself for flavour, needs to be of the very best quality, daisy fresh and perfectly cooked.

Cook the fillets simply in a steaming basket over boiling water, or alternatively wrap them in spinach or lettuce leaves to make small parcels.

Of course, there is no reason why you cannot add a cholesterol-laden butter or hollandaise sauce to steamed fish for added richness and flavour.

Poaching

Place the fish fillets in a frying pan or baking dish, folding the thin fillet-ends under to prevent overcooking. Pour in a hot poaching liquid (which may be a court bouillon, stock, milk or wine and water). If poaching in the oven, cover with foil. Cook very gently. The liquid should tremble without bubbling. Cooking fast will toughen and shred fish.

Timing

As a general rule allow 8 minutes for every 450 g/1 lb of fish when steaming or poaching, providing that the liquid is already hot when you immerse the fish in it. Small thin fillets will cook much faster than large, thick ones. so allow 1 minute for every 25 g/1 oz.

Oven poaching can be slightly slower than pan-poaching because it is easier to get the liquid just trembling on the hob than it is in a coolish oven. But if the oven is set at 180 C/350 F/Gas 4, the dish is covered with foil and the court bouillon or cooking liquid is near boiling point at the start of cooking, the timings will be roughly similar.

When cooked (test by pressing with your finger – if cooked the fillet feels firm but not squashy), lift the fillets out with a perforated spoon and drain them briefly on absorbent paper.

Frying, Baking & Grilling Flat Fish

Grilling

Small fish are best grilled on the bone, as this helps to stop them curling under the heat. Long thin fillets need slashing at intervals to prevent warping, but small thickish cuts can be left whole. I like to leave the skin on these to protect the flesh and keep it moist, and because when cooked it is deliciously crisp and crackly.

Slash the fillets diagonally. Cut deeply but not right through the flesh. Brush both sides with butter or olive oil. Grill the flesh side first then turn over and grill the skin fiercely.

Grilling fish is very fast. Small thin fillets will cook in 4 minutes or less under fierce heat. Very thin fillets need not be

turned over – the bottom bakes on the hot grill tray while the top browns. Thicker fillets and whole fish will need to be turned over half way through grilling time.

Whole small fish will cook in about 10 minutes. Once browned, they should be moved further away from the heat to allow the inside to cook before the skin is scorched. It is often more convenient to finish the cooking in the oven, or to forget grilling altogether and bake the fish in a hot oven. Larger flat fish, like baby turbot, won't fit on the grill pan anyway, so must be cut into steaks or thick fillets.

Baking

Fillets or whole flat fish can be baked in foil with freshly-grated root ginger, chopped fresh tarragon, lemon juice, chopped skinned tomato or grated cheese for extra flavour.

When baking fish unwrapped, allow 8-12 minutes cooking time for small fillets at 200 C/400 F/Gas 6. For whole fish weighing 1.1 kg/2 lb or more allow about 15 minutes cooking time per 450 g/1 lb at 180 C/350 F/Gas 4. To test to see how well done it is, press gently with a finger. Cooked fish will feel firm and resilient, while raw fish will feel squashy.

Frying

Deep frying is an excellent traditional method of cooking fish providing that the fat or oil is fresh. Stale oil has ruined many a fish and chip shop.

To pan fry, dust each fillet in well-seasoned flour and fry in hot butter, keeping the fat just sizzling. Turn the fish once, so that each side is lightly browned. Serve with lemon wedges.

Poaching, Microwaving & Baking Round Fish

Poaching

Like flat fish, round fish can quickly become dry and tough if overcooked, so poaching is an ideal method of cooking. The fish is kept moist, immersed in a flavoured liquid, which can be either stock, court bouillon or wine and water, and cooked very gently so that the water is barely moving – no bubbles at all.

Cutlets can be poached in a sauté pan, but whole fish need a large pan or stockpot with the fish curled inside to fit. To cook a large fish, you will need a fish kettle. Lay the fish flat or in an 'S' shape.

Cold poached fish: Cover with cooled stock or court bouillon, bring the liquid to the boil and turn down the heat so that the liquid is barely agitating – not bubbling at all. Cook for 4 minutes for every 450 g/1 lb, remove from the heat and leave the fish to cool in the liquid.

Hot poached fish: When cooking a fish to be served hot, start with hot poaching liquid. Immerse the fish in the liquid, bring it to the boil and then poach gently for 6 minutes for every 450 g/1 lb (add on an extra 6 minutes for a fish weighing more than 3.6 kg/8 lb). Remove the cooked fish from the pan and drain it on absorbent paper to remove the excess stock before serving.

Microwaving

Fish cooks perfectly in the microwave, producing tender, succulent flesh which is full of flavour. But do be careful to slash the skin two or three times before cooking to prevent a build up of pressure that might cause it to split.

To poach a whole fish in the microwave, curl it into a large microwave-proof bowl and pour 3-4 tbls liquid such as court bouillon, stock or water over the top. Cover the dish and microwave at HIGH (100%) allowing about 4-5 minutes for every 450 g/1 lb of fish. Check with a fork to check that the fish is done – the flesh should flake but still be slightly underdone near the centre. Leave to sit, covered, for 5-10 minutes after microwaving to allow it to finish cooking.

An even better way of cooking fish in the microwave, however, is to bake it. Arrange whole fish head to tail in an oval or oblong microwave-proof dish, then add a little melted butter and some vegetables and herbs for flavour. Shield the head and tail with small pieces of smooth foil to avoid overcooking. Cover and microwave at HIGH (100%), allowing 4-6 minutes per 450 g/1 lb. Turn the fish over and rearrange halfway through microwaving.

Baking

Pan-baked fish makes a complete supper in one dish. Lay the cleaned fish on a bed of grated carrot and courgette. Season with salt, black pepper and lime juice. Brush with butter or oil, cover and bake.

To foil-bake fish, butter or oil the foil and season the fish with salt, pepper, lemon juice and fresh herbs. A small whole fish or 225 g/8 oz cutlet will take 10 minutes in an oven preheated to 200 C/400 F/Gas 6. Cook a medium-sized fish weighing between 450 g/1 lb and 900 g/2 lb in an oven preheated to 190 C/375 F/Gas 5 for 20-30 minutes. A large fish weighing between 1.4 kg/3 lb and 1.8 kg/4 lb will take 45-60 minutes in an oven preheated to 180 C/350 F/Gas 4. The fish should feel firm when cooked.

Barbecuing, Grilling & Pan-Frying Round Fish

Barbecuing

The smoky flavour and charcoaled, crisp skin of barbecued fish is delicious. Stuff whole fish with fresh herbs and slices of lemon or lime and brush liberally with oil, or marinate first in a spicy oil and lemon juice mixture overnight. To prevent the fish falling apart you can wrap it in well-oiled foil but you will not get a crisp skin. A fish-shaped griddle is helpful. It opens out like tongs – the fish is sandwiched in between and is far easier to lift and turn.

Grilling

Fresh fillets, cutlets or small whole fish are best grilled quickly, so preheat the grill to the highest temperature. Use equal-sized fish that will cook in the same time. Brush the fish with oil or melted butter and season with salt, pepper, paprika, or a few crushed herbs. A 350-450 g/12 oz-1 lb fish will need 6 minutes per side; steaks 2.5-4 cm/1-1½ in thick will need 3 minutes per side. Fillets 175 g/6 oz in weight will need only 1½-2 minutes grilling on each side.

Pan-Frying

Pan-frying is quick and a sauce can be produced from the juices. Trout and mullet are good cooked this way, but oily fish are better grilled. Fish is usually fried in clarified butter – normal butter tastes better but tends to burn. Pat the fish dry with absorbent paper and fry plainly or coat in seasoned flour, ground almonds or rolled oats first. Brown on both sides, then turn the heat down to cook through – a 225 g/8 oz trout will need 7 minutes per side.

POULTRY

Choosing a bird
Most chickens are sold young and tender. The elderly boiling fowl of wonderful flavour (but fearsome toughness) is rare today. When buying chicken, however, remember fresh chickens generally have better flavour than frozen ones and corn-fed birds (with yellow skins) are, I think, the best of all. All fresh chickens should have smooth soft skins without hairy legs or bruises, and frozen chickens should have no icy water lying in the tray.

Good for you
Chicken is an excellent source of protein, and is relatively low in fat – especially without the skin. The fatty skin can be removed before cooking, but I have to say that most of the flavour is in the skin.

Take care
Any form of food poisoning is a pretty nasty business. The most likely cause, where chicken is involved, is from salmonella bacteria which are very toxic.

In fact almost all chickens sold contain some salmonella, but usually nowhere near enough to cause trouble. So don't allow the bacteria to multiply. Keep the chicken refrigerated at all times and thaw frozen birds thoroughly before cooking. Always use clean kitchen tools (and hands), and wash all of your equipment thoroughly after use. Cook the flesh right through and, above all, don't leave leftovers sitting about. Refrigerate or freeze as soon as they are cool.

Jointing a Chicken

1 Turn the chicken over so the backbone is uppermost. Cut through to the bone along the spine. Where the thigh joins the backbone, cut round the fleshy 'oyster' on each side to loosen it from the carcass. The 'oysters' should then come away when the legs are severed.

2 Turn the bird over again and pull a leg away from the body. Cut through the skin as far round the leg as possible, close to the body. Pull the leg away and twist so that the thigh bone is exposed. Cut the leg off between the thigh bone and carcass. Repeat on the other side.

3 Now for the breast. Carefully cut down each side of the breastbone to free the flesh a little. Use scissors to cut through the small bones that are close to the breast. Cut away the breastbone.

4 Open up the bird. Cut each wing and breast off the carcass with a pair of kitchen scissors, starting at the tail end of the bird and cutting up through the wing bone near the neck.

5 Cut the wing joint in two, leaving about one third of the breast attached to the wing. Cut off the almost meatless pinions (which can go in the stock-pot along with the carcass) from each wing.

6 Lay the legs down on the board and cut through the joint where the thigh and lower leg bones meet. Turn over to complete the cut if necessary. Chop the feet bones off the drumsticks with the heel end of a heavy knife or cleaver.

Boning a Chicken Leg

1 Using a heavy knife or a pair of poultry shears, chop off the joint at the end of the drumstick bone.

2 With a small knife or boning knife, cut along the thigh and drumstick through to the bone.

3 Open the leg out and scrape the flesh away from the bones until they are free. Trim away any sinew and fat. Leave the skin on to hold the leg together.

Boning a Chicken Breast

1 Using a small sharp knife, start close to the bone and ease the flesh away from the breastbone.

2 Hold the breastbone in one hand and continue to scrape the flesh from the ribs using the tip of the knife. Take care not to dislodge the fillet which is attached to the underside of the breast.

3 At the wing joint, cut away the carcass and wing to free the boneless breast. Pull skin from breast, salting it first to get a good grip. Trim any fat and membranes from the breast meat.

Open Boning a Whole Bird

  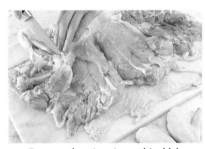

1 Lay the chicken breast-side down and, using a small, sharp knife, cut along the backbone. With the point of the knife release the 'oysters'. Keeping the blade close to the ribcage, scrape and ease the meat away from the bones until you meet the wing and leg joints. Cut through these, leaving the limbs attached to the skin and flesh. Cut the remaining flesh away from the ribcage, working down towards the breastbone, taking care not to pierce the skin.

2 Remove the ribcage by carefully scraping between the skin and the ridge of the breastbone.

3 Remove the wing tips and 'ankle' joints. Then, with the bird lying skin-side down and flat open, cut through to the bones along the lengths of wings and legs. With the point of the knife, cut the meat away from bones until they can be pulled free. Remove sinews. Stuff, roll and tie in shape with string.

Roasting Chicken

Roast chicken is justifiably an all-time favourite – and perfect juicy flesh and crackly skin are easy to achieve. Lightly brush the chicken with butter (or oil or bacon fat, or even walnut or sesame oil for a change), and put into a greased tin, then into a pre-heated oven.

For a version of French roast that produces delicious juices to serve instead of gravy, pour a glass of white wine and a glass of stock into the roasting tin with the chicken. Before serving, skim off the fat and season the juices.

Timing

A small bird weighing 1-1.5 kg/2-3 lb will take approximately an hour to cook in an oven preheated to 200 C/400 F/Gas 6, whereas a medium-sized bird will take half an hour longer. Large birds weighing up to 2.5 kg/6 lb will take 2-2½ hours to cook.

When calculating cooking times, remember that a meat stuffing will add approximately half an hour to the usual cooking time.

PRUE'S TIP

A no-fuss method of basting is to soak a square of muslin or a yellow or blue J-cloth (red dyes run!) in melted fat and lay it over the bird. The cloth will do the basting, and also stop fat from splattering the oven.

Stuffing

Don't overstuff poultry, especially if the stuffing mixture contains a cereal like rice, which swells during cooking. Also, an overstuffed bird will take so long to cook that the breast will be overdone and dry.

1 Spoon the chilled stuffing in the neck hole of the chicken. Never use warm stuffing unless cooking immediately.

2 Extra stuffing can go in the body cavity – clean it thoroughly first by wiping with damp absorbent paper.

Trussing

I seldom truss anything. Trussed legs take so long to cook that the breast tends to overcook to dryness. But if you do want to truss a bird, the following method is quick and easy to do. Be sure not to use plastic string as it will melt in the oven.

1 Make a loop around the parson's nose, cross the string round and over the chicken drumsticks. Pull tight.

2 Turn the bird over and loop one end of the string around a wing. Tuck in the neck flap. Pull the string over and tie around the other wing to secure it.

Serving Chicken

Making Gravy

To make gravy, remove the roast chicken from the pan and keep it warm. Skim off most of the fat and stir in 1-2 tsp flour. Stir over a medium heat until golden brown, then add 200 ml/7 fl oz stock and stir until boiling.

Carving

1 Start carving with the breast towards you. Steady the bird with a carving fork and cut through the skin between the thigh and breast. Bend the thigh outwards and cut through the joint.

2 Slice down through the corner of the breast towards the wing. Move the wing to find the joint then cut through it. Carve the breast then turn the bird round so the neck end is towards you and repeat the process.

Microwaving Chicken

Chicken cooks very well in the microwave but tends not to brown as it would in the oven. To add extra flavour and colour, try using a tasty glaze or marinade.

To glaze a chicken for microwaving, mix equal quantities of clear honey, Worcestershire sauce and soy sauce together in a bowl. Brush over the breast, legs and wings before cooking.

Alternatively, you can pep up your chicken with a spicy marinade. Mix 1 tbls Dijon mustard, 1 crushed clove of garlic, ½ tsp ground cumin and a large pinch of paprika together and spread over the chicken before cooking.

Whole Birds

Protect the wings and drumstick tips with small strips of foil shiny-side in. Place on a microwave-proof roasting rack, cover and microwave on HIGH (100%) turning over halfway through the cooking time. Wrap the cooked chicken in foil and leave to stand for 10-15 minutes before serving.

If you use a microwave thermometer to test if the bird is cooked, the temperature should be 82-85 C/180-185 F rising to 87-92 C/190-200 F after the standing time. A small bird that weighs less than 1.5 kg/3 lb will take approximately 25 minutes, a medium one weighing 1.5-2 kg/3-5 lb about 45 minutes and a large bird weighing up to 2.5 kg/6 lb about 55 minutes.

Portions, Drumsticks & Breasts

Chicken pieces should be arranged on a microwave-proof roasting rack or shallow dish with the thinner parts towards the centre. Cover and microwave. Two chicken breasts will take 5-7 minutes to cook through, whereas four breasts will take 9-11 minutes. Two drumsticks will cook in about 3 minutes, but 4 will take about 5-7 minutes. When the pieces are cooked, cover with foil and leave them to stand for 5 minutes before serving.

Grilling, Barbecuing & Poaching Chicken

Grilling & Barbecuing

Grilling is without a doubt one of the best cooking methods for bringing out the flavour of chicken. Whether you have an electric or gas grill, the results will be equally good, although nothing beats the aroma of chicken cooked over a barbecue. Marinate the meat beforehand in olive oil and herbs and baste using a rosemary twig.

A spatchcocked chicken weighing 450-900 g/1-2 lb will cook under the grill or on the barbeque in about 25-35 minutes. Chicken portions will take 12-25 minutes and drumsticks 8-12 minutes.

Spatchcocking

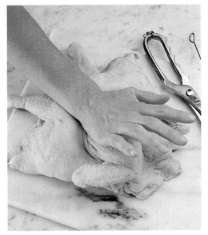

To open out a small chicken for fast grilling, cut along both sides of the backbone with poultry shears or strong scissors. Open the bird out as far as possible. Thump firmly with the heel of your hand and flatten the breastbone, wishbone and ribcage. Push a skewer through the nearest leg, both breasts and then the far leg to hold the bird open flat.

Poaching

The simplest way of poaching chicken is to put the untrussed bird into a large saucepan. You can add chopped carrots and onions, a stock cube and a bundle of herbs to improve the flavour. Cover with cold water, bring to the boil, then cook gently (with the water trembling rather than bubbling) until cooked. Young birds will take 1-1½ hours, while older birds will need 2½-3 hours. To test if the chicken is cooked, move the leg. It should wobble freely, with the bone feeling loose.

Cool the chicken quickly to stop germs breeding. Put the saucepan in a plastic bowl of cold water in the sink and leave the cold tap dripping into the bowl.

LAMB

You cannot fail with roast lamb. Overcook it, so the flesh falls off the bone and is dark and crackly, and you have an authentic Greek-style dish. Undercook it, so that it is positively bloody and barely hot in the middle, and it can be served in a classic French style. Roast lamb is wonderful either way (and anywhere in between).

The other great thing about lamb, of course, is that it will taste superb however little you do to it. For a simple French flavour, stud a leg with tiny sprigs of rosemary and slivers of garlic. Or you can marinate the meat with spices, oils, herbs and yoghurt and then roast it in the Indian style.

Buy the best
The first rule of good cooking is to buy good ingredients. Find a reliable butcher or use a supermarket where turnover is fast and you can be sure the meat is fresh. Lamb should have only a slight smell and that smell should be fresh and pleasant. The fat should be firm, the skin neither slimy nor obviously dried out and the flesh an attractive rosy pink.

The chill factor
Although British lamb is known for its flavour and quality, imported and frozen New Zealand lamb can be surprisingly good. You will find that joints are smaller since New Zealand lambs are generally smaller animals than British ones. But if you're like me you'll find that frozen lamb lacks the flavour of fresh, especially if it is thawed very quickly. Whenever possible, thaw lamb very slowly, so that it loses the minimum amount of liquid and flavour. A good guide is to allow 5 hours for each 450g/1 lb in the fridge or 2 hours for each 450g/1 lb at room temperature. If time is short though, you can place the joint under cold running water.

Don't cook lamb from frozen. Not only will it turn out tough, but it may well burn on the outside and be unpleasantly raw in the middle.

Large Cuts

1 Middle neck Also called the scrag, this joint is economical with a good flavour, but it needs slow cooking.

2 Shoulder This is the front leg, which also comes whole or, if large, halved into the blade joint and knuckle joint. The meat is good for roasting, but fattier than that from the leg.

3 Best end of neck A very popular cut with a fine grain and tender meat. It consists of 6-8 cutlets joined by the backbone (chine bone) which needs to be cut through by your butcher for quick and easy carving.

4 Breast This is the belly of the sheep. It can be boned, stuffed and rolled, and is a relatively cheap cut of meat that benefits from slow cooking.

5 Loin This is the back of the lamb and is another top quality cut with sweet, tender meat. If serving a whole loin, ask the butcher to cut through the backbone. When two loins are joined together, they

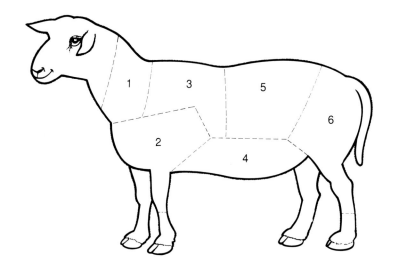

are called a saddle of lamb and are sometimes sold with the kidneys attached.
6 Leg The back leg (which includes the buttock) is sold whole, or halved into fillet and knuckle end. The meat is of top quality, lean and ideal for roasting.

Chops & Steaks

Lamb steaks, chops and cutlets will take anything from 2-10 minutes to cook depending on thickness, heat, and how pink you like them. Always start with fierce heat, brown both sides, then turn down the heat if the cut is thick and needs further cooking. To test for doneness, press with a finger. Very rare lamb feels soft, pink lamb a little firmer and well done lamb resistant, almost bouncy.

Lamb is particularly good flavoured with herbs, mustard, garlic, or with sweet jellies like redcurrant or crabapple.

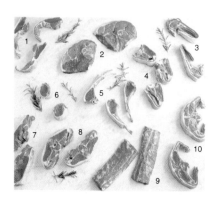

Grilling & Frying Times

1 Boned loin chop	5-10 mins
2 Gigot steak	5-10 mins
3 English cutlet	5-10 mins
4 Loin chop	5-10 mins
5 Cutlet	5 mins
6 Noisette	2-5 mins
7 Chump chop	10 mins
8 Barnsley chop	5-10 mins
9 Collop or escalope	2-5 mins
10 Butterfly chop	5-10 mins

Boning a Shoulder of Lamb

There is no mystery to boning meat. Generally it's simply a matter of cutting the meat away from the bone until the bone is free. You'll find that it's well worth the effort as carving a boned joint is very quick and easy. Take the opportunity to add some flavour by brushing the opened-out shoulder with redcurrant jelly, or scattering it with some chopped fresh herbs and orange slices.

1 Lay the lamb joint skin side down with the end with the round bone facing away from you. Feel for the flat end of the shoulder blade under the meat and, using a sharp, rigid boning knife, carefully cut the flesh away from the top and bottom of this blade bone.

2 When you reach the ball joint at the thin end of the blade, twist it several times and cut through any sinews holding the bone. Then remove it.

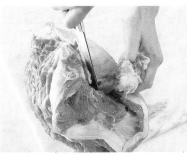

3 Open up the flesh where the blade bone has been removed and gradually scrape flesh away from the bone until the whole bone appears and you reach the second joint. Twist and cut any sinews, then remove the bone.

4 The remaining bone runs at a right angle. Slice through the meat along the bone, turn the meat skin side up and scrape the rest of the meat away from the bone and remove it.

5 Stuff or flavour the boned joint as desired, then roll up and tie securely before cooking.

Boning a Leg of Lamb

1 Feel where the shank bone is and make a cut along the side with the least meat on it. With the shank bone end towards you, scrape away the meat down to the joint. Cut through any sinews at the joint and remove the bone.

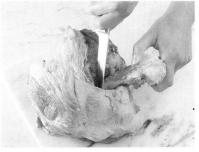

2 With the joint the same way up continue scraping down the remaining bone, keeping the knife next to the bone and using the sharp tip to scrape away the flesh as far as you can.

3 Turn the joint up the other way and ease the knife round hip bone. Work down the bone and pull it out. Stuff the leg if desired, then roll up the boned meat, tuck in the ends and secure them neatly with skewers before roasting.

Preparing Lamb for Roasting

Joints of roast lamb are not only delicious to eat but beautifully simple to cook as well. Bring the joint to room temperature before cooking and make sure you pre-heat the oven.

The easiest way to roast a joint of lamb is simply to place the lamb in a roasting dish, pour a little oil over the top and season with salt and pepper.

An alternative is to roast lamb on a rack. Although you miss out on the brown sticky bits which go towards making fantastic gravy, this technique does have its advantages. Firstly, you can get the underside brown: nice if you want a golden, crispy skin. Also, you can put root vegetables, French style, in the pan under the rack so that the meat juices drip on to them giving them a delicious taste.

Leg

Remove the knuckle bone and cut away the skin and excess fat. Make several slits and insert sprigs of rosemary and slivers of garlic. Roast the knuckle bone in the dish with the leg.

Shoulder

Using a sharp knife, cut the meat away from the blade bone to loosen it. Twist until the bone works itself free. Then pull it out or remove after roasting.

Special-Occasion Roasts

Rack of Lamb
This is an easy and popular way of preparing best end of neck.

1 Cut through the fat to the top of the rib bones, then neatly trim off the upper 5 cm/2 in of fat.

2 Trim away the meat between the joint's exposed bones and then scrape the bones clean. Place the rack bony-side down and make criss-cross scores in the fat to give the rack a decorative effect when roasted. Wrap the fat-free rib ends in some foil to prevent burning.

Guard of Honour
You will need 2 matching racks (best ends of neck) for this, preferably from the same animal so that they interlock neatly. Ask the butcher to cut the chine bone.

1 Place the rack skin-side up and use a knife to prise a corner of the skin away from the fat. Strip the skin back using the knife to help. Trim meat and fat between the bones and scrape clean. Score diagonal lines into the fat.

2 Interlock the two racks, fatty side outwards. Tie at intervals with string. Prevent the rib ends from burning by wrapping each bone with foil. Season.

Crown Roast
You also need 2 best ends of neck for this impressive roast. Fill the centre with a herb or fruit stuffing to give it extra flavour.

1 Trim the meat from the tops of the bones and scrape clean. Sew the joints together end-to-end, sewing around the last bone of each joint to secure.

2 Stand the tied joints upright and bend them round to make a circle. Stitch the free ends together and then tie around the middle to hold the crown in shape. If you wish, you can cut between the bones at the base to help the crown stand easily. Season inside and out.

Roasting Lamb

Place the prepared roast in an oven pre-heated to 200 C/400 F/Gas 6. If you want your roast rare, cook it for 18 minutes per 450 g/1 lb. For a medium roast, cook 24 minutes per 450 g/1 lb, and for a well-done roast, cook 28-30 minutes per 450 g/1 lb. To check if the roast is cooked, prick the flesh deeply with a skewer or thin knife. If the juices run red, the roast is still too raw. If they are pink it will be nicely rare. Almost clear juices mean a medium-cooked joint, whereas almost no juice at all means your roast is well-done. Remember that a boned, stuffed joint will take longer to cook than a joint of meat on the bone, because the bone conducts the heat.

Settling

After roasting, turn the oven off and leave the meat to settle for 10-15 minutes. This allows the juices to permeate nicely, makes carving easier and gives you a chance to make a quick gravy.

Making Gravy

It's hard not to make good gravy with lamb. As the meat cooks, the juices from the joint become stuck to the pan. By deglazing the pan after cooking – adding lamb stock and then stirring vigorously over a moderate heat – a good gravy is almost certainly guaranteed.

Pour off the excess fat from the roasting pan but leave the meat juices. Add 1 tbls flour and a pinch of mustard powder and stir over a moderate heat until smooth.

Stir in ½ tsp tomato purée and then add 300 ml/½ pt lamb stock. Stir until boiling and season to taste with salt and ground black pepper. Boil rapidly until well reduced and syrupy. Cut 25 g/1 oz butter into small cubes and whisk into the sauce one at a time to make a rich gravy.

P R U E ' S   T I P
Don't wrap the joint in foil for roasting – it will cook wetly rather than roast. The point about roasting is that it uses dry heat and gives a good crusty outside. If the joint is browning too quickly and you need to protect it, lay foil on loosely so air can still circulate.

S E R V I N G   N O T E
Roast lamb is traditionally served accompanied by mint sauce or redcurrant jelly.

Carving Lamb

There is nothing difficult about carving, but because of its mystique the task can be daunting, especially in front of a table of hungry diners! So here is my rather unorthodox advice for large joints.

Poke about with the carving fork to find where the bone is, and carve towards the bone if possible. Of course, this is difficult if the bone is close to the surface, so you may have to cut diagonally towards the bone, at a slant or even parallel to it. Meat fibres run parallel to the bone so cutting towards the bone cuts across the fibres and gives the most tender meat.

Cold meat is generally sliced more thinly than hot meat. If you are like me, you will cut the thinnest slices of meat that you can (this is easier to do with a really sharp knife). Thin slices of meat are economical as you need less meat to cover the plate – and the recipients think they are getting more. Accompanied by fresh vegetables and a tasty gravy everyone will be satisfied!

P R U E ' S   T I P
If you don't know what you are faced with, or where the bones are, just cut a thin slice and have a look. If it is a stringy slice, cut at another angle, across the fibres.

Shoulder

Cut a wedge-shaped slice from the centre of the shoulder. Continue cutting slices from either side of the first cut. (If you have removed the blade bone, slice across the meat until you reach the main bone). When all the meat from one side has been removed, turn the shoulder round and carry on carving.

Leg

Put the leg, rounded side up, on a carving-board. Carve a thin, wedge-shaped slice from the centre to the bone, then carve from either side of the first cut. Turn over, hold the shank and carve horizontal slices.

Best End of Neck

Remove the half-severed chine bone (if left attached for cooking). Hold with a carving fork and cut down between the rib bones vertically to separate the joint into chops.

PORK

It is surprising that the home cook's Sunday lunch is most likely to be roast beef or chicken when a leg of pork topped with crunchy crackling, accompanied by the appetising aroma of sage and the smell of real pork gravy, is so tempting. Concern about undercooked pork and uncertainty about buying it might account for this unpopularity. Quality does vary more in pork than it does in chicken and lamb, but good quality, lean pork is always worth searching for.

Buying pork

Unfortunately, there is no way to guarantee pork won't be dry and stringy. A reliable butcher or supermarket is your best bet. Pork should be pale-fleshed (never bloody or slimy), should smell sweet. The fat should be bright white. Check the butchering, too. What looks like a juicy joint could be cut so that the fat top is 50% of the whole piece. Allow about 225 g/8 oz boneless pork per person or, 275-350 g/10-12 oz on the bone.

Keeping pork

A couple of days in the fridge will not hurt pork. Cover large joints with foil and put smaller pieces in polythene bags. If the pork smells a little strong and not as fresh as it should do, wash it under cold water, then rub a mixture of vinegar and salt into it. If the smell persists, return to the shop and complain! If you are keeping the pork for 3 or 4 days, freeze it. Joints and portions can be frozen for up to 6 months; offal, mince and sausages for 3 months.

Large Cuts

1 Neck end Can be sold whole or in two sections – the (English) spare rib and the blade. The spare rib slices into large meaty chops interlaced with fat. The blade is a thin meaty joint covered on one side with skin and includes the shoulder bone. The whole joint can be boned and roasted, the spare rib roasted whole or grilled as chops and the blade roasted whole.

2 Foreloin Similar to the best end of lamb, with an L-shaped bone. This can be roasted whole, sliced into chops or prepared as for a crown roast of lamb.

3 Middle loin Consists of loin chops and the fillet, which is a long, tender, thin, lean piece of meat lying beneath the middle loin. The kidney is sometimes attached to the joint. The middle loin can be roasted whole on the bone, or off the bone and rolled. The fillet can be roasted whole.

4 Chump end Consists of chump chops which are slightly fattier and meatier than loin chops. It can also be roasted whole.

5 Fillet end of leg A flat circular joint with a lot of lean meat surrounded by skin. It's good for roasting on or off the bone.

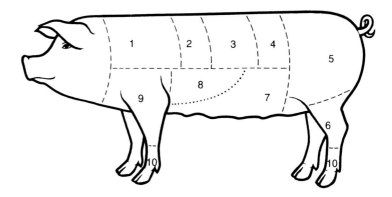

6 Knuckle end of leg Good for roasting on the bone, or it can be boned and rolled.

7 Belly This is a thin flat joint of meat interlaced with fat and cartilage. The thick end near the front leg is meatier than the end nearest the hind leg. It can be boned and rolled, or sliced between the bones for roasting with a barbecue marinade.

8 American spare ribs A thin joint with a lot of bones joined by a little meat. It is usually sliced up between the bones and sold for roasting, barbecuing or grilling.

9 Hand & spring Consists of some belly and the front leg with a bit of bone. It is usually boned and rolled for roasting.

10 Trotters These can be coated in breadcrumbs and grilled or used for making jellied stock.

Steaks, Cutlets & Chops

Frying

Put a spoonful of oil or dripping in a heavy-based frying-pan and heat before adding the meat. Fry the meat quickly to seal in the juices, turning the heat down only when the meat is brown on both sides. Continue cooking on a low heat. To tell if the pork is cooked, press with a finger. It should feel firm, almost bouncy.

Grilling

Preheat the grill to maximum before grilling. Start grilling as close as possible to the heat until the meat is brown. Turn and brown the other side. Thin cuts of meat should be ready to serve at this point. For thicker cuts reduce the heat to finish cooking more gently.

Grilling & Frying Times

1 English spare rib chop	15-20 mins
2 Tenderloin or fillet	10-15 mins
3 Leg escalope	4-5 mins
4 Chump chop	15-20 mins
5 Boneless loin chops	10-15 mins
6 American spare ribs	20-25 mins
7 Loin chops	20-25 mins

Boning a Loin of Pork

Boned loin of pork can be rolled with a savoury stuffing to make the meat go further. Try sage, onion and pear, prune and apple or mushroom and thyme.

1 Stand the loin with the ribs uppermost. Remove the kidney if there is one. Hold the joint steady and use a small sharp knife to cut close to either side of each rib. Do not cut any deeper into the flesh than is necessary.

2 Prise the ribs upwards with your fingers and cut along the underside of each rib, working from the thin edge down towards the long spinal bone. Twist the ribs free with one hand while holding the spine steady with the other. Loosen the fillet (if present) which you will find is attached to the spine by connective tissue. Cut through this, keeping the knife close to the bone. Pull the fillet away from the spine but do not detach it.

3 Loosen the spine by cutting around the vertebrae which extend from the spine. Remove the spine by lifting it as you cut away the meat, keeping your cuts close to the bone. Turn the loin over and score through the skin neatly before rolling. To roll the joint, start with the long side from which the spine was removed and roll it towards the thinner side. To secure in place, tie at regular intervals along its length.

Boning Other Cuts

Belly

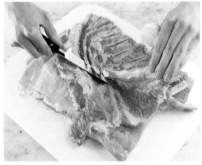

1 Cut either side of each rib to where it joins the cartilage. Then cut along the underside of the ribs and cartilage until the bones and cartilage come free.

2 With meat skin-side down, cut the skin away from the meat, rolling up the meat as you go.

English Spare Rib

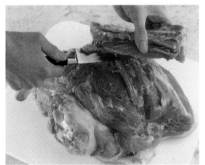

1 Lay the joint skin-side down and remove the spinal bone to which a few rib bones will be attached. Do this by cutting along the underside of these rib bones, keeping the knife close to the bone. Work around the spine and remove in one piece. Loosen the thin end of the blade bone. Keeping the knife close to the bone, cut either side of the blade until it is almost free.

2 Now loosen the thicker or knuckle end of the blade bone. Make a cut through the meat, deep enough to reveal the knuckle end. Trim away as much of the meat as possible and remove the bone.

PRUE'S TIP

Use the bones for stock which can be used to make sauces to accompany the roasts.

243

Roasting Pork

A perfectly roasted joint of pork is cooked slowly and thoroughly, and uncovered.

Preparing

Take the meat out of the fridge and let it come up to room temperature. If the joint is frozen, allow it time to thaw in the fridge first. For joints under 1.8 kg/4 lb, a night in the fridge will suffice. Up to 2.8 kg/6 lb requires a day and a night, while a 3.6 kg/8 lb joint will need about 60 hours and a 4.5 kg/10 lb leg will take at least 3 days and nights.

Timing

For rolled and stuffed joints, cook at 190 C/375 F/Gas 5 for 30 minutes per 450 g/1 lb plus an extra 20-30 minutes. Joints on the bone should be cooked at 200 C/400 F/Gas 6 for 30 minutes per 450 g/1 lb, plus an extra 30 minutes. For boned joints omit the extra 30 minutes. Check it is cooked by piercing with a skewer – the juices should be clear.

Making Crackling

Aside from the belly, the rind on all cuts makes good crackling. Ensure that the rind has been scored through the skin and just into the fat in thin parallel lines. Pour half a kettleful of boiling water over the scored skin to open up the slits, then pat dry with absorbent paper. Brush the rind with oil and rub in salt and pepper to season. For a crispier crackling do not baste during roasting.

Making Gravy

To make an unusual gravy to accompany roast pork, pour off the roasting fat, leaving the pork juices. Stir in 1 tbls flour. Then add 300 ml/½ pt dry white wine or cider with 2 tsp freshly chopped sage to the roasting tin. Season with salt and black pepper and bring to the boil. Boil until thick and syrupy.

Carving Pork

Loin

1 First remove the crackling. Then remove the chine bone from the joint with a carving knife and discard.

2 Cut the meat away from the bones in one piece, then carve it into thin slices and serve.

Hand & Spring

1 First remove the crackling and then carve slices from either side of the bone with a carving knife.

2 Then carve horizontal slices along the length of the bone on either side of the joint and serve.

Fillet End of Leg

First remove the crackling. Starting from the thicker end, carve along the length of the joint by cutting down to the bone. Then cut along the bone to release the slices. Turn the joint over and repeat.

PRUE'S TIP
An alternative way of carving the loin is to remove the chine bone and then carve the whole joint into chops by cutting through the crackling between the bones.

WATCHPOINT
Pork must always be thoroughly cooked right through to the centre.

Ham

Hams are the hind legs of the pig that have been brined or cured in dry salt. They are often salted and smoked according to local traditions and are usually eaten cold after cooking on or off the bone. The most famous British hams are the well-hung Bradenham hams and the mild, sweet York hams. American Virginia hams owe their sweet flavour to the pigs' diet of peanuts and peaches. The ham is cured in salt and sugar, and smoked over apple and hickory wood for a month. The continental Parma and prosciutto hams (from Italy) and Bayonne hams (from France) are specially salted and smoked but not cooked.

Preparing

Soak the uncooked ham for 2-3 hours in cold water to remove some of the excess salt. Weigh the ham and calculate the cooking time, allowing 25 minutes per 450 g/1 lb for joints weighing up to 4.5 kg/10 lb and approximately 15-20 minutes per 450 g/1 lb for larger joints.

Cooking

1 Put the ham in a large pan, cover with cold water and bring to the boil. Discard the water, cover with fresh cold water, bring to the boil and simmer gently for half the calculated cooking time.

2 Remove the ham from the pan, wrap it loosely in foil and put in a roasting tin. Bake at 180 C/350 F/Gas 4 until 30 minutes before the end of the total calculated cooking time.

3 Unwrap the ham, remove the foil and then carefully remove the skin from the joint with a knife.

4 Return the ham to the pan and spread it with 4-5 tbls Dijon mustard. Press plenty of demerara sugar all over the surface and protect the leg bone with a piece of foil. Return to the oven for the rest of the cooking time and until richly coloured. Cool and slice.

Gammon & Bacon

Gammon

This is also the hind leg of the pig but it is cured while still attached to the rest of the animal. Gammon can be bought whole, or divided up into different joints.

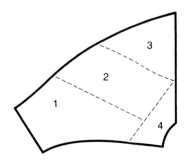

1 Gammon hock (or knuckle)
2 Middle gammon
3 Corner gammon
4 Gammon slipper

Bacon

This is pork which is cured in entire sides from which the tail, trotters and fillet have been removed. All bacon is salted and some is also smoked.

The microwave will cook bacon rashers well. Snip the rind with scissors before cooking, lay on a microwave rack between 2 sheets of absorbent paper and cook on HIGH (100%). Remove the paper as soon as the bacon is cooked.

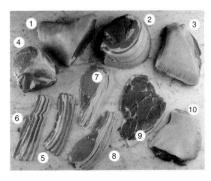

Cuts of Bacon

1 Forehock knuckle This makes good stock for soups and stews or can be boned and rolled for boiling.
2 Boned and rolled collar Bacon from the neck end of a pig. It is sold on the bone or boned and rolled, as pictured. It is generally used whole for baking as a cheap alternative to gammon.
3 Butt Part of the hand and spring and used for stewing.
4 Slipper A small joint that is perfect for boiling or baking.
5 Smoked streaky rashers
6 Unsmoked streaky rashers
7 Unsmoked back rashers
8 Smoked back rashers
9 Collar rashers Part of the collar and ideal for grilling.
10 Small hock Used in the same way as the butt.

VEAL

Veal at its best is tender, succulent to the point of stickiness and truly delicious. Yet quality and price vary. The best milk-fed (usually Dutch) veal is very pale and very expensive, but essential for fillets and steaks which will be quickly cooked. Veal for these dishes will come from the loin. Grass-fed veal (usually English) is less delicate and pinker. It is good in pies and casseroles as it needs slow cooking.

Track it down

Small cuts of veal, such as escalopes, are easy to find, but you may have to order larger cuts from the butcher. Both milk- and grass-fed veal should smell milky and fresh. Large pieces of veal may be stored for a few days, but cook sliced veal within 24 hours. Veal has little fat so to counter-act dryness wrap roasting veal in pork or beef fat and do not overcook.

Taking stock

The delicious stocks that can be made from veal bones are as good a reason as any to learn how to bone your own veal joints. Veal bones produce a clear stock that sets to a jelly and has a pronounced, but light flavour. Its gelatinous power makes it most chefs' favourite base for stocks and soups. Veal stock is also perfect for use in rich game casseroles.

Large Cuts

1 Calf's head This used to be served stuffed but most people would find it unpalatable nowadays. The upper part of the neck is known as the scrag end – a bony, untidy piece of meat. However, it can be used to add flavour to casseroles.

2 Middle neck Chops from this cut are meatier than the scrag end, making them better value. You can use them to make stews and casseroles.

3 Shoulder This can be stewed or roasted either on the bone or boned and rolled. It is a juicy, flavoursome cut of meat. The lower part of the shoulder (the hock) is better braised and stewed.

4 Best end This makes a delicious roast.

5 Breast Particularly good roasted if boned, stuffed and rolled. It is tender and full of flavour.

6 Loin This is the best cut for roasting either on the bone or boned and rolled. Small thickish steaks or cutlets for frying and grilling come from this cut. Tenderloin medallions are small, lean steaks cut from the fillet end of the loin.

7 Top of the leg This joint can be roasted whole. Escalopes – thin slices of veal – are cut from the thickest part of this joint. These choice cuts are perfect grilled.

8 Knuckle end of leg The bones of this cut are neat and rounded, and the meat is full of flavour. It is best either braised or casseroled.

Escalopes

Perfect escalopes are hard to come by anywhere except in Italy because butchers do not like to cut slices from their best joints. But do insist on meat cut from a single piece of loin or cushion end of the rump – not sliced across two or three sinewy divisions. And make sure the butcher cuts against the grain.

It is usual to beat out veal escalopes thinly to tenderise the meat before crumbing and cooking, but I prefer them only lightly beaten. If they are too thin you get more egg and breadcrumb than meat. Besides, you haven't a hope of not over-cooking anything that's paper thin.

Preparing

Sandwich veal escalopes between two layers of cling film. Beat gently with a rolling pin to an even thickness.

Cooking

To make Wiener Schnitzel, dip the escalopes first into seasoned flour, then into beaten egg, then into fine breadcrumbs. Fry each side quickly in hot clarified butter.

For a cordon bleu escalope, sandwich a thin slice of Gruyère cheese and a slice of ham inside a veal escalope. Dip in flour, then egg and then breadcrumbs, then repeat the egg and crumbs to build up a thicker crust so that the melted cheese doesn't seep out. Deep fry in oil or fry in hot clarified butter for 4 minutes.

Boning a Breast of Veal

1 Lay the breast of veal flat on a board and, using a sharp, rigid boning knife, cut the thin outer skin away from the fat with a sawing motion.

2 Lift back the flap of fat to expose the rib bones underneath. Trim away the excess fat according to whether you prefer lean or fatty meat.

3 Using a short, sharp knife, cut along the sides of the rib bones. Working the knife underneath, loosen the meat around the central bone, cutting it free from any connecting gristle.

Cooking Veal

Roasting

Veal, unlike most meat is best cooked in a slowish oven. It lacks the fat content that benefits from searing heat – you are not trying to produce crisp crackling, or to brown and melt excess fat. In fact you want to keep what little internal fat there is safely inside the meat – hence the rather low cooking temperatures.

Flavouring

Because veal flesh is mild in flavour, it is often filled with sweet or spicy stuffings. Try sorrel or spinach with sausagemeat and onion. Or serve it with a lemon or herb sauce, or with a gravy sweetened with a little clear jam or jelly. The juiciest cuts for roasting are the shoulder and breast, but the loin and the cushion from the rump, and topside are the largest pieces of lean meat. These are inclined to dryness so need barding as for beef (see page 249), slowish cooking, and above all must not be overcooked. The English have a horror of pink veal, but I have an even greater horror of stringy overcooked veal. Do stop while the meat is still juicy.

Timing

To roast veal, first preheat the oven to 170 C/325 F/Gas 3. Weigh the roast and put on a rack in a roasting pan. Spread the surface of the meat with butter and put rindless bacon or pork fat over the top of the veal or cook in a roasting bag. Put in the oven and roast according to weight – for thick joints, either on the bone or boned and rolled, allow 30 minutes per 450 g/1 lb. Thin joints such as unrolled breast and best end will take about 22 minutes per 450 g/1 lb. To test for doneness, pierce the meat with a skewer.

If it is cooked the juices will run clear. Leave to rest for 15-20 minutes in a warm place before carving.

Roast veal is, in fact, often baked rather than truly roasted. It may be French roasted with wine or tomatoes in the pan, wrapped in foil or even pot roasted in a lidded pot.

Making Gravy

Use veal bones to make a stock and boil down to 150 ml/¼ pt. Melt 1 tbls butter, stir in 1 tbls flour and fry until pale brown. Add the stock and 3 tbls white wine. Stir, boil hard for 5 minutes then add ½ tsp Dijon mustard and 5 tbls cream. Simmer for 10 minutes.

Stewing

Osso Bucco is a deep-flavoured, classic Italian veal and tomato stew – the name literally means bone with a hole. The cut used in this recipe is the knuckle – its muscular flesh, tendons and connective tissue start off as tough as rubber but end up as soft as butter.

OSSO BUCCO

Preparation time: 5 mins
Cooking time: 2 hours
Serves 4

INGREDIENTS

350 g/12 oz ripe tomatoes
3 tbls olive oil
1 large onion, finely chopped
1 large carrot, finely chopped
2 cloves of garlic, crushed
4 large meaty slices of knuckle veal
15 g/½ oz flour
2 tsp tomato purée
150 ml/¼ pint dry white wine
300 ml/½ pt veal stock
Salt and ground black pepper
A bouquet garni

1 Dip the tomatoes into boiling water for 5 seconds. Skin and chop them. Put 1 tbls of oil into a casserole, add the onion, carrot and garlic and cover. Cook on a gentle heat without browning.

2 In a large pan, brown the meat on both sides in 2 tbls of oil, two pieces at a time. Put on a plate when brown.

3 Sprinkle the flour into the pan. Stir well. Add the cooked vegetables, purée, tomatoes, wine, stock, salt and pepper and bring to the boil. Put the meat back into the casserole, add the bouquet garni, cover and simmer for 1½ hours.

4 Remove the veal and keep warm. Boil the sauce rapidly until thick. Remove the bouquet garni. Use a whisk to break up the sauce, but don't sieve it. Pour over the meat and serve.

BEEF

The colour of beef when you buy it varies from deep pink to very dark red, and depends on how old the animal was, its breed, whether it was male or female and how long it has been hung (this should be an absolute minimum of 8 days). Ideally, the meat should be marbled with tiny streaks of fat which will dissolve during cooking and tenderise it. The colour of the fat varies from yellow to white.

In general, the meat which comes from the hindquarter of the animal is tender and is very good for roasting and grilling, while cuts from the forequarter generally have more flavour, but are tougher and need slow moist cooking.

Packaging points
If you buy direct from a butcher, the meat will be just wrapped in paper and popped into a plastic bag. Supermarkets, however, often use CAP (controlled atmosphere packaging) where the meat is put into rigid containers and then sealed with clear plastic. Meat packed in polystyrene trays and covered with plastic wrap, however, will colour more quickly and has a shorter shelf life than that in a CAP box. Remove the wrappings, cover loosely with foil or greaseproof paper and store near the bottom of the fridge. Joints will keep for up to 4 days, chopped meat for up to 2 days and minced beef for 1 day.

Freezing beef
Wipe the meat with a clean damp cloth and double-wrap in polythene. Freeze large joints for up to 1 year and chopped or minced beef for up to 4 months.

Large Cuts

1 **Neck** Buy cubed or minced. Makes a rich gravy when cooked slowly.
2 **Clod** Buy and use as you would neck.
3 **Chuck** Sold cubed, sliced and minced. Needs slow cooking.
4 **Blade** Sold as a braising cut, or cubed for steak and kidney pie filling. Cook slowly.
5 **Rib** The whole of the rib has 13 individual ribs – the first three of these are with the chuck and these bones are removed. Forerib – sold as the first four ribs – is the traditional roast, usually cooked on the bone but it can also be boned and rolled. Back rib is the next three ribs which have less bone but the same flavour as the forerib. Wing rib is a large, expensive tender cut with the last three ribs and part of the sirloin.
6 **Sirloin** This is a tender prime cut that can be roasted or grilled. It includes porterhouse, T-bone and fillet steak.
7 **Rump** Lean prime meat. Rump steaks can be grilled and fried; barded lean joints can be roasted.
8 **Topside and silverside** Topside is a lean cut, best pot roasted or roasted rare.

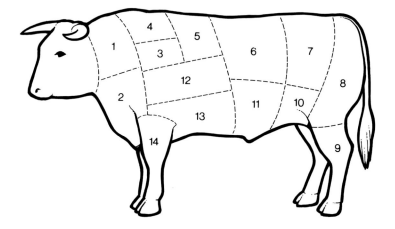

Silverside can be fresh or salted, poached, braised or slow roasted.
9 **Leg** The hind leg. A lean meat, which is sliced or cubed for use in casseroles.
10 & 11 **Flank** This is an inexpensive, coarse-grained meat. Buy sliced or cubed and use for stews, or boned and rolled and use for pot roasts.

12 **Top rib** Lean meat, sold boned and rolled for pot roasts or sliced for braising.
13 **Brisket** A coarse-grained and fatty meat, but this adds to the flavour. Sold boned and rolled, salted for boiling or fresh for pot roasts. Also sliced for braising.
14 **Shin** This is taken from the foreleg and is sold cubed or sliced. Cook slowly.

Steaks

Some steaks will contain a little fat 'marbling' – don't be put off by this – it helps the flavour. To keep steak in the fridge, brush with oil and cover loosely with foil, or spread thickly with dripping or butter. Never wrap it in cling film or put it in a plastic box.

When slicing fillet into steaks, trim off the membrane and the chain (a very thin fillet running the length of the main fillet) before cutting the slices.

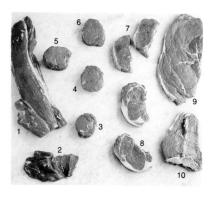

Types of steak
1 Whole fillet
2 Fillet end
3 Medallion
4 Mignon
5 Chateaubriand
6 Fillet steak
7 Porterhouse steak
8 Sirloin
9 Rump steak
10 T-bone steak

Barding & Larding

Very lean joints like topside and rump, which don't have any fat covering the outside, need extra help to keep the meat moist during cooking. Barding is almost always done by the butcher wherever you buy the meat, but it's a technique that's worth knowing how to do yourself. Larding however, is often a matter of preference and is only done by specialist butchers. The fat for both larding and barding is usually fat salt pork which is beaten out flat before using. Suet or streaky bacon can also be used for barding.

PRUE'S TIP

To give the meat a fragrant flavour, lay a few sprigs of fresh thyme and parsley, or some grated fresh root ginger and crushed garlic, over the meat before covering with barding fat. If the meat is already barded, cut the string and remove the fat, then replace over the herbs or ginger and garlic, and re-tie.

Barding

Beat out a piece of fat salt pork or suet very thinly. Wrap the sheet of fat around the meat joint and tie securely in several places with string. Alternatively, you can use several slices of streaky bacon.

Larding

You need a good-sized piece of fat salt pork which has been flattened to about 6 mm/¼ in thick, (available from most butchers, but you will need to order it in advance). Cut the fat into thin strips 6mm/¼ in wide and 5 cm/2 in long. Secure a strip in a larding needle (available from speciality kitchen shops) and thread it through the top 1 cm/⅓ in of the meat, weaving it in and out. You will need several strips of fat to complete the row. Start the next row and thread it to create a basket-work effect.

Cooking en Croûte

When I first started cooking for a living, Filet de Boeuf en Croûte was my speciality. It was less expensive then and few people worried about the cholesterol content of butter-laden puff pastry, fried mushrooms and beef fillet. I seldom cook it now, but when I'm feeling extravagant and in need of a treat, it's just the ticket.

Originally, the technique of cooking meat in pastry was devised to protect the meat from the blaze of an open fire. Meat cooked in this way – so neither aroma nor juices could escape – tasted better and stayed moister than open-roasted joints. The pastry was not meant to be eaten – indeed it was almost inedible, a flour-and-water dough which baked into a brick-hard crust. But gradually cooks realised that an edible crust would do the job just as well – and feed more people. I don't think I'm alone in liking the pastry as much as the meat!

En croûte dishes can be prepared in advance, stored in the fridge and cooked at the last minute. The pastry will stop the meat from drying out.

Fillet of beef is the quickest, tenderest and most popular beef joint to use en croûte, but it is by no means the only option. Topside is wonderfully lean, and sirloin, well trimmed, also makes an impressive and delicious dish.

BEEF EN CROUTE

Preparation time: 40 mins
+ cooling
Cooking time: 1 hour 35 mins
Serves 4-6

INGREDIENTS

2 tbls beef dripping

1.4 kg/3 lb sirloin,
trimmed of all fat and gristle

1 quantity brioche dough
(see page 283) made using only 3 tsp sugar

6 tbls fresh white breadcrumbs

3 slices cooked tongue

4 tbls ready-made mustard

1 thin slice cooked ham

FOR THE GARNISH
Flat-leaved parsley

1 Preheat oven to 190 C/375 F/ Gas 5. Heat the beef dripping in a large saucepan until it is just smoking, then quickly fry the beef to brown all sides without cooking the inside. Set aside to cool.

2 Roll out the brioche as thinly as possible. Spread the breadcrumbs down the centre, and lay the tongue slices on top of the crumbs.

3 Spread mustard over the beef and lay it on the tongue. Lay the ham on top. Bring up the sides of the brioche round joint. Press joins together to seal.

4 Make a criss-cross pattern in the pastry with a knife. Bake in the oven for 1½ hours. Garnish and serve.

Frying & Grilling

The reason steaks, chops and cutlets are often so much better in steakhouses and restaurants is that the chef will grill or fry them really fiercely. If the pan or grill isn't hot enough, the warm juices will run out before the outside has been seared to contain them. When this happens, the meat 'stews' in the leaking juices, the moisture evaporates, the inside ends up dry, and the outside grey.

When the heat is fierce, however, the juices are driven away from the heat. When you turn the steak over, that side becomes seared too and the juices are trapped. Of course some will escape if you allow the steak to cool, but the inside will still be juicy.

Many domestic grills are feeble beyond belief. If yours won't brown one side of a chop or steak well in 3 minutes, use a good heavy-based frying-pan instead.

Jabbing with a fork while the meat is cooking is counter-productive. It makes holes for the juices to run out, and too much pushing and turning the meat doesn't give it a chance to brown.

If you like crisp fat and rare steak cut the fat from the meat and start frying it before the lean meat. Or hold the steak with tongs to fry the fat first.

All steaks, especially large ones, benefit from a few minutes 'rest' after cooking to allow the juices to spread evenly through-out the meat, rather than the outside being dry and the middle being moist.

Flavouring & Tenderising

Marinating tenderises steak wonderfully, and will flavour and preserve it too. Wine, vinegar, lemon and other acids tenderise it, while oil keeps it fresh by keeping out air. Herbs, garlic and spices provide flavour.

Alternatively, if you haven't time to marinate, bash tough steak with a wet mallet to tenderise it.

Grilling & Frying Times

Whole fillet	Rare – 9 mins
	Medium – 11 mins
	Well-done – 15 mins
Fillet steak	Rare – 2 mins
	Medium – 3 mins
	Well-done – 4 mins
Sirloin	Rare – 4 mins
	Medium – 5 mins
	Well-done – 7 mins
T-bone steak	Rare – 6 mins
	Medium – 8 mins
	Well-done – 12 mins

Degrees of Doneness

'Blue'	Inside raw and juices not hot enough to run
Rare	Inside red and with the juices running freely
Medium	Inside pink and juices running gently
Well-done	Inside just slightly pink and juices set
Overdone	Inside grey and most of the juices lost

PEPPERED STEAKS

INGREDIENTS

| 4 steaks |
| 2 tbls black peppercorns |
| 2 tbls oil |
| 1 tbls brandy |

1 Trim the steaks and dry on absorbent paper. Coarsely crush the peppercorns and press evenly onto both sides of each steak. Set aside at room temperature for 30 minutes to absorb the flavour.

2 Heat the oil in a heavy-based frying-pan and then add the steaks and cook as desired. Transfer the steaks to a plate and keep warm.

3 Add 50 ml/2 fl oz water and the brandy to the pan and scrape up any sediment from the bottom with a wooden spatula. Boil until syrupy, season with salt and pour over the steaks to serve.

Pot Roasting

The beef should be boned, trimmed of excess fat, rolled and tied with string.

POT ROAST BEEF

Preparation time: 20 mins
Cooking time: 3¼ hours
Serves 6-8

INGREDIENTS

| 1.8 kg/4 lb topside, top rib or brisket, rolled |
| 3 tbls oil or half oil and half beef dripping |
| 1 onion, finely chopped |
| 1 large carrot, finely chopped |
| 2 celery stalks, finely chopped |
| 1 clove of garlic, crushed |
| 300 ml/½ pt red wine |
| 1 bay leaf |
| 400 g/14 oz tinned tomatoes |
| Salt and ground black pepper |

1 Preheat oven to 170 C/325 F/Gas 3. Heat the oil or oil and dripping in a deep, flameproof casserole. Fry the meat quickly over high heat on a hob, turning to brown on all sides.

2 Remove the meat from the casserole. Add all the vegetables and garlic and cook until soft. Add rest of ingredients. Bring to the boil.

3 Return the meat and any juices to the casserole, season and cover. Cook in the oven for about 3 hours, turning the meat halfway through.

4 Take the meat out and put on a serving plate. Keep hot. Remove the bay leaf from the casserole and purée all the vegetables and juices in a blender or through a sieve. Reheat in a pan, spooning off any surplus fat. Slice the meat thinly and pour the purée over the meat to serve.

PRUE'S TIP

Don't be tempted to use undrinkable wine for cooking – it will taste just as rancid whether you are drinking it or cooking with it.

Roasting Beef

A perfectly roasted joint of beef, browned on the outside, juicy and tender within, is easy to achieve if you follow these guidelines. Use high quality beef, like rib, sirloin, rump and topside. Large joints are better to roast than smaller ones as these can shrink too much during cooking.

Preparing

Allow 350 g/12 oz per person for joints on the bone and about 175-225 g/6-8 oz for boneless meat. Take the meat out of the fridge (defrost if necessary) and let it come up to room temperature – about 2 hours. If it is a rib joint, partly cut through the chine bone, then remove when cooked. Wipe clean and rub with ground pepper and some oil if it's very lean and not barded or larded. Stand the joint on a rack in a roasting tin. Rub a little salt on the fat but not into the meat. Always place the joint in a preheated oven, and be sure to baste during cooking.

Flavouring

Mix a little plain flour, mustard powder and pepper together and rub into the fat and meat as soon as it is taken out of the fridge. The meat will absorb the flavours and when it is cooked, will produce a wonderful tasty gravy.

Is it done?

To check how cooked the meat is, push a metal skewer into the thickest part – the colour of the juices which ooze out will tell you if it's done. Rare meat and the juices will be red, medium will be pink and well-done will be clear.

Timing

There are two methods of calculating the cooking time when roasting beef, one using a high heat and the other a lower oven temperature.

High heat: It is best to start the meat off at 220 C/425 F/Gas 7 for 15 minutes, then reduce to 180 C/350 F/Gas 4 and, for every 450 g/1 lb of meat, cook as follows:

Boneless	Rare – 10 mins
	Medium – 15 mins
	Well-done – 20 mins
On the bone	Rare – 15 mins
	Medium – 20 mins
	Well-done – 25 mins

Low heat: For every 450 g/1 lb of meat, cook at 170 C/325 F/Gas 3 for 25 minutes if you want a medium roast and 35 minutes if you want your roast well done. This method cooks the meat consistently, but will not produce rare meat.

Serving Beef

When the meat is cooked, cover it with foil and leave it to stand for 15 minutes, by which time the juices will have settled and the meat will be a lot easier to carve into lovely thin slices.

Carving Boned & Rolled Joints

Boned and rolled joints are obviously much easier to carve than those with the bones still in them. Remove the string and either carve across the meat, or stand the joint on its side on part of the fat, and carve downwards.

V A R I A T I O N

Skin and seed a tomato, add it to the gravy while it is cooking and simmer gently until it dissolves – it will give the gravy a subtle flavour.

S E R V I N G   N O T E

Roast beef is traditionally served accompanied by Yorkshire puddings (see page 267) and horseradish sauce (see page 298).

Carving Ribs

1 Stand the joint fat side up with the chine bone to your right. Cut off the chine bone.

2 Run the knife closely around the main rib bone, to separate the meat from it. Then carve the meat into thin slices.

Making Gravy

Pour off most of the fat from the roasting tin, leaving about 2 tbls. Save this meat dripping for the Yorkshire puddings. Put the tin over a low heat and stir in 2 tbls flour. (If you have coated the meat with flour before cooking, you will only need 1 tbls flour here.) Cook, stirring, until lightly browned. Gradually stir in 300 ml/½ pint beef stock (or vegetable cooking water) and a few tablespoons of wine for extra flavour. Pour in the meat juices that have collected on the serving plate as well. Scrape the tin to loosen all the bits, and bring to the boil, stirring. Season well and simmer for about 5 minutes, stirring.

GAME

The distinction between game and other meat has become a little blurred. Game used to mean wild things, but now a lot is farmed, including venison, quail, pigeon, partridge and guinea fowl. Even birds that are shot, such as pheasants and grouse, are protected, fed and looked after, ready for the start of the season.

How high?

Traditionally game is eaten after being hung, or matured, for anything from a few days for tiny birds like woodcock, to several weeks for venison. Hanging allows the gamy flavour to develop, but hanging for too long will result in the flesh going blue or green and smelling foul rather than high. Personally I like venison fairly high, and game birds almost as fresh as chickens.

Check it over

Your best bet is to ask your butcher, poulterer or even supermarket manager for young, fresh game. Once it has been plucked and dressed it is pretty difficult to tell what you are getting. If you are buying game ready for the pot, look for undamaged flesh with no blue or green blotches and, in birds, look for a smooth dry skin. A wet and slimy skin means that the bird has probably been frozen and defrosted fairly recently.

Refrigeration rules

Treat plucked and dressed game in the same way as any fresh meat – take it out of the plastic wrapper when you get it home, and put it on a plate in the refrigerator until you are ready to cook it. If you are not planning on cooking it for a day or two, cover loosely with foil to protect it and prevent the flesh drying out.

Game Birds

If the bird is in the feather, and hung, gut it. However, woodcocks and snipe have so little 'trail' no one bothers about it.

Cleaning

1 Make a small cut from the anus (politely called the 'vent') towards the breast, keeping the cut as small as possible. Cover your hand with a wet J-cloth and work up under the breastbone, loosening the entrails as you go. Draw them out. Rinse out the cavity and dry with a cloth.

2 Chop off the head with a heavy knife. Turn the bird breast-side down, and cut through the neck skin from the head end to where it meets the body. Peel the skin off the neck, leaving it attached to the body. Chop off the neck as close to the body as possible. Leave the feet on if roasting whole.

Plucking

Start at the head and pluck feathers one by one. Pull out in the direction they grow.

Singeing

Any stubbly remnants of feathers can be singed off over a gas flame.

Trussing

Tie the legs and parson's nose together with string.

Barding

Tie pork back fat or bacon fat over the breast as a self-baster during roasting.

Roasting

The following times are for rare red-meat birds, and just pink quail and guinea fowl. Allow 25% more cooking time for well-done birds. Roast on 200 C/400 F/Gas 6.

Quail	12 mins
Snipe	15 mins
Woodcock	20 mins
Pigeon	22 mins
Small duck (eg teal)	25 mins
Large duck (eg mallard)	35 mins
Partridge	25 mins
Grouse	35 mins
Pheasant	40 mins
Guinea fowl	45 mins

ROAST GROUSE

Preparation time: 20 mins
Cooking time: 30 mins
Serves 2

INGREDIENTS
2 young grouse, barded with fatty bacon
25 g/1 oz butter
2 small peeled onions,
each stuck with 3 cloves
Large bunch of fresh watercress

1 Preheat oven to 200 C/400 F/Gas 6. Put the grouse side-by-side, but not touching, in a small roasting tin. Tuck half the butter and one clove-studded onion into the vent of each bird. Roast in the centre of the oven for 30 minutes.

2 Remove from the oven and test for doneness by sticking a thin skewer into a thigh. The juices should run out pink rather than dark red. Transfer to a hot platter.

3 Twist the stalks off the watercress bunch and use to garnish the birds before serving.

Rabbit & Hare

Hares have rich, very gamy flesh, more akin to venison than to rabbit, which closely resembles chicken. Indeed, in the days when rabbits were cheaper than chicken, cooks frequently sold rabbit disguised as chicken in pies and casseroles, the only sure identification being the very different bones, which were carefully removed. You might try the same trick if your family are squeamish. It works. I know because I've got away with it successfully on a rabbit-hating husband.

Paunching
Paunch rabbits fresh; hares once they have been hung. Split the abdomen along the length of the body and pull out the entrails. Clean inside with a damp cloth.

Skinning
Cut off the head and tail and work the skin off like a vest.

WATCHPOINT
Always inspect the hare or rabbit liver. If it is discoloured, blotchy or looks diseased, throw the animal away immediately.

PRUE'S TIP
Wild rabbit can be too strongly flavoured. To reduce the strength of the flavour, soak overnight in salted water in the fridge.

Jointing
Fresh rabbit can be bought ready-jointed from many butchers. But if you choose to buy it whole, or are given one, it can be jointed quite simply. The same technique can be used to joint a hare and both can be frozen for up to 3 months. For convenience, interleave the joints with greased freezer tissue to make them easily accessible. That way you can use them as you need them.

1 Place the rabbit on a board and cut off the head with a large, sharp cook's knife. Cut off the forelimbs of the rabbit just behind the shoulders. Chop in half by splitting along backbone.

2 Cut the rabbit through the ribs about halfway along the middle of the back. Using the heel of your hand on the back of the knife, push down through the base of the back to remove the hindquarters. Split the hindquarters in two down the centre.

3 Follow the above steps to give 6 decent-sized portions. For pies or casseroles, where you need smaller pieces, chop each piece in half again

Venison

Young farmed venison is only slightly more flavoured than beef, but the flavour will develop with hanging. Venison is a lean meat and tends to be dry.

Cooking
Roasting joints include the loin, whole saddle, neck and haunch, but should be from young animals only and well barded. Tougher cuts benefit from marinating. Small chops, venison steaks from the loin, fillet or haunch can all be quickly fried. They are best well marinated before cooking. Very well hung and marinated saddle or haunch of older animals can be pot roasted. Marinate and sear before cooking, then use the marinade in the cooking liquid. Fresh vegetables and herbs add extra flavour. Any venison cut may be casseroled, but those from older animals should be hung and marinated first.

Barding

Sprinkle the surface of the meat with herbs and seasonings, then wrap large thin slices of pork back fat around the meat and tie securely with string.

Larding

Use a larding needle to thread thin strips of back fat through the meat, spacing them regularly.

OFFAL

Kidneys

Calves' kidneys are undoubtedly the best sort to use. To prepare them, cut across into slices, removing the membrane and central core as you go, and any white tissue or fat.

To grill kidneys, first heat the grill to maximum. Then brush the kidneys and the grill tray with butter. Grill the kidneys as close to the heat as you can, turning them once when just brown. Remove from the grill while the middle of the kidney is still pink and serve immediately.

To fry, heat butter or olive oil in the frying-pan. Make sure the kidneys are dry when you put them in the pan. Leave them to fry undisturbed until you can see the moisture on the top side rising to the surface. Then turn them over and increase the heat. Kidneys are not easy to fry because they are quite wet, so keep the heat up so that they don't stew in their own juices.

Liver

Brush slices of liver with melted butter, then fry or grill for 2-3 minutes. Chicken livers are full of B vitamins, iron, iodine and protein. They are delicious sliced, sautéed, eaten on toast or made into pâté.

Other Offal

Sweetbreads
These are, in fact, the pancreatic and thymus glands and a great delicacy – certainly well worth overcoming any squeamishness you might feel.

To prepare sweetbreads, cover in cold water and leave to soak for up to 3 hours, changing the water as it becomes pink. Put into a pan and cover with water. Bring very slowly to simmering point. Drain, then pick off any stringy bits of membrane. Place on a tray and put another tray weighted with 2 tins of food, or another heavy object, on top. Leave to chill for 1 hour until cold. Dry well. Dust in flour, shaking off any excess. Fry in hot butter until pale brown and continue cooking for about 4 minutes until firm.

Brains
These are softer and creamier than sweetbreads. Prepare in exactly the same way but press with a lighter weight. One set of brains will serve 2 people.

Brains can be fried in the same way as sweetbreads, but should take about 2-3 minutes on each side. To make brains in black butter, remove the cooked brains from the pan, add more butter and turn up the heat until the butter goes brown and grainy. Tip in the brains to coat with butter and serve sprinkled with finely chopped parsley. Alternatively, they are also excellent crumbed. Dust with flour, then dip in egg and roll in breadcrumbs. Breaded brains should take about 8 minutes to fry in hot butter.

Tongue
Tongues are bought either salted or fresh, and must then be cooked before pressing for eating cold or using in other recipes. Ask the butcher if a salted tongue needs to be soaked before cooking. It may not if it has been only lightly brined. If it does, cover it with cold water and leave to soak overnight in the fridge. If you're short on time, put the tongue in a pan, cover with cold water, bring slowly to simmering point and discard the water.

Not surprisingly, beef tongues are large and strong flavoured. If possible, use veal tongues – they are larger than lamb's tongues, more subtly flavoured than beef tongues and and far superior to either.

To boil veal tongues, wash them and put them in a pan with plenty of water, a few roughly chopped carrots and sliced onions, a bunch of fresh herbs and a few allspice berries, peppercorns and whole cloves. Bring slowly to the boil and simmer gently, skimming off any froth as it forms, until the meat is tender. They will take up to 2½ hours to cook. When checking for readiness, test the tip of the tongue rather than the thicker fatty parts as this takes longer to cook. Cool in liquid. While still just warm, peel the tough outer skin off the tongues using your fingers.

SAUSAGES

The sausage was invented as a way to use up meat scraps and for making tough cuts palatable. It has come a long way since then, and a good sausage is truly a treat. But cheap sausages lack flavour, and are usually so full of cereal that they burst in the pan. The only way to guarantee a good sausage is to buy it from a respected sausage specialist or make it yourself. This is easiest with a sausage filler, which comes as an attachment to some food processors. Alternatively, roll skinless sausages by hand or use an opened-out roasting bag as a temporary skin while you poach the filling to firmness.

Skinless Sausages

It's easy to make sausages without skins – just make the mixture sticky enough to hold together on its own and take great care when frying.

FRESH PORK SAUSAGES

Preparation time: 10 mins
Makes 6-8 sausages

INGREDIENTS
1 thin slice wholemeal bread, roughly broken up into small pieces
3 fresh sage leaves
1 egg yolk
2 tbls milk
¼ tsp salt
¼ tsp ground black pepper
450 g/1 lb coarsely-minced pork belly

1 Liquidise the broken bread with the fresh sage until you have fine crumbs. Tip the herby crumbs into a large bowl and add the egg yolk, the milk, the salt and the pepper.

2 Work in the minced pork, using twisting motions of your hand (with the fingers spread out), to ensure thorough and even mixing.

3 Take small handfuls of the mixture and roll into sausages. Make sure the sausages are flat at the ends, not tapered, and that they are of even thickness. It is very easy to get them too fat in the middle and too thin at the ends.

PRUE'S TIP

If you don't have a liquidiser, use ½ tsp dried sage and 2 heaped tsp dried white crumbs soaked in milk to replace the fresh sage and the bread.

Poached Sausages

Another way to make sausages if you don't have a sausage filler is to wrap the mixture in an oven bag or some cling film and poach until firm.

SEAFOOD SAUSAGES

Preparation time: 45 mins
Cooking time: 25-30 mins
Makes 24 small sausages

INGREDIENTS
225 g/8 oz white crabmeat
100 g/4 oz raw scampi, peeled
225 g/8 oz turbot, skinned and boned
2 egg whites
300 ml/½ pt double cream
Salt and ground white pepper
1 egg, beaten
150 g/5 oz fine white breadcrumbs
Butter, for frying

1 Purée the seafood and fish until smooth. Chill, then beat in the egg whites, cream and seasoning. Using a felt-tip pen, indicate the length of sausage on a piece of paper. Open out a roasting bag and lay over the paper so that you can see the marks. Then pipe the mixture between the two marks.

2 Bring the roasting bag up to enclose the sausage. Twist the ends to secure the shape, then tie them together. Repeat until all the mixture is used.

3 Bring a shallow pan of water to the boil. Turn the heat down so the water barely moves (if it simmers or boils the sausages will burst). Poach the sausages in the water for 4-5 minutes, until just firm. Lift out, cool, then refrigerate until well chilled.

4 Slit each roasting bag with a knife and remove the sausage. Dip in beaten egg, then roll in breadcrumbs. Fry very gently in butter, turning until golden all over. Serve immediately.

STOCKS & SAUCES

A good sauce, really professionally made, smooth and deep-flavoured, is a little miracle. It will turn a poached egg into a feast or a boring bit of chicken into something pretty special. Taste will come, as always, from good ingredients. Meatless bones from a roasted young chicken will obviously not make as good a stock as a whole raw boiling fowl. Lightly salted, fresh butter gives a better flavour than margarine. Fresh herbs are better than dried and so on.

Stock secrets

Behind every great sauce and many a soup lies a strong, carefully made stock.

However, the intense real flavour of a good cook's brown stock is not the easiest, or the quickest, thing to achieve. Top chefs tend their stocks as nurses watch over babies in Intensive Care, with many a visit, much checking and adjusting, and constant clucking vigilance. The secret of a good stock is in the slow gentle simmering. If the liquid is the slightest bit greasy, vigorous boiling will produce a murky, fatty-tasting broth. Skimming, for meat stocks, is also vital.

When making stocks and sauces, make sure that you taste them regularly. It's the only way to tell whether or not you've got them just right.

Special sauces

Once you understand the basic principles of making sauces, you need not stick to making only the classics. You can swap milk for stock and vice-versa, or, best of all, use the juices from the meat or fish you are cooking to add flavour to the sauce. You can add wine or liqueur, herbs or spices to suit your taste. You can take a flour-thickened sauce and cross it with a butter emulsion to make the hybrid known as sauce bâtarde. I use this sauce a lot. It combines the luxury of a butter emulsion with the stability of a flour-based sauce. But just one tiny word of warning – simple flavours work best.

Quick Pan Sauces

These simple sauces are quick to make, yet they sacrifice nothing in flavour. They all serve 4-6 people.

Mustard & Cream Sauce

Quickly pan-fry thin slices of pork fillet in 50 g/2 oz clarified butter to brown both sides. Place in an ovenproof dish and keep warm. Add 150 ml/¼ pt Classic Brown Stock (see page 259), 150 ml/¼ pt double cream and 1 tbls Dijon mustard. Boil, stirring until syrupy. Adjust seasoning.

Redcurrant & Ginger Sauce

Pan-fry lamb cutlets in clarified butter to brown both sides. Keep warm while you make the sauce. Add 150 ml/¼ pt Classic Brown Stock (see page 259), 1 tbls redcurrant jelly and a pinch of ginger to the pan. Boil hard until syrupy.

Raspberry Vinegar Sauce

Quick fry thin slices of veal liver in 50 g/2 oz clarified butter. Put on a warm plate. Add 2 tbls raspberry vinegar to the pan. Boil down to 2 tsp. Add 150 ml/¼ pt double cream, salt and pepper and bring to the boil. Serve over the liver.

Garlic & Yoghurt Sauce

Pan-fry chicken livers in 50 g/2 oz clarified butter until brown. Add 1 clove of crushed garlic and fry for 30 seconds. Stir in 3 tbls strained Greek yoghurt and salt and pepper. Serve on toast as a starter.

Red Wine & Mushroom Sauce

Pan-fry steak medallions quickly in clarified butter to brown both sides. Keep warm. Fry 100 g/4 oz sliced mushrooms in the pan fat. Add a glass of red wine and boil to reduce to 1 tbls. Add 150 ml/¼ pt stock and 1 tbls freshly chopped parsley. Boil, stir and spoon on to the steaks.

Orange & Thyme Sauce

Skin and core pigs' kidneys. Slice thinly. Pan-fry quickly in 50 g/2 oz clarified butter, tossing to brown evenly. Add the juice of ½ an orange with 1 tsp finely grated zest, 2 tbls veal demi-glace (see page 260), and 1 tsp chopped thyme. Boil and whisk in 25 g/1 oz chilled butter, in bits. Serve spooned over kidneys.

Rich Butter Sauce

Fry chicken thighs in 50 g/2 oz clarified butter until browned. Lower heat and cook for 15 minutes. Pour off all but 3 tbls of the fat. Add 1 tbls lemon juice and boil until almost evaporated. Lift out the chicken and keep warm. Add 150 ml/¼ pt Classic Brown Stock (see page 259) and boil down to 2 tbls, stirring constantly. Whisk in 50-75 g/2-3 oz chilled butter, bit by bit. Pour over the chicken and serve.

Creamy Garlic Sauce

Poach fish fillets in unsalted water with a glass of dry white wine. When cooked, reduce liquid to 150 ml/¼ pt and add a garlic Boursin cheese. Whisk until smooth and hot. To avoid curdling, do not boil.

Vegetable Sauces

This fresh-tasting tomato sauce is a world away from the ready-made kind that comes in bottles.

TOMATO SAUCE

INGREDIENTS

400 g/14 oz tinned tomatoes
1 small onion, chopped
1 carrot, chopped
1 stick of celery, chopped
½ a clove of garlic, crushed
1 bay leaf
2-3 fresh parsley stalks
Salt and ground black pepper
Juice of ½ a lemon
Dash of Worcestershire sauce
1 tsp sugar
1 tsp freshly chopped basil

1 Put all the ingredients in a heavy-based pan and simmer over medium heat for 30 minutes.

2 Strain the sauce through a sieve and return it to the pan. It should coat and cling to the back of a spoon. If the sauce is too thin, reduce it by boiling rapidly. Check the seasoning and add more salt and pepper to taste before serving.

SOUBISE SAUCE

Serve this simple and highly-flavoured onion sauce with vegetables, fish or meat.

INGREDIENTS

1 large Spanish onion, chopped
50 g/2 oz butter
1½ tbls flour
300 ml/½ pt creamy milk
Salt and ground white pepper
1 bay leaf
2 tbls double cream

1 Put the onion into a saucepan with the butter and 300 ml/½ pt water. Simmer until the onion is soft and the water evaporated.

2 Stir in the flour, cook for 30 seconds, then add the milk, bay leaf, salt and pepper. Stir until boiling and simmer for 2 minutes. Stir in the double cream. Remove bay leaf and liquidise if desired.

Fish Stocks & Sauces

If boiled down to a thick syrup this simple fish stock is called glace de poisson and used, in small amounts, to flavour soups and sauces. Freeze in ice cube trays for later use. A few cubes can be quickly defrosted whenever needed.

FISH STOCK

INGREDIENTS

Fish bones, heads, skins, seafood shells
Sliced onion, carrot and celery stalks
Parsley stalks
1 bay leaf
Pinch of thyme
White peppercorns

1 Put all the stock ingredients in a pan, cover with water and simmer for 20 minutes.

2 Strain the stock. If you prefer, it can be strengthened in flavour by reducing.

WATCHPOINT

Never simmer fish stock for longer than 20 minutes or the bones will give the stock a bitter flavour.

FISH ASPIC

Thick coatings of aspic jelly went out with the ark, but a fine layer brushed over a cold salmon or trout looks really attractive. Aspic jelly is lighter than decorating cold fish with mayonnaise, prevents the fish from drying out, and allows you to show off the prettiness of the food.

INGREDIENTS

1.2 L/2 pt cold fish stock
25 g/1 oz gelatine
White and crushed shells of 2 eggs

1 Skim any fat from the stock and put into a 2.3 L/4 pt pan. Sprinkle over the gelatine and whisk in the egg white and crushed egg shells.

2 Whisk over a gentle heat until the mixture boils and rises. Remove from the heat and let the mixture subside, ensuring the egg white crust remains intact. Bring to the boil twice more.

3 Cool for 10 minutes. Clean a sieve with boiling water, line with a double layer of muslin or J-cloth and strain the liquid through, allowing the egg-white crust to slip into the muslin last. Strain once more through the muslin and egg white. Refrigerate until ready to use.

COURT BOUILLON

Court bouillon is a slightly acidulated liquid used for poaching fish or sometimes as a base for fish soups. Vinegar is usually used to acidulate but white wine can be used instead. Vegetables and herbs are used to add flavour.

INGREDIENTS

300 ml/½ pt wine vinegar
3 bay leaves
2 onions, sliced
Large handful of fresh parsley
2 carrots, sliced
1 leek, sliced
12 black peppercorns

1 Put everything in a large saucepan, add 4.6 L/8 pt water and simmer for 20-30 minutes. Cool and strain.

PRUE'S TIP

It may sound odd to whisk raw egg whites and crushed shells into the stock when making aspic, but there is a good reason. As the proteins in the egg coagulate, they attract unwanted sediment which then rises to the surface to form a crust. Repeated boilings attract even more and after final straining, the aspic is clear. This process is called clarification.

Chicken Stocks & Sauces

It makes me cross when I find I have bought a chicken without giblets, as they are so useful for making flavoured stocks, sauces and gravies. Try this simple recipe as an alternative to your usual gravy next time you roast a chicken.

GIBLET GRAVY

Preparation time: 10 mins
Cooking time: 1 hour 10 mins
Makes 900 ml/1½ pt

INGREDIENTS

Chicken giblets
600 ml/1 pt chicken stock
1 onion, sliced
1 bouquet garni
1 carrot, sliced
1 celery stalk, sliced
15 g/½ oz butter
1 tsp potato starch or cornflour

1 While the chicken is roasting, simmer the neck, heart and gizzard in the stock with the onion, bouquet garni, carrot and celery.

2 After 1 hour strain the stock. Chop the heart and gizzard. Slice the liver and sauté in the butter.

3 Add juices from the roast chicken to the stock and bring to the boil. Mix the potato starch or cornflour with 2 tbls water and stir into the gravy. Stir over a medium heat for 2 minutes, add the chopped heart and gizzard with the sautéed liver and pour into a gravy boat.

WHITE STOCK

Preparation time: 5 mins
Cooking time: 3 hours
Makes 900 ml/1½ pt

INGREDIENTS

2 onions, sliced
1 carrot, sliced
1 leek, sliced
Handful of fresh parsley stalks
1 bay leaf
6 peppercorns
2 raw chicken carcasses
1 veal bone

1 Put all the ingredients into a large pan with 1.2 L/2 pt cold water and bring to the boil slowly. Skim off any scum or fat. Simmer for 3 hours, skimming occasionally.

2 Strain, cool and lift off any solidified fat. Chill until required or boil vigorously to reduce to 300 ml/½ pt. Concentrated, the stock will keep for up to 10 days.

Coating Poultry

For a really impressive presentation, coat boned and stuffed poultry in a chaudfroid sauce. This is a rich white sauce made with stock and thickened with liquid aspic.

CHAUDFROID SAUCE

Preparation time: 30 mins
Cooking time: 10 mins
Makes 450 ml/¾ pt

INGREDIENTS

1 bay leaf
4 black peppercorns
1 slice of onion
Blade of mace
Sprig of parsley
300 ml/½ pt milk
20 g/¾ oz butter
20 g/¾ oz flour
Salt and ground black pepper
75 ml/3 fl oz prepared aspic
3 tbls double cream

1 Put the bay leaf, peppercorns, onion, mace and parsley together with the milk in a small saucepan. Bring slowly to the boil and then set aside to cool for 20 minutes. Strain. Melt the butter, stir in the flour and cook for 30 seconds. Remove the pan from the heat and slowly add the strained milk, beating well between each addition so that you get a smooth silky sauce. Return the pan to a gentle heat and cook until thickened, stirring all the time. Season well with salt and pepper.

2 Beat the prepared aspic into the white sauce, followed by the cream, making sure that the sauce is very smooth. Set the pan over a bowl of crushed ice and stir until it starts to set. Remove the pan and stir until the sauce resembles thick cream.

PRUE'S TIP
If the sauce looks lumpy, blend it briefly in a liquidiser until it is smooth.

Meat Stock

This versatile stock can be used in many dishes – as long as you don't make it with distinctively flavoured pork, mutton or lamb. Some bones, such as veal bones, which give the subtlest deep-flavoured jellying stock are not always easy to find in small quantities, so it's worth ordering in bulk for the freezer. In any case, stock-making is such a performance it's worth making extra.

CLASSIC BROWN STOCK

Preparation time: 20 mins
Cooking time: 3¾ – 12¾ hours
Makes 1 L/1¾ pint

INGREDIENTS
2 onions, unpeeled and chopped
2 carrots, chopped
2 sticks celery, chopped
2 tbls beef dripping
2.3 kg/5 lb marrow bones
(or beef, veal or game bones)
225 g/8 oz raw meat, preferably beef, diced
Handful of parsley stalks
1 bay leaf
½ tsp black peppercorns
1 sprig of fresh thyme

1 Preheat oven to 200 C/400 F/Gas 6. Gently fry the vegetables in the dripping in a large heavy based pan, stirring continuously, until they are an even brown.

2 Place the bones and raw meat in a roasting tin. Heat in the oven for 35-45 minutes or until a dark even brown. Turn occasionally.

3 Place all ingredients in the pan with the vegetables and about 2.3 L/4 pt water. Simmer gently for at least 3 hours, preferably 8-12 hours, skimming off any surface scum. Top up the water level when necessary. Strain the stock and skim off any remaining fat or lift off with absorbent paper.

FREEZER TIP
Make plenty of stock, skim off the fat and strain, then boil down to a syrupy glaze. Pour into ice-cube trays and freeze for easy defrosting at a later date.

Thickening & Clarifying Stock

The two ways of thickening stock for casseroles and soups are by slaking or making beurre manié.

Slaking
Heat 300 ml/½ pt stock. Mix 1 tsp cornflour or arrowroot with 1 tbls cold water and stir half of the stock into it. Tip the mixture back into the pan and stir over the heat until boiling and thickened.

Using Beurre Manie
Work 15 g/½ oz butter and 15 g/½ oz flour into a smooth paste. Gradually add to 600 ml/1 pt hot stock, whisking until boiling and thickened.

Clarifying Stock
It really is worth setting some time aside and making the effort to clarify the stock as described below. This method will give you a wonderful, crystal clear stock which can be left to set into a decorative jelly.

1 To clarify 1.2 L/2 pt stock, put the stock, 2 egg whites and 2 crushed eggshells in a clean pan. Whisk until the egg-white head rises up in the pan. Remove from heat to allow the head time to subside in the pan.

2 After 10 minutes return to a gentle heat and slowly bring to the boil again, this time not whisking. Heat and rest twice more.

3 Strain through double muslin over a sieve into a large clean bowl. Try to let the egg-white head slip into the sieve first to act as a filter.

WATCHPOINT
Never add salt when making stock. You may want to reduce it and this could make it over-salty.

Foundation Sauce

Once you know how to make sauce espagnole or demi-glace, there's no limit to the number of other sauces you can make. The method for sauce espagnole is described below. Demi-glace (half glaze) refers to the final stage of perfection of a sauce espagnole – when the sauce becomes syrupy.

SAUCE ESPAGNOLE

Preparation time: 20 mins
Cooking time: 1 hour
Makes About 600 ml/1 pt

INGREDIENTS

100 g/4 oz lean bacon, diced
4 carrots, diced
2 large onions, chopped
2 sticks celery, chopped
4 tbls oil
2 tbls flour
1.2 L/2 pt strong brown stock
2 tsp tomato purée
50 g/2 oz mushrooms (or stalks and peelings), chopped
Handful of fresh parsley sprigs
2 bay leaves

1 Gently brown the bacon, carrots, onions and celery in the oil in a saucepan for 10 minutes or until very soft and brown all over.

2 Stir in the flour. Brown again for 2 minutes, stirring and scraping the pan bottom, until russet brown.

3 Add most of the stock, the tomato purée, mushrooms, and herbs. Simmer for 30 minutes.

4 Skim the sauce by tipping in some cold stock, removing scum as it rises. Repeat twice while the sauce simmers.

5 Push juices through a conical strainer. Reduce by half. It is at demi-glace stage when it coats the back of a spoon.

Espagnole Variations

The following classic sauces are variations on the basic sauce espagnole recipe, and are very easy to concoct. They all make enough to serve 4-6 people.

Sauce Robert

Simmer 2 finely chopped shallots in 3 tbls white wine and 1 tbls white wine vinegar until the liquid has almost evaporated and the shallots are soft. Add 1 tbls Dijon mustard and 300 ml/½ pt Sauce Espagnole. Serve with pork chops, mashed potatoes, carrots and Dijon mustard.

Sauce Bordelaise

Sweat 2 chopped shallots in 15g/½ oz butter. Add a glass of claret and reduce to 1 tbls. Add 300 ml/½ pt Sauce Espagnole and a pinch of chopped fresh thyme. Simmer for 15 minutes until thick and syrupy. Serve with sirloin steak, potatoes, mushrooms and mangetout.

Sauce Estragon

Make 150 ml/¼ pt Sauce Espagnole, then add 2 tbls chopped tarragon and 150 ml/¼ pt double cream. Simmer until the sauce is syrupy. Serve with fried chicken and garnish with tarragon.

Sauce Chasseur

Sweat 25 g/1 oz chopped onions or shallots in 15 g/½ oz butter. Add to this 75 g/3 oz sliced mushrooms, and fry for 3 minutes. Add a glass of white wine, boil until almost evaporated. Add 300 ml/½ pt Sauce Espagnole and a seeded, skinned tomato, cut into julienne strips. Serve with châteaubriand steak and vegetables.

Sauce Madère

Add a glass of Madeira to 300 ml/½ pt Sauce Espagnole and allow to simmer for 15 minutes. Beat in 25 g/1 oz butter, bit by bit. Serve on grilled pheasant breast with game chips and fresh vegetables.

Making White & Butter Sauces

I like butter sauces in small quantities for special occasions and the flour-based thickened sauces (white sauce, egg sauce, parsley sauce, cheese sauce) for casual entertaining and family fare. The flour-thickened ones are much better-tempered for a start. They never curdle, they reheat easily, and they taste wonderful.

Equipment
Heavy-based saucepans, especially copper ones, or non-stick ones are best for making sauces. Enamel burns. The best shape of pan for sauces is the sauteuse, which has sloping sides. It splashes less than a straight-sided pan. For a smooth, shiny finish, whizz white sauces briefly in the liquidiser before serving.

Keeping Sauces
To prevent a skin forming on leftover sauces, stretch cling film over the jug (not touching the sauce), or put a wet circle of greaseproof paper on the surface. Remove the paper or cling film and reheat the sauce before serving. Flour-based sauces can be reheated in a microwave (stirring once or twice) or over direct heat. Butter emulsions are difficult to reheat – they tend to separate. It is better to keep them warm in a bain-marie, giving them a stir each time you pass. They are served warm anyway, so will keep well over a pan of hot (rather than boiling) water.

Freezing
Flour-based sauces come out of the freezer in an unhappy state – lumpy and watery. But they will reconstitute perfectly if whisked to the boil. Emulsions can not be frozen – they curdle irredeemably.

Thickening
To make a good white sauce you must get the consistency right – thickening is essential. The three basic techniques for this are reduction, roux and beurre manié.

Reduction is when you boil a sauce until some of the liquid evaporates, leaving less liquid with a more intense flavour.

A roux is a sauce based on equal amounts of fat and flour. As the fat melts in the hot liquid, the flour is evenly distributed. The most usual roux is the 'blond' one, when the flour is fried very briefly in butter. For brown sauces the flour is fried until brown.

Beurre manié translates as 'kneaded butter'. This method is similar to roux in using an equal mixture of flour and butter, but the butter is softened rather than melted. The flour is worked into it to make a thick paste, then small pieces of the paste are whisked into the hot liquid until it is the correct consistency. Use to thicken thin sauces, soups and stews.

Clarifying Butter
Clarified butter is an essential ingredient in many sauces. To clarify butter, line a small sieve with a doubled-over piece of muslin and set over a basin. Place the butter in a small pan over a gentle heat and when it is completely melted, pour it through the muslin and sieve. Discard the foamy white deposits.

Beurre Blanc

Also known as butter sauce, beurre blanc is the most fashionable of chef's sauces and is easy to make. The thing to remember is that when the sauce consists mostly of liquid, you can boil it as you whisk. But, as the butter begins to outweigh the liquid, the heat must be gentler.

BASIC BEURRE BLANC

Preparation time: 5 mins
Cooking time: 15 mins
Makes 175 ml/6 fl oz

INGREDIENTS
225 g/8 oz unsalted butter
1 tbls chopped shallot
3 tbls wine vinegar
Salt and ground white pepper
Squeeze of lemon juice

1 Chill the butter and cut it into 3 lengthways, then across into small blocks. Keep cold.

2 Put the shallot, vinegar and 3 tbls water into a frying-pan and reduce by boiling down to 2 tbls.

3 Lower the heat. Gradually add the butter, piece by piece, whisking vigorously with a wire whisk all the time. The process should take about 5 mins and the sauce should become thick, creamy and pale – rather like a thin hollandaise. Add salt, pepper and lemon juice before serving.

PRUE'S TIP
Chilled butter is easier to work with. It takes a few seconds longer to melt, giving you time to whisk it to an emulsion.

VARIATIONS

• Cheat's Beurre Blanc
Follow the Basic Beurre Blanc recipe, but whisk 3 tbls of stock and a heaped teaspoon of Beurre Manié (see page 259) into the reduced vinegar and bring to the boil before adding the butter. The little bit of flour will help stabilise the sauce.

• Sauce Bâtarde
Make a Velouté Sauce (see page 263) and then whisk in 100 g/4 oz butter, following the same method as for the Basic Beurre Blanc recipe.

• Green Sauce Bâtarde
Liquidise a handful of blanched, well-drained watercress or spinach leaves and stir into the Sauce Bâtarde.

• Weight Watchers' Sauce
Substitute fromage blanc for the butter in the Basic Beurre Blanc recipe. Don't let the mixture boil.

Hollandaise Sauces

To achieve success with hollandaise sauce, keep it at the right temperature – hot enough to slightly thicken the yolks but not hot enough scramble them.

BASIC HOLLANDAISE

Preparation time: 5 mins
Cooking time: 15 mins
Makes 150 ml/¼ pt

INGREDIENTS

3 tbls white wine vinegar
6 peppercorns
1 bay leaf
Blade of mace
2 egg yolks
Salt
100 g/4 oz softened butter
Juice of 1 lemon

1 Boil vinegar, peppercorns, bay leaf and mace in a small heavy saucepan and reduce by boiling to about 1 tbls. Cream the egg yolks with a pinch of salt and a knob of butter in a small bowl. Set this in a bain-marie on a gentle heat. Whisk until slightly thickened, but don't let the water boil.

2 Strain the reduced vinegar onto the egg yolk mixture, whisking constantly. Whisk in the softened butter bit by bit.

3 When the sauce is light and thick, take it off the heat and whisk for 1 minute. Add lemon juice, and salt if necessary. Keep warm until needed by standing the bowl in hot water.

VARIATION

To make hollandaise in a liquidiser, put 1 tbls wine vinegar and 2 tbls lemon juice in a small pan and bring to the boil. Melt 175 g/6 oz clarified butter. Meanwhile, put 3 egg yolks and a pinch of salt in the liquidiser and blend briefly. With the mixer still going, gradually add the hot vinegar and lemon juice. Very slowly (with the machine still running) pour the melted clarified butter onto the egg yolks. Adjust the seasoning and serve.

BEARNAISE SAUCE

Similar to hollandaise, and just as rich, is béarnaise. But the addition of shallots, tarragon and chervil give it a freshness and 'bite' that makes it perfect with meat, chicken or fish dishes.

INGREDIENTS

1 tbls chopped shallots
3 tbls chopped chervil
3 tbls chopped tarragon
1 sprig of thyme
1 bay leaf
2½ tbls vinegar
Salt and ground white pepper
125 g/4½ oz butter, cut in to small pieces
2 egg yolks

1 Put the shallots, thyme, bay leaf, vinegar, salt and pepper and 2 tbls each of the chervil and tarragon in a pan and reduce by two thirds. Allow to cool slightly.

2 Mix the egg yolks with 1 tbls water, add to the pan and whisk over a very low heat. When thickened, gradually add the butter, whisking continuously. Adjust seasoning. Stir in remaining herbs.

Mousseline Sauces

The advent of the liquidiser and the electric whisk has brought back into fashion sauce mousseline which is an airy, almost bubbly sauce. It can still be made in the traditional way though – with a lightweight balloon whisk and a strong whisking arm!

BASIC MOUSSELINE

Preparation time: 2 mins
Cooking time: 10 mins
Makes 150 ml/¼ pt

INGREDIENTS

2 eggs
1 egg yolk
1 tsp white wine vinegar
3 tbls concentrated fish, veal or chicken stock
Salt and ground black pepper
50 g/2 oz unsalted butter, softened

1 Put the eggs, egg yolk, vinegar, stock and seasoning in a bowl and set over a pan of simmering water.

2 Whisk steadily until thick and mousse-like. Take off the heat and whisk in the butter, bit by bit.

3 To serve chilled, continue whisking until the sauce is cold, then refrigerate, whisking occasionally.

WATCHPOINT

Don't let the bottom of the bowl touch the simmering water.

VARIATIONS

Try one of the following variations to the Basic Mousseline recipe:

• Stir in 1-2 tbls of half-whipped cream at the last stage.

• For a Pepper Mousseline, sprinkle over drained green and red peppercorns.

• Use lemon juice instead of stock.

• Pour the sauce onto heated dinner plates and scatter with diced, cooked vegetables before laying cooked chicken or fish on top.

Béchamel Sauces

Béchamel is the French version of white sauce. The milk is infused with onion, mace, peppercorns, bay leaf and parsley before being thickened with a roux.

BASIC BECHAMEL

Preparation time: 10 mins
Cooking time: 10 mins
Makes 300 ml/½ pt

INGREDIENTS

300 ml/½ pt milk
Slice of onion
Blade of mace
Few fresh parsley stalks
4 peppercorns
1 bay leaf
20 g/¾ oz butter
20 g/¾ oz flour
1 tbls cream
Salt and ground white pepper

1 Place the milk with the onion, mace, parsley, peppercorns and bay leaf in a saucepan and slowly bring to simmering point.

2 Reduce the heat and allow the flavour to infuse for about 8-10 minutes. Strain.

3 Make a blond roux: melt the butter in a thick-based saucepan, stir in the flour and cook, stirring, over moderate heat for 1 minute.

4 Remove from the heat. Gradually whisk the infused milk into the roux, a little at a time, adding more milk when the last addition is thoroughly mixed in. Return the sauce to the heat and stir or whisk until boiling. Simmer for 2-3 minutes and then add the cream. Taste and adjust the seasoning accordingly before serving.

VARIATIONS

• Parsley Sauce
Proceed as for the Basic Béchamel recipe, putting the parsley stalks (but not the leaves) into the milk. Finally, add the parsley leaves, finely chopped. Season with salt and pepper.

• Green Sauce
Boil 225 g/8 oz trimmed spinach until wilted. Drain and dry on a cloth. Liquidise with one quantity of Basic Béchamel.

• Mornay Sauce
Make the roux with 40 g/1½ oz butter and 40 g/1½ oz flour and add 600 ml/1 pt milk, as for béchamel. Remove from the heat and add 75 g/3 oz grated Gruyère and 25 g/1 oz grated Parmesan. Season with salt and pepper.

Velouté Sauces

Velouté is made with stock, instead of the milk used in béchamel. Veal, chicken or pale meat stocks are all 'white' stocks rather than beefy brown ones.

BASIC VELOUTE

Preparation time: 15 mins
Cooking time: 10 mins
Makes 300 ml/½ pt

INGREDIENTS

20 g/¾ oz butter
20 g/¾ oz flour
300 ml/½ pt white stock, strained and well skimmed
Salt and ground white pepper
Few drops of lemon juice

1 Make a blond roux: melt the butter in a pan, add the flour and cook, stirring, over a gentle heat until pale biscuit-coloured. Remove the pan from the heat.

2 Gradually whisk in the stock. Bring to the boil, stirring until thickened. Simmer until slightly syrupy. Taste and add seasoning and lemon juice.

POULETTE SAUCE

INGREDIENTS

2 egg yolks
2 tbls cream
250 ml/9 fl oz hot chicken velouté sauce
25 g/1 oz butter, diced
Dash of fresh lemon juice

1 Mix together the egg yolks, cream and 50 ml/2 fl oz of the hot chicken velouté sauce.

2 Pour into a pan and add the remaining velouté sauce. Stir over a gentle heat until blended. Off the heat whisk in the diced butter and a dash of fresh lemon juice before serving.

VARIATIONS

• Fish Velouté
Make fish stock and use instead of white stock in the Basic Veloute recipe.

• Aurore Sauce
Whisk 2 tbls tomato purée and 25 g/1 oz butter into Basic or Fish Velouté.

• Suprême Sauce
Add 125 ml/4 fl oz double cream to one quantity of Basic Velouté and boil hard, stirring, to reduce and thicken.

• Microwave Velouté
Using the same ingredients as for Basic Velouté, melt the butter in a microwave-proof jug at HIGH (100%) for 30 seconds. Stir in the flour. Whisk in the stock and cook for a further 3 minutes, whisking every 30 seconds.

PRUE'S TIP

Long slow simmering produces a shiny velouté sauce with a delicious concentrated flavour.

CHEESE COOKERY

I think if I had to forego all but one of the great protein sources (meat, fish, eggs and cheese) the one I'd hold onto is cheese.

Cheese please

The flavours and textures provided by cheese are as varied as one could wish, and the list of uses for the cook is endless. Cheese grates, crumbles, melts, stretches, bakes, grills – even fries. It is good on its own, with salads, with starch (think of macaroni cheese or a hefty wholemeal sandwich), good as a delicate mousse or a silky sauce, good in pastry and good in stuffings. It mixes well with fish, poultry, fruit or fresh vegetables. I'd say cheese is pretty nearly indispensable, and I've no intention of dispensing with any of it. Life just wouldn't be the same without it.

Keep it cool

There's a lot of rubbish talked about storing cheese, with admonitions not to refrigerate it. This is the crassest nonsense. The maker refrigerates it, the distributor refrigerates it, the wholesaler refrigerates it and the shop you buy it from refrigerates it. It is just plain daft to then leave it in a warm kitchen to go sweaty and rancid before you eat it. If the cheese is in perfect condition when you buy it, the best way to keep it that way is well-wrapped in the fridge. Even runny-in-the-middle cheeses like Camembert and Brie should be served coolish. Left in a warm room they will flow all over the place in an hour or so.

European Cheeses

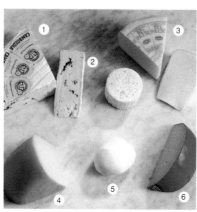

1 Ricotta A soft, unripened cheese from Italy with a mild flavour, similar to cottage cheese. Sold in an upturned basket shape from the basket it was moulded in.

2 Goat's cheese There are numerous types, the flavour depending on the age of the cheese. Young cheeses are soft, maturing to a harder texture with moulds developing on the surface. Illustrated here is Crottin de chèvre.

3 Jarlsberg A semi-hard cheese from Norway. Mildly flavoured and with fairly largish holes.

4 Parmesan A hard cheese used in Italian cooking. Older cheeses, matured for up to 3 years, are used for grating, while younger cheeses can be eaten at the table.

5 Tilsit A semi-hard cheese with a supple texture, often with small holes. It has a strong flavour and is made in Germany.

6 Feta A soft, unpressed Greek white cheese, it can be made with goat's, cow's or sheep's milk. Sold in brine, it is mild and salty.

1 Cambozola This creamy, mild, blue Brie is not often used in cooking – it is more frequently a star of the cheeseboard.

2 Peppered Boursin This creamy soft cheese is perfect for sauces, and is also delicious as a spread on toast.

3 Bel paese A semi-soft, good melting cheese from Italy. Very creamy with a dense texture and mild taste.

4 Gouda A semi-hard Dutch cheese with a yellow wax coating. When young it has a mild flavour. It is also available matured when the flavour is much stronger.

5 Mozzarella A soft mild cheese, often sold in little purse shapes immersed in brine to keep them moist. Can be made with cow's or buffalo's milk.

6 Edam Another semi-hard cheese from Holland, sold in a large ball covered in red wax. Suitable for almost any dish, it has a bland flavour, which like Gouda, strengthens on maturing.

The Perfect Cheeseboard

The trick to producing an appetising cheeseboard is to have a few large pieces of cheese rather than lots of little bits – which tend to look like off-cuts or leftovers. A large slice of one good cheese is better than 4 small ones.

PRUE'S TIP

Choose interesting fruit that goes well with cheese, like figs, fresh dates, crispy apples, pears and grapes. Leave plenty of space for cutting the cheeses and decorate with fig and vine leaves.

Melting Cheese

Melted cheese is unbeatably warming and sustaining on winter nights. It is also highly indigestible. Do not eat dishes such as raclette or fondue at bedtime and do not wash them down with ice-cold drinks. The cheese will form an indigestible lump in the tum, hardened by icy beer or wine.

Raclette

Raclette is cheese toasted until it melts and drips. Gruyère, Emmental or Tilsit are the usual cheeses. Swiss restaurants often have a special toaster that grills the cut half of a cheese. More simply, however, melt the thinly sliced cheese in a buttered dish in the oven.

Fondue

A good fondue is a lovely way to feed friends informally. Classic Gruyère fondue is the best but almost any cheese will produce a smooth, hot dip. Beware of letting your bread fall off the fork into the fondue pot. Traditionally women have to kiss every man in the room, and men buy the next bottle of wine!

PRUE'S TIP
To prevent curdling, stir 1 tsp cornflour mixed with 1 tbls milk into the fondue.

SWISS CHEESE FONDUE

Preparation time: 5 mins
Cooking time: 7 mins
Serves 4

INGREDIENTS

½ a clove of garlic
150 ml/¼ pt dry white wine
225 g/8 oz Gruyère, diced
Ground white pepper
Pinch of grated nutmeg
1 tbls kirsch
Cubes of bread, to serve

1 Rub the inside of the fondue pot with the cut clove of garlic. Put the pan on the burner.

2 Pour in the wine and add the cheese. Add pepper and a grating of nutmeg. Stir while bringing gently to the boil.

3 Add the kirsch and simmer for 2 minutes. Serve guests with long-handled forks and cubes of bread.

Other Cheese Treats

Potted Cheese

Mix 175 g/6 oz leftover cheese (grated or mashed) with 75 g/3 oz softened butter, pepper, salt and chopped fresh herbs. Press into 2 ramekins. Serve on toast. If not for immediate use, omit the herbs and cover the top with a thin layer of clarified butter.

Camembert Fritters

Cut Camembert into small wedges. Dip the cheese first in egg, then in dried breadcrumbs. Place in the freezer and chill until almost frozen. Deep-fry in oil at high temperature (190 C/375 F) until the coating is golden brown. Drain and serve with a sweet, fruity sauce. Garnish with lamb's lettuce.

Party Brie

Slice a round Italian loaf of bread horizontally. Hollow out the bottom half. Sprinkle with fresh thyme and fit a small whole Brie into it. Replace the bread lid and bake at 180 C/350 F/Gas 4 for about 15 mins to heat the bread and just warm the cheese. Serve in slices with grapes and green salad leaves.

PRUE'S TIP
Use a Camembert or small Brie in a cottage loaf to make enough to serve 8-10 people.

EGG COOKERY

Eggs are extremely versatile and nutritious. They are full of protein, vitamins and minerals and relatively low in calories – an average egg has only 80. Eggs come in many types and sizes, from tiny quail eggs to large goose and duck eggs. The more unusual kinds may only be available through farms.

Bacteria are present in almost all food and eggs are no exception. But they are dangerous only if allowed to reach toxic levels. Time, warmth and moisture all promote the growth of bacteria, so use only fresh eggs (check the sell-by date) and always store them in your fridge.

Babies, young children, elderly people and pregnant mums are most susceptible to food poisoning, so eliminate any risks by making sure eggs they eat are cooked thoroughly. Worries about raw yolks in mayonnaise can be allayed by adding vinegar to the yolk, which will kill any bacteria present. Meringue and icings aren't a problem, as the high proportion of sugar makes a hostile environment for bacteria. Never use old, dirty or cracked eggs and make sure that all equipment that comes into contact with them – including your hands – is thoroughly clean.

To test for freshness, put an egg into a bowl of cold water. Fresh eggs will lie flat on the bottom, 2-3 week old eggs will tilt up and bad eggs will float.

Omelettes

Make sure you use a heavy-based pan when cooking omelettes so the heat is evenly distributed.

FRENCH OMELETTE

Preparation time: 5 mins
Cooking time: 4-5 mins
Serves 2

INGREDIENTS

4 eggs
Salt and ground black pepper
15 g/½ oz butter

1 Break the eggs into a bowl and stir together with a fork. Stir in 2 tbls water and season. Heat an empty heavy-based pan, add the butter and melt over a medium heat. Swirl to coat the base and sides of the pan then pour in the eggs.

2 Stir with the back of a fork until starting to set, then pull in the sides, tipping the pan to let the raw egg run underneath. Cook for 2-3 minutes. Fold in three and serve.

Savoury Soufflés

Contrary to popular belief, soufflés are extremely easy to make. Start with these foolproof individual soufflés. They use a basic cheese soufflé mixture, baked once, then soaked in cream and baked again.

CHEESE SOUFFLES

Preparation time: 30 mins + cooling
Cooking time: 35 mins
Serves 6

INGREDIENTS

300 ml/½ pt milk
Slice of onion
Pinch of nutmeg
50 g/2 oz butter, plus extra for greasing
50 g/2 oz flour
Pinch of English mustard powder
175 g/6 oz mature Cheddar cheese, grated
4 egg yolks
Salt and ground black pepper
5 egg whites
350 ml/12 fl oz single cream

1 Preheat oven to 180 C/350 F/Gas 4. Heat the milk slowly with the onion slice and nutmeg, then strain. Grease 6 small teacups.

2 Melt the butter then stir in the flour and mustard. Cook for 30 seconds and remove from the heat. Stir in the milk, return to the heat and stir for 30 seconds. Add 100 g/4 oz of the cheese, the egg yolks and salt and pepper. Whisk the egg whites until stiff then fold into the cheese mixture.

3 Fill two thirds of each cup with the cheese mixture. Stand the cups in a roasting tin. Pour boiling water into the tin then bake for 15 minutes or until the soufflés are risen and set. Allow them to sink and cool.

4 Set the oven to 220 C/425 F/Gas 7. Butter a shallow ovenproof serving dish. Turn the soufflés out then put them upside down on the dish. Sprinkle the remaining cheese on top. Season the cream with salt and pepper and pour it over the soufflés. Bake for 10 minutes until a pale golden colour.

Pancakes & Crêpes

The secret of a good pancake lies in the batter. Once you can make a smooth batter then elegant crêpes are within reach. Making a perfect French crêpe – so thin that tossing it is nigh impossible – is a skill easily mastered. But you do need an even-bottomed frying-pan. A heavy one is best, because you can make thick pancakes like drop scones in it too. They would burn in a thin pan. I use the same frying-pan, an ancient iron one, for everything – omelettes and crêpes included. The idea that omelette and crêpe pans should be kept just for these things is a myth.

BASIC PANCAKES

Preparation time: 5 mins
+ resting
Makes 450 ml/¾ pt

INGREDIENTS
100 g/4 oz flour
Pinch of salt
1 large egg
1 egg yolk
300 ml/½ pt milk
1 tbls oil, plus extra for greasing

1 Sieve the flour and salt together into a large bowl and make a well in the centre of the flour.

2 Into this well, break the egg then add the egg yolk and pour in a little of the milk.

3 Using a whisk, mix the egg and milk together and then gradually draw in the flour from the sides as you beat in more milk until you have a batter which is the consistency of half-whipped cream. Beat the batter until smooth then stir in the oil.

4 Continue to beat in the remaining milk – the batter should now be the consistency of thin cream. Cover the bowl and set the batter aside for 30 minutes – this will give the cooked batter more lightness.

5 Heat a frying-pan. When hot, wipe lightly with a little oil and pour in 25-35 ml/1-1½ fl oz batter. Swirl the pan around so the batter is spread evenly over the base. Place over the heat and cook for 1 minute.

6 Slide a palette knife under the pancake, flip it over and cook the other side until golden brown. Slide the finished pancake onto a plate. Repeat the process with the remaining batter.

BASIC CREPES

Preparation time: 5 mins
+ resting
Cooking time: 20 mins
Makes 16 crepes

INGREDIENTS
100 g/4 oz flour
1 tbls caster sugar
3 large eggs
300 ml/½ pt milk
75 g/3 oz butter, melted, plus extra for greasing

1 Sieve the flour into a large bowl and stir in the caster sugar. Make a well in the centre and break the eggs into it.

2 Add a little milk to the eggs and mix them together lightly. Gradually draw the flour in from around the sides and beat in more milk until the batter reaches the consistency of half-whipped cream. Beat well, stir in the melted butter and remaining milk.

3 Set the batter aside for 30 minutes, brush pan with melted butter and then cook as for the Basic Pancakes.

VARIATIONS
Vary the Basic Crêpe recipe with one of the following:
• Replace 2 tbls of the milk with brandy, Grand Marnier, rum or kirsch.
• Add the finely grated zest of 1 large orange or lemon.
• Add ½ tsp allspice to the flour.

Other Batters

Once you've mastered this basic batter try adding fruit and flavourings for variety.

BASIC FRITTER BATTER

Preparation time: 10 mins
+ resting

INGREDIENTS
100 g/4 oz flour
Pinch of salt
1 large egg, separated
150 ml/¼ pt milk
1 tbls oil or melted butter

1 Sieve the flour and salt together into a bowl. Make a well and add the egg yolk and milk to make a thick batter.

2 Beat until smooth, add the rest of the milk and oil or melted butter and set aside for 30 minutes. Whisk the egg white. Fold the egg white into the batter and use it immediately.

PRUE'S TIP
It is much quicker and easier to make Basic Fritter Batter in a blender or food processor. Simply put all the ingredients, except the egg white, into the machine and whizz for a short time. Transfer the batter to a bowl, whisk the egg whites with a hand whisk until stiff but not dry and fold in.

YORKSHIRE PUDDINGS

INGREDIENTS
100 g/4 oz flour
A pinch of salt
1 or 2 eggs
Approximately 150 ml/¼ pt milk
Beef dripping, for greasing

1 Sift flour and salt into a bowl. Make a well, add the eggs and milk and beat vigorously. Stand for 1 hour.

2 Grease patty tins with dripping. Pop in the hot oven when your beef joint comes out – by the time the meat has rested they will be puffed up and browned to perfection.

PIZZA & PASTA

It's easy to find an instant appetite for freshly made pizza and pasta with their delicious toppings and sauces.

Pizza treats

Start with a traditional yeast dough base (or use a packet of bread mix). Alternatively, use an incredibly quick scone base which is cooked in a frying-pan, then covered with a smooth tomato sauce and topped with your favourite ingredients. Any of the following ingredients can be used for the topping: sliced button mushrooms, onion, peppers, pepperoni sausage, cheese, sweetcorn, ham, crumbled bacon, prawns, crab, tuna, spinach, artichoke hearts, eggs, chicken, beef, anchovies, olives, capers and herbs.

Pasta perfection

Fresh pasta is now readily available in supermarkets and delicatessens and does have a special taste and texture – really quite different from the dried stuff. However, they can be substituted for each other. Fresh pasta is generally sold as tagliatelle, lasagne sheets, ravioli and tortellini. Dried pasta comes in many different shapes and sizes.

Home-made pasta is even better and is extremely simple to make.

Make your own

There really is nothing to making your own pasta dough, it's simply a matter of mixing flour and eggs together and then rolling out the dough before cutting and curling it into a range of shapes and sizes. The most important thing to remember is to roll the pasta as thinly as possible. Thick pasta tastes like it looks – heavy. For a special meal try colouring the dough before rolling with spinach or tomato purée, or even squid ink.

Pasta machines

Speciality kitchen stores sell hand-operated pasta machines which work like an old fashioned mangle. You feed a flattened piece of dough through the machine several times until it is really thin. If you make a lot of pasta, there are electric machines which will do the whole job for you. These have attachments to make pasta of different shapes and sizes.

Types of Pasta

Sheets & Strips

1 Lasagne Large sheets of dried pasta, either plain or verde (green) or with holes.
2 Lasagnette Large sheets of pasta, like lasagne but with wavy edges.
3 Pappardelle Similar to lasagnette, but in long narrow strips.
4 Cannelloni Large hollow tubes, suitable for stuffing.
5 Tagliatelle Narrow pasta ribbons, sold in round 'nests'.

Shaped Pasta

1 Pastini Tiny shapes like grains of rice, usually added to soups.
2 Vemicelli Thin spaghetti, sold in 'nests'.
3 Spaghetti Long thin strands of pasta.
4 Bigoli Whole-wheat spaghetti.
5 Farfalle Bows and butterflies, available in various sizes..

6 Malloreddus Seashells with wavy edges.
7 Conchiglie Shell-like shapes.
8 Lumache Little snail-shell shapes.
9 Penne Quills, either ridged or smooth.
10 Rigatoni Short ridged tubes.
11 Fusilli Twists, shown here coloured with spinach and tomato.

Making Pasta Dough

When making plain egg pasta, try to use fresh eggs – golden yolks will give the pasta a lovely sunny colour.

BASIC PASTA DOUGH

Preparation time: 1¾ hours
+ drying
Makes 450 g/1 lb

INGREDIENTS
450 g/1 lb strong white flour,
plus extra for dusting

| 1 tsp salt |
| 4 eggs |
| 1 tbls olive oil |

1 Sift the flour and salt into a large bowl, make a well in the centre. Add eggs, oil and 3 tbls cold water.

2 Gradually work the flour into the liquid until it holds together. Knead the dough on a chopping board or work surface. Using the heel of your hand, push the dough away from you, then pull it back with your fingertips. Give the dough a quarter of a turn each time. Continue kneading the dough for 15 minutes until smooth and elastic: little air bubbles under the surface will indicate when it is ready.

3 Wrap the dough loosely in a polythene bag and leave at room temperature for 1 hour, or overnight in the fridge.

4 Divide the dough into four pieces and keep three in the bag while you are working with the first. Roll out on a floured surface as thinly as possible. Leave for 10 minutes before cutting.

VARIATIONS
To make green pasta, follow the Basic Pasta Dough recipe, but use 350 g/12 oz strong white flour, ¾ tsp salt, 2 eggs, 1 tbls double cream and about 5 tbls puréed cooked spinach. To make red pasta, blend the eggs and oil with 3 tbls tomato purée before adding to the flour.

Shaping Pasta

Shaping Tagliatelle

Roll the sheet up like a Swiss roll and using a sharp knife, cut across into 12 mm/½ in widths. Unroll them as you cut them. Lay on a clean cloth, cover with another cloth and leave to dry for a minimum of 1 hour, but not longer than overnight.

Shaping Lasagne

Cut the dough with a sharp knife into neat rectangles about 6.5 cm/2½ in by 12.5 cm/5 in. Lay on a clean cloth, cover and leave to dry out as for tagliatelle.

Shaping Tortellini

Use a 5 cm/2 in smooth-edged cutter to stamp out little circles from the dough. Place 1 tsp of filling on each circle, fold over and seal to make semi-circles. You may need a little beaten egg or water to seal the edges. Wrap each one around your index finger and press the ends together. Lay on a clean cloth, cover and leave to dry out, as for tagliatelle.

To make the stuffing for tortellini, gently fry 1 skinned chicken breast in 25 g/1 oz butter and 1 tbls oil for 10 minutes. Chop roughly then pass through a mincer with 75 g/3 oz cooked ham and 75 g/3 oz mortadella sausage. Add 75 g/3 oz grated Parmesan cheese and 2 beaten eggs. Mix to a smooth paste. Cool, then chill until needed.

Cooking & Serving Pasta

Both fresh and dried pasta are cooked and served in the same way. Allow 50-75 g/2-3 oz dried pasta and anything up to 225 g/8 oz fresh pasta per person.

Cooking

There are two ways of cooking pasta. One is to cook it in boiling water and the other, which only applies to large sheets of pasta such as lasagna and lasagnette, is to layer it with a sauce and bake it in the oven. Tubes should be cooked before stuffing. When using dried pasta, look for the brands labelled 'no cook'. These will be as happy in the sauce as the fresh one.

To cook in water, for every 450 g/1 lb pasta, bring 3.4 L/6 pt water and 2 tsp salt to the boil in a large pan. Add 1 tbls oil to stop the pasta from sticking together. When the water is at a rolling boil, add the pasta. Pasta shapes are gradually emptied into the pan of boiling water (slowly, to

maintain the temperature) but long shapes like spaghetti need to be held in a bundle and gently eased into the pan. As it softens it will relax into the water. Once it is submerged, give it a stir with a fork to loosen it. Never cover pasta while it is cooking – it will inevitably boil over in a starchy froth.

Cook dried pasta for 10-12 minutes and fresh pasta for 3-8, depending on the size of the strips or shapes.

Microwaving

To microwave dried pasta, pour 1.7 L/3 pt boiling water into a microwave-proof bowl. Heat on HIGH (100%) for 2 minutes. Add salt, oil and 225 g/8 oz pasta. Cook on HIGH (100%) uncovered for 5 minutes. Cover, stand for 5 minutes. To microwave fresh pasta, cook uncovered in the boiling water on HIGH (100%) for 1 minute. Stand for 1-2 minutes.

Serving

The pasta should be soft but firm to the bite. Drain in a colander, tip back into the pan, add a knob of butter and shake over a low heat for a minute. The Italians have a general rule that says smooth sauces should be served with pasta shapes and narrow tubes, while thicker sauces are used with flat pasta.

Pizza Toppings

One 23 cm/9 in pizza will serve one person as a meal, or can serve up to four people as a snack.

Basic Tomato Sauce

Fry 1 chopped onion and 1 crushed garlic clove in 2 tbls olive oil until soft. Add 450 g/1 lb skinned and chopped fresh tomatoes or 400g/14 oz tinned tomatoes, 1 tsp dried herbs (basil, oregano, parsley) 1 tsp sugar, salt and black pepper to taste. Simmer for 15 minutes then sieve.

Siciliana

Spread the base with tomato sauce. Top with green, red and yellow peppers which have been softened in a little olive oil, slices of pepperoni sausage and sliced button mushrooms, then sliced tomatoes and sliced mozzarella.

Nettuno

Spread the base with tomato sauce and top with tuna, grated cheese, anchovies, tomato slices and black olives. Garnish with basil.

Fiorentina

Spread the base with tomato sauce. Top with sliced tomatoes and cooked red, yellow and green peppers. Add cooked spinach and sliced mozzarella. Bake for 15 minutes, then break an egg on top. Cook until egg is set.

Quattro Formaggio

Spread the base thinly with tomato sauce. Sprinkle grated Gruyère on to a quarter of the dough, crumbled Gorgonzola, grated Parmesan and sliced bel paese onto the other three quarters. Make a cross of anchovies, bake and then garnish with a sprig of fresh basil.

Traditional Pizza Bases

This dough is made with yeast – use fresh, dried or fast action.

BASIC PIZZA BASE

Preparation time: 2 hours
Cooking time: 15-20 mins
Makes Four 23 cm/9 in bases

INGREDIENTS

700 g/1 lb 8 oz strong white flour
2 tsp salt
20 g/¾ oz fresh yeast or
10 g/⅓ oz dried yeast and ½ tsp sugar or
1 sachet (6 g/¼ oz) fast action dried yeast
Flour, for dusting
Oil, for brushing

1 Sift the flour and salt into a large warmed bowl. If using fresh yeast, mash it with 150 ml/¼ pt of lukewarm water and leave in a warm place for 10-15 minutes until frothy. If using dried yeast, add the sugar to the water, sprinkle over the yeast and leave until frothy. If using fast action dried yeast simply stir into the flour.

2 Add the yeast mixture and 300 ml/½ pt lukewarm water to the flour to make 450 ml/¾ pt total.

3 Mix to a dough in the bowl then knead on a lightly floured surface. Push the dough away from you with the heel of your hand. Use your fingers to bring the dough up and towards you then push away again. Knead for 10 minutes until smooth and elastic.

4 Shape into a neat ball, put it into a lightly-oiled bowl and cover with cling film. Leave in a warm place for about 1 hour or until doubled in size.

5 Knead the dough again until smooth then divide into 4 pieces. Roll each piece into a 23 cm/9 in circle and place on greased baking sheets. Leave for 20 minutes to rise again.

6 Brush with oil, cover with the chosen topping and bake at 220 C/425 F/Gas 7 for 15-20 minutes until lightly browned.

PRUE'S TIP
There is no need to add sugar to fresh yeast to activate it. Always add fast action dried yeast directly with the flour.

Pan-Cooked Pizza Bases

This pizza with its crisp, scone-like base, is cooked in a frying-pan – perfect when time is tight.

BASIC PAN-PIZZA BASE

Preparation time: 10 mins
Cooking time: 20 mins
Makes One 23 cm/9 in base

INGREDIENTS

175 g/6 oz self-raising flour
½ tsp salt
40 g/1½ oz butter
1 egg
2 tbls milk
Oil, for frying

1 Sift the flour and salt into a bowl. Add the butter and rub in until the mixture looks like breadcrumbs.

2 Add the egg and milk and mix to a dough. Form into a ball then roll out to a 23 cm/9 in circle.

3 Brush a large frying-pan with oil and lift the dough into it. Neaten the edges then cook over a high heat for about 5-7 minutes or until the base has browned evenly.

4 Brush the top with oil, cover with the chosen topping and place under hot grill for about 10 minutes or until the topping is cooked.

VARIATION
Add some chopped fresh or dried herbs to the dough before cooking.

BREAD

Doughs & don'ts

For every person who finds bread making as easy as pie, there's one who thinks it's beyond them.

The first thing to discover is why people fail with bread. I did for years for three reasons. The first was that I bought the wrong flour – good bread needs strong flour. The second reason was that the oven heat was too low which meant the crust was thick and the bread coarse and crumbly. Thirdly, I believed those recipes that tell you bread is cooked as soon as it 'sounds hollow when tapped'. Even half-cooked bread sounds hollow to me. I now wait until the loaf feels light as well.

Once you know your ingredients and have mastered the techniques, you'll find that bread making is simple, and can even be therapeutic.

Using yeast

This is the traditional raising agent for making bread. Fresh yeast looks like putty and has a pleasant, sweet smell. Avoid stale yeast which has turned brown and dry. It will have lost its efficiency. Store fresh yeast in the fridge in small plastic bags for up to 2 weeks or freeze it, wrapped, for 2-3 months. Freeze in convenient 25 g/1 oz

pieces; when ready to use, thaw for 20-30 minutes. Dried yeast needs to be reconstituted before using by mixing it with a little sugar and some warm liquid. Leave in a warm place for 15-20 minutes until frothy. Fast-action dried yeast can be stirred straight into the flour. Don't keep opened sachets for more than 4 months.

Get the ratio right

For every 1.4 kg/3 lb of strong white flour, use 25 g/1 oz fresh yeast or 15 g/½ oz dried yeast mixed with 900 ml/1½ pt warm liquid. For the same amount of brown flour, use 50 g/2 oz fresh yeast or 25 g/1 oz dried yeast mixed with 900 ml/1½ pt warm liquid.

Go for gluten

It is the gluten in flour that gives dough its stretchability and makes it rise, so choose high gluten strong or bread flours. Whole-wheat/wholemeal flour consists of the whole wheat grain and makes a fairly dense loaf with a pleasant nutty taste. Wheatmeal/brown flour has a small amount of the bran and germ removed. Loaves made with this have a smooth crust and lighter texture. Strong plain white flour is excellent for light, airy bread and sweet loaves. Rye flour contains no gluten. Mix with strong white flour.

Other ingredients

Salt adds flavour and prevents the yeast from working too quickly and spoiling the texture of the loaf. Measure accurately: too much stops the yeast from working properly, too little produces a tacky dough which is difficult to handle. A standard proportion is 1 tsp per 450 g/1 lb flour.

Sugar acts as food for the yeast and helps the dough get off to a good start. It is especially important when using dried yeast. Fat or oil adds flavour, gives a silky texture and helps it keep. Either water or milk is also needed – the temperature should be tepid – about 38 C/100 F.

Techniques & Tips

Adding Flour to Liquid

Prepare the yeast liquid according to the instructions on page 273, then stir in the flour using a round-ended knife. Form into a ball. The dough should be soft and dry enough not to stick.

Kneading

This distributes the yeast throughout the dough and stretches the gluten. Stretch the dough out on a floured surface, fold it in two, squash it back into a ball, give it a quarter turn and then repeat. Continue in this way for 10 minutes.

Rising

Shape the kneaded dough into a ball and place in a lightly oiled bowl. Cover with a piece of oiled cling film or place in an oiled plastic bag to prevent a skin forming. Leave until doubled in size This will take 1-1½ hours in an airing cupboard, 1½-2 hours at room temperature, 4 hours in a cool place, such as larder and up to 12 hours in the fridge. Don't leave in too warm a place or allow to over-rise since this will spoil the dough.

Microwaving

Use the microwave to speed up rising. Place kneaded dough in a bowl, cover with cling film and microwave on HIGH (100%) for 15 seconds. Set aside for 5-10 minutes, then repeat. You can use the microwave for the second proving as well, but don't use metal loaf tins.

Knocking Back & Shaping

Tip the dough out and work until back to its original size. Add flavourings. Shape and place in tins or on baking trays. These should be greased and dusted with flour.

Proving

Cover dough with oiled cling film or a plastic bag and leave in a warm place until doubled in size – about 30 minutes for rolls and ¾-1 hour for a large loaf.

Baking

The rule of thumb is the plainer the dough the hotter the oven. Even a rich dough needs a moderately hot oven (about 190 C/375 F/Gas 5), while plain loaves should be cooked in a very hot oven (about 230 C/450 F/Gas 8). To test if it is cooked, turn out of the tin. The loaf should sound hollow when tapped and feel light.

Making Bread

If it's your first time making bread, try this basic recipe first. Once you've got the hang of it, try experimenting with a variety of different flavourings and shapes – the scope for invention is endless.

BASIC WHITE BREAD

Preparation time: 25 mins
+ proving
Cooking time: 35-45 mins
Makes 3 loaves

INGREDIENTS

25 g/1 oz fresh yeast or 15 g/½ oz dried yeast and 2 tsp caster sugar
2 tbls oil, plus extra to grease
4 tsp salt
1 tbls sugar
1.4 kg/3 lb strong white flour

1 Mix fresh yeast with 900 ml/1½ pt warm water or mix dried yeast with caster sugar and 450 ml/¾ pt water and leave in a warm place for 15 minutes.

2 Pour yeast liquid or, if using dried yeast, the yeast liquid plus 450 ml/¾ pt warm water, into a large bowl and stir in the oil, salt and sugar. Add 90% of the strong white flour and mix well to make a soft dough, adding more flour if necessary.

3 Form into a ball and knead for about 10 minutes until smooth and elastic. Place in an oiled bowl, cover with oiled cling film and leave to rise until doubled in size.

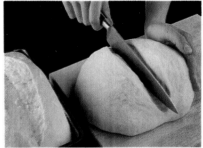

4 Grease and flour three 900 g/2 lb loaf tins if using. Knock back dough and knead for 2-3 minutes. Divide into three and place in the tins or shape into rounds and place on greased baking tray. Cover loosely with oiled cling film and leave the dough to prove in a warm place for ¾-1 hour or until doubled in size. Preheat the oven to 220 C/425 F/Gas 7. Make a lengthways cut in each and dust with flour.

5 Bake for 35-45 minutes. To test if cooked, turn out into oven-gloved hand. It should feel light and sound hollow when tapped. Cool on a wire rack.

PRUE'S TIP
If you're short of time or energy a good food processor will knead about 225-350 g/8-12 oz of dough in 1 minute.

Variations

Toppings
Normally toppings are added before the final rising but they can also be added just before baking. Be gentle when brushing toppings onto a loaf so as not to knock out the air. For a shiny top use beaten egg. Egg yolk alone gives a particularly shiny finish. Milk gives a softer, slightly silky texture, while sugar syrup gives shine and sweetness. Brush on just before baking or alternatively wait until the loaf is three-quarters cooked, then glaze it and return to the oven. Caraway or poppy seeds can be thickly sprinkled on sweet or plain loaves. Brush the loaf with water and then scatter the seeds on top.

Savoury Flavours
Knead chopped olives, chopped walnuts, flaked almonds, pine kernels, caraway or sunflower seeds into Basic White Bread or Traditional Brown Bread after the first rising. Alternatively, stir herbs or spices thoroughly into the flour before adding it to the yeast liquid.

Sweet Flavours
Add sultanas, chopped dried apricots or dates plus mixed spice or cinnamon to any basic dough.

Cheese & Onion Bread
For one large loaf, take ⅓ of the risen Basic White Bread dough, and knead into it 50 g/2 oz grated Cheddar cheese and 1 small chopped, lightly fried and cooled onion. Shape and leave to prove. Before baking, brush with beaten egg and sprinkle with about 25 g/1 oz grated cheese.

Basic Milk Bread
For three large loaves follow the recipe for Basic White Bread but rub 100 g/4 oz butter into the flour instead of oil. Make up liquid using half warm water and half warm milk and add to the flour. Put the dough into three prepared 900 g/2 lb tins and brush with beaten egg or milk before cooking at 200 C/400 F/Gas 6 for 55 minutes. For richer loaves, add 2 lightly beaten eggs.

Traditional Brown Bread
Follow the recipe for Basic White Bread but use 900 g/2 lb brown flour and 450 g/1 lb strong white flour. For Granary Bread use half strong white and half granary flour.

Rolls
Shape one quantity of Basic White Bread dough into 36 balls. Brush with beaten egg, sprinkle with poppy, sesame or caraway seeds and place on prepared baking trays. Cover with oiled cling film and leave to rise for about 30 minutes. Bake at 220 C/425 F/Gas 7 for 25-30 minutes. For crusty rolls, omit toppings and brush with water straight after baking.

Bap Rolls
Use half the quantity of Milk Bread dough. Shape risen dough into eighteen 12 mm/½ in thick rounds. Leave to prove then dust with flour. Bake for 15 minutes at 200 C/400 F/Gas 6. Cover with a towel after cooking for a soft crust.

PASTRIES & PIES

It used to be said that you could tell a good cook by her pastry. Today, with perfectly good frozen and chilled pastries available in every supermarket, home pastry making is in decline. Yet real, homemade pastry is a delicious treat, and a skill well worth mastering.

There are so many rules in pastry books that you could be forgiven for thinking the process is so packed with danger and difficulty that the best answer might be a trip to the supermarket. Not so. Pastry making is very easy, and most rules are breakable. I used to know a countrywoman, Bett, who broke them all, yet made the most wonderful pastry. She never used a recipe, never sifted the flour, only bothered to rub the fat into the flour until it resembled small rocks rather than fine breadcrumbs and never measured any of the ingredients!

With that sort of spirit but a less cavalier technique, perfect pastry can be yours.

Types of pastry

Choux pastry is probably the easiest to make provided you take care to follow the exact quantities. It can be used for the most stunning of pâtisseries, from éclairs to light-as-air profiteroles.

Rich shortcrust pastry has a deliciously light texture and a slightly sweet flavour. For more golden pastry, use wholemeal flour or add 1 tsp of cinnamon or mixed spice. Rich almond pastry is also light and deliciously crumbly, and can be made simply and successfully providing, as always, water, mixing implements and hands are kept as cold as possible.

The joy of layered pastries such as flaky and puff is in their texture. For maximum volume you get maximum lightness – fine layers piled one upon the other and seemingly held up by air.

As far as savoury pastries are concerned, proper old-fashioned suet crust – crumbly, savoury crisp on the outside and soft and moist inside – is an English speciality I'd hate to see disappear. The French pâte à pâte is the greedy gastronome's answer to English hot-water crust. It is rich and delicious, but robust enough to hold a heavy filling. And for something a little different, try a simple potato pastry.

Lining Tins & Baking Blind

Baking Blind

This is when you pre-cook a pastry case before the filling is added. The uncooked pastry case is pricked with a fork, lined with greaseproof paper and weighed down with baking beans. This stops the case bubbling up while cooking. Baking blind will stop the pastry from becoming soggy when it is filled: also, a filling will often cook more quickly than a case.

Baking Times

Blind bake almond and shortcrust pastry cases according to the following chart. Pre-heat the oven to 220 C/425 F/Gas 7.

15-18 cm/6-7 in flans	20 mins
20-25 cm/8-10 in flans	25 mins
30-35 cm/12-14 in flans	30 mins
Tartlets/barquettes	10-15 mins

Lining Tins

Roll the pastry out onto a lightly floured surface. The best thickness is about 3 mm/⅛ in. It is important not to stretch the pastry to fit the tin – ease it gently into the tin, pushing it down into the sides. If time allows, chill the lined tin in the fridge before baking blind to firm it up and help it keep its shape.

Lining Large Flan Tins

1 Roll out the pastry, then flop half back over the rolling pin. Lift the pastry onto the tin.

2 Ease the pastry into the tin, pushing it gently downwards into the sides.

3 Simply roll the pin over the tin to trim off the excess pastry. This pushes the pastry more firmly into the sides.

4 Prick all over the base of the lined tin with a fork. Line with greaseproof paper and fill will baking beans.

5 Chill the lined tin for 30 minutes before baking or wrap with cling film and freeze. Thaw for 15 minutes and allow 10 minutes extra cooking time.

6 About 10 minutes before the end of cooking, remove beans and paper. Return the tin to the oven. This will give the pastry plenty of time to dry out.

Lining Tartlet Tins

Barquette (boat-shaped) moulds lined with pastry and filled with fruit are ideal for party desserts. Lift the pastry onto tins and ease it into them. Trim off excess. The pastry should be pricked, then the tins lined and filled with beans.

Once the bases are cooked, try brushing them with melted chocolate and leave them to dry – this prevents the filling from making the pastry soggy.

Rich Pastries

Rich pastries have a reputation for being hard to handle. Their high fat content means that if the dough becomes too warm, they seem to melt in your hand rather than in the mouth as they're supposed to. The secret to success is to handle the pastry as lightly as possible.

BASIC ALMOND PASTRY

Preparation time: 10 mins
+ chilling
Makes About 400 g/14 oz

INGREDIENTS

175 g/6 oz flour	
Pinch of salt	
65 g/2½ oz ground almonds	
50 g/2 oz caster sugar	
2 egg yolks	
2 drops vanilla essence	
75 g/3 oz unsalted butter, softened	

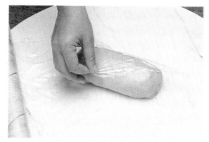

1 Sift the flour and salt onto a work surface and sprinkle the ground almonds over the top. Make a large well in the centre and add the sugar, egg yolks and vanilla essence. Using the fingertips of one hand, mix the sugar and egg yolks together until the mixture is creamy.

2 Add the softened butter and keep mixing, gradually incorporating all the flour and ground almonds.

3 Knead the mixture gently to a paste, then wrap in cling film and relax in the fridge for about 30 minutes.

PRUE'S TIP
You can make this rich pastry in a food processor. Process all the ingredients in short bursts until they form a ball.

VARIATION
- **Pâte Sucrée**
You can make this classic French pastry by omitting the ground almonds from the Basic Almond Pastry recipe and adding an extra egg yolk and another 25 g/1 oz caster sugar.

Shortcrust Pastries

Rich shortcrust pastry is basically a shortcrust pastry mixture made with butter plus an egg yolk. Make sure everything is cool and don't overwork the mixture. Rinse your hands in cold water before you start and chill the dough before cooking. The made-up pastry can be stored in the fridge for 3-4 days. Use this pastry for flans and double-crust pies. Use wholemeal flour instead of plain for a darker pastry.

RICH SHORTCRUST

Preparation time: 10 mins
+ chilling
Makes About 350 g/12 oz

INGREDIENTS

225 g/8 oz flour	
Pinch of salt	
115 g/4½ oz butter	
1 egg yolk	
2 tbls iced water	

1 Sift the flour and salt into a bowl and rub in the butter. Mix the egg yolk with the chilled water and add to the flour and butter mixture.

2 Mix to a firm dough, first by mixing with a round-ended knife and then finishing off with one hand. You may need to add more water, but go easy here: the pastry shouldn't be too damp as this will produce a tougher texture. Wrap the pastry in cling film and chill in the fridge for 30 minutes.

VARIATION
- **Basic Shortcrust Pastry**
Make a basic shortcrust by following the Rich Shortcrust recipe but replacing the egg yolk with a little extra iced water – about 1-1½ tbls. For the fat use half butter or block margarine with half shortening or lard.

PRUE'S TIP
If you're convinced that you can't make pastry, try flinging all the ingredients into a food processor. Whizz merrily until a ball of pastry forms, but beware of over-processing as it will make the pastry grey and tough.

Choux Pastry

There is only one vital rule to making choux pastry: follow the instructions carefully. Don't guess the quantities, don't tip the flour in before the water is boiling and don't add all the egg at once.

BASIC CHOUX PASTRY

Preparation time: 8 mins
+ cooling
Cooking time: 3 mins
Makes About 450 g/1 lb

INGREDIENTS

75 g/3 oz butter
95 g/3¾ oz flour, sifted
Pinch of salt
3 eggs

1 Place the butter and 215 ml/7½ fl oz water in a heavy saucepan. Bring slowly to the boil to give the butter time to melt completely.

2 When the mixture is boiling. Shoot in all the flour at once and take the pan off the heat.

3 Working as fast as you can, beat the mixture with a wooden spoon: it will soon become thick and smooth and leave the sides of the pan. Beat in the salt.

4 Stand the bottom of the saucepan in a basin of cold water to bring down the temperature.

5 Beat the eggs together in a basin. When the flour mixture is cool, beat in the eggs, a little at a time, making sure the egg is well mixed in before adding more. If the eggs are large, it may not be necessary to add all of them. The mixture should be of a dropping consistency.

P R U E ' S   T I P
A dropping consistency means the mixture should fall off the spoon rather reluctantly, all in one blob. Avoid adding too much egg.

Flaky Pastry

Light and layered, flaky pastry is traditionally used for pie toppings for both sweet and savoury dishes.

BASIC FLAKY PASTRY

Preparation time: 25 mins
+ resting
Makes 400 g/14 oz

INGREDIENTS

225 g/8 oz flour
Pinch of salt
75 g/3 oz butter
150 ml/¼ pt iced water
75 g/3 oz lard

P R U E ' S   T I P
If the fats are too cold they will be difficult to blend, too soft and the pastry will be hard to handle.

W A T C H P O I N T
Layered pastries need a hot oven because a sudden blast of great heat is needed to expand the carefully trapped air in the pastry, which will force the layers to rise. Too cool an oven will produce unrisen, heavy and soggy pastry. Also, the butter will melt before the flour cooks and holds it in place, making the pastry greasy.

1 Sift the flour and salt, rub in half the butter and enough water to bind. Knead until smooth. Roll into a rectangle and dot the top ⅔ with half the lard. Fold in three.

2 Press the edges well to seal them. This prevents the fat escaping during rolling.

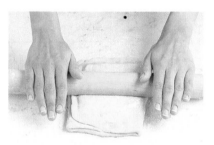

3 Give the pastry a quarter turn and carefully roll it out flat again to make the same-size rectangle as it made before.

4 Dot the top two-thirds again with the remaining butter and fold as before: bring the unbuttered side up and the top buttered side down.

5 Turn, roll out and dot with the remaining lard. Fold and roll once more. Fold, then leave to chill for 15 minutes. Roll out once more.

Puff Pastry

Puff pastry is the most spectacular and best of the layered pastries, but is also the trickiest to make. When first making it, cut the fat content by about 50 g/2 oz. This will make handling easier, and you will learn the technique without tears. Once that works, start to use the full quantity of butter to make glorious butter pastries. To thaw frozen pastry, allow 1 hour at room temperature or about 4 hours in the fridge.

BASIC PUFF PASTRY

Preparation time: 50 mins
+ chilling
Makes 450 g/1 lb

INGREDIENTS

225 g/8 oz flour, plus extra for dusting
Pinch of salt
25 g/1 oz lard
150 ml/¼ pt iced water
200 g/7 oz softened butter

PRUE'S TIP

When making puff pastry it is easy to forget how many turns it has been given. To avoid confusion, mark the pastry by pressing 2, 3, 4 etc fingertips into it before wrapping and chilling.

1 Sift the flour with the salt into a bowl. Rub in the lard and add enough water to bind the mixture. Form into a ball and knead for 3-5 minutes until smooth and elastic.

2 Roll the dough out to a rectangle 12.5 cm/5 in by 25 cm/10 in and then roll the middle third out a little wider than the rest as shown.

3 Wrap the butter in greaseproof paper and tap with a rolling-pin to shape it into a 10 cm/4 in by 7.5 cm/3 in block. Place on the centre of the pastry and fold the side flaps over to enclose it.

4 Fold both top and bottom over to enclose the butter tightly. Press the edges together with the rolling-pin. Give the pastry a half-turn so that the short sides are at the top and bottom.

5 Tap the parcel with the rolling-pin to flatten the butter a little, then roll out quickly and lightly until the pastry is 3 times as long as it is wide. Fold it in 3 again, then seal the edges again by pressing gently but firmly with the rolling-pin.

6 Give it a half turn again so that the short sides are at top and bottom. Wrap the pastry and let it rest in the fridge for 30 minutes.

7 Roll out again and repeat the rolling and folding process 6 times. Wrap well and chill between each rolling and folding if the butter shows signs of melting or squeezing out.

Variation

Try this quick and easy alternative to the traditional puff pastry method.

ROUGH PUFF PASTRY

Preparation time: 30 min
+ chilling
Makes 275 g/10 oz

INGREDIENTS

175 g/6 oz flour, plus extra for dusting
Pinch of salt
100 g/4 oz butter

1 Sift the flour and salt into a bowl. Cut the butter into small pieces and add them to the flour. Add iced water, mixing with a knife.

2 Gather the paste into a ball, wrap and chill for about 10 minutes. Roll the pastry out on a floured board into a 15 cm/6 in by 10 cm/4 in rectangle. Now proceed with rolling and folding as for Basic Puff Pastry, repeating the process 3 times. Chill the wrapped pastry between turns if necessary.

Suet Pastry

Suet is bought by the packet – ready shredded and convenient. But it is cheaper from the butcher. If you have a food processor, ask for beef suet and shred it yourself. You can also chop it by hand.

Vegetarian suet is also available. It is usually made from palm oil and can be used to make pastry in exactly the same way as beef suet.

Baking

Baked suet pastry is slightly drier than steamed and has a crisp cakey crust. It makes a good topping for 'cobbler'. Cover a rich stew with rounds cut from thickly rolled-out suet pastry to make a tasty dish.

Steaming

This is the classic cooking method for suet pastry and is best for dishes with lengthy cooking times like steak and kidney pudding. The long cooking means the pastry has time to brown and flake rather than being solidly doughy.

BASIC SUET PASTRY

Preparation time: 5 mins
Makes 575 g/1 lb 4 oz

INGREDIENTS
175 g/6 oz suet
350 g/12 oz self-raising flour, plus extra for dusting
½ tsp salt

1 If you are using fresh suet, chop it into chunks first, then process in a food processor or blender until thoroughly shredded.

2 Mix shredded suet, flour and salt together in a bowl. Add enough water to form a soft dough and knead briefly on a floured surface before rolling out.

PRUE'S TIP
If you shred your own suet, don't worry about taking out fine membrane and slight discolourations before processing. After chopping they become practically invisible.

WATCHPOINT
As with most pastries using a chemical raising agent (the baking powder in the self-raising flour), this pastry should be baked as soon as possible after it is made. If you want to make it up ahead of time, prepare and cook the whole dish. It will reheat perfectly well in the oven or in the microwave.

Other Savoury Pastries

Potato pastry is a light, crisp and nutty pastry. But remember to work the grated potato in by hand – processing will turn it horribly gluey.

POTATO PASTRY

Preparation time: 15 mins
Makes About 300 g/12 oz

INGREDIENTS
100 g/4 oz butter
100 g/4 oz granary flour
100 g/4 oz raw potato, grated
Pinch of salt

1 Rub the butter into the flour until it resembles fine breadcrumbs. Work in the grated potato and the salt. Knead briefly until smooth. Shape into a ball and chill for 10 minutes.

WATCHPOINT
Do not make this kind of pastry too far in advance as the raw potato turns black very quickly.

HERB PATE A PATE

Preparation time: 10 mins + chilling
Makes 450 g/1 lb

INGREDIENTS
275 g/10 oz flour
1 tbls chopped dried herbs, including thyme, basil, bay leaves, rosemary, savory
½ tsp salt
175 g/6 oz soft butter
2 egg yolks

1 Sift the flour onto the work surface and sprinkle with the dried herbs and the salt.

2 Make a well in the middle of the flour and drop the butter and yolks into it. Work the butter and yolks together with just the fingertips of one hand, gradually drawing in the surrounding flour. The pastry should be soft and malleable. Add more flour if it is too sticky, or a little water if it is too dry. Wrap in cling film and leave to chill in the fridge for 30 minutes until firm.

PRUE'S TIP
Pâte à pâte can be made in a food processor but, as with all pastry making, great care should be take not to overmix.

CAKES

Who can resist a good cake? Just a taste tends to lead to a slice, followed by surreptitious little slivers until only crumbs remain. Which, of course, need eating up on the waste-not-want-not principle.

Since home-made cakes are a million light-years away from commercial cakes, making them yourself is a good idea. With fruit cakes you can put less sugar in them for a start and be sure they contain real eggs, real booze and good fruit.

Sponges, which double as both a dessert and a cake, are fairly delicate, so benefit from being made at home and eaten on the day they are made. Yeast cakes are just plain delicious and there's nothing quite like the smell of freshly-risen yeast to give any kitchen a homely air.

Fruit Cakes

Fruit cakes are delicious, and easy to make, whether they are rich and dark, laced with booze and stiff with fruit, or pale, light, and barely speckled with pale but tasty fruit like sultanas or pineapple.

Naughty Nibbles

If you make the fruit cake in a ring mould, you get a 'sailing cake' – the idea being that you can break off chunks to eat without the benefit of plate or knife – ideal if battling with the high seas or having a quick, illegal munch behind the gym. Fruit cakes can be steamed as well as baked. I always steam the ring-mould ones, because it is impossible to line them effectively with paper.

Storing & Freezing

Double-wrap in foil and store in a cake tin or a sealed polythene bag. Rich cakes will keep for up to 1 year and lighter ones with not much fruit for up to 1 week. Fruit cakes freeze better than anything and if you really want to, you can make 3 years' Christmas cakes in one go.

Preparing Tins

Fruit cakes have long cooking times, so line the tin completely with greased greaseproof paper to prevent the edges from overcooking.

Lining a Round Tin

First brush the tin with melted lard or oil. Cut a piece of greaseproof paper slightly longer than the circumference of the tin and 7.5 cm/3 in deeper than its depth. Fold paper back 2.5 cm/1 in along one of the long edges. Snip at intervals up to the crease. Bend paper to fit inside tin, with snipped edge lying neatly in the bottom. Cut out a circle of greaseproof using the tin as a guide, lay in tin and grease.

Lining a Square Tin

First grease the tin. Then lay the tin on a large sheet of greaseproof paper and trace around the base with a pencil. Cut out a larger square around the drawn one, to include the depth of the tin plus 5 cm/2 in. Cut into each corner as far as the traced line of the centre square. Fold the paper along the drawn lines and along the corner edges and form it into a box. Drop into the tin, pencil-side down. Smooth sides.

Preparing Dried Fruit

Rinse and dry glacé and crystallised fruit to remove sugary coating. To prevent larger fruit from sinking, chop and toss in some of the measured flour before mixing in.

Testing for Doneness

Push a fine skewer into the centre of the cake. If the cake is cooked, the skewer will come out clean. If there are traces of uncooked mixture on the skewer, return the cake to the oven for another 20 minutes or so.

Adding Alcohol

Adding additonal brandy during storing time will help to keep cakes moist and will enrich and improve the flavour. Pierce the cake with a thin skewer and trickle 2-3 tbls of brandy over the surface of the cake. Repeat weekly. If you prefer, you can use rum or sherry instead.

Rich Fruit Cake

This recipe is suitable for one 18 cm/7 in square or a 20 cm/8 in round cake.

BASIC RICH FRUIT CAKE

Preparation time: 15 mins
Cooking time: 3-3½ hours
Serves 10-12

INGREDIENTS

175 g/6 oz butter, softened,
plus extra for greasing
200 g/7 oz flour
1 tsp ground mixed spice or allspice
350 g/12 oz currants
225 g/8 oz sultanas
100 g/4 oz raisins
60 g/2½ oz glacé cherries
60 g/2½ oz mixed peel
175 g/6 oz soft brown sugar
Grated zest of 1 lemon
1 tbls black treacle
4 large eggs
50 g/2 oz ground almonds
60 g/2½ oz blanched almonds, chopped
2 tbls brandy

1 Preheat oven to 150 C/275 F/Gas 1. Grease and line the tin and use string to tie a piece of thick newspaper around the outside of the tin.

2 Sift the flour with the spice and set aside. Wash, dry and chop the fruit. Toss in a little of the sifted flour. Cream the butter with the sugar until light and fluffy and then add the lemon zest and treacle.

3 Beat the eggs, one at a time, adding a little flour with each egg. Fold in the remaining flour with the ground almonds, followed by the fruit, nuts and brandy and mix thoroughly.

4 Spoon the mixture into the prepared cake tin. Level the top and then make a dip in the centre of the mixture. Bake in the centre of the oven for 3 hours and then test with a skewer. If not cooked, return to the oven and test again after 30 minutes. Leave in the tin for 30 minutes. Cool on a wire rack.

Light Fruit Cake

This recipe makes the right quantity of mixture for an 18 cm/7 in square tin or a 20 cm/8 in round tin.

BASIC LIGHT FRUIT CAKE

Preparation time: 15 mins
Cooking time: 2 hours
Serves 10

INGREDIENTS

225 g/8 oz butter, softened,
plus extra for greasing
225 g/8 oz caster sugar
4 eggs, beaten
350 g/12 oz flour
2 tsp baking powder
100 g/4 oz ground almonds
100 g/4 oz glacé cherries
100 g/4 oz crystallised pineapple
100 g/4 oz crystallised ginger
100 g/4 oz sultanas
50 g/2 oz angelica,
chopped to the size of the sultanas
Grated zest of 1 orange

1 Preheat oven to 160 C/300 F/Gas 2. Grease and line a cake tin. Cream the butter and sugar together in a large bowl until pale and fluffy. Gradually beat in the eggs, adding a little flour to stop curdling.

2 Sift the remaining flour with the baking powder and fold into the mixture with the ground almonds. Chop the cherries, pineapple and ginger and fold in with the sultanas, angelica and the orange zest and spoon into the prepared cake tin.

3 Level the surface, make a slight hollow in the centre of the mixture and bake on the centre shelf for 2 hours. If the cake top gets too brown, cover with a double piece of greaseproof paper for the rest of the cooking time.

VARIATIONS
For a slightly different flavour, replace the angelica, cherries, pineapple, ginger and sultanas with any of the following:
• 350 g/12 oz chopped dates and 175 g/6 oz chopped walnuts.
•175 g/6 oz each red, green and yellow glacé cherries. Halve and coat in flour before adding.
•100 g/4 oz dried apricots, 100 g/4 oz dried apples and 275 g/10 oz dried figs, all chopped.

Gateau Sponges

At the heart of every good gateau lies a moist and light sponge base. No matter how stunning the beautifully arranged top, a dry or undercooked sponge will spoil a potential masterpiece. Fortunately it's easy to achieve perfect sponges – as long as you stick to the recipe and use the correct size tin. As a rough guide, a 3-egg quantity of mixture is enough for an 18 cm/7 in tin or a 23 cm/9 in ring tin, and a 4-egg quantity fills a 20 cm/8 in tin. All conventionally cooked sponge bases freeze well without decorations for up to three months and thaw quickly when needed.

Lining Tins

If possible use a buckle or loose-bottomed tin. These make it easy to remove the cake without damaging it. To prepare the tin, brush it lightly with a little oil. Butter tends to make the cake stick. Leave ring tins unlined, but for other tins line the base with a circle of greaseproof paper and then brush again with oil. Mix 1 tbls each of flour and caster sugar together, tip into the tin and twist it to coat. Tip out excess. The sugar gives the cake mixture something to cling to as it climbs up the side of the tin.

Levelling the Surface

To ensure that the cake has a level top after cooking, pour the mixture into the tin, level the surface, and then hollow out the centre slightly. As the cake rises, it will fill out the hollow.

Cooling

Cool the cooked cake in the tin for 5 minutes and then remove the outside ring by releasing the clip. The bottom can then be removed and the cake left to cool on a wire rack. Before icing the cake flip it over and carefully peel off the paper.

Victoria Sponge

The creaming together of fat and sugar is the method used to make this cake and incorporate air and lightness, although self-raising flour ensures a successful rise. Simple and speedy, it's an ever-popular tea-time treat.

BASIC SPONGE

Preparation time: 30 mins
Cooking time: 25 mins
Serves 4

INGREDIENTS

175 g/6 oz butter
175 g/6 oz caster sugar
3 large eggs
175 g/6 oz self-raising flour
3 tbls strawberry jam
225 ml/8 oz fl oz whipped cream
Icing sugar, to dust
Oil, caster sugar, flour for greasing

1 Preheat oven to 190 C/375 F/Gas 5. Grease and base-line two 18 cm/7 in sandwich tins. Dust with sugar and flour and tip out excess.

2 Put the butter and sugar in a bowl and cream together until light and fluffy. Slowly beat in the eggs, one at a time. Sift the flour and fold in.

3 Divide the mixture equally between the two tins and bake for 20-25 minutes or until the surface of the cake springs back when pressed.

4 Cool for 5 minutes then turn out onto a wire rack to go cold. Sandwich cakes together with jam and whipped cream and dust the top lightly with icing sugar.

PRUE'S TIP

For an all-in-one method sift 1 tsp baking powder with the flour and put in the bowl of a food mixer with all the other ingredients. Beat for 1 minute until smooth and well combined, and then continue as for the basic recipe.

WATCHPOINT

Be careful to beat the eggs in slowly to avoid the mixture curdling. If your mixture does curdle though, don't panic. Bake in the oven as usual, it will not rise as high as it should but the result will still be perfectly acceptable.

Whisked Sponge

A whisked sponge is a fat-free cake which relies entirely on air as the raising agent. The air is trapped within the eggs during whisking and as the air expands in the heat of the oven the cake rises.

BASIC WHISKED SPONGE

Preparation time: 15 mins
Cooking time: 30 mins
Serves 4

INGREDIENTS

3 eggs
75 g/3 oz caster sugar
75 g/3 oz flour, sifted
A pinch of salt
Oil, caster sugar, flour for greasing

1 Preheat oven to 180 C/350 F/Gas 4. Brush an 18 cm/7 in spring-form or loose-bottomed tin with oil, line the base with greaseproof paper, coat with oil and sugar and flour.

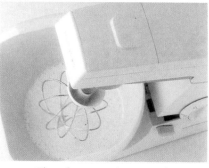

2 Place the eggs and sugar in the bowl of a food mixer and whisk until they turn pale, thick and fluffy and the mixture leaves a trail when the whisk is lifted.

3 Then add the sifted flour and salt and fold in carefully with a large metal spoon.

4 Pour the mixture into the prepared tin and bake for 30 minutes or until the cake has shrunk away from the sides and springs back when pressed lightly with the fingertips. Leave to cool in the tin for 5 minutes and then turn out onto a wire rack to cool.

PRUE'S TIP

For extra protection cut a strip of greaseproof paper and line the sides of the tin as well – the cake should shrink away from the sides as it cooks.

Genoese Sponge

The classic Genoese sponge is a whisked sponge with a little melted butter folded into the whisked mixture with the flour. The butter gives a richer flavour, a moister texture and also improves the keeping quality of the cake. A Genoese sponge will keep for a day or two before going dry. If you use a hand whisk, you will get greater volume if the bowl is set over a pan of simmering water. A 'Genoese fine' is richer and uses 90 g/3½ oz of melted butter.

BASIC GENOESE SPONGE

Preparation time: 30 mins
Cooking time: 40-45 mins
Serves 6

INGREDIENTS

4 eggs
115 g/4½ oz caster sugar
Pinch of salt
115 g/4½ oz flour, sifted
50 g/2 oz butter, melted
Oil, caster sugar, flour for greasing

1 Preheat oven to 190 C/375 F/Gas 5. Grease, line and flour a 20 cm/8 in spring-form or loose-bottomed tin.

2 Put the eggs and sugar in a bowl and set over a saucepan of simmering water, ensuring that the base of the bowl does not touch the water. Whisk the mixture until it is pale and thick, has doubled in volume and leaves a trail on the surface.

3 Remove the bowl from the saucepan and continue to whisk until the mixture is cool. Fold in the salt and half the sifted flour with a large metal spoon. Pour the melted butter around the edge and fold in, followed by the remaining flour.

4 Scrape the mixture into the prepared tin and bake for 30-35 minutes, or until the cake has shrunk away from the sides. Leave to cool in the tin for 5 minutes and then turn the sponge out onto a wire rack to become completely cold before serving.

WATCHPOINT

The butter should be runny but not hot and must be poured around the edges of the bowl and not into the centre of the mixture which would cause too much air to be lost. Fold the butter in quickly and smoothly with a metal spoon.

Yeast Cakes

One of the revelations for a stranger to the Continent is the range of sweet breads and yeasted cakes in the bakeries and pâtisseries. Brioche, streusel cake, plum cake, stollen, rum baba or savarin are all marvellous affairs, with the wholesomeness of bread yet the extravagance and sheer wickedness of good pâtisserie.

Perhaps the best thing, from the busy cook's point of view, is that these cakes freeze well. Last Christmas, I discovered an unidentifiable package in the freezer which turned out to be year-old stollen. It emerged quite unharmed.

SWEET YEAST DOUGH

Preparation time: 20 mins
+ rising
Makes 1 loaf or cake

INGREDIENTS

125 ml/4 fl oz milk
15 g/½ oz fresh yeast
275 g/10 oz flour
25 g/1 oz butter
40 g/1½ oz caster sugar
Pinch of salt
1 egg

1 Warm the milk until hand-hot. Whisk in the yeast and 2 tbls of the flour. Leave to rise in a warm place for 30 minutes or until the mixture is thick and puffy.

2 Rub the butter into the flour until the mixture resembles fine breadcrumbs. Add the sugar and salt.

3 Add the egg to the flour mixture with the puffy paste (the starter) and work to a soft pliable dough.

4 Knead well for 5 minutes. Cover and leave to rise in a warm place for 30 minutes or until approximately doubled in bulk.

5 Knead again for 2-3 minutes, then use in your recipe. Leave to rise for a further 10-15 minutes just before baking.

PRUE'S TIP
All baking equipment and ingredients should be at room temperature. The warmth will encourage speedy action from the yeast.

Brioche

Brioche dough is used for individual breakfast buns, for large tea breads (excellent sliced, toasted and buttered) and to envelope terrines, sausages, pâtés and fish, so it is definitely worth knowing how to make a good one.

BASIC BRIOCHE BUNS

Preparation time: 20 mins
+ rising
Cooking time: 10 minutes
Makes 10

INGREDIENTS

Oil, for greasing
7 g/¼ oz fresh yeast
250 g/9 oz flour, plus extra for dusting
40 g/1½ oz caster sugar
Pinch of salt
2 eggs, beaten
50 g/2 oz butter, melted

1 Lightly grease 10 small brioche tins with oil. Mix the yeast with 2 tbls warm water and a pinch of sugar.

2 Sift the flour, caster sugar and the pinch of salt together into a large bowl and make a well in the centre of the mixture with your fingertips.

3 Pour the eggs, butter and the yeast mixture into the well and mix together with the fingers of one hand until smooth and soft.

4 Knead on a floured board until smooth and very elastic. Put in a greased bowl, cover and leave in a warm place for 1 hour.

5 Knead the dough for 2 minutes, then divide into 10 pieces. Take three-quarters of each piece and roll into a smooth ball. Put into the brioche tins. Push a floured finger into the top of each. Roll the rest of the dough into small balls with pointed tips. Put the tip into the hole in the top of each brioche bun and put the brioche tins in a baking tray.

6 Preheat oven to 230 C/450 F/Gas 8. Cover the buns lightly with greased cling film and leave to rise in a warm place for 15 minutes or until doubled in size. Remove cling film. Bake in oven for 10 minutes.

PRUE'S TIP
Brioche dough can be very slack and difficult to knead at first. It may be easier to slap it about in a bowl rather than on a board.

SERVING NOTE
Plain brioche is superb simply eaten with butter and fruit conserve for breakfast. Brioche also combines well with ham and Gruyère. Hollow out the small buns and use them to hold a seafood, pâté or mushroom filling.

DESSERTS

I have friends for whom the entire rest of the meal – no matter how delicious – is a bore and a chore, undergone only as a means to the dessert served at the end. Whether you're cooking them or eating them, one of the delights of desserts and puddings is the variety of tastes, textures and techniques they offer.

Keep your cool

Since the advent of the electric sorbetière, making ice creams has become child's play. Now you can merrily tip such unlikely mixtures as puréed cucumber with mint, or plain yoghurt and honey into one of those miracle machines and, because it stirs as it freezes, the result will be smooth. But traditional methods work just as well. There are many ways of making ices. You can make a custard with milk or cream and eggs, or a mousse mixture by whisking eggs and sugar over heat, or a flavoured meringue mixture, or even a simple syrup to produce a sorbet. The classic rich ices, with real cream and eggs are still the smoothest and the best.

Light as air

Sweet soufflés, contrary to popular myth, are easy to make. The fact is, hot air rises. And if you get air into your mixture and then bake it, it's bound to rise. Of course it will sink too eventually, but all good soufflés sink. If a soufflé stays up indefinitely it is either horribly full of flour, or overcooked beyond redemption. But the hot air will not leak out and cause collapse instantly. If you take the soufflé straight from the oven to the table, there will be plenty of time for your guests to admire its glory before it starts to sink.

Mousses & jellies

Summer or winter, there is something wonderfully special about a mousse or jelly. Mousses are as light as air, but have a rich, luxurious taste, while a good home-made fruit jelly has a fresh, tangy flavour nothing like the coloured and flavoured packet versions you find in the shops.

Meringue magic

Meringue is a wonderfully frivolous thing. Piled in voluminous mountains on flans and tarts, snow-white and crisp for petit fours or pale beige and sticky for a tea-time treat, it is almost everyone's favourite.

Sweet Soufflés

When making a soufflé, always remember to get your oven hot and dish ready before you start whisking the egg whites. Get the basic mixture ready before the whites are whisked. Whisk the whites until they are stiff to trap the maximum amount of air in them. Don't overfold when adding whites to the soufflé mixture – too much stirring knocks out the air. And always put the mixture straight into the oven once the dish is filled.

There are few puddings as impressive as a family-size classic vanilla soufflé standing two inches above the dish, and just wobbling enough for the diners to guess at a moist, soft middle and crisp, sugary edge. Serve hot, straight from the oven.

BASIC VANILLA SOUFFLE

Preparation time: 30 mins
+ cooling
Cooking time: 40-45 mins
Serves 6

INGREDIENTS

50 g/2 oz melted butter, plus extra for greasing
75 g/3 oz caster sugar, plus extra for dusting
½ vanilla pod, split
225 ml/8 fl oz milk
50 g/2 oz flour
5 egg whites
4 egg yolks
Icing sugar, to decorate

1 Heat oven to 200 C/400 F/Gas 6. Tie a paper collar round a 1.3 L/2¼ pt soufflé dish. Brush with butter and dust with caster sugar.

2 Scald the vanilla pod with the milk and strain. Stir the flour into the butter, add the milk and stir over a low heat until thick. Beat until smooth, then add one of the egg whites and beat well. Allow the mixture to cool, then add the egg yolks, one at a time, beating well until smooth.

3 Whisk the remaining egg whites and sugar together until stiff peaks form. Stir quarter of the egg white mixture into the milk custard mixture. Fold in the remaining egg white mixture.

4 Turn the vanilla soufflé mix into the prepared soufflé dish. Bake for 30-35 minutes, dust with icing sugar and serve immediately.

Meringue Notes

Meringue is not every cook's favourite. 'They come out flat', 'They leak', 'They stick', 'You need a hammer to break them', are just some of the complaints. Yet, meringue really is easy to make. Around 99% of all failures are entirely due to underwhisking. Simply remember you cannot overwhisk meringue, and other problems like oven temperature and undercooking, are easily cured. Follow these steps and you will be sure of success.

Ingredients

Caster sugar is the best kind to use for light white meringues, although icing sugar used in meringue cuite (professional chefs' meringue) gives a distinctive chalky texture and will hold its shape better. Soft brown sugar produces a meringue with a pale beige colour and toffee-like taste. Use a 50/50 mix with caster sugar to help the meringue dry out.

A teaspoon of vinegar or lemon juice is said to make the whites whisk to a greater volume. I don't always bother, although they certainly don't do any harm! There is also the theory that slightly stale eggs are easier to whisk. They are, but only if whisked by hand, so don't reject any day old eggs you might have.

Equipment

The theory is that if you rub a copper bowl with lemon juice and whip the egg whites in it, the copper reacts with the acid and the egg whites and produces a lighter mixture. We did some tests using hand-held wire balloon whisks, rotary whisks and electric whisks in a variety of copper, plastic, stainless steel and glass bowls. Any difference in the volume was not measurable.

Paper or Foil?

Because meringues, especially large ones, are inclined to stick, edible rice paper is a good surface to cook them on. Just tear the paper around the bottom of the meringues when they are cooked but leave it on the bases. Baking parchment works like a dream, never sticking, and foil and greaseproof paper are acceptable if properly prepared. Lightly oil them first and dust with flour.

Testing

Cooked meringues should lift off the baking tray easily. If they feel light and dry but are sticking, break one open: a toffee-like middle can be delicious, but dry meringues store better.

Freezing & Storing

Cooked, crisp, dry meringue keeps well. Just store in an airtight tin or bag like biscuits. Soft cooked meringue, like that on the top of a pie, keeps for a day or two in the fridge but loses its crisp crust. Raw meringue freezes brilliantly and can be baked from frozen – on pie tops for example. Filled meringues soften after 4-5 hours and are best freshly filled.

Making Meringue

This is the most straightforward kind of meringue. Use it for cream-filled glossy shells and pie toppings. It's an ideal way to use up leftover frozen egg whites, and the cooked meringues keep for a month in an airtight tin.

BASIC MERINGUE

Preparation time: 20 mins
Cooking time: 2 hours
Makes 50 miniature shells
or 16 large shells

INGREDIENTS
4 egg whites
225 g/8 oz caster sugar

1 Preheat oven to 130 C/250 F/Gas ½. Cover two baking trays with baking parchment. Whisk the egg whites until stiff but not dry.

2 Add half of the sugar to the stiff egg whites and whisk again until the mixture is very stiff and glossy.

3 Carefully fold in the rest of the sugar with a large metal spoon using a cutting action. Take care not to knock any air from the mixture.

4 Spoon the meringue onto the lined baking trays using two dessert spoons for each large shell, or two teaspoons for tiny meringues. Leave plenty of room to allow them to expand.

5 Bake for up to 2 hours or until the meringues are dry right through. Remove from the paper and cool on a wire rack. If the paper sticks, tear around each meringue before peeling away.

Custard-Based Ice Cream

You won't want to eat ordinary, ready-made ice cream after you've tried delicious custard-based ice creams. They are rich and smooth and once you've mastered the straightforward technique, the scope for experimenting with different flavours is almost endless.

VANILLA ICE CREAM

Preparation time: 5-10 minutes
+ freezing
Cooking time: 10 minutes
Serves 6

INGREDIENTS
300 ml/½ pt milk
150 ml/¼ pt single cream
100 g/4 oz caster sugar
4 egg yolks
Few drops of vanilla essence

1 Put the milk, cream and sugar together in a heavy saucepan and slowly bring to the boil. Meanwhile beat yolks with the vanilla.

2 Pour the boiling cream mixture onto the yolks, stirring constantly. Leave to cool.

3 Pour the mixture into a shallow container and freeze until frozen around the edges.

4 Transfer the ice cream to a bowl and whisk with a rotary beater or electric whisk until smooth, pale and creamy. Pour back into a deeper container and refreeze. Whisk once more and refreeze if the ice cream is still not smooth enough.

Meringue-Based Ice Cream

The lightest of the ice creams made with meringue. It won't need beating during freezing. Meringue-based ice cream is always very sweet and therefore needs a sharp fruit flavour.

RASPBERRY ICE CREAM

Preparation time: 10-15 mins
+ freezing
Cooking time: 20 mins
Serves 6

INGREDIENTS
225 g/8 oz raspberries
225 g/8 oz caster sugar
4 egg whites
300 ml/½ pt double cream

1 Purée the raspberries in a liquidiser or food processor and sieve to remove the seeds.

2 Put the sugar and 150 ml/¼ pt water in a saucepan over a gentle heat until the sugar has dissolved. Then bring to the boil and boil rapidly until it reaches a temperature of 116 C/240 F or until a small amount of the boiling syrup will roll into a soft ball when plunged into a bowl of cold water.

3 Whisk the egg whites in a large bowl until stiff and then gradually pour on the sugar syrup, whisking all the time. Continue to whisk until very stiff, shiny and cool.

4 Whip the cream until floppy but not stiff and fold into the meringue mixture. Fold in the fruit purée.

5 Pour into a rigid container and freeze for at least 4 hours or until the ice cream is firm.

PRUE'S TIP
If making ice cream by hand, chill bowls and the whisk in the freezer beforehand so that the ice cream won't melt during rewhisking. With most ices, the trick is to beat, stir or whisk frequently during the freezing process. As a general rule, the more you whisk, the airier and smoother your ice will be.

FREEZER TIP
If ices are served straight from the freezer, they will be too hard to scoop and will be so cold you will be unable to taste a thing. Transfer them to the fridge 30 minutes before serving. This develops (or ripens) the flavour.

SERVING NOTE
When ice cream is stiff enough to hold its shape, 'marble' or streak it with sweetened fruit purée.

Mousses & Jellies

Mousses and jellies have one big difference between them. Mousses, unlike jellies, have whisked egg whites folded into them to give a light, fluffy texture, with egg yolks and whipped cream added for a richer flavour.

Setting

Both mousses and jellies have a setting agent in common – gelatine. Gelatine is extracted from boiled bones of animals. Unappetising though this sounds, it's such a versatile ingredient! But gone are the days when you had to boil beef bones to extract the gelatinous juices. Now you can just use magic packets of powder which easily set hot and cold desserts.

Gelatine

Gelatine comes in two forms, French leaf or sheet gelatine is generally considered to be the best quality. Powdered gelatine, sold in sachets, on the other hand, is more easily obtainable and the one which most cooks will use. An alternative to animal gelatine, useful for vegetarians, is agar-agar, a jellying agent extracted from seaweed.

Dissolving Gelatine

Place a little liquid in a saucepan, sprinkle over the gelatine and stir. Leave until spongy – about 5 minutes – then stir over low heat until dissolved. Do not boil. Use 4 tbls liquid to 4 tsp gelatine.

Using Gelatine

To set 600 ml/1 pt of liquid, you will need 5 sheets (20 g/¾ oz) of French leaf gelatine or one 4 tsp sachet (15 g/½ oz) of powdered gelatine. If adding whipped cream or whisked egg white to a mousse, fold in just as the gelatine begins to set or the jelly mixture will sink and you'll get a solid layer on the bottom and the cream or egg white on top. A jelly or mousse will take 1½-2 hours to set in the fridge. To unmould a jelly, dip in hot water, invert onto a serving plate and give a sharp shake so the jelly is released.

Using Agar-Agar

Made from seaweed, this vegetarian product works exactly like gelatine, but needs to be boiled with some or all of the liquid ingredients in a recipe before it can set. Use 2 tsp per 600 ml/1 pt of liquid. Agar-agar is most commonly available from wholefood or health food shops.

WATCHPOINT

Don't let the gelatine boil or its setting qualities will be destroyed.

MICROWAVE TIP

Gelatine can be quickly dissolved in the microwave. Soak 1 sachet in 4 tbls water, and microwave on HIGH (100%) for about 30-35 seconds, taking care not to let the water boil.

Basic Recipes

Fruit purées can be made from fresh, frozen, canned or even dried fruit. Don't add cream and egg white until the purée is nearly set and never while it is still warm.

RASPBERRY MOUSSE

Preparation time: 20 mins
+ chilling
Cooking time: 5 mins
Serves 4-6

INGREDIENTS

225 g/8 oz frozen raspberries, defrosted
75-100 g/3-4 oz caster sugar
4 tsp (1 sachet) powdered gelatine
Juice of ½ an orange
150 ml/¼ pt double cream
1 egg white
Toasted flaked almonds
and whole raspberries, to decorate

1 Rub the raspberries through a nylon sieve, pressing through as much fruit as possible. Discard the seeds left in the sieve.

2 Place the sugar and 4 tbls water in a pan and heat very gently until the sugar dissolves. Stir into purée.

3 Sprinkle gelatine over orange juice in a pan, set aside briefly, then dissolve over low heat. Blend in a little of the raspberry mixture and then add the rest. Pour into a mixing bowl.

4 As the raspberry mixture begins to set, whip cream and whisk egg white. Fold in cream (saving some for decoration) then egg white.

5 Turn into one large or six individual serving dishes. Chill for 1-2 hours and then pipe reserved cream around the edge, sprinkle with flaked almonds and decorate with raspberries to serve.

ORANGE JELLY

Preparation time: 5 mins
+ chilling
Cooking time: 1 min
Serves 6

INGREDIENTS

750 ml/1¼ pt orange juice
4 tsp (1 sachet) powdered gelatine

1 Pour 4 tbls of the orange juice in a small pan. Sprinkle over gelatine. Stir and set aside for 5 minutes.

2 Place the pan over a low heat, stirring continuously until all the gelatine has completely dissolved.

3 Stir in remaining orange juice. Set aside, stirring occasionally. Pour into jelly mould. Chill to set.

4 To serve, loosen the jelly round the edges with a knife. Place a serving plate over the jelly mould, turn upside down and give a sharp shake. Carefully remove the mould. If the jelly sticks, dip the mould briefly in hot water.

SWEET SAUCES

Perfection in sweet sauces is usually easier and quicker to achieve than it is with complicated or subtle savoury sauces. And they are universally popular. Few people who have accepted ice cream then turn down the sauce. So there is seldom the frustration of having carefully planned some wonderful combination, only to have the best part of it – the sauce – dismissed with a wave of the hand.

Home-made goodness

Commercial sauces tend to have far too much sugar added to them. One of the advantages of the real thing is that you can sweeten to your taste. Also most sweet sauces – except custard – freeze rather well, so you can stock up the freezer for a rainy day. Being high in sugar, sweet sauces do not freeze rock hard, and thaw conveniently fast.

Flights of fancy

Chefs use sweet sauces for their finest flights of fancy – perhaps using two contrasting sauces on one plate, elegantly patterned or feathered to please the nouvelle cuisine gastro-critic. And there is no reason why home cooks should not do the same, for pattern-making on a plate is extremely easy, and spectacular plates produce admiring silences!

Custard Sauces

The classic crème anglaise is one of the truly English sauces admired the world over. And with good reason. Silky smooth, rich and faintly tinged with vanilla, it is a very good sauce indeed. But it is also very difficult to make. What you need above all is patience. If you try to hurry the slow heating and thickening process, even in a double boiler, curdling will result.

It takes 20 minutes to stir crème anglaise to perfection, which is why packet custard is so popular. And, I must say, though the real thing is unbeatable, a bit of cheating is what most chefs do. Some use packet custard and add a bit of orange zest or a fresh vanilla pod to the heating milk to flavour it, some add cream or kirsch. But the commonest cheat in top restaurants is to make classic custard with eggs but add a bit of cornflour to the milk. This ensures that the sauce thickens without the risk of curdling.

P R U E ' S   T I P

For a fashionably flecked sauce, split the vanilla pod and let the seeds escape into the custard.

V A R I A T I O N S

• Cheat's Custard
Mix a heaped teaspoon of cornflour with a little of the milk in the Créme Anglaise recipe before heating it. Stir into the milk with the vanilla pod. Bring to the boil until bubbling. Cool slightly. Pour onto sugar and yolks. Proceed with the recipe.

• Instant Creamy Custard
Make packet custard with 25% of the milk replaced by single cream, or make the custard and add a few spoonfuls of cream at the end.

CRÈME ANGLAISE

Preparation time: 2 mins
Cooking time: 25 mins
Makes Approx 450 ml/¾ pt

INGREDIENTS

| 3 egg yolks |
| 1 tbls caster sugar |
| 300 ml/½ pt milk |
| 1 vanilla pod |

1 Mix the yolks and sugar together. Warm the milk and vanilla until hot, but nowhere near boiling.

2 Pour the milk onto the yolks, stirring. Place the bowl over a pan of very gently simmering water. Do not boil the water. Stir steadily until the custard thickens. When the custard reaches coating consistency, place the bowl in a larger bowl of icy water to prevent over-heating.

ICED SABAYON

This is one of the most exciting of sauces, yet the technique is easy to master. The whisking over heat must be slow and steady, otherwise the mixture will separate.

Preparation time: 10 mins
Cooking time: 10 mins
Serves 4

INGREDIENTS

| 2 eggs |
| 2 egg yolks |
| 2 tbls caster sugar |
| 2 tbls Cointreau |
| 185 ml/6½ fl oz half-whipped cream |

1 Whisk together eggs, egg yolks and sugar with the Cointreau in a bowl over a pan of simmering water.

2 When thick, remove from the heat and set in a bowl of iced water. Keep whisking until cool, then fold in the half-whipped cream.

W A T C H P O I N T

Weightwatchers beware: the caster sugar helps the custard thicken without curdling – mighty difficult to do if you use an artificial sweetener.

Sweet White Sauces

Sweet white sauce is cheap and very easy to make and provides the ideal base for many other sweet sauces.

BASIC SWEET SAUCE

Cooking time: 5 mins
Makes 300 ml/½ pt

INGREDIENTS

20 g/¾ oz butter
20 g/¾ oz flour
300 ml/½ pt milk
1 tbls sugar
4 drops vanilla essence

1 Melt the butter, add flour and cook for 30 seconds to make a roux. Off the heat, stir in the milk until smooth, then return to the heat. Add sugar and vanilla. Bring to the boil, stirring.

COFFEE SAUCE

Cooking time: 10 mins
+ infusing and cooling
Makes 500 ml/¾ pt

INGREDIENTS

300 ml/½ pt milk
150 ml/¼ pt single cream
1 vanilla pod
6 cardamom pods
20 g/¾ oz butter
20 g/¾ oz flour
2 tbls finely ground fresh coffee
2 tbls muscovado sugar
Ice cream, to serve

1 In a heavy pan, bring the milk, the single cream, the vanilla pod and the cardamom pods slowly to the boil. Leave for 30 minutes to infuse.

2 Melt the butter in a pan, add the flour and cook for 30 seconds. Strain in the infused milk and stir until boiling and thick.

3 Once thickened, stir in the coffee and the muscovado sugar. Leave to cool, covered with cling film. Serve poured over ice cream.

VARIATIONS
The Basic Sweet Sauce recipe can be easily adapted to complement your favourite dessert.
• For an orange flavour, infuse the milk by gently heating with the thinly pared rind of 2 oranges before straining into the roux. Just before serving add 3 tbls cream and 1 tbls orange flower water, available from chemists.
• For a lemon flavour, add up to half a jar of lemon curd to the Basic Sweet Sauce once it has been thickened.

PRUE'S TIP
You can use cornflour instead of a roux. In a pan, mix 2 tsp cornflour with a little milk taken from the 300 ml/½ pt. Stir in the rest, add the sugar and vanilla and stir until boiling and thickened.

Chocolate Sauces

Chocolate sauces vary from the moderately cheap, made with cocoa and golden syrup, to the hugely expensive, made with costly chocolate and real brandy. I like both sorts – and everything in between.

VARIATIONS
• To make a boozy chocolate sauce, add rum whisky, brandy or curaçao to your Ultimate or Quick Chocolate Sauce.
• To make mocha sauce, use strong black coffee to replace the water in the Ultimate Chocolate Sauce. Or increase the coffee quantity from ¼ tsp to 1 tsp in the Quick Chocolate Sauce.

PRUE'S TIP
Block chocolate sets when cold, so cold chocolate sauces will need extra water as well as some cocoa powder. A combination of 100 g/4 oz dark block chocolate, 2 tsp cocoa, 1 tsp sugar and 300 ml/½ pt water will give the right consistency when chilled.

ULTIMATE CHOCOLATE SAUCE

Cooking time: 5-7 mins
Makes 125 ml/¼ pt

INGREDIENTS

225 g/8 oz dark sweetened eating chocolate
2 tbls Tia Maria

1 Heat 6 tbls water in a heavy-based pan. Break up the chocolate, add to pan and stir over heat until smooth. Add the Tia Maria and serve hot.

QUICK CHOCOLATE SAUCE

Cooking time: 5 mins
Makes 350 ml/12 fl oz

INGREDIENTS

1 tbls cocoa powder
1 tbls cornflour
¼ tsp instant coffee
1½ tbls sugar
300 ml/½ pt milk
1 tsp butter

1 Mix the cocoa, cornflour, coffee and sugar together in a saucepan. Stir in enough milk to make a paste. When smooth, add the rest of the milk and stir until boiling. Add butter.

Fruity Sauces

Fruity sauces range from the wonderfully jammy sauces traditionally served with baked and steamed puddings, to the exotic, fresh and tart modern sauces which give colour and interest to dinner party desserts. The fruit used can be fresh, either raw or cooked, dried or in jam form. If the sauce is to be made in advance, sweeten with caster sugar then cook and purée the fruit. Keep refrigerated or frozen. Raw soft fruit can be liquidised or pressed through a sieve to produce delicious instant coulis. Sweeten uncooked sauces with icing sugar.

Quick Fruit Sauces

Mango Sauce
Peel raw mango, slice the flesh off and liquidise. Add sifted icing sugar to taste.

Sauce Cardinale
Push ripe raspberries through a sieve to purée. Sweeten with icicng sugar.

Blackcurrant Coulis
Cook blackcurrants with sugar. Push through a conical sieve with a rounded ladle. Then boil down until it gets to a syrupy consistency.

Variations

STRAWBERRY SAUCE

Preparation time: 10 mins
Makes 300 ml/½ pt

INGREDIENTS
75 g/3 oz strawberries
25 g/1 oz icing sugar
½ tbls kirsch
150 ml/¼ pt double cream

1 Liquidise the strawberries with the sugar and kirsch. Half whip the cream and stir in the purée.

HOT ORANGE SAUCE

Preparation time: 2 mins
Cooking time: 5 mins
Makes 300 ml/½ pt

INGREDIENTS
300 ml/½ pt orange juice
2 tsp cornflour
3 tsp caster sugar

1 Mix 2 tbls orange juice with the cornflour and sugar. Heat the rest of the orange juice, and gradually add the cornflour mixture. Return to the pan and stir until boiling.

SUMMER SAUCE

Preparation time: 5 mins
+ sugaring
Cooking time: 10 mins
Makes 600 ml/1 pt

INGREDIENTS
350 g/12 oz mixed soft fruit, including strawberries, raspberries, blueberries, redcurrants
75 g/3 oz caster sugar
Ice cream, to serve

1 Place the mixed fruit in a glass or china bowl. Sprinkle the sugar over the fruit and leave aside for about 1-2 hours or until the juice runs.

2 Tip the fruit and sugar into a saucepan and stew gently, shaking the pan rather than stirring to avoid damaging the fruit as much as possible.

3 When the fruit is soft and the juices are syrupy, serve immediately with ice cream.

PEACH, ALMOND & BRANDY SAUCE

Preparation time: 2 hours
Cooking time: 15 minutes
Makes 600 ml/1 pt

INGREDIENTS
100 g/4 oz dried peaches
150 ml/¼ pt orange juice
50 g/2 oz sugar
1 tbls brandy
25 g/1 oz blanched almonds, cut into slivers
Fromage frais, to serve

1 Just cover the peaches with hot water and leave to soak. After 2 hours add the orange juice and stew until soft, then purée or liquidise. Return to the pan.

2 Add the sugar, simmer until syrupy, adding water if the purée is too thick. Then add the brandy and the slivered almonds. Serve hot with fromage frais.

ICINGS, FILLINGS & GLAZES

Decorating cakes can be fun, and it is not difficult. It is also one of those areas of food presentation where a little skill and patience can make a world of difference to the end result. But if you haven't time to make homemade icing or marzipan, try decorating a fruit cake using one of these easy methods.

Cover the cake with icing, then encrust it thickly all over with Smarties. It will look like one of the Queen Mum's jolliest hats. Don't do this more than a few hours ahead, because the colour of the Smarties will leak into the icing.

Cover the top of the cake with almonds as for Dundee cake.

Line up rows of walnut halves, dried halved apricots, Brazil nuts, hazelnuts and glacé cherries. Glaze heavily with apricot jam once the cake has cooked and cooled.

Alternatively, glaze the cake with warm sieved apricot jam, and decorate with glacé fruits. Or, if the cake is to be eaten soon, try fresh fruit such as cherries, or edible flowers with non-toxic leaves.

Marzipan

Real marzipan made with freshly ground almonds is a glorious thing. It costs an arm and a leg, but I think it is worth every penny. You can also make a sweet nut paste – which is what marzipan is – with other nuts.

There are two basic methods for making marzipan. One, the cooked one, takes longer to mix, but is quicker and easier to use. Being pliable and warm, it doesn't tear, and holes are easy to patch. The 'quick' marzipan is easier to mix, and can be done in a food processor, but it is trickier to use. I tend to use the cooked version for large cakes and the uncooked one for small cakes, or for adding a layer of marzipan, like a sandwich filling, in the middle of the cake mixture before baking. After covering, leave the cake in a cool, airy place for 1 week to dry. Over-moist marzipan discolours the icing.

Quantity Guide
The following chart tells you how much marzipan you will need for different cake sizes. To tot up how much your marzipan will weigh, add together the ingredients, allowing 50 g/2 oz per egg.

18 cm/7 in round 15 cm/6 in square	450 g/1 lb
23 cm/9 in round 20 cm/8 in square	900 g/2 lb
25 cm/10 in round 23 cm/9 in square	1.1 kg/2 lb 8 oz
28 cm/11 in round 25 cm/10 in square	1.4 kg/3 lb

COOKED MARZIPAN

Preparation time: 20 mins
Cooking time: 5 mins
Makes 700 g/1 lb 8 oz

INGREDIENTS
2 eggs
175 g/6 oz caster sugar
175 g/6 oz icing sugar
350 g/12 oz ground almonds
4 drops vanilla essence
1 tsp lemon juice

1 Lightly beat the eggs together in a large bowl. Sift the sugars together and add to the eggs. Place the bowl over a pan of boiling water and whisk until creamy. Remove from the heat.

2 Add the ground almonds, vanilla essence and lemon juice and beat briefly with a wooden spoon. It should now be a soft paste.

3 Lightly dust a working surface with icing sugar, turn out the paste and knead until just smooth. Overworking will draw out the oil from the almonts and give a greasy paste.

UNCOOKED MARZIPAN

This will cover a 23 cm/9 in round or 20 cm/8 in square cake.

Preparation time: 10 mins
Makes 1 kg/2 lb 4 oz

INGREDIENTS
225 g/8 oz caster sugar
225 g/8 oz icing sugar
450 g/1 lb ground almonds
2 egg yolks
2 whole eggs
2 tsp lemon juice
6 drops vanilla essence

1 Sift the caster sugar and the icing sugar together into a large bowl and stir in the ground almonds. Mix together the egg yolks, whole eggs, lemon juice and vanilla essence.

2 Make a well in the centre of the dry ingredients, pour in the egg mixture and gradually mix together. Lightly dust a working surface with icing sugar and knead the marzipan until smooth.

P R U E ' S   T I P
Use cooked marzipan while still lukewarm and very pliable. To store, wrap tightly in cling film and either refrigerate or freeze until needed. Bring to room temperature and knead briefly before using but do not overwork.

Gâteau Icings

Fresh fruit gâteaux are best with whipped cream, but flavoured cakes such as chocolate or walnut are delicious with butter icing or crème au beurre with a complementary flavouring. Glacé icing gives a smooth, shiny finish. All recipes provide enough icing to cover a 18 cm/7 in cake.

GLACE ICING

Preparation time: 5 mins

INGREDIENTS
225 g/8 oz icing sugar
3-4 tbls boiling water

1 Sift the sugar into a bowl and beat in enough boiling water so that the icing leaves a ribbon trail on itself when the spoon is lifted. Add a suitable flavouring to complement the cake.

BUTTER ICING

Preparation time: 5 mins

INGREDIENTS
50 g/2 oz butter
100 g/4 oz icing sugar, sifted
1 egg yolk, beaten

1 Cream the butter and sugar together in a bowl and stir in the yolk slowly to make a firm icing.

VARIATIONS
Vary Butter Icing to suit your cake:
• Add the finely grated zest of 1 lemon or orange.
• Beat 25 g/1 oz melted chocolate into the icing.

CREME AU BEURRE

Preparation time: 10 mins
Cooking time: 10 mins

INGREDIENTS
2 egg yolks
50 g/2 oz sugar
150 g/5 oz butter, softened

1 Whisk the egg yolks in a bowl. Dissolve the sugar in 50 ml/2 fl oz of water in a pan. Bring to the boil until a sugar thermometer reads no more than 115 C/240 F. Test by dropping a little into cold water – it should form a ball.

2 Remove pan from heat and add the syrup to the egg and whisk with an electric mixer until it turns pale and mousse-like. Cream the butter until pale and fluffy and slowly beat into mousse mixture. Add a flavouring to complement the cake, if desired.

Other Icings

Thick royal icing is wonderfully quick to use and it's fun roughing it up with a fork. It gives a professional coat for important cakes and is the classic icing for piping. This recipe makes enough to cover a 20 cm/8 in round cake, sufficient for 2 coats and a simple decoration.

ROYAL ICING

INGREDIENTS
3 egg whites
700 g/1 lb 8 oz icing sugar
1 tsp lemon juice
2 drops blue food colouring
1 tsp glycerine

1 Beat the egg whites and 350 g /12 oz of the icing sugar together with a wooden spoon. Add the lemon juice, food colouring and glycerine. Gradually stir in 350 g/12 oz more icing sugar until it produces firm peaks when the spoon or blades are lifted. Do not beat vigorously as this produces small air bubbles in the icing. If using an electric mixer go as slowly as possible.

HOME-MADE FONDANT

Preparation time: 30 mins
Makes 1 lb 8 oz

INGREDIENTS
75 g/3 oz lard or white vegetable fat
3 tbls lemon juice
500 g/1 lb 2 oz icing sugar

1 Put the lard or vegetable fat, lemon juice and 2 tbls water into a pan. Heat until the fat has melted.

2 Sieve 275 g/10 oz of icing sugar into the pan and bring to the boil, stirring until smooth. Remove from heat.

3 Gradually add the rest of the icing sugar, 1 tbls at a time, and beat until all the sugar is incorporated. This is easiest in a food mixer, on a slow speed.

4 Dust a clean pastry board or smooth surface with icing sugar. Turn the fondant out onto the surface and knead until cool.

QUICK AMERICAN FROSTING

Preparation time: 15 mins
Makes 8 oz

INGREDIENTS
175 g/6 oz caster sugar
⅛ tsp cream of tartar
Pinch of salt
1 egg white
Few drops of vanilla essence

1 Put the caster sugar, cream of tartar, salt, egg white and vanilla essence in a medium-sized bowl with 2 tbls water. Beat vigorously for 1 minute. Place the bowl over a pan of simmering water and continue beating for 7 minutes.

2 Remove the bowl from the heat and continue beating until the frosting is thick enough to spread over a cake.

Crème Pâtissière

This is the glorious creamy mixture found nestling under rows of glazed fruit in French tarts. It is simplicity itself to make and has a multitude of uses – pipe it into choux buns and cream horns, layer it with jam between pastry or sponges. Don't worry if the custard goes lumpy when you add the milk: as the flour cooks and as you keep beating, it will become smooth.

CREME PATISSIERE

Preparation time: 15 mins
Cooking time: 10 mins
Makes 450 ml/¾ pt

INGREDIENTS

450 ml/¾ pt milk
5 cm/2 in piece of vanilla pod, split, or a few drops of vanilla essence
5 egg yolks
100 g/4 oz caster sugar
2 tbls flour, sifted
1 tbls cornflour, sifted

1 Bring the milk and vanilla pod to simmering point in a saucepan. Remove from the heat and leave to infuse for 10 minutes. Whisk the egg yolks and sugar until pale and thick, then whisk in the flour and cornflour.

2 Take the vanilla pod out of the milk and pour the milk slowly onto the thickened egg yolk mixture, whisking constantly.

3 Pour the mixture back into the saucepan and bring to the boil. Simmer for a few minutes to cook the flour, beating constantly with a wooden spoon to get rid of any lumps.

PRUE'S TIP
To prevent a skin from forming on the top of the custard as it cools, cover the surface with a cut-out circle of greaseproof paper.

VARIATIONS
• For a ginger flavour, infuse no more than a 1.5 cm/½ in piece of peeled and chopped fresh root ginger in the milk instead of the vanilla pod.
• Alternatively, liqueur can be beaten into the custard before cooling.

Glazes

A glaze gives a fruit flan a professional finish and helps to preserve and intensify the colour of the fruit. The glaze needs to be fairly thick to cover the whole surface area so you'll probably need to spoon it over the fruit. It should be syrupy.

PRUE'S TIP
Apricot glaze can also be brushed over a cooked, unfilled pastry case. It will act as a seal against wet sweet fillings.

APRICOT GLAZE

Cooking time: 2 mins

INGREDIENTS

3 tbls apricot jam
Juice of ½ a lemon

1 Place the jam, lemon juice and 2 tbls water in a heavy saucepan. Bring to the boil over a low heat, stirring gently.

2 Sieve the glaze into a bowl. While still warm, spoon over the arranged fruit. If using fruit that discolours quickly like banana, spoon the glaze over as soon as the fruit is in position.

VARIATIONS
• Redcurrant jelly can be heated with water in the same way as apricot glaze, but it does not need to be sieved. It has to be almost cold before it is the right consistency for glazing fruit.
• Marmalade can be used in place of apricot jam.
• Melt clear honey with a dash of lemon juice for a rich, dark glaze. Don't use set honey as it will turn cloudy when cold.

MICROWAVE TIP
Put ingredients in a medium-sized bowl with 1 extra tbls water. Microwave on HIGH (100 %) for 30-40 seconds, stirring halfway through cooking time.

SWEETS

Most of us have tried our hand at making fudge and toffee, but with a little practice you can also make professional-looking, filled chocolates and truffles. They're deceptively easy, and you can make them as stylish as you like. Fill them with a selection of chopped nuts or dried fruits, or try marzipan or truffle mixture. They are cheaper than commercially made sweets and make a delightful gift.

Remember not to store the finished chocolates in the fridge as they may sweat, causing the chocolate to lose its shine. Truffles are best stored in their paper cases, either layered with greaseproof paper or between sheets of cardboard. Wrap fudge in cellophane or greaseproof paper and store in a cool place in an airtight tin. It will keep for up to two weeks – but if your house is anything like mine I'm sure it will be gone long gone before then.

Toffee

Make sure you use double cream when making toffee – its high fat content is needed to withstand the rapid boiling.

BASIC TOFFEE

Preparation time: 10 mins
+ cooling
Cooking time: 20 mins
Makes About 50 squares

INGREDIENTS

25 g/1 oz butter, plus extra for greasing
250 g/9 oz sugar
225 ml/8 fl oz double cream
25 g/1 oz clear honey
3 drops of vanilla essence
¼ tsp cream of tartar

1 Line an 18 cm/7 in square tin with buttered greaseproof paper. Put the butter, sugar, cream, honey and vanilla essence in a pan and stir over a medium heat until the sugar has dissolved. Brush sides of pan with a wet pastry brush to remove any crystals.

2 Bring to the boil and stir in the cream of tartar. Boil steadily, stirring occasionally, until a teaspoon of the mixture dropped into iced water forms a firm ball, then dip the pan in cold water to stop the mixture cooking any further.

3 Pour the syrup into the tin. Leave to cool, then score into 2.5 cm/1 in squares. When set, unmould and cut into pieces. Wrap each piece in cellophane or waxed paper.

Fudge

Smooth and firm, with a light grainy texture – this is how perfect fudge should be. And it's so easy to achieve, just remember to cook at the right temperature and not to overbeat.

BASIC FUDGE

Preparation time: 5 mins
Cooking time: 25 mins
Makes About 50 squares

INGREDIENTS

Oil, for greasing
450 g/1 lb sugar
75 g/3 oz butter
150 ml/¼ pt milk
175 ml/6 fl oz evaporated milk
3 drops of vanilla essence
75 g/3 oz raisins
3 tbls rum

1 Lightly oil a shallow 18 cm/7 in square tin. Put the sugar, butter, milk and evaporated milk in a heavy-based pan and heat over a gentle heat, stirring all the time, until all the sugar has dissolved. Bring to the boil without stirring, then reduce the heat to a steady boil. Continue cooking until the syrup reaches a temperature of 116 C/240 F – a soft ball will form when a little mixture is dropped into a bowl of cold water. Stir gently a few times during the cooking process.

2 Remove the pan from the heat and add the vanilla essence, raisins and rum. Beat the mixture vigorously with a wooden spoon until it becomes thick and grainy.

3 Pour the mixture into the prepared tin and score the surface into 2.5 cm/1 in squares. Cut up when cold, and store in an airtight container until ready to use.

V A R I A T I O N S
Try adding the following instead of the rum and raisins:
• 150 g/5 oz melted plain chocolate. Add 50 g/2 oz chopped nuts if wished.
• 100 g/4 oz chopped glacé cherries. Add 3 tbls kirsch for extra flavour.

Truffles

Truffles are possibly one of the simplest sweetmeats to make. If you want to dip them in melted chocolate, use a fork, or a special round, spiralled metal implement to hold them securely and allow the chocolate to drip back into the pan. For square shapes, a special fork with elongated prongs is used, so the sweets are well supported.

BASIC TRUFFLES

Preparation time: 15 mins
+ chilling
Makes About 30

INGREDIENTS
225 g/8 oz plain, milk or white chocolate
2 egg yolks
25 g/1 oz butter
1 tbls double cream
50 g/2 oz ground almonds
2 tbls dark or light rum
4 tbls cocoa powder, for coating

1 Melt the chocolate in a bowl set over a pan of hot water. Add the egg yolks, butter, cream, almonds and rum and beat together to combine.

2 Chill the mixture until it is firm enough to handle. This will take about 30 minutes. Then form teaspoonsful into balls. Roll in the cocoa and place in paper sweet cases. Chill truffles until required.

VARIATIONS
To vary the flavour of your truffles, try one of the following:
• Replace the rum with a flavoured liqueur such as cherry brandy, Cointreau or Amaretto.
• Wrap the truffle mixture around pricked cherries that have soaked overnight in brandy or kirsch. Drain well before using.
• Coat truffles in icing sugar, chocolate vermicelli, dessicated coconut or mixed chopped nuts instead of the cocoa.
• Dip the truffles into 100 g/4 oz melted chocolate. If using white chocolate you can then dip in 4 tbls caster sugar.

Chocolates

Chocolate moulds are reusable and can be bought at cake decorating or specialist cookware shops.

FILLED CHOCOLATES

Preparation time: 20 mins
+ chilling
Makes 24

INGREDIENTS
100 g/4 oz plain, milk or white chocolate, melted

FOR THE FILLING
50 g/2 oz chopped nuts, maraschino cherries, glacé fruit, marzipan or truffle mixture

FOR THE DECORATION
Melted plain or white chocolate, whole nuts or crystallised violet and rose petals

1 Use two sets of chocolate moulds, cleaned and dried. Pour 1 tsp melted chocolate into each shape then brush the chocolate up the sides to the top using a paintbrush.

2 Turn the moulds upside-down on a piece of baking parchment and chill until set. Remove the paper and spoon a little filling mixture into each hollow centre.

3 Fill to the top with melted chocolate. Scrape across the surface with a round-bladed knife to remove excess chocolate. Chill until set. To unmould the chocolate, tap gently on the work surface. If any chocolates refuse to come out chill for a further 3-5 minutes then try again.

4 Decorate with plain or white chocolate piped using a fine star nozzle. Alternatively, top with whole nuts or crystallised petals.

PRESERVES

Home-made preserves, made with nothing but fresh fruit and sugar, are unbeatable. And if you're lucky enough to have home-grown or cheaply picked fruit, they can be less than half the price of their commercial equivalents.

In a jam

There is always the danger of jams fermenting. To prevent this they must set. Three things are necessary: pectin, sugar and acid. You also need to kill off any organisms which might make the jam go bad, and then make sure that no new ones get in. The mixture should be heated to its setting point –105 C/220 F. If it has reached this temperature and won't set, don't keep boiling – you'll get a caramel-flavoured syrup, then burnt sugar. Stop, cool the jam and re-boil when you have bought pectin or added high-pectin fruit.

Plenty of pectin

If you have never made jams before, start with blackcurrants, plums, raspberries or apricots – they are high in pectin and never fail. Strawberries are tricky for jam making as they are hard to keep whole, are low in pectin and inclined to lose their brilliant, natural colour.

Testing for pectin

When making jam, you can test the concentration of pectin by putting a teaspoon of the simmered fruit juice (before you add the sugar) into a glass. Add a tablespoon of methylated spirits. Allow to cool. If there is enough pectin the juice will have clotted into a single lump. The juice is low in pectin if there are several small clots or none at all. Boil it hard for 10 minutes to concentrate it, and then test again. If it still refuses to set, redress the balance by adding high-pectin fruit now, or commercial pectin at the end. A general guide is 150 ml/¼ pt pectin to 1.8 kg/4 lb fruit. Don't eat this mixture.

Picking fruit

Fruit for jams and jellies needs to be just ripe as this is when the pectin content is highest. Pick it over carefully, but avoid washing (the boiling will sterilise it). Just make sure it is free of leaves and creepy-crawlies. Frozen fruit works perfectly. To prepare the fruit, cut it to the size that you want it in the finished jam. Halve plums and apricots, slice peaches and finely shred orange or lemon rind for marmalade. Remove stalks from raspberries and strawberries, leaving the fruit whole. Top and tail gooseberries.

Sticky business

Only highly refined sugars produce clear scum-free jams. The cheapest is granulated so use that. Avoid brown sugar as it spoils the look of the jam and produces too caramelly a taste. Most acid fruits require an equal weight of sugar to fruit. You can reduce the sugar but do not use less than 3 parts sugar to 4 parts fruit or the jam will not set.

Acid ingredients

Fruits for jam must contain enough acid to react with the pectin and sugar to get a set. Most fruits high in pectin are also pretty acidic, but some, like apricots may need added lemon juice, tartaric acid or ascorbic acid (vitamin C).

Jam

Almost all jams are made by first cooking the fruit, then adding the sugar and boiling the mixture until it is pulpy and will set. Once you have mastered this Basic Plum Jam you will feel confident enough to experiment with both low- and high-pectin fruits.

BASIC PLUM JAM

Preparation time: 40 mins
Cooking time: 15-20 mins
Makes 1.8 kg/4 lb

INGREDIENTS
900 g/2 lb granulated sugar
900 g/2 lb ripe plums

1 Sterilise and dry four 450 g/1 lb jam jars and their lids, a funnel and a spoon for skimming. Warm the dry jars in a low oven. Put the sugar into a roasting tin and warm it up in a low oven for 5-10 minutes.

2 Halve the plums and stone them. Simmer them, stirring regularly, in 300 ml/½ pt water until soft.

3 Add the warm sugar and stir until it is dissolved. Boil rapidly until 105 C /220 F is reached, or until the jam is ready to set.

4 To test for setting, chill a saucer in the fridge. Put a teaspoon of the jam onto the cold saucer and return to the fridge. When cold, the jam should have a skin on top which will wrinkle when pushed with a finger. If not setting, boil for another 5 minutes and test again.

5 Leave the jam for 10 minutes to thicken up a little (otherwise the whole fruit may rise in the jars). Skim off any scum after the 10 minutes.

6 Pour or ladle the jam into the warm jars. Wipe the jars with a wet cloth then seal and label.

PRUE'S TIP
The best airtight seal is provided by metal screwtop lids, screwed on while the jam is hot so that the air contracts as it cools and forms a tight seal. Paper covers work too, providing the jams are to be stored level and undisturbed.

Jellies

Jellies are similar to jams, but more costly to make as only the simmered fruit juice and not the whole fruit is used. Sugar is added and the mixture boiled until it sets.

Don't worry about stalks and leaves – they will be strained out later. If some of the fruit is very tough, stew it first. Add the softer fruit later.

Hedgerow Jelly

To make hedgerow jelly, use a mixture of any of the following fruits: blackberries, sloes, rowan berries, hips, hawthorn berries, crab-apples, elderberries, quinces and bullaces (wild plums). Put them all into a large pan, making sure tough fruit, like sloes and crab-apples, are at the bottom. Add enough water to the pan to come halfway up the fruit. Cover and simmer slowly until the fruit is soft and pulpy. Fit a jelly bag over a large container and ladle juice into the bag. Leave to drip overnight. Measure the juice and add 450 g/1 lb sugar for each 600 ml/1 pt of liquid. Boil until it sets.

Preserves

Some fruit, such as figs, do not set very easily but can be made into preserves. Unlike jam, the mixture is boiled gently to a syrupy consistency. However, they do not keep very well and should be refrigerated after opening. Use glass jars with metal screwtops.

Fig Preserve

To make Fig Preserve, use 900 g/2 lb ripe figs, the juice of 2 lemons, 900 g/2 lb sugar and 150 ml/¼ pt of water. Proceed as you would for jam but go slowly until all the sugar dissolves.

Passionfruit Preserve

To make Passionfruit Preserve, scoop the flesh and seeds from the fruit. Add the juice of 1 lemon and 225 g/8 oz sugar to each 300 ml/½ pt pulp and proceed in the same way as for jam.

Citrus curds are among the simplest of preserves to make. Their storage period is short, however – 3 weeks in the fridge – so they are best made in small quantities and used quickly.

LEMON CURD

Preparation time: 10 mins
Cooking time: 10 mins
Makes 575 g/1 lb 4 oz

INGREDIENTS

2 large lemons	
75 g/3 oz butter	
225 g/8 oz granulated sugar	
3 eggs, beaten	

1 Finely grate the zest of the lemons, taking care to grate zest only, not pith. Squeeze the juice.

2 Put the zest, juice, butter, sugar and eggs into a saucepan and heat gently, stirring until thick.

3 Pour through a funnel into sterilised jars and allow to cool. Cover and store in the fridge for up to 3 weeks.

PRUE'S TIP
Don't worry about curdling. You can always strain the curd.

Marmalades

Jams made with citrus fruits are called marmalades. Seville oranges are the most popular choice of fruit for making into marmalade because of their strong flavour, but grapefruit and limes are also delicious. Marmalades can be chunky, like jams, or strained like jellies, depending on your taste. Try this basic recipe for a start.

ORANGE MARMALADE

Preparation time: 20 mins
+ soaking
Cooking time: 2 hours 20 mins
Makes 2.8 kg/6 lb

INGREDIENTS

900 g/2 lb Seville oranges	
2 lemons	
1.8 kg/4 lb sugar	

1 Cut the fruit in half and roughly squeeze into a large bowl. Remove the pips and tie them in a piece of muslin. Slice the fruit skins, finely or in chunks as wished, and add them to the juice with the bag of pips and 2.8 L/5 pt water.

2 Transfer to a preserving pan or saucepan and simmer gently until the rind is soft and transparent – about 2 hours. Remove the pips. Warm the sugar in a low oven for 20 minutes. Tip into the orange pulp. Stir. Bring slowly to the boil.

3 Once the sugar has dissolved, boil rapidly until setting point is reached: 105 C/220 F on a sugar thermometer, or when a little marmalade dropped on a chilled saucer and cooled, wrinkles when pushed. This may take up to 20 minutes, but test after 5 minutes and then at 3-minute intervals.

4 Allow to cool for 10 minutes then ladle through a funnel into warm, dry sterilised jars. Cover with waxed discs and cellophane and leave for 24 hours. Label and store in a cool place.

PICKLES & RELISHES

Although you will more often than not spoon relishes straight from the jar you bought in the supermarket, if you go to the trouble of making them for yourself at home you will certainly appreciate the difference in flavour and freshness.

HORSERADISH SAUCE

Preparation time: 5 mins

INGREDIENTS

| 1 tsp white wine vinegar |
| Squeeze of lemon juice |
| 1 tsp Dijon mustard |
| Salt and ground black pepper |
| 2 tbls grated horseradish |
| 150 ml/¼ pt double cream |

1 Mix together the vinegar, lemon juice, Dijon mustard, salt, pepper and grated horseradish. Whip the double cream and fold into the horseradish.

GRAINY MUSTARD

The interesting texture and tangy flavour of home-made mustard can pep up even the blandest dish.

Preparation time: 45 mins
+ marinating
Makes 600 ml/1 pt

INGREDIENTS

| 50 g/2 oz black mustard seeds |
| 50 g/2 oz white mustard seeds |
| 1 tbls mustard powder |
| 150 ml/¼ pt white wine |
| 125 ml/4 fl oz white wine vinegar or cider vinegar |
| 100 g/4 oz honey |
| 1 tbls salt |

1 Process the mustard seeds and powder, then add the wine. Stir the blended seeds, powder and wine thoroughly. Leave for 30 minutes.

2 Blend the mustard mixture until it becomes a paste. Add the vinegar, honey and salt and combine. Pour into pots and leave for 2-3 weeks.

VARIATIONS
Tarragon and honey or black olive and dill seed make two excellent combinations for flavouring home-made mustards.

MINT SAUCE

Preparation time: 2 mins
+ standing

INGREDIENTS

| 100 g/4 oz fresh mint, finely chopped |
| 150 ml/¼ pt malt vinegar |
| 2 tsp caster sugar |

1 Put the mint into a screw-top jar. Add the malt vinegar and the caster sugar. Shake, then leave to stand for 15-20 minutes. It will keep in the fridge for up to 4 months.

MINT JELLY

Preparation time: 2 mins
+ cooling
Cooking time: 2 mins
Makes 175 g/6 oz

INGREDIENTS

| 175 g/6 oz bottled apple jelly |
| 2 tbls chopped fresh mint |

1 Heat the apple jelly in a pan over a low heat until melted. Stir in the mint, cool for 20 minutes and pour into a jar. This will keep for up to 14 days in the fridge. If you have no apple jelly, use fresh or canned apple sauce, but cool and serve on the same day.

Tomato Relishes

Home-made ketchup is delicious and contains no artificial additives! The taste, as ever, depends on good ingredients.

TOMATO KETCHUP

Preparation time: 30 mins
Cooking time: 1-1½ hours
Makes 1 L/1¾ pt

INGREDIENTS

| 2.8 kg/6 lb ripe tomatoes, skinned and chopped |
| 225 g/8 oz sugar |
| 20 g/¾ oz salt |
| Pinch of cayenne pepper |
| ½ tsp ground ginger |
| ½ tsp paprika |
| ½ tsp ground mace |
| ½ tsp ground cloves |
| 300 ml/½ pt distilled malt vinegar |

1 Cook the tomatoes until soft. Sieve into a pan. Add the other ingredients. Boil gently, stirring occasionally until thick and creamy.

2 Sterilise the bottles and lids in boiling water for 15 minutes. Pour the sauce into the bottles to 2.5 cm/1 in from the rim. Screw on the lids, then unscrew a half turn.

3 Stand bottles on a trivet in a pan of water. Bring the water to 70 C/160 F and maintain for 30 minutes. Lift out the bottles and tighten lids.

FRESH TOMATO RELISH

Preparation time: 10 mins

INGREDIENTS

| 575 g/1 lb 4 oz fresh tomatoes, skinned, seeded and chopped |
| 1 finely chopped onion |
| Pinch of sugar |
| 15 g/½ oz butter |
| Chopped fresh basil |

1 Simmer the chopped tomatoes with the onion and sugar in the butter until pulpy and thick. Add a pinch of chopped basil at the last minute.

PRUE'S TIP
To make a tomato coulis add only half the onion and purée the sauce in a blender when cooked.

Chutneys

Keep home-made chutney for 3 months before eating to allow it to mellow.

APRICOT, ORANGE & ONION CHUTNEY

Preparation time: 30 mins
+ soaking
Cooking time: 30-40 mins
Makes 2.3 kg/5 lb

INGREDIENTS

450 g/1 lb dried apricots
2 oranges
700 g/1½ lb onions, sliced
450 g/1 lb granulated sugar
225 g/8 oz sultanas
900 ml/1½ pt malt vinegar
2 tsp salt
1 tsp mustard seeds
1 tsp ground turmeric
2 green chillies, split
2 cloves garlic, crushed

1 Soak the apricots in warm water for 2 hours. Use a potato peeler to pare the orange zest finely away from the pith of the oranges. Cut the zest into very fine strips, using a sharp knife.

2 Peel the pith from the oranges and discard it. Chop the orange flesh discarding the membrane. Drain apricots and chop into chunks. Combine all ingredients in a pan and simmer for 30-40 minutes until thick and syrupy.

3 Using a measuring jug, pour the chutney into sterile, dry, warm jars. Cover with clamp-tops or tight-fitting lids to seal.

WATCHPOINT

Avoid non-stainless utensils when making pickles and chutneys. The vinegar reacts with the metal to produce a metallic taste, and slightly poisonous pickles and chutneys. When storing, don't use unvarnished metal lids for stoppers.

QUICK MANGO RELISH

INGREDIENTS

1 ripe mango
2 fresh green chillies, seeded and chopped
1 onion, chopped
1 tbls chopped fresh coriander
½ tsp salt
2 tbls desiccated coconut

1 Peel the mango and chop the flesh. Reserve half and blend the other half with the rest of the ingredients to make a sauce. Stir in the reserved chopped mango and chill.

Pickles

Use good quality vinegars for pickling – brown malt vinegar is fine, but for light-coloured vegetables, choose either white malt vinegar or wine vinegar.

PICKLED ONIONS

Preparation time: 20 mins
+ pickling
Cooking time: 15 mins
Makes 1.8 kg/4 lb

INGREDIENTS

1.8 kg/4 lb pickling onions

FOR THE PICKLING VINEGAR
1.2 L/2 pt malt vinegar
3 blades of mace
1 cinnamon stick
2 tsp allspice berries
½ tsp black peppercorns
2 tsp mustard seeds
4 cloves
1 split chilli
15 g/½ oz root ginger, sliced

FOR THE BRINE
225 g/8 oz salt
2.3 L/4 pt boiling water

1 Put the vinegar, mace, cinnamon, berries, peppercorns, mustard, cloves, chilli and ginger in a pan and heat gently until just at simmering point. Leave the pickling vinegar until cold.

2 Combine the salt and boiling water in a large heatproof bowl and stir to dissolve. Leave this brine until cold. Scald the onions in boiling water, drain, then remove the skins.

3 Prick the onions all over with a stainless steel skewer. Put in a bowl and add the brine. Weight the onions down with a saucer to ensure they are all submerged, and leave for 48 hours.

4 Drain the onions and pat dry. Pack into jars. Pour vinegar over the top, being careful to allow only clear liquid onto the onions. Strain if necessary. Leave to mature for 3 months before eating, but use within a year.

LIME PICKLE

Preparation time: 15 mins
+ salting
Makes 900 g/2 lb

INGREDIENTS

1 lemon
3 limes
50 g/2 oz salt
2 tsp mustard seeds, dry roasted
2 fresh green chillies
300 ml/½ pt sesame oil

1 Wash the fruit and dry thoroughly as any moisture will turn the pickle mouldy. Slice the fruit into wedges and place in a colander. Sprinkle with the salt and leave to drain for 24 hours.

2 Layer the fruit in 2 sterilised jars with the mustard seeds. Pop 1 chilli in each jar and pour over the oil to cover the fruit. Seal securely and leave to mature for 2-4 weeks – the skins will have softened when it is ready to eat.

STUFFINGS & MARINADES

Stuffings are principally used to add flavour to the finished dish and are useful for making poultry and joints of meat go further. As the stuffing may make up half the dish, it must be wonderful, not too heavy and bready. Fresh bright vegetables make light stuffings, or use other meats – whole chicken breasts or diced, cooked bacon in a sausagemeat base. Try spicy rice or lentils, or maybe even something surprising like a combination of olives, ham and spinach.

Marinating is an excellent way of pepping up cheaper cuts of meat. A good marinade will not only add flavour, but the acids in the vinegar, onion, lemon and wine will also help to tenderise the meat, while the oil will preserve it by keeping out the air. Experiment with different herbs, and spices to suit the meat and the meal you are planning.

Stuffings

SAGE, ONION & PEAR STUFFING

INGREDIENTS

2 onions, finely chopped
25 g/1 oz butter
100 g/4 oz fresh white breadcrumbs
2 tbls chopped fresh sage
Salt and ground black pepper
1 large or 2 small pears, peeled, cored and cut into small dice
A little beaten egg

1 Sauté the onions in the butter until soft and just coloured. Leave to cool and then mix with the breadcrumbs, sage, salt and pepper and pears. Bind with the egg and use as required.

MARJORAM & CHERVIL STUFFING

INGREDIENTS

1 small onion, finely chopped
25 g/1 oz butter
100 g/4 oz pork sausagemeat
50 g/20 oz fresh white breadcrumbs
Grated zest of 1 lemon
1 tbls chopped fresh marjoram
1 tbls chopped fresh chervil
Salt and ground black pepper
A little beaten egg

1 Sauté the onion in the butter until softened. Cool and then mix with the sausagemeat, breadcrumbs, lemon zest, marjoram and chervil. Season to taste and bind with the beaten egg.

PRUNE & APPLE STUFFING

INGREDIENTS

1 small onion, finely chopped
25 g/1 oz butter
100 g/4 oz fresh white breadcrumbs
100 g/4 oz pitted prunes, chopped
1 cooking apple, peeled, cored and chopped
Pinch each of allspice, ground turmeric and cinnamon
Salt and ground black pepper
A little beaten egg

1 Sauté the onion in the butter until soft. Cool and then add the breadcrumbs, prunes, apple, spices, salt and pepper. Bind the mixture with a little beaten egg.

Marinades

BASIC MARINADE FOR STEAK

INGREDIENTS

3 tbls olive oil
2 cloves garlic, crushed
2 tsp dry English mustard
1 tbls sugar
1 tbls vinegar
2 shallots, chopped
1 tsp dried thyme

1 Mix all the ingredients together well and pour over the meat. Marinate for at least 2 hours. Drain before frying.

BASIL & GARLIC MARINADE

INGREDIENTS

3 tbls olive oil
4 tbls chopped fresh basil
2 cloves garlic, crushed
6 black peppercorns, crushed
1/4 tsp salt

1 Combine oil, basil, garlic, peppercorns, and salt. Marinate the meat in this mixture for at least 2 hours, turning regularly.

RED WINE & MUSTARD SEED MARINADE

INGREDIENTS

2 onions, sliced
150 ml/1/4 pt red wine
150 ml/1/4 pt olive oil
1 tbls sugar
1 tsp mustard seeds
1 bay leaf, crushed

1 Mix the onions with the olive oil, red wine, sugar, mustard seeds and bay leaf. Mix well with the meat and put in a covered or sealed container. Refrigerate for between 24 hours and 3 days. Turn the meat occasionally.

PRETTY PRESENTATION

Ice Bowls

Pretty coloured food and flowers suspended in clear ice make colourful containers and are worth the effort to make. They cost next to nothing and can transform an ordinary fruit salad or iced soup into a spectacular dish.

The main points to remember when making these impressive containers is that the two bowls you use must be the same shape, one smaller than the other and the rims must be level when filled with water. Whenever possible use glass bowls so that you can see the pattern while you are arranging it. Plastic bowls can be used if necessary and are easier to unmould. You can make individual ice bowls in the same way as large ice bowls. Try using yoghurt, cottage cheese or coleslaw containers.

You will also need two broad elastic bands or sticky tape and flowers, fruit or herbs, to decorate. Use rose petals, sweetpeas, freesias, lavender and nasturtiums in bowls used to serve fruit salads, ice creams and sorbets. Or try sliced strawberries, kiwi fruit, oranges, lemons, limes, star fruit and sprigs of red- or blackcurrants. For salad bowls and chilled soup bowls use rosemary sprigs, mint leaves, dill fronds and borage leaves.

1 Fill the larger bowl ⅓ full with cold tap water or still mineral water. Push the smaller bowl into the water and secure in place with the elastic bands or sticky tape, ensuring that the two bowl rims are level. The water should now come about ⅔ of the way up the bowls.

2 Push the decorations into the water between the two bowls. Place in the freezer overnight or until frozen.

PRUE'S TIP
You can use a few drops of food colouring to tint the water a pale pink, green or orange.

3 Add another layer of decorations and gently pour in a cupful of very cold water or enough to just cover the decorations. Freeze again. Then fill to the top with more iced water and freeze again.

4 To unmould the bowl, fill the smaller bowl with tepid water, twist to loosen and remove. Dip the bottom of the larger bowl in tepid water to loosen then remove this too. Make sure the water isn't too hot or the bowl will crack. Keep the ice bowl in the freezer until required.

WATCHPOINT
Before freezing ice bowls check there are no air bubbles as these will melt and produce a hole.

Fanning

This simple technique can be applied to a variety of fresh fruit and vegetables with stunning results. Equipped with a small pointed knife you can conjure up a fanned garnish in a matter of seconds.

Strawberries

Choose fruit that is just ripe and still has the stalk attached. Lay the fruit on a chopping board and cut downwards into thin slices, leaving the stalk end intact. Gently press sideways to fan open.

Avocado Pears

Peel the skin from a halved avocado and place cut-side down on a chopping board. Cut even slits along the flesh, leaving the narrow end uncut. Using the flat of your hand, gently push the slices apart to form a fan.

If the avocado is too firm to fan, slice it in half lengthways and then across into to crescents instead. Then slide a palette knife underneath and fan with your fingers. Slide onto a plate.

Peaches & Nectarines

Carefully cut the fruit in half lengthways and twist apart. Discard the stone. Leaving the skin on, cut in half again. Make thin cuts along the length of each quarter, leaving one end intact. Gently fan apart.

Chicken Breasts

Lay the cooked breast on a board and cut diagonally into 12 mm/½ in slices. Lift onto the plate and ease the segments apart at one end.

Pastry Presentation

When you are making pies, tarts or flans, there are usually scraps of pastry left over. A light knead, a quick roll of the pin and a dash of imagination can turn the scraps into delightful decorations to make your pies a picture.

For leftover puff and rough puff pastry, make sure you lay the pieces flat on top of each other and roll out gently. Kneading them together will destroy their delicate layers. When the pie is decorated, refrigerate for 10 minutes or so – the chilling will help keep its shape. For a pretty effect, use diluted food colouring to paint the pastry before baking.

Shapes

Use pastry cutters or a small a knife to cut out shapes, or mould them freehand. Choose shapes to reflect the filling – fish shapes for fish pies, or a bouquet of little vegetables for a vegetable pie.

Flowering Centrepieces

To make a chrysanthemum, cut a strip of pastry 15 cm/6 in by 5 cm/2 in. Cut slits along one side, graded from short to long. Brush the base with beaten egg and roll up the pastry, starting from the long cuts. Ease the fronds apart and sit upright on the pie vent.

To make a rose, cut out the petals with a sharp-pointed knife. Loosely fold one petal over and pinch at the base. Fold another petal round it to enclose the cut edges, and gradually build up the rose until the outside petals are almost flat.

Leaves & Fruit

When making leaves, roll out the pastry as thinly as possible or they will lose their shape when cooked. Use a leaf-shaped cutter or cut the pastry into strips, then cut diagonally into even-sized diamonds. Mark the veins with the blade of a knife

To make apples, roll out small balls of pastry and brush with diluted red food colouring. Use cloves as the apple stalks. Roll pastry under the palm of your hand for the branches. Curve the branch around the centre of the pie, and place the apple and leaves along it.

Finishing Touches

After decorating pies and tarts, brush with a glaze to give the cooked dish a golden colour. Use beaten egg or egg yolk diluted with a little water or milk, or just use milk. If wished, add a pinch of salt for savoury pies and caster sugar for dessert pies.

'Knocking up' & Crimping Edges

Use these techniques to seal double layers of flaky pastry. 'Knock up' the edges of the pie with the blade of a knife – the cuts help the pastry rise. Push gently with thumb and forefinger and drag a dessert knife back between to crimp edges.

Decorative Ideas

Try using 3 long strips of pastry, pinched together at one end and plaited to decorate the edge of a pie.

Alternatively, pinch up the edge of a double crust pie and, using two fingers, push in opposite directions to give a wavy effect. Roll out tiny balls of dough and place them in the spaces the curves make.

To make holly, cut out the leaves with a pastry cutter or make freehand. Roll balls of dough for the berries. Use 2 leaves and 3-4 berries to make each 'sprig' and arrange 'sprigs' around the pie edge.

Fish Parcel

To decorate a fish-shaped pie use a sharp knife to score out the tail markings and mouth, and crimp the bottom edges. Roll out a pastry eye. Use the point of a knife to score semi-circles into the pastry to represent the fish scales.

PRUE'S TIP

For oak leaves and acorns, cut out the leaves with a pastry cutter or freehand. Make little cups, roll balls of dough for the acorn and place inside the cups. Use 3 leaves and place an acorn in the centre. Place around the edge of the pie.

Chocolate Tricks

Few people can resist a dessert or pastry decorated with chocolate. With the following chocolate tricks you can transform ordinary cakes into luscious, mouth-watering gateaux and give simple desserts that professional touch.

Types of Chocolate

Choose a chocolate to suit the job in hand. Chocolate-flavoured cake covering is made with vegetable oils, melts easily and is very easy to work with. Plain dark dessert chocolate has a bittersweet flavour. Plain dark cooking chocolate has the best quality and flavour of all the dark chocolates. Milk chocolate contains less cocoa and more milk and is particularly good for piping. White chocolate is made with vegetable fat, full cream milk, cocoa butter and sugar. It has a very sweet flavour.

Melting Chocolate

The two main things to remember when melting chocolate are to melt it slowly and never let it get too hot. Simply break the chocolate into small pieces and place in a bowl over a saucepan of cold water, or in the top of a double boiler. The base of the bowl should not touch the water. Heat the water gently and let it just simmer. When the chocolate has melted, remove the pan from the heat and stir the chocolate until it is smooth and glossy. If it starts to harden just reheat it in the same way and try again.

Making Curls & Caraque

Chocolate curls or the larger caraque can be made by melting the chocolate then pouring it onto a marble slab, melamine board or clean work surface. Using a big knife, pare long curls off the surface of the chocolate, carefully adjusting the angle of the knife as you work.

Alternatively, pare away curls from a block of chocolate using a vegetable peeler.

Making Chocolate Leaves

Choose well-defined leaves such as rose or bay. Wash and dry the leaves, then dip the underside into the melted chocolate or paint it on with a brush. Allow excess chocolate to drain back into the bowl, or scrape leaf gently on the side of the bowl to achieve a smooth surface. Place on a lined baking tray to set, chocolate side up. When set, peel away the leaf. If you want a realistic curved appearance, lay them over a wooden rolling pin while they set.

Making Chocolate Cases

Chocolate cases can be used as containers for ice creams, sorbets, mousses or fruit. To make them, brush the inside of petit fours cases, tartlet tins or bun cases with 2 or 3 coatings of melted chocolate, allowing the chocolate to harden between each coating. Place on a baking tray to harden and store in a cool place. Do not refrigerate or the chocolate will develop a 'bloom'.

Dipping Fruit

Dip the tips of fruits such as strawberries, cherries, orange segments, pineapple triangles, physalis (Cape gooseberries), and grapes into melted chocolate. The fruit should not be wet or the chocolate will not grip. Once dipped, hold the fruit for a few seconds to allow it to drip and begin to harden, then lay it on a baking tray lined with baking parchment.

Piping Chocolate

Piped chocolate is an effective way of decorating cakes and desserts. Fill a greaseproof piping bag with melted chocolate which has cooled and thickened slightly. Snip a small piece from the end.

Shapes

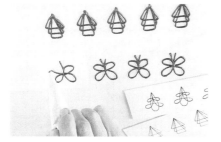

Draw shapes on a piece of white paper. Slip under a piece of baking parchment and use as a guide as you pipe onto the parchment. Allow to set, then peel off.

Straight Lines

Pipe in neat lines, working towards yourself, keeping the piping bag close to the surface. For a criss-cross effect, give a quarter turn and repeat.

Feathering

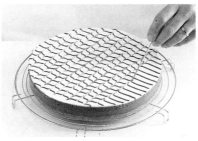

First pipe some neat horizontal lines, then draw a skewer back and forth evenly over the lines to create a feathered effect.

Writing

Mark out with pin pricks first. For joined-up writing, always start from the top of the letter and let the writing flow. For individual letters, put the tip of the bag at the top of a letter. Lift the bag, squeezing gently as you begin to form the letter. When you reach the bottom of the letter, stop squeezing and lift the bag away.

Sauce Presentation

There are hundreds of simple chefs' tricks which help make little puddings and desserts look amazingly elegant and up-to-date. Sauces can be patterned and swirled, feathered or spotted very easily and to great effect.

Double Flavours

Imagine the plate is a compass. Pour a pool of crème anglaise at north and south and matching pools of blackcurrant coulis at east and west. Unmould a blackcurrant jelly in the centre.

Spotty Sauce

Cover one side of the plate with passion fruit sauce with the seeds in it. Cover the other with double cream. Dot the cream with melted chocolate, dropped from a piping bag. It will set into little buttons as it hits the cold cream. Spoon chocolate mousse in the middle.

Feathering

Pour raspberry coulis onto a plate around ice-cream. Spoon on 1 tsp double cream. Draw a cocktail stick through the cream.

Shiny Set Sauce

Choose a clear fruit sauce and add 1 tsp powdered gelatine for 300 ml/½ pt liquid. Sprinkle on the gelatine, leave 10 minutes to soak, then reheat gently until clear. Pour a thin layer onto cold plates and leave to set. Decorate with tiny mint leaves around the edge, adding a layer of just liquid sauce to stick in place. Refrigerate until stuck. Cover with another thin layer of sauce (if necessary reheat to liquefy) and leave to set. Put a tiny fruit tartlet in the middle.

Flambés

Flambé is a French culinary term which means to flame food with spirits. This process should lightly singe the surface of the food, giving a wonderful aroma and delicious flavour.

The spirit can be heated separately in a metal ladle or in a small saucepan, ignited and then carefully poured, flaming, over the food on its serving dish or plates. This is the ideal method for flaming your Christmas pudding. It is best to light the spirit at the table rather than moving with the lighted flame.

To flame food in its cooking pan pour the spirit onto the hot sizzling food to heat through and then ignite with a match or long taper. The food will continue flaming until the alcohol is burned off leaving the flavour of the spirit behind. This method can be used to flame food in a sauce or can be used for seared meat like chicken or steak, before cream or stock is added to the dish.

Fruit liqueurs are best on desserts, and brandy, sherry or port can be used for both desserts and savoury dishes.

Matching Flavours

Follow this chart to make sure you choose a suitable liqueur for your flambé.

Marsala	Fruit and creamy desserts
Kirsch	Cherries and fresh fruit desserts Almond and chocolate desserts
Cointreau or Grand Marnier	Crêpes and citrus desserts Poultry
Apricot Brandy	Almonds, apricots and oranges Lamb
Madeira	Beef, game and ham
Sherry, Port, Brandy	All savoury dishes and desserts

WATCHPOINT
It is best to light the spirit at the table rather than moving with the lighted flame. Watch out for curtains, napkins and tablecloths.

CREATIVE COVER-UPS

Countless disasters can befall the unsuspecting cook, yet with common sense and a little imagination it is possible to avert all but the most dire of culinary crises.

Don't panic

Not enough food to go round? Bulk out dishes with compatible ingredients or make another vegetable side dish or salad to fill people up. Slice a small joint thinly, cover it with a good, rich sauce and serve with extra vegetables.

If flavour is lacking, turn to your storecupboard for inspiration. Don't forget your food processor or blender if you are short of time, the sauce is lumpy or you need a quick soup.

If you have forgotten to turn the oven on and want to eat in a hurry, or if it breaks down part-way through an important dinner party, most dishes can be cooked on the hob, in a slightly different form. Cut meat up into small pieces and it will cook more quickly.

If you haven't catered for a vegetarian guest, some meat dishes can be adapted. Alternatively, try serving cottage cheese, snipped chives, and drained, tinned sweetcorn tossed together with chopped hard-boiled egg, seasoned with salt and pepper and attractively garnished.

If you drop food, as long as there is no broken glass or china, it is usually possible to reassemble it and disguise with garnishes, cream or a sauce.

Storecupboard standbys

You are more likely to keep your calm and produce an inspired concoction from a kitchen well stocked with ingredients. Useful items to keep in your storecupboard or fridge are cheese, cornflour, dried herbs and spices, lentils, olives, pasta, pesto, redcurrant jelly, rice, nuts and seeds, soy sauce, stock cubes and Tabasco, tins of fruit, vegetables, kidney beans, haricot beans, chickpeas, tuna and tomato purée.

Useful items to keep in your freezer are ice cream, whipping cream, herb croûtons, stock, a variety of frozen vegetables, prawns and crabmeat.

Oranges, lemons, garlic and onions can all pep up bland food. Parsley, watercress and cucumber can mask many disasters.

Sauces

Sauces are temperamental with the potential to either burn, curdle or go lumpy, so you may find the following points helpful.

Burning

This is acceptable for gravies or brown sauces providing they aren't charcoaled. If you burn a white or sweet sauce, remove from the heat and pour into a clean pan, taking care not to scrape off any of the burnt sauce. Continue on a gentle heat.

Too Thin

With bèchamel sauce, cheese sauce or custard, blend a little cornflour with cold milk and stir into the sauce until boiling. For gravies, tomato or sweet and sour sauces do the same but add a dash of soy sauce at the same time for extra colour.

Alternatively, make a Beurre Manié (see page 261) and stir into the sauce in small lumps. It will give a better flavour than cornflour but must be thoroughly cooked or you'll get the taste of raw flour.

Curdling

Egg-based sauces often curdle. For hot sauces this can be prevented by stirring 1 tsp cornflour into the egg yolks before you start making the sauce.

Make mayonnaise and hollandaise in a blender, slowly pouring the melted butter or oil onto the whisked egg yolks. If you make the sauce conventionally and it begins to curdle, plunge the pan immediately into cold water, or remove from the heat and add 1 tbls cold water. If the sauce has curdled allow it to cool slightly and then start again using another egg yolk and very gradually adding the curdled mixture. Whisk all the time or place in a blender until the mixture comes together to give the sauce a smooth consistency.

Too Fatty

Excess fat from sauces and gravies can be soaked up by laying absorbent paper or a slice of bread on the surface of the sauce.

Lacking Flavour

Add redcurrant jelly or sherry to a brown sauce for roast lamb or duck. With stir-fried pork, use soy sauce, sherry and a splash of sesame oil, and for beef, red wine or port. Add cheese or herbs to white sauce for vegetables and white wine if it's for fish.

Vegetables

Hot Vegetables
Overcooking is the most common fate to befall vegetables. The following ideas will mask uninspiring vegetables.

Vegetable Gratin

Chop and boil or steam not-quite-fresh vegetables as usual. Put in a heatproof serving dish and sprinkle with a mixture of breadcrumbs, crushed nuts and grated Cheddar cheese. Cook under a hot grill until golden brown.

Cold Vegetables
Heat up cold or leftover vegetables by tossing them in a pan with a little garlic lightly fried in oil.

Vegetable Purées

An excellent way to serve overcooked vegetables such as broccoli, cauliflower, Brussels sprouts, carrots, parsnips, swedes or turnips is to make a purée. Mash the vegetables with butter, cream, salt and pepper. Serve sprinkled with sesame seeds, chopped nuts or a mixture of breadcrumbs and grated cheese. Add a pinch of nutmeg to a purée of swede or turnip. If a purée tastes too strong, stir in a little mashed potato to absorb some of the flavour.

Cheat's Ratatouille
Rescue overcooked courgettes by adding to sautéed onion and garlic, tinned tomatoes and herbs.

Salads
As a rule, don't make salads from vegetables that are not fresh. However, limp lettuce can be refreshed by washing it in iced water. Shake it dry and chill it in a large plastic bag for 1-2 hours. Tired watercress improves if put upside down in water in the fridge for 1 hour. If it's still flagging, use for a refreshing soup.

Avocados
Bullet-like avocados will ripen over a couple of days. But if you want to eat them straight away, remove the flesh, chop roughly and mix with cooked chopped streaky bacon, prawns or diced chicken. Add some breadcrumbs, cream and seasoning. Pile back into shells and bake in oven for 10 minutes.

Disguise over-ripe avocados with a creamy dressing of mayonnaise or soured cream. If they are badly discoloured, make guacamole dip by mashing the good flesh with lemon juice, grated onions, chopped tomatoes, Tabasco and chopped fresh coriander.

Fish, Meat & Poultry

Freshness
If you are worried about the freshness of fish or shellfish it is best to throw it out immediately. Fish which smells only slightly can be partially freshened by soaking in vinegar and water for 10 mins.

If meat or poultry smells a bit high, wash it in cold water and vinegar. Rinse several times under cold water. Throw it out if you still have any doubts at all, especially with chicken and especially if it still smells. Ensure that you cook the meat very well.

Filleting & Skinning
Filleting fish is not easy and can result in a mess of small fish pieces. If so, poach or steam it. Once cooked, arrange neatly on a serving dish and smother with a sauce. The skin will come off cooked fish easily while it is still hot.

Tough Meat

If you suspect meat is tough, beat steaks or marinate joints before cooking or casserole very slowly. Slice steak into thin strips and cook with onions, mushrooms and paprika until tender. Remove from the heat and add a swirl of cream to make a delicious stroganoff.

Marinating
If you have failed to notice that a recipe calls for meat to be marinated, don't give up. Score the meat with a sharp knife so that the marinade can penetrate easily and then marinate, at room temperature, for as long as possible. The dish should still have a good flavour.

Frozen Meat

Some meat can be used from frozen, but do not cook larger frozen joints or poultry. By the time the inside is cooked, the outside will be tough. Defrosting can be speeded up by putting the meat in cold water. Remove any giblets from chicken as soon as possible. Rinse out the cavity with warm water and cook when cold, but not frozen.

Undercooking
Never undercook pork or poultry. If roasts are too rare, wrap them in foil and stand in a warm place for 20 minutes. The inside will continue cooking, without overcooking the outside.

Cakes & Desserts

Gelatine

If, after many hours in the fridge, a mousse is still unset, turn it out and add a little gelatine dissolved in water. Taste the mixture – if you can taste the gelatine add extra flavouring. If the mousse is half-set you can present it in attractive spoonfuls on individual plates. If you turn out a sloppy mousse, put it straight in the freezer to set. But don't decorate the top or the weight may make the mousse collapse altogether.

Cakes

Sometimes cakes will go wrong for no apparent reason – they may sink in the middle or have a dry texture.

Slice up a failed sponge to make a trifle or slice it in half and sprinkle each half with liqueur. Assemble with thick layers of fruit and decorate with whipped cream.

A dry overcooked fruit cake is very uninteresting. For rich fruit cakes, make deep holes in the cake and drizzle with sherry or brandy. If it is not needed immediately, wrap the cake in foil and leave for 1-2 days. Don't try this with light fruit cakes – they will just become soggy. Instead, serve them in thin slices, spread with butter, as you would a tea bread.

Meringues

Egg whites for meringues need to be beaten until very stiff. With an electric whisk this is very easy, by hand it's hard work. Any oil in the egg will prevent stiffening, so make sure the bowl is clean and remove any bits of egg yolk with a piece of eggshell. Ideally meringues should be white and dry and keep their shape. If they do collapse or crumble when removed from the baking tray, crush and use in a gateau with cream and fruit. Misshapen meringues can also be piled together with cream or icecream and drizzled with a fruit or caramel sauce.

Other Disasters

Pastry

Undercooked pastry is horrible, but over-cooked pastry just becomes very crispy, so if in doubt, cook for a little longer. To prevent soggy bottoms in pastry that hasn't been baked blind stand the dish on a baking sheet that has been heated at the same time as the oven.

Tears and holes in the bottom of pies can be easily patched with spare bits of pastry. Dampen with water and stick down with your thumb. Holes that appear on the top can be neatly covered with strips or fancy decorations of pastry. Always glue down decorations with beaten egg and brush the surface of the pie with a glaze.

Pâté

Pâté sometimes has an unpleasantly strong liver flavour so taste the mixture before cooking and if necessary add 2-3 tbls double cream and 1-2 tbls lemon juice. Brandy will also help neutralise the taste of liver, while garlic and herbs add their own flavour. If the texture of pâté is too crumbly, you can either return it to the tin and pour over a good meat stock that will gel when re-chilled, or purée it in a blender and chill for at least 30 minutes before serving. Either way, the pâté will taste just as good.

Beans

Red kidney beans are a problem if they are undercooked – they are potentially toxic. Soaking speeds cooking – but if you have forgotten to do this boil them for 3 minutes and leave in fresh water for 1 hour. Then cook in fresh water until tender. Don't salt beans while they are cooking or soaking as it will toughen the skin.

Rice

Rice is only too easy to overcook. Rinse or soak it in water before cooking to remove excess starch. Drain the moment the rice is tender. Add some butter or oil and keep warm in a covered container in the oven. Do not stand the rice in water. If it has turned stodgy, rinse it in boiling water so that you can separate the grains, and then stir in butter or oil.

Pasta

Lasagne and spaghetti do have a tendency to stick together so always add a little oil to the water. Feed lasagne sheets into the water one by one, and stir spaghetti water vigorously to separate the strands. If the pasta still sticks, rinse well in boiling water to separate and add a knob of butter. When they are still warm, lasagne sheets can be gently pulled apart under warm water. Keep them separate on a clean tea-towel.

MICRO-NOTES

Although we tend to think of the microwave as a complex gadget it is no more complicated than a food processor. When used to complement a conventional cooker, it is the ultimate kitchen tool.

Adapting recipes

Microwaved food usually requires less liquid and seasoning than that cooked in a conventional oven and as a general rule will only need a third to a quarter of the cooking time. Cooking will be slower if you have a large quantity of food. Test food often to prevent over-cooking. Remove the food when nearly cooked, wrap it in foil and allow it to stand. This allows the food to finish cooking completely.

Care with containers

Once you've bought a microwave there's no need to rush out and buy special cooking containers – just remember never to use metal in the microwave. Ovenproof glass and china work well as long as they don't have a metal trim. Porous earthenware may slow down the rate of cooking. Plastic, paper, wood and wicker should only be used for short periods. However, strong boil-in-bags or roasting bags are microwave-proof as long as they are pierced and tied with string, not wire.

Cover it up

Covering will prevent the surface of food from drying out, will speed up cooking and will help keep the oven clean. Cling film is very useful, but buy non-PVC which is safe, and do not allow it to touch the surface of the food. Pierce before using to allow the steam to escape. Ovenproof casserole lids or upturned plates make convenient lids if you have to stir the food frequently. Clear plastic domes are good for covering large items like joints of meat. Absorbent paper is good for stopping cakes, bread and pastry from turning soggy during reheating. Use greaseproof paper for food which may spit hot fat. Protect very thin parts of food from over-cooking with a little foil, shiny side down. Foil should never touch the sides of the cooker.

Place it properly

Position food so that the thickest part is on the outside of the dish. If you have several small items such as lamb chops or chicken legs, arrange them in a circle around the edge.

Toss & turn

Most food needs to be stirred or turned during cooking to heat it through evenly, as the edges cook much faster than the middle of a dish.

Golden brown

To brown microwaved foods, grill briefly before or after cooking, cook in a special microwave browning dish, coat with a suitable brown seasoning or include darker ingredients in the recipe.

The big thaw

To defrost, turn the microwave down to the lowest setting and, between bursts of energy, allow the food to rest with the microwave off. If you turn the heat up, the outside of the food will cook while the inside remains frozen.

Reheating tips

Be careful not to overcook small items of food when reheating. Cover to prevent drying out and stir or rearrange halfway through cooking.

Clean it up

Wipe up any spills as they occur otherwise they will tend to dry on and be more difficult to remove. Always wipe with warm water and detergent – never with a scouring pad or an abrasive cleaner. To loosen dried-on food, microwave a cup of water for a few minutes until steamy. Leave for 2 minutes before wiping. To remove smells, microwave slices of lemon for 2 minutes then leave for 1 hour.

Bread, Butter & Beans

Bread

To thaw a sliced or unsliced loaf, leave wrapped but remove the fastening tag and open the end of the bag. Set the microwave on DEFROST (30%) for 3-4 minutes until no longer frosty but still cool. Leave to stand for 5-10 minutes.

To warm bread rolls, place in a basket or on a plate and microwave on HIGH (100%) for 20-30 seconds. Take care not to over-microwave bread or it will go stale very quickly.

To make dried breadcrumbs, place a thick slice of bread on a plate and microwave on HIGH (100 %) for 2-3 minutes until just dry. Stand for 2-3 minutes and then process into fine crumbs.

Proving Dough

Microwaving can speed up this process. Give the dough 3-4 minute bursts on LOW. Leave to stand 10-15 minutes and repeat until doubled in size.

Butter

To soften butter, unwrap and microwave on DEFROST (30%) for 5-10 seconds for each 50 g/2 oz in weight. Stand for 2-3 minutes.

To melt 25 g/1 oz butter, microwave on DEFROST (30%) for 20-30 seconds. To melt 100 g/4 oz butter, microwave for 1-1½ minutes at the same temperature.

Dried Beans

Speed up the soaking process by putting dried beans in a bowl and covering them with boiling water. Cover and microwave on HIGH (100%) for 5 minutes. Stand for 1½ hours.

Sweets & Sauces

Caramel

Place 150 ml/¼ pt hot water and 150 g/5 oz sugar in a large non-plastic bowl. Microwave on HIGH (100%) for 3-4 minutes, stirring occasionally, until sugar is dissolved. Then microwave for 10-13 minutes until the syrup turns a caramel colour. Cool slightly and then stir in 3-4 tbls hot water. Watch carefully towards the end – the syrup will turn golden very quickly.

Custard

To make egg custard, microwave 600 ml/1 pt milk on HIGH (100%) for 4 minutes. Beat 4 egg yolks together with 3 tbls sugar in a large bowl and gradually beat in the hot milk. Heat on MEDIUM (50%) for 5-6 minutes, stirring every minute, until it coats the back of a spoon.

For a quick custard, put 1 tbls custard powder and 1 tbls sugar in a jug. Mix in 600 ml/1 pt milk and microwave on HIGH (100%) for 5-6 minutes, stirring.

Chocolate

Put chocolate pieces in a microwave-proof bowl. Heat on MEDIUM (50%) until they begin to lose their shape. For 50 g/2 oz this should take 2-3 minutes, for 100 g/4 oz about 4 minutes. Allow to stand 1-2 minutes before using.

Sugar

To soften brown sugars that have gone hard, place 225 g/8 oz in a bowl and sprinkle with 1 tbls water. Cover with cling film and microwave on HIGH (100%) for 15-30 seconds. Stand for 5 minutes. Ensure sugar does not melt.

Ice Creams & Sorbets

To soften a carton of ice cream or sorbet, microwave on DEFROST (30%) for 2-3 minutes, turning after 1½ minutes. Individual portions take 30-45 seconds.

Gelatine

To dissolve 1 sachet (15 g/½ oz)of gelatine, put 4 tbls cold water in a cup or jug. Sprinkle with gelatine. Stir and then microwave on HIGH (100%) for 30-35 seconds or until dissolved. Do not boil.

When using jelly cubes, place in a bowl with 150 ml/¼ pt cold water. Cook on HIGH (100%) for 1½-2 minutes. Stir well.

Fruits & Nuts

Citrus Fruit

Use the microwave for drying the zest and extracting more juice from citrus fruit.

Juice: microwave the whole fruit on HIGH (100%) for 20-30 seconds. This will make the fruit easier to squeeze.

Zest: finely grate the zest of 2 or 3 lemons, limes or oranges. Line a plate with absorbent paper and place a glass of water in the centre. Spread the zest evenly over the plate and microwave on HIGH (100%) for 4-6 minutes, separating the particles with your fingertips every minute. Remove when it feels dry. Stand for 1-2 hours until brittle. Use only half the amount specified in a recipe.

Dried Fruit

Save hours of soaking by plumping up fruit in the microwave.

Apricots, pears, prunes, figs: cover 225 g/8 oz fruit with 250 ml/8 fl oz water, wine or fruit juice. Cover with cling film and microwave on HIGH (100%) for 5-6 minutes, stirring once.

Raisins, sultanas, currants: spread 100 g/4 oz fruit in a shallow dish and add 4 tbls cold water or fruit juice. Cover with cling film and microwave on HIGH (100%) for 2-3 minutes until plump. Remove the fruit once softened and don't allow liquid to boil dry.

Nuts

Any kind of nut – almonds, cashews, hazelnuts or pine kernels can be quickly toasted in the microwave. Blanch to remove skins and chop or split nuts. Place in a shallow dish and cook on HIGH (100%) according to weight, stirring half-way through. For 50 g/2 oz cook 4-5 minutes. For 75 g/3 oz cook 6-7 minutes

Coconut: it is easy to burn coconut, so put the flakes in a roasting bag with a non-metallic tie. Cook on MEDIUM (50%) for 30 seconds or until coconut is lightly browned, shaking the bag every 15 seconds. Stand for 2-3 minutes.

WINE NOTES

Four factors separate any bottle of wine from its neighbours on a wine merchant's shelf or restaurant list. Knowing where a wine comes from will provide an idea of its style. The kind of grape, when mentioned, can be helpful, as different grapes have different flavours and characteristics. The date on the bottle will make a difference as older wine may be softer than younger wine and the weather in some vintages may have been better than others. And finally, there is the producer's name – a restaurant is only as good as its cook, and similarly the quality of a wine depends on its maker. And price plays no part in it, as there are poor pricey wines and lovely inexpensive ones.

Keep it cool
Wines are happiest living in the kind of environment human beings detest. They like dark, damp, cool places through which a gentle breeze blows occasionally. They hate disturbance and change. As a general rule, the warmer the environment, the faster the wine will age. The ideal temperature is 7-10 C/45-50 F. Try using a cupboard or rack in the garage.

Let it breathe
Red wines are drunk at just below room temperature – 15-16 C/60-62 F. Whites, rosés and sparkling wines should be served at 8-10 C/46-50 F. Surprisingly, the quickest way to chill wine is not in the freezer. Ten minutes in a bucket of cold water or basin filled with ice cubes will be far more effective. To warm a red wine, leave the bottle in tepid – not warm – water for five minutes. Open white wines just before serving, but full-flavoured red wines benefit from being opened an hour or two before they are to be drunk.

Glasses with class
Although there is a traditional style of glass for every style of wine, a single set of glasses can suffice. Just be sure to choose a set which are narrower at the rim that in the bowl.

Wine for Fish & Shellfish

Anyone who has tried drinking claret with sardines will have discovered that the two combine to produce a nasty, metallic taste.

The solution to this problem is to choose the right wine to go with the right fish. Oily fish like sardines work well with crisp dry whites such as Muscadet or Vinho Verde.

Some grilled fish taste far fishier than others. With sea bass, try a lighter Chardonnay, a traditonal white Rioja (such as Marqués de Murrieta) or a good Soave such as Pieropan. Turbot and trout are both perfect accompanied by dry German Riesling.

Poached salmon is subtly flavoured and calls for dry white wine without too rich a style and without too much acidity.

Try a lighter Chardonnay such as a Mâcon-Villages, a good Soave, or a white Château-du-Pape.

The various types of seafood and shellfish require very different wine styles. Oysters need emphatically dry whites such as Muscadet, Sancerre, Chablis, Verdicchio or Frascati. Scallops can handle a slightly richer style – try a light Italian Chardonnay or Pinot Blanc – and lobster can be perfect with Tokay from Alsace.

Lastly, when looking for a wine to accompany smoked salmon, stay in Alsace, but try a Pinot Gris. Alternatively, try a white Rhône.

Wine for Poultry & Game

Roasted or sautéed chicken or turkey are well balanced by a medium-weight Chardonnay, by a Riesling from Alsace or Germany or by light reds.

For creamy chicken dishes try a fresh, goosberryish Sauvignon, a young Alsace or a dry Vouvray. Roast duck goes well with fruity wine, such as a top quality Beaujolais, blackcurranty red wines from the Loire and light Bordeaux.

Match venison with spicy wines from France (Cahors, Madiran, Hermitage and Châteauneuf), California (Cabernet) and Italy (Barolo). Rabbit suits rustic wines like Bairrada and Douro from Portugal and Barbera and fuller Chiantis from Italy.

The most gamy birds are perfect with spicy wines of the northern Rhône – Hermitage and Côte-Rôtie – Australian Syrah or Californian Zinfandel. Less pungent game birds suit Burgundy, St Emilion and Pomerol from Bordeaux.

Wine for Meat & Foreign Foods

Matching Meats

Tradition dictates that red meat calls for red wine, but the kind of red wine depends on the type of meat and the sauce in which it has been prepared.

If the sauce has been made with a wine from a particular region, there is an argument for serving it with a wine from the same region. A creamy sauce, however, needs a soft wine with plenty of fresh, fruity acidity to cut through the richness, and a rich, meaty casserole requires heartier wines such as Châteauneuf-du-Pape, Barolo, a rich Burgundy such as Gevrey-Chambertine, or a Bordeaux from St Emilion.

Roast beef and steaks prepared without sauce go well with full-flavoured, but not overly spicy Bordeaux, Burgundy, Rioja, richer Beaujolais Crus, Chianti or Douro and lighter Zinfandels from California.

Lamb teams well with a rich Rioja or a red wine from Provençe and pork can be paired with red or white wines. For white, try a rich Chardonnay, a traditional Rioja, a Tokay or a Pinot Blanc from Alsace or a drier Riesling from Germany. If you prefer

red, then go for a medium-bodied wine such as a Dolcetto, a Valpolicella or Chianti, a red Loire or a Beaujolais.

Foreign Favours

In some parts of the world, such as India and China, wine has no traditional place at all. Consequently, their style of cooking can offer something of a challenge when it comes to selecting a wine.

Some curries are so dominated by the flavour of peppers and spice that it is certainly not worth choosing a top quality wine. Go instead for fruity, spicy wines, such as chilled Beaujolais Nouveau, red

Loires, young Rhônes or Australian Shiraz, dry German Reislings – or a light, off-dry rosé such as Mateus.

For milder curries try Dolcetto, Valpolicella and Bairrada, while creamy ones are well suited to Sauvignons.

Creole, Chinese and Thai food often combine so many sweet, sour and savoury flavours that it is best to go for a very tasty wine. My favourite is Sauvignon Blanc from New Zealand, but Alsace Gewürztraminer and southern French rosés are lovely – as is chilled Asti Spumante. The same applies to Japanese food, though sake rice wine is traditional.

Wine for Desserts & Cheeses

Dessert Wines

According to some rule books all desserts deserve to be served with Sauternes – except those which involve chocolate or ginger. Both chocolate and ginger are believed to be incompatible with any wine. But although at its most spicy, ginger overpowers almost any other flavour, at its mildest, it can be matched by late-harvest Gewürztraminer. And, surprisingly, chocolate can be lovely with Australian or Californian Orange Muscats, or with fruity Cabernet Sauvignon from California.

Fresh fruit tarts and mousses need fruity wines. A sweet Riesling (such as German Auslese) or Muscat (a late-harvest Alsace,

a Beaumes-de-Venise from the Rhône, or a Moscatel de Setúbal from Portugal) can be the perfect accompaniment.

Creamy desserts such as syllabub and crème brulée are better served by sweet wines from the Loire, or by Sauternes.

Hearty steamed or baked sponge puddings can be much sweeter than one expects and anything other than a very intense wine can be overshadowed completely. Sweet Hungarian Tokay or Boal or Malmsey Madeira can be perfect, but my favourite accompaniment is rich Australian Liqueur Muscat.

Wine for Cheese

Despite the commonly held belief that red wines are the perfect partner for cheese, objective tastings prove that white wines often fare better – particularly with high-fat cheeses.

In the Loire, the winegrowers of Sancerre believe their dry, gooseberryish wine to be the only match for the goats' cheese which is made in their region. However, Pouilly Blanc Fumé, Sauvignon Blanc from New Zealand and good Chablis can be successful too. These dry wines also go well with Dutch cheeses.

One of the great wine-and-cheese

partnerships is Roquefort and Sauternes. The combination of honeyed sweetness and salty tang is perfect. For variety, however, you can swap the Roquefort for a similar blue cheese and replace the Sauternes with a late-harvest Riesling or even a moelleux wine from the Loire. And don't forget that other time-honoured favourite, Stilton and port.

Soft French cheeses are natural partners to gentle, fruity red Burgundy. Bordeaux can go with Cheddar, provided the wine comes from St Emilion or Pomerol, both of which areas use the rich-flavoured Merlot grape. But my own first choice to go with Cheddar cheese would be port (vintage or tawny) or, alternatively, you could try Madeira.

GLOSSARY

Al dente
An Italian term used to describe food, such as pasta, cooked until it is just tender but firm to the bite.

Aspic
Clear savoury jelly made from clarified meat or fish stock.

Bain-marie
A pan or dish in which water is kept hot. Used for delicate mixtures such as sauces and custards.

Bake blind
To bake a pastry case weighted down with greaseproof paper and beans.

Bard
To tie bacon or pork fat over part or all of a piece of meat, poultry or game before roasting. This keeps the flesh from drying out and makes basting unnecessary.

Bavarois
A creamy custard dessert that has been set with gelatine.

Beurre manié
The French term for kneaded butter which consists of equal parts butter and flour worked to a smooth paste; used to thicken sauces.

Blanch
To plunge food into boiling water for a short period of time. Meats such as sweetbreads are blanched to make the flesh firm and preserve their whiteness; bacon may be blanched to remove excess saltiness; some vegetables need to be blanched to prepare them for freezing.

Bouqet garni
A bunch of herbs, usually parsley, thyme and bay leaf, tied together or wrapped in muslin. It is added to a savoury dish whilst cooking and removed before serving. Other herbs that may be added vary according to taste.

Canelle knife
A small tool used for cutting grooves in fruit and vegetables such as cucumbers, carrots, courgettes, lemons and limes.

Caramelise
To boil sugar, or sugar syrup, until it is a brown toffee. The resulting caramel is used to coat moulds for puddings. Also, to sprinkle sugar over a pudding and grill until it is melted to a caramel topping.

Caul
Fatty membrane from the lower portion of pig's or sheep's bowel that is used to wrap and bard meat and fish dishes which need long cooking.

Chine
To remove the backbone from a rib roast or rack of lamb before cooking to make it much easier to carve and simplify serving the joint.

Clarify
To remove all impurities. Butter is clarified by being heated until it foams and is then skimmed or strained through muslin. Stock for consommé or aspic is clarified by being whisked with egg whites and shells over heat and then strained in a similar manner.

Consommé
Clear soup made from clarified stock; it may also be set to a jelly and then served cold.

Court bouillon
A slightly acidulated, aromatic liquid used for poaching, usually fish and seafood, but also some types of meat and vegetables.

Crême pâtissière
The French term for confectioner's custard, a thick custard used as a filling for cakes and pastries.

Crêpe
Large, wafer-thin French pancakes which may be filled with a sweet or savoury mixture.

Crimper
A serrated tong-like tool which is used in cake decorating.

Croquette
A chilled savoury mixture rolled into a cylinder, coated with egg and breadcrumbs and deep-fried.

Croustade
A fried or baked bread case or pastry crust, in which hot savoury mixtrues are served.

Croûte
A pastry case in which food is cooked (such as beef en croûte); or toasted bread base on which the food can be served.

Croûton
Fried bread dice used to garnish soups or other dishes.

Crystallise
This applies to fruit or flowers that are either brushed with egg white then dipped in sugar or boiled repeatedly in sugar syrup.

Deglaze
To dilute, usually with wine or stock, the sediment and concentrated meat juices left in a pan after cooking (particularily if sautéed and roasted), to make a gravy or sauce that can be served with the meat dish.

Dégorger
To prepare vegetables such as aubergines and cucumbers by lightly salting and leaving for an hour or so to remove any strong taste or excess liquid they may contain. It also applies to some meats.

Duxelles
A mixture of very finely chopped mushrooms, shallots (and sometimes ham), butter and seasoning; used to flavour soups and sauces or as a stuffing for meat and savoury pastries.

Emulsion
A smooth liquid such as mayonnaise, containing tiny drops of oil or fat distributed smoothly and evenly throughout another liquid.

Farce
A French term that is used to describe stuffing or forcemeat.

Flambé
French for flamed. To set alight a spirit such as brandy and pour, flaming, over food. The alcohol is burned off leaving just the flavour of the spirit.

Fold
To incorporate a light airy mixture, such as whisked egg whites, into a heavier one without a stirring or beating action which might result in loss of air.

Fumet
A strong, well-reduced stock made from fish or game.

Galantine
Meat which has been boned, stuffed and rolled, wrapped in muslin, poached and served cold.

Glace de viande/de poisson
Brown meat or fish stock which has been simmered until reduced to a thick, syrupy consistency.

Hard ball
The point at which, after prolonged boiling, sugar syrup reaches a temperature of about 120-124 C/250-255 F and drops of the syrup form hard balls when dropped into water.

Hard crack
The temperature at which drops of sugar syrup become brittle like glass (approximately 150-160 C/300-320 F). The syrup should be watched carefully to prevent it turning to caramel or burning.

Hors d'oeuvre
A term used to describe the first course or starter, and often used to refer to a selection of bite-sized tidbits served with drinks. The tidbits are often biscuit, bread or pastry based.

Julienne
This term refers to thin matchstick-sized sliced or very fine shreds of meat, chicken or vegetables.

Lard
To thread narrow strips of bacon through lean meat before cooking. These lardons give the meat flavour and keep it moist while cooking.

Lardons
Narrow strips of larding fat. Also, fried bacon strips used as a garnish.

Liaison
Thickening agent, such as beurre manié, roux, egg yolk and cream, or blood. Used for soups, sauces and other liquids.

Macerate
To soak food in the syrup or liquid in which it will be served.

Marinade
A seasoned, acidulated liquid, cooked or uncooked, in which foods are soaked to be preserved, tenderised and/or flavoured before cooking. Marinades can be used as a base for sauces.

Médaillon
Medallions – small pieces of meat or sometimes vegetable; also a small, round biscuit.

Mousseline
Generally, a mixture which has had whipped cream added to it. Also, little moulds made from poultry or fish, enriched with cream and served either hot or cold.

Noisette
A rolled lamb chop, cut from a rack which has been first boned, then rolled and tied.

Nouvelle cuisine
A style of cooking that promotes light and delicate dishes using unusual combinations of extremely fresh ingredients.

Oyster
Small piece of meat, shaped like an oyster, found on either side of the backbone of a chicken, turkey or other birds.

Papillote, en
Fish or poultry cooked in a parcel of oiled greaseproof paper.

Paupiette
A thin slice of meat, such as veal escalope, rolled around a stuffing and tied up before cooking.

Pulses
The dried seeds of leguminous plants such as peas, beans and lentils.

Reduce
To boil down liquids or sauces to form a reduction either to thicken the consistency or strengthen and concentrate the flavour.

Refresh
To rinse freshly-cooked vegetables briefly under cold water before serving. Prevents further cooking and sets the colour.

Render
To melt down pork or beef fat in order to make dripping.

Roux
A mixture of butter and flour which forms the base, and thickening agent, for a sauce.

Rust
The underside of a bacon rasher or ham, opposite the rind. This should be cut away.

Setting point
The point at which jam or marmalade will set. This usually happens at 105 C/220 F but check by putting a little jam on a cold saucer and placing it in the fridge for a few minutes. When cold the jam should have a skin which will wrinkle when pushed.

Slake
To mix thickening agents, like cornflour, in a little cold liquid until smooth before adding to the hot liquid to be thickened.

Soft ball
The stage at which a small amount of boiling sugar syrup will roll into a soft ball if plunged into a bowl of cold water. This usually happens when syrup has reached between 116-118 C/240-244 F.

Soft crack
The stage at which a drop of sugar syrup in cold water hardens immediately, usually between 130-135 C/265-275 F.

Souse
To seep or cook food in a marinade.

Spun sugar
Sugar syrup boiled to the crack stage, worked to give fine, glass-like threads. Used to decorate desserts.

Strudel pastry
A rich, paper-thin dough rolled around a sweet or savoury filling before baking or frying.

Syrup
Sugar and water that is boiled to thicken the consistency.

Terrine
A seasoned and flavoured mixture of minced meat, fish or vegetables cooked covered in the oven.

Tomalley
The greenish liver of a lobster – can be used with roe in lobster butter.

Yoghurt
Milk based and set to a solid with a live bacterial culture.

Zest
The thinly pared or grated coloured outer skin of an orange, lemon or lime without any of the bitter white pith; used for adding a citrus flavour to sweet and savoury dishes.

Zester
A small tool used to remove the outer zest from citrus fruit.

WEIGHTS AND MEASURES

Metric and Imperial weights and measures are given throughout this book. Don't switch from one to the other within a recipe as they are not interchangeable.

All spoon measurements are level, all flour plain, all sugar granulated and all eggs medium unless otherwise stated. In all recipes we used a 5 ml teaspoon and a 15 ml tablespoon.

Microwave tips have been tested using a 650 watt microwave oven. Add 15 seconds per minute for 600 watt ovens and reduce the timings by 5-10 seconds per minute for 700 watt ovens.

QUICK MEASURES

➤ 1 rounded tbls flour is equal to 15 g/½ oz
➤ 1 tbls caster or granulated sugar is equal to 15 g/½ oz
➤ 2 tbls dry breadcrumbs are equal to 15 g/½ oz
➤ 1 tbls dried currants, raisins or sultanas is equal to 15 g/½ oz
➤ 2 tbls mixed, chopped nuts are equal to 15 g/½ oz

MICROWAVE POWER SETTINGS

Power Level	Percentage	Numerical Setting
HIGH	100%	9
MEDIUM HIGH	75%	7
MEDIUM	50%	5
DEFROST	30%	3
LOW	10%	1

OVEN TEMPERATURES

°C	°F	Gas Mark	
70 C	150 F	Low	-
80 C	175 F	Low	-
90 C	190 F	Low	-
100 C	200 F	¼	-
110 C	225 F	¼	Very slow
130 C	250 F	½	Very slow
150 C	275 F	1	Slow
160 C	300 F	2	Moderately slow
170 C	325 F	3	Moderately slow
180 C	350 F	4	Moderate
190 C	375 F	5	Moderately hot
200 C	400 F	6	Hot
220 C	425 F	7	Hot
230 C	450 F	8	Very hot
240 C	475 F	9	Very hot

AUSTRALIAN CUP CONVERSIONS

	Metric	Imp
1 cup flour	150 g	5 oz
1 cup sugar, granulated	225 g	8 oz
1 cup sugar, caster	225 g	8 oz
1 cup sugar, icing	175 g	6 oz
1 cup sugar, soft brown	175 g	6 oz
1 cup butter	225 g	8 oz
1 cup honey, treacle	350 g	12 oz
1 cup fresh breadcrumbs	50 g	2 oz
1 cup uncooked rice	200 g	7 oz
1 cup dried fruit	175 g	6 oz
1 cup chopped nuts	100 g	4 oz
1 cup dessiccated coconut	75 g	3 oz
1 cup liquid	250 ml	9 fl oz

SOLID WEIGHT CONVERSIONS

METRIC	IMPERIAL
15 g	½ oz
25 g	1 oz
50 g	2 oz
100 g	4 oz/¼ lb
175 g	6 oz
225 g	8 oz/½ lb
350 g	12 oz
450 g	1 lb
575 g	1¼ lb
700 g	1½ lb
800 g	1¾ lb
900 g	2 lb

LIQUID VOLUME CONVERSIONS

METRIC	IMPERIAL
25 ml	1 fl oz
50 ml	2 fl oz
125 ml	4 fl oz
150 ml	5 fl oz/¼ pt
175 ml	6 fl oz
225 ml	8 fl oz
300 ml	10 fl oz/½ pt
450 ml	15 fl oz/¾ pt
600 ml	20 fl oz/1 pt
900 ml	1½ pt
1.2 L	2 pt
1.7 L	3 pt

INDEX

A

Antipasto, mixed meat, 25
Apple
Crème brûlée, 170
French apple tart, 200
Peach and apple tray bake, 193
Pork with apple cups, 114
Prune and apple stuffing, 300
Apricots
Baklava, 194
Fig and apricot nectar, 159
Filo pork and, 112
Glaze, 293
Orange and onion chutney, 299
Tartes Tatin, 169
Veal, chestnut and apricot pie, 106
Aubergines
in olive oil, 128
with olives, 146
Plantains and, 121
Avocados
Carrot and avocado salad, 138
Creative cover-ups, 306
Dip, 21
Fanning, 301
and grape salad, 141
Guacamole, 20, 306
Prawn and avocado bake, 30

B

Bacon
Celery hearts and, 147
Cuts, 245
Baking
Blind, 274
Bread, 272
Fish, 232, 233
Baklava, apricot, 194
Barbecuing
Chicken, 237
Fish, 233
Sizzling barbecue ribs, 90
Thai barbecue chicken, 70
Barding
Beef, 249
Game, 252
Venison, 253
Batter
Cherry clafoutis, 199
Crêpes, basic, 267
Fritter, 267
Pancakes, basic, 267
Yorkshire puddings, 267
Beans
Types of, 222-3
Hot Sicilian bean salad, 143
Beef
Buying, 248

Cannelloni, 92
Carving, 251
Curry, 99
Cuts, 248
en croûte, 249
in Guinness, 100
Mignon fillets and sauces, 116
Mustard beef rolls, 93
Peppered sirloin steak, 117, 250
Pot roast, 250
Preparing, 249
Roasting, 251
Serving, 251
Sirloin in whisky sauce, 97
Steak and kidney mini pies, 103
Vegetable dolmas, 148
Berryfruits
Berryfruit baskets, 167
Blackcurrant coulis, 290
Cheesecake with strawberries, 182
Fruity meringue rings, 166
Hedgerow crumble, 184
Hedgerow jelly, 297
Raspberry mousse, 287
Sauce cardinale, 290
Strawberry coulis, 160
Strawberry gratin, 168
Summer sauce, 290
Turkey and cranberry pie, 77
Biscuits
Brandysnap baskets, 162
Choc-chip oaties, 221
Cigarettes russes, 164
Florentines, 189
Langues de chat, 161
Palmiers, 188
Viennese, 188
Boning
Chicken, 235
Fish, 230, 231
Lamb, 239
Pork, 243
Veal, 247
Brains
Cooking, 254
Preparing, 254
Bread
Bread and butter pudding, 185
Brown, traditional, 273
Cheese and onion, 273
Ingredients, 272
Making, 272
Milk, basic, 273
Rolls, 273
Toppings, 273
Using yeast, 272, 273
White, basic, 273
Buns, Chelsea, 191

Butter
Beurre manié, 259
Clarifying, 261
Sauces, 261

C

Cabbage in mustard seeds, 144
Cakes
Adding alcohol, 279
Black Forest gâteau, 211
Brioche, 283
Carrot and walnut, 205
Chocolate pizza, 207
Chocolate roulade, 210
Coffee gâteau, 206
Creative cover-ups, 307
Dundee, 204
Eccles cakes, 190
Fruit, 280
Genoese sponge, basic, 282
Mint brownies, 190
Peach and apple tray bake, 193
Preparing fruit, 279
Preparing tins, 279, 281
Rich chocolate, 208
Sponge, basic, 281
Storing and freezing, 279
Streusel tray bake, 192
Sweet yeast dough, basic, 283
Victoria sponge, basic, 281
Whisked sponge, 282
Yeast cakes, 283
Cannelloni, beef, 92
Caramel
Caramelised rice pudding, 184
Peaches in, 158
Carrots
Carrot and avocado salad, 138
Carrot and walnut cake, 205
Potato and carrot bake, 150
Carving
Beef, 251
Chicken, 236
Lamb, 241
Pork, 244
Celery
Hearts and bacon, 147
and Stilton soup, 13
Cheese
Börek, 28
Camembert fritters, 265
Celery and Stilton soup, 13
Curd tartlets, 195
Feta and tomato salad, 140
Fondue, 265
Halloumi and tomato salad, 142
Ham and cheese gougère, 102
Party Brie, 265

Perfect cheeseboard, the 264
Potted cheese, 265
Raclette, 265
Sauce, 92
Savoury Easter pie, 132
Soufflés, 256
Spinach and cheese pasties, 134
Swiss cheese fondue, 265
Types of, 264
Cheesecakes
Chocolate, 181
Serious, 202
with strawberries, 182
Chicken
Boning, 235
Buying, 234
Canton lemon, 72
Coronation, 69
Country stuffed, 79
Creative cover-ups, 306
Fanning, 301
French roast, 80
Goujons, 28
Italian-style, 74
Jointing, 234
Korma, 71
and leek galantine, 78
Cooking, 237
Microwaving, 237
Nasi goreng, 153
with olives, 82
and onion quiche, 76
Pancake rolls, 68
Parsley chicken choux, 41
Poussins with grapes, 86
with Prawns, 72
Roasting, 236
Serving, 236
Spatchcocking, 237
Stuffed drumsticks, 68
Thai barbecue, 70
Yoghurt-baked, 70
Chocolate
Caraque, 303
Cheesecake, 181
Chip oaties, 221
Dipping fruit in, 303
Filled chocolates, 295
Leaves, 303
Melting, 303
Mint brownies, 190
Mousse, 171
and nut loaf, 178
Piping, 303
Pizza, 207
Pudding, 180
Rich chocolate cake, 208
Rich chocolate torte, 179
Roulade, 210
Sauces, 172, 176, 289
Soufflés, 172
Chorizo mushrooms, 22
Chow mein, vegetable, 120
Chowder, crab, 19
Chutneys
Apricot, orange and onion chutney, 299
Quick mango relish, 299

Clams
Herbed clams and prawns, 33
Marinière, 46
Preparing, 225
Clarifying
Butter, 261
Stocks, 259
Coconut
Chickpeas in, 122
Cod in, 52
Cod in coconut milk, 52
Coffee
Gâteau, 16
Sauce, 289
Consommé
Basic, 16
à la julienne, 16
Monte Carlo, 16
Courgettes
Italienne, 149
Vegetable dolmas, 148
Crab
Chowder, 19
Dressed crab, 226
Preparing, 226
Wontons, 37
Creative cover-ups, 305-7
Crème brûlée
Apple, 170
Classic, 170
Crêpes
Basic, 267
Pecan-stuffed, 175
Crudités, and tricolour dips, 21
Crumble, hedgerow, 184
Curry
Beef, 99
Chicken korma, 71
Curried pumpkin, 127
Powder, 215
Quick fish, 51
Spicy mixed vegetables, 123
Vegetable and cashew, 124

D
Dhal, lemon and mint, 122
Dips
Avocado, 21
Boursin cheese, 23
Chinese, 21
Garlic, 28
Guacamole, 20, 306
Hummus, 223
Prawn and lemon, 21
Tricolour, 21
Tzatziki, 91
Dolmas, vegetable, 148
Dressings
Mayonnaise, classic, 219
Oriental, 138
Tarragon wine, 142
Vinaigrette, classic, 219
Yoghurt, 219
Zesty lime, 219
Duck
in bitter orange, 73
Peking, 84

E
Eggs
Crêpes, basic, 267
Fritter batter, basic, 267
Omelettes, 266
Pancakes, basic, 267
Soufflés, cheese, 266
Yorkshire puddings, 267
En croûte
Beef, 249
Lamb in a jacket, 108
Salmon, 64

F
Falafel, 223
Figs
and apricot nectar, 159
Preserve, 297
Filo pastry
Apricot baklava, 194
Cheese börek, 28
Pork and apricots, 112
Samosas, mini, 29
Seafood baskets, 38
Fish
Aspic, 257
Buying, 227
Cooking, 232-3
Creative cover-ups, 306
Family fishcake, 54
Filleting, 230
French fish soup, 18
Grilled fish steaks, 56
Italian fish stew, 53
Kebabs, 42
Mixed fish kebabs, 42
Mixed fish pie, 65
Parcel, 302
Preparing, 230-1
Quick fish curry, 51
Seafood baskets, 38
Seafood sausages, 255
Smoked fish platter, 26
Stuffing, 231
Thai-baked fish, 61
Types of, 227-8
See also under Shellfish and individual fish
Flambés, 304
Flans
Chicken and onion quiche, 76
Onion and caraway, 134
Fondue, Swiss cheese, 265
Fritter batter, 267
Fruit cakes
Basic, 280
Variations, 280
Frying
Beef, 250
Fish, 232
Lamb, 238
Pork, 242
Fudge, 294

G
Galantine, chicken and leek, 78
Game
Buying, 252

Hot game pie, 104
Preparing, 252
See also under individual game
Gammon
Cuts, 245
Glazed, 115
Garlic
and basil marinade, 300
Mushrooms, 23
Pâté, coarse, 22
Sauce, 28
Using, 216
Gazpacho, 10
Gelatine, 287
Goose, roast, with sage, 83
Gougère, ham and cheese, 102
Goujons, chicken, 28
Grains
Buying, 220
Types of, 221
Grapes
Avocado and grape salad, 141
Poussins with, 86
Gratin
Potato, 153
Strawberry, 168
Gravy, 236, 241, 244, 247, 251, 258
Grilling
Beef, 250
Chicken, 237
Fish, 232, 233
Lamb, 238
Pork, 242
Grouse, roast, 252
Guacamole, 20
Guard of honour, (lamb), 240

H

Haddock
Family fishcake, 54
Smoked haddock soufflé, 40
Halibut, 227
Grilled fish steaks, 56
Ham
and cheese gougère, 102
Cooking, 245
Glazed gammon, 115
Hare, preparing, 253
Herbs
Basil and garlic marinade, 300
Bouquet garni, 214
Freezing and drying, 214
Herb pâte à pâté, 278
Herbed clams and prawns, 35
Juniper and rosemary marinade, 113
Lemon and herb stuffing, 108
Lemon and mint dahl, 122
Lettuce and chive salad, 139
Marjoram and chervil stuffing, 300
Mint brownies, 190
Mint jelly, 298
Mint and rosemary stuffing, 79
Mint sauce, 298
Orange and thyme sauce, 256
Parsley chicken choux, 41
Pesto sauce, 42
Roast goose with sage, 83

Sage, apple and prune stuffing, 83
Sage, onion and pear stuffing, 360
Sage and raisin stuffing, 114
Salmon and tarragon parcels, 39
Shrimp and tarragon stuffing, 39
Spinach and sorrel ravioli, 131
Tarragon lamb chops, 96
Types of, 214
Using, 214
Honeyed pear pie, 197
Hummus, 223

I

Ice bowls, 301
Ice creams
Raspberry, meringue-based, 286
Rhubarb, 164
Vanilla, custard-based, 286
Icings, fillings and glazes
American frosting, quick, 292
Apricot glaze, 293
Butter icing, 292
Chocolate glaze, 179
Chocolate icing, 208
Crème au beurre, 206, 292
Crème pâtissière, 293
Fondant, home-made, 292
Glacé icing, 292
Marzipan, 291
Pineapple frosting, 205
Royal icing, 292

J

Jams,
Making, 296
Plum jam, basic, 296
Jellies
Hedgerow, 297
Orange, 287
Port, 165
Using agar-agar, 287
Using gelatine, 287

K

Kebabs
Middle Eastern, 91
Mixed fish, 42
Shish, 42
Kidneys
Cooking, 254
Preparing, 254
Steak and kidney mini pies, 103
Koulibiaca, vegetarian, 135

L

Lamb
Boning, 239
Buying, 238
Carving, 241
Crown roast, 240
Cuts, 238
French roast, 110
Grilling, 238
Guard of honour, 240
in a jacket, 108
Middle Eastern kebabs, 91
Noisettes, 94

Rack of, 240
Roasting, 241
Shish kebabs, 42
Tarragon lamb chops, 96
Vegetable dolmas, 148
Walnut-stuffed, 109
Langoustines, baked, 31
Larding
Beef, 249
Venison, 253
Leeks
Chicken and leek galantine, 78
and sweet potato soup, 15
Lemon
Baked lemon and lime pie, 196
Canton lemon chicken, 72
Curd, 297
Lemony potatoes, 151
and mint dahl, 122
Sole with lemon sauce, 55
Lime
Baked lemon and lime pie, 196
Lime pickle, 299
Liver
Cooking, 254
Preparing, 254
Lobster, preparing, 224

M

Mangoes
Mango relish, 299
Mango sauce, 290
Marinades
Basil and garlic, 300
Garlic and white wine, 70
Ginger and chilli, 61
Juniper berry and rosemary, 113
Marinade for steak, basic, 300
Olive oil and lemon juice, 42
Red wine and mustard seed, 300
Marmalade, basic, 297
Marrow, stuffed, 129
Marzipan
Cooked, 291
Uncooked, 291
Mayonnaise, classic, 219
Meringues
Basic, 285
Creative cover-ups, 307
Fruity meringue rings, 166
Raspberry ice cream, 286
Microwaving
Bread, 272, 308
Chicken, 237
Fish, 233
Sauces, 309
Techniques, 308-9
Mint
Brownies, 190
Jelly, 298
Lemon and mint dahl, 122
Sauce, 298
Molluscs, preparing, 225
See also under Mussels and Clams
Monkfish
Seafood baskets, 38
in yoghurt, 50

Mousses
Chocolate, 171
Making, 287
Raspberry, 287
Salmon, 30
Using agar-agar, 287
Using gelatine, 287
Mullet
Red mullet in orange, 60
Types, 228
Mushrooms
Boats, 24
Chorizo, 22
Garlic, 23
Soup, 14
Mussels
Moules marinière, 34
Preparing, 225
Saffron, 47
Seafood baskets, 38

N
Nasi goreng, 155
Nectarines
Curd tartlets, 195
Fanning, 301
Pork chops, 95
Noisettes, lamb, 94
Nuts
Almond praline, 173
Carrot and walnut cake, 205
Chestnut stuffing, 79
Chocolate and nut loaf, 178
Hazelnut profiteroles, 176
Peach, almond and brandy sauce, 290
Peach and almond tart, 198
Pecan and cranberry stuffing, 82
Pecan-stuffed crêpes, 175
Turkey with pecan nuts, 82
Veal, chestnut and apricot pie, 106
Vegetable and cashew curry, 124
Walnut and apple stuffing, 109
Walnut and orange tart, 203
Walnut-stuffed lamb, 109

O
Octopus, preparing, 229
Offal
Cooking, 254
Types of, 254
Oils
Herbal, 217
Hot Chilli, 217
Peppercorn, 217
Types of, 217
Olives
Aubergines with, 146
Chicken with, 82
Omelettes, 266
Onions
Apricot, orange and onion chutney, 299
and caraway flan, 34
Chicken and onion quiche, 76
Dicing, 216
Pickled, 299
Sage, onion and pear stuffing, 300
Using, 216

Oranges
Apricot, orange and onion chutney, 299
Duck in bitter orange, 73
Glazed potatoes, 151
Hot orange sauce, 290
Marmalade, 297
Orange Jelly, 287
Red mullet in orange, 60
and thyme sauce, 256
Walnut and orange tart, 203
Osso bucco, 247

P
Paella, Spanish, 48
Pancake rolls
Chicken, 68
Chinese, 36
Pancakes
Basic, 267
Chinese, 84
Pan-frying
Fish, 233
Sauces, 256
Parsnip chips, 150
Passionfruit
Hearts, 160
Preserve, 297
Pasta
Beef cannelloni, 92
Cooking and serving, 270
Creative cover-ups, 307
Dough, 269
Shaping, 269
Spinach and sorrel ravioli, 131
Types of, 268
Pasties, spinach and cheese, 133
Pastry
Almond, basic, 198, 275
Amaretto choux, 177
Baking blind, 274
Choux, basic, 276
Creative cover-ups, 307
Crimping edges, 302
Filo, 28, 29, 38, 112, 194
See also under Filo pastry
Flaky, basic, 276
Ham and cheese gougère, 102
Hazelnut profiteroles, 176
Herb pâte à pâté, 278
Knocking up, 302
Lining tins, 274
Parsley chicken choux, 41
Pâte sucrée, 275
Potato, 278
Presentation, 302
Puff, basic, 277
Rough puff, 277
Shortcrust, 275
Suet, 278
Types of, 274
Pâté
Coarse garlic, 22
Creative cover-ups, 307
Paunching, rabbit and hare, 253
Peaches
and almond tart, 198
and apple tray bake, 193

in caramel, 158
Fanning, 301
Pears
Honeyed pear pie, 197
Pork and pear pie, 105
Sage, onion and pear stuffing, 300
Sauternes pears, 160
Peas
French petits pois, 144
Types of dried, 222
Peppers
Provençal pepper salad, 143
Red pepper sauce, 116
Vegetable dolmas, 148
Pheasant
Preparing, 252
Roast, 87
Pickles
Lime pickle, 299
Pickled onions, 299
Pies
Baked lemon and lime, 196
Honeyed pear, 197
Hot game, 104
Mixed fish, 65
Pork and pear, 105
Presentation, 302
Savoury Easter, 132
Steak and kidney mini, 103
Turkey and cranberry, 77
Veal, chestnut and apricot, 106
Pizza
Bases, 271
Chocolate, 207
Fiorentina, 270
Nettuno, 270
Preparing, 268
Quattro formaggio, 270
Siciliana, 270
Plantains and aubergines, 121
Plum
Jam, basic, 296
Sauce, Chinese, 84
Poaching
Chicken, 237
Fish, 232, 233
Pork
with apple cups, 114
Boning, 243
Buying, 242
Carving, 244
Chinese pancake rolls, 36
Cuts, 242
Filo pork and apricots, 112
Frying and grilling, 242
Milk roasted, 113
Nectarine pork chops, 95
and pear pie, 105
Roasting, 244
Sesame toasts, 26
Sizzling barbecue ribs, 90
Sweet and sour, 98
Potatoes
and carrot bake, 150
Gratin, 153
Lemony, 151
Orange-glazed, 151

Prawns
and avocado bake, 30
Chicken with, 72
Chinese pancake rolls, 36
Herbed clams and, 33
and lemon dip, 21
Seafood baskets, 38
Sesame toasts, 26
Presentation
Chocolate, 303
Fanning, 301
Flambés, 304
Ice bowls, 301
Pastry, 302
Piping chocolate, 303
Sauces, 304
Preserves
Jam, basic plum 296
Jellies, basic, 297
Lemon curd, 297
Marmalade, orange, 297
Testing for pectin, 296
Profiteroles, hazelnut, 176
Puddings
Bread and butter, 185
Chocolate, 180
Ginger, 174
Hedgerow crumble, 184
Rice, basic, 220
Rice, caramelised, 184
Pulses
Chickpeas, 222
Chickpeas in coconut, 122
Cooking, 223
Falafel, 223
Hummus, 223
Lemon and mint dahl, 122
Lentils, 222
Storing, 222
Types of bean, 222
Types of pea, 222
Pumpkin
Chilli pumpkin soup, 14
Curried, 127

R

Rabbit and hare, preparing, 253
Rack of lamb, 240
Raclette, 265
Ravioli, spinach and sorrel, 131
Relishes
Apricot, orange and onion chutney, 299
Fresh tomato relish, 298
Grainy mustard, 298
Horseradish sauce, 298
Mint jelly, 298
Mint sauce, 298
Quick mango relish, 299
Tomato ketchup, 298
Rhubarb ice cream, 164
Ribs, sizzling barbecue, 90
Rice
Caramelised rice pudding, 184
Caraway-spiked wild rice, 154
Cooking, 220
Creative cover-ups, 307
Nasi goreng, 155

Pudding, 220
Serving, 220
Spanish paella, 48
Stuffed tomatoes, 126
Stuffed vine leaves, 126
Types of, 220
Vegetable dolmas, 148
Yellow, 154
Roasting
Beef, 251
Chicken, 236
Game, 252
Lamb, 240-1
Pork, 244
Veal, 247
Roulade, chocolate, 210

S

Salads
Avocado and grape, 141
Carrot and avocado, 141
Feta and tomato, 140
Halloumi and tomato, 242
Hot Sicilian bean, 143
Lamb's lettuce, 139
Lettuce and chive, 139
Oriental, 138
Preparing leaves, 218
Provençal pepper, 143
Salmon and vegetable, 142
Tabouli, 140
Types of leaves, 218
Salmon
Chaudfroid, 62
en croûte, 64
Mousses, 30
Russian tartlets, 27
and tarragon parcels, 39
and vegetable salad, 142
Samosas, mini, 29
Sauces, making
Creative cover-ups, 305
Microwave tips, 309
Preparation, 256
Presentation, 304
Thickening, 261, 305
Sauces, savoury
Aurore, 263
Bâtarde, 256, 261
Béarnaise, 116, 262
Béchamel, basic, 263
Beurre blanc, 261
Bordelaise, 260
Brandy, 117
Butter, 261
Chasseur, 260
Chaudfroid, 258
Cheese, 92
Chinese plum, 84
Creamy garlic, 256
Demi-glace, 260
Espagnole, 260
Estragon, 260
Garlic and yoghurt, 256
Green, 263
Green avocado, 130
Hollandaise, basic, 262

Horseradish, 298
Lemon, 55
Lemon chilli, 72
Madère, 260
Mornay, 263
Mousseline, basic, 262
Mustard and cream, 256
Orange and thyme, 256
Parsley, 263
Peanut, 70
Pesto, 42
Piquant, 32
Poulette, 263
Red Leicester, 129
Red pepper, 116
Red pepper and tomato, 130
Red wine and mushroom, 256
Redcurrant and ginger, 256
Rich butter, 256
Robert, 260
Rouille, 18
Soubise, 257
Suprême, 263
Sweet and sour, 37
Thai, 61
Tomato, 257, 270
Velouté, basic, 263
Sauces, sweet
Blackcurrant coulis, 290
Brandy, 117
Cardinale, 290
Cheat's custard, 288
Chocolate, 172, 176, 289
Coffee, 289
Crème anglaise, 288
Fruity, 290
Ginger, 174
Grand Marnier, 160
Mango, 290
Orange, hot, 290
Peach, almond and brandy, 290
Sabayon, 168, 288
Strawberry, 290
Strawberry coulis, 160
Summer, 290
Toffee, 173
Vanilla cream, 169
White sauce, sweet, 289
Sausages
Chorizo mushrooms, 22
Fresh pork, 255
Seafood, 255
Scaling fish, 230
Sea bass, 228
Thai-baked fish, 61
Sesame toasts, 26
Shellfish
Buying, 224
Seafood baskets, 38
Seafood sausages, 255
See also under individual shellfish
Shish kebabs, 42
Shrimp family
Cooking, 225
Preparing, 225
Types of, 225
See also under Prawns and Langoustines

Skinning
Fish, 230
Rabbit and hare, 253
Sole
Florentine, 58
with lemon sauce, 55
skinning, 230
Types of, 227
Soufflés
Cheese, 266
Chocolate, 172
Hot toffee, 173
Smoked haddock, 40
Vanilla, 284
Soups
Celery and Stilton, 13
Chilli pumpkin, 14
Classic consommé, 16
Consommé à la julienne, 16
Consommé Monte Carlo, 16
Crab chowder, 19
Cream of spinach, 12
Cream of tomato, 11
French fish, 18
Gazpacho, 10
Leek and sweet potato, 15
Mushroom, 14
Spices
Cabbage and mustard seeds, 144
Caraway-spiked wild rice, 154
Chilli pumpkin soup, 14
Curry powder, 215
Garam masala, 215
Garlic and basil marinade, 300
Ginger and chilli marinade, 61
Grainy mustard, 298
Hot chilli oil, 217
Onion and caraway flan, 134
Peppercorn oil, 217
Peppered sirloin steak, 117
Red wine and mustard marinade, 300
Saffron mussels, 47
Spicy mixed vegetables, 123
Spinach with nutmeg, 146
Types of, 215
Using, 215
Spinach
and cheese pasties, 1345
Cream of spinach soup, 12
with nutmeg, 146
Savoury Easter pie, 132
and sorrel ravioli, 131
Stuffed trout, 59
Squid
Golden, 32
Preparing, 229
Stir-fried vegetables, 145
Stocks
Clarifying, 259
Classic brown, 259
Court bouillon, 62, 257
Fish, 257
Giblet gravy, 258
Preparation, 256
Slaking, 259
Thickening, 259
White, 258

Strawberries
Cheesecake with, 182
Coulis, 160
Fanning, 301
Gratin, 168
Sauce, 290
Stuffings
Apricot and pine kernel, 112
Chestnut, 79
Lemon and herb, 108
Lime and coriander, 68
Marjoram and chervil, 300
Mint and rosemary, 79
Pecan and cranberry, 82
Prune and apple, 300
Rice and pine kernel, 126
Sage, apple and prune, 83
Sage, onion and pear, 300
Sage and raisin, 114
Shrimp and tarragon, 39
Walnut and apple, 109
Sweet potato and leek soup, 15
Sweet and sour pork, 98
Sweetbreads
Bonne femme, 43
Cooking, 254
Preparing, 254
Sweets
Chocolates, filled, 295
Fudge, basic, 294
Toffee, basic, 294
Truffles, basic, 295
Swiss cheese fondue, 265

T

Tabouli, 140
Tacos with sauces, 130
Taramasalata, 20
Tarts
Apricot tartes Tatin, 169
Curd tartlets, 195
French apple tart, 200
Peach and almond, 198
Peach and apple tray bake, 193
Russian tartlets, 27
Walnut and orange, 203
Toffee
Basic, 294
Hot toffee soufflés, 173
Tomato
Basic sauce, 270
Cream of tomato soup, 11
Feta and tomato salad, 140
Halloumi and tomato salad, 142
Ketchup, 298
Relish, 298
Stuffed, 126
Tongue
Cooking, 254
Preparation, 254
Trout
Gutting, 231
Rainbow, 228
Salmon, 228
Sea, 228
Spinach-stuffed, 59
Truffles, basic, 295

Tuna, 229
Provençal platter, 57
Turkey
and cranberry pie, 77
with pecans, 82
Tzatziki, 91

V
Veal
Boning, 247
Buying, 246
Chestnut and apricot pie, 106
Cooking, 246, 247
Cuts, 246
Demi-glace, 260
Escalopes, 246
Osso bucco, 247
Stewing, 247
Vegetables
Buttery vegetable layers, 148
and cashew curry, 124
Cheat's ratatouille, 306
Chow mein, 120
Creative cover-ups, 306
Dolmas, 148
Glazed, 152
Salmon and vegetable salad, 142
Savoury Easter pie, 132
Spicy mixed, 123
Stir-fried, 145
Vegetarian koulibiaca, 135
See also under individual vegetables
Venison
Cooking, 253
Larding, 253
Vine leaves, stuffed, 126
Vinegars
Herb, 217
Raspberry vinegar, 217
Types of, 217

W
Wine
with cheeses, 311
with desserts, 311
with fish and shellfish, 310
with foreign foods, 311
with game, 310
Glasses, 310
with meat, 311
with poultry, 310
Red wine and mustard marinade, 300
Serving, 310
Storing, 310
White wine and garlic marinade, 70
Wontons, crab, 37

Y
Yeast, using, 272, 273
Yoghurt
Baked chicken, 70
Dressing, 219
Monkfish in, 50
Yorkshire puddings, 267

Z
Zabaglione, 161